Advance Praise for
Appearing and Empty

"*Appearing and Empty*, the ninth volume in H. H. the Dalai Lama and Ven. Thubten Chodron's extraordinary *Library of Wisdom and Compassion*, is largely devoted to a discussion of various Indian Buddhist perspectives on the two truths: conventional and ultimate. These concepts are the interpretive key to understanding how Buddhists make sense of the world and especially how they learn to distinguish between appearance and reality—through both philosophical analysis and insight meditation—in order to realize perfect wisdom and win spiritual freedom. There is also a wonderfully detailed exploration of the schools of Chinese Buddhism and their take on key issues in Buddhist theory and practice. Incisive, illuminating, and highly readable, *Appearing and Empty* is a welcome addition to the bookshelves of followers of the Dalai Lama and students of Buddhism everywhere."
—Roger R. Jackson, John W. Nason Professor of Asian Studies and Religion, emeritus, Carleton College

"Sravasti Abbey is a beautiful and secluded place with a wonderful, panoramic view of the outer world. Within its walls the nuns, led by Gelongma Thubten Chodron, practice Dharma, mirroring the Mahāyāna ideal explained in this book. I highly recommend *Appearing and Empty* to anyone who wishes to gain in-depth insight into Lama Tsongkhapa's understanding of the union of appearance and emptiness. This is facilitated by a presentation of emptiness in other Buddhist traditions, leading readers along a path to spiritual realization."
—Geshe Kalsang Damdul, former director of the Institute of Buddhist Dialectics

THE LIBRARY OF WISDOM AND COMPASSION

The Library of Wisdom and Compassion is a special multivolume series in which His Holiness the Dalai Lama shares the Buddha's teachings on the complete path to full awakening that he himself has practiced his entire life. The topics are arranged especially for people not born in Buddhist cultures and are peppered with the Dalai Lama's unique outlook. Assisted by his long-term disciple, the American nun Thubten Chodron, the Dalai Lama sets the context for practicing the Buddha's teachings in modern times and then unveils the path of wisdom and compassion that leads to a meaningful life, a sense of personal fulfillment, and full awakening. This series is an important bridge from introductory to profound topics for those seeking an in-depth explanation from a contemporary perspective.

Volumes:

1. *Approaching the Buddhist Path*
2. *The Foundation of Buddhist Practice*
3. *Saṃsāra, Nirvāṇa, and Buddha Nature*
4. *Following in the Buddha's Footsteps*
5. *In Praise of Great Compassion*
6. *Courageous Compassion*
7. *Searching for the Self*
8. *Realizing the Profound View*
9. *Appearing and Empty*

Volume 10 to come!

THE LIBRARY OF WISDOM AND COMPASSION • VOLUME 9

Appearing and Empty

Bhikṣu Tenzin Gyatso,
the Fourteenth Dalai Lama

and

Bhikṣuṇī Thubten Chodron

Wisdom

Wisdom Publications
132 Perry Street
New York, NY 10014 USA
wisdomexperience.org

Library of Congress Cataloging-in-Publication Data
Names: Bstan-'dzin-rgya-mtsho, Dalai Lama XIV, 1935– author. |
 Thubten Chodron, 1950– author.
Title: Appearing and empty / Bhikṣu Tenzin Gyatso and Bhikṣuṇī Thubten Chodron.
Description: First edition. | Somerville: Wisdom Publications, 2023. |
 Series: The library of wisdom and compassion; volume 9 |
 Includes bibliographical references and index.
Identifiers: LCCN 2022056898 (print) | LCCN 2022056899 (ebook) |
 ISBN 9781614298878 (hardcover) | ISBN 9781614299004 (ebook)
Subjects: LCSH: Mādhyamika (Buddhism) | Truth—Religious aspects—Buddhism
Classification: LCC BQ7476 .B78 2023 (print) | LCC BQ7476 (ebook) |
 DDC 294.3/92—dc23/eng/20230222
LC record available at https://lccn.loc.gov/2022056898
LC ebook record available at https://lccn.loc.gov/2022056899

ISBN 978-1-61429-887-8 ebook ISBN 978-1-61429-900-4

27 26 25 24 23
5 4 3 2 1

Photo credits: cover, courtesy of the Office of His Holiness the Dalai Lama; pp. vi, xviii, 14, 178, 236, 398, Ānandajoti Bhikkhu / PhotoDharma.net; p. 40, Tibetan Nuns Project | TNP.org; p. 208, Olivier Adam Photography
Cover and interior design by Gopa & Ted 2. Interior typeset by PerfecType.

Printed on acid-free paper that meets the guidelines for permanence and durability of the Production Guidelines for Book Longevity of the Council on Library Resources.

Printed in Canada.

Publisher's Acknowledgment

The publisher gratefully acknowledges the generous help of the Hershey Foundation in sponsoring the production of this book.

Contents

Preface

GIVEN THE EMPHASIS that Madhyamaka has in the Tibetan Buddhist community nowadays, I was surprised, during one of our interviews for the *Library of Wisdom and Compassion*, when His Holiness remarked that until the time of the Sakya sage Rendawa and his student Tsongkhapa, epistemology, not Madhyamaka, was the most popular topic in Tibet. Thanks to their interest in Madhyamaka, it has become a great topic of debate and discussion ever since, not only in monastic communities in Tibet, India, and Mongolia but also internationally as Buddhists, philosophers, and scientists delve into it.

Madhyamaka's early spread to China gave rise to translations of Nāgārjuna's and Āryadeva's texts by the great translator Kumārajīva and his team. Yet it was the Yogācāra and Tathāgatagarbha philosophies that later won the hearts of the Chinese. Nevertheless, Madhyamaka has influenced the indigenous Buddhist traditions in China, and renewed interest in it has arisen in Chinese Buddhism beginning in the twentieth century when Fazun Shih and other Chinese monks studied in Tibetan monasteries such as Drepung. In recent years, Yinshun Shih (1906–2005), who systematized a lamrim for Chinese Buddhists, has further contributed to this by widely teaching Madhyamaka philosophy.

As with the Pāli tradition, Buddhism in China has many sects to meet the interests and dispositions of diverse spiritual seekers. All of these are to be respected because they originate from the same Teacher, the Buddha. This volume and the entire *Library of Wisdom and Compassion* were written with this in mind.

Overview of This Book

Appearing and Empty continues the Madhyamaka teachings begun in the previous two volumes of the series, *Searching for the Self* and *Realizing the Profound View.* The first three chapters of this book emphasize the two truths—ultimate and veiled truths—and their compatibility. What does it mean to be true? True to whom? True to what kinds of cognizers? Chapters 4 and 5 discuss reliable cognizers. How can we validate our cognitions if things exist only by mere dependent designation on the conventional level and ultimately lack any self-nature?

Chapters 6–9 explore the assertions of the Yogācāra and Svātantrika Madhyamaka tenet systems and how they explain what exists, how it exists, and how it is perceived. These chapters also explore the topics where these systems and the Prāsaṅgika Madhyamaka system differ, which sharpens our understanding of reality. The debates among previous masters who hold diverse views have clarified many points for Buddhists of future generations, even though these masters frequently reached different conclusions. Studying these points of debate expands our wisdom and intelligence and reveals aspects of the Dharma that we may never have thought about left to our own devices. The essence of the debates is presented without going into the complex details, which you can find in other texts, some of which are mentioned in the recommended reading at the end of this volume.

Chapter 10 discusses Prāsaṅgikas' unique positions, which depend on their distinctive views about the object of negation and the ultimate truth. Various traditions' views of insight meditation, its union with serenity, and how to realize the ultimate nature are covered in chapters 11 and 12.

We then turn to Buddhism in China, which is predominantly the Sanskrit tradition, explaining in chapter 13 the ten principal schools that were popular in China, many of which are also popular in Tibet. This includes discussion on sudden and gradual awakening in both Chinese and Tibetan schools and is followed in chapter 14 with an exploration of the three philosophies emphasized today in Chinese Buddhism—Madhyamaka, Yogācāra, and Tathāgatagarbha. We'll then look at some of the Chinese indigenous schools—Chan (Zen), Huayan, Pureland, and Tiantai—before exploring Chinese Madhyamaka more closely. The volume ends with a chapter on Buddhism today in China.

How This Book Came About

The story of the origins of the *Library of Wisdom and Compassion* was shared in volume 1, *Approaching the Buddhist Path*, and elaborated on in volume 7, *Searching for the Self*. My initial request to His Holiness was to write a short text that Tibetan lamas could use when teaching non-Tibetans—people who come to the Dharma with very different preconceptions and assumptions than those growing up as Tibetan Buddhists. His Holiness's response was to ask me to write a longer volume based on his teachings. That gradually grew in length, especially after he expressed the wish that teachings from the Pāli tradition and Buddhism in China be included. Over my objection, he also insisted that I be a co-author as well as editor.

His Holiness gave me a letter requesting Theravāda monks to instruct me. Thus I spent two weeks studying and practicing with Ajahn Anan at Wat Marp Jan in Thailand. This was followed by studying Bhikkhu Bodhi's lengthy series of oral teachings on Majjhima Nikāya and later corresponding with him to ask questions. This led to reading about the Pāli Abhidharma, participating in a vipassanā retreat, and discussing the Dharma with Western monastics whom I met at our annual Western Buddhist Monastic Gatherings. Having taught the Dharma in Singapore for almost two years, I also got to know monks from the Theravāda tradition, participated in panel discussions with them, and was invited to speak at their temples.

My knowledge of the Chinese tradition began with going to Taiwan in 1986 to receive full ordination. It continued during my time teaching in Singapore and expanded during the 1996 conference Life as a Western Buddhist Nun, where Bhikṣuṇī Master Wu Yin from Luminary Temple in Taiwan taught Vinaya. Over the years, Sravasti Abbey has developed a close relationship with Master Wu Yin and her students, who helped arrange interviews with monastics and professors of Madhyamaka and Tathāgatagarbha when I visited Taiwan. I've also enjoyed many discussions with monastic friends from the Pāli and Chinese traditions. The study and engagement with the Pāli tradition and Chinese Buddhists has helped my own Dharma practice considerably.

Please Note

Although this series is coauthored, the vast majority of the material is His Holiness's teachings. I researched and wrote the parts about Buddhism in China, the Pāli tradition, and some other passages; I also composed the reflections. For ease of reading, most honorifics have been omitted, but that does not diminish the great respect we have for the excellent sages, learned adepts, practitioners, and scholars. Foreign terms are given in italics parenthetically at their first usage. Unless otherwise noted with "P," "C," or "T," indicating Pāli, Chinese, or Tibetan, respectively, italicized terms are Sanskrit. When two italicized terms are listed, the first is Sanskrit, the second Pāli. For consistency, Sanskrit spelling is given for Sanskrit and Pāli terms in common usage (nirvāṇa, Dharma, arhat, ārya, sūtra, and so forth), except in citations from Pāli scriptures. To maintain the flow of a passage, it is not always possible to gloss all new terms on their first usage, so a glossary is provided.

"Sūtra" often refers to Sūtrayāna (Sūtra Vehicle) and "Tantra" to Tantrayāna (Tantric Vehicle). When these two words are not capitalized, they refer to the sūtra and tantra scriptures. "Mahāyāna" refers principally to the path to buddhahood as well as the attainment of a buddha's qualities and activities as explained in the Sanskrit tradition.[1] In general, the meaning of all philosophical terms accords with the presentation of the Prāsaṅgika Madhyamaka tenet system as understood by Tsongkhapa. Other presentations of Prāsaṅgika Madhyamaka also exist in the Tibetan community. Unless otherwise noted, the personal pronoun "I" refers to His Holiness.

Appreciation

My deepest respect goes to Śākyamuni Buddha and all the buddhas, bodhisattvas, and arhats who embody the Dharma and compassionately teach and guide us confused beings who seek happiness but are ignorant of the means to create its causes. I also bow to all the realized lineage masters of all Buddhist traditions through whose kindness the Buddhadharma still exists in our world.

The *Library of Wisdom and Compassion* consists of many volumes. For their aid in this ninth volume, I want to express my gratitude to His Holiness's translators—Geshe Lhakdor, Geshe Dorji Damdul, and Mr. Tenzin Tsepak. I am grateful to Geshe Kelsang Wangmo for carefully checking the manuscript and offering many useful suggestions, to Dr. Guy Newland for reading the manuscript and answering many questions, and to Samdhong Rinpoche for clarifying important points. I appreciate Bhikkhu Bodhi's clear teachings on the Pāli tradition, his generously answering my many questions, and his looking over the sections on the Pāli tradition before publication. I am also indebted to Bhikṣuṇī Master Wu Yin, Bhikṣuṇī Jendy Shih, Prof. Lin Cheng-kuo, Prof. Wan Jing-Chuang, Bhikṣu Houkuan Shih, and Dr. Matthew Orsborne for sharing their knowledge and practice of Chinese Buddhism and Madhyamaka. Appreciation goes to Own Su-jei for translating some of these interviews, and special thanks to Bhikṣu Jianhu Shih for sharing his knowledge and practice of the Chinese Buddhist traditions and checking those portions of this volume.

The staff at the Private Office of His Holiness kindly facilitated the interviews with His Holiness, Sravasti Abbey supported me while I worked on this volume, and Mary Petrusewicz skillfully edited this book. I thank everyone at Wisdom Publications who contributed to the successful production of this series. All errors are my own.

Enjoy this book and the Buddhadharma!

Bhikṣuṇī Thubten Chodron
Sravasti Abbey

Abbreviations

AN — Aṅguttara Nikāya. Translated by Bhikkhu Bodhi in *The Numerical Discourses of the Buddha*. Boston: Wisdom Publications, 2012.

BCA — *Bodhicaryāvatāra*, by Śāntideva. Translated by Stephen Batchelor in *A Guide to the Bodhisattva's Way of Life*. Dharamsala: Library of Tibetan Works and Archives, 2007.

BV — *Commentary on Bodhicitta* (*Bodhicittavivāraṇa*), by Nāgārjuna. Translated by Geshe Thupten Jinpa.

C. — Chinese

CE — "Cataphatic Emptiness: rGyal-tshab on the Buddha-essence Theory of Asaṅga's *Ratnagotravibhāgavyākhyā*," by Bo Jiang. PhD diss., Columbia University, 2008.

CŚ — *The Four Hundred* (*Catuḥśataka*), by Āryadeva. Translated by Ruth Sonam in *Yogic Deeds of Bodhisattvas*. Ithaca, NY: Snow Lion Publications, 1994.

DAE — *Dependent Arising and Emptiness: A Tibetan Buddhist Interpretation of Mādhyamika Philosophy*, by Elizabeth Napper. Boston: Wisdom Publications, 2002.

Dhp — Dhammapada.

EBM — *Essentials of Buddhist Meditation*, by Zhiyi. Translated by Bhikṣu Dharmamitra. Seattle, WA: Kalavinka Press, 2008.

EY *Emptiness Yoga*, by Jeffrey Hopkins. Ithaca, NY: Snow Lion Publications, 1987.

FEW *Tsong-kha-pa's Final Exposition of Wisdom*, by Jeffrey Hopkins. Ithaca, NY: Snow Lion Publications, 2008.

GR *Illuminating the Intent: An Exposition of Candrakīrti's "Entering the Middle Way"* (*Dgongs pa rab gsal*), by Tsongkhapa. Translated by Thupten Jinpa. Somerville, MA: Wisdom Publications, 2021.

HSY *How to See Yourself as You Really Are*, by His Holiness the Dalai Lama. Translated by Jeffrey Hopkins. New York: Atria Books, 2006.

J. Japanese

K. Korean

LC *The Great Treatise on the Stages of the Path* (*Lam rim chen mo*), by Tsongkhapa. 3 vols. Translated by Joshua Cutler et al. Ithaca, NY: Snow Lion Publications, 2000–2004.

MMA *Supplement to the "Treatise on the Middle Way"* (*Madhyamakāvatāra, Dbu ma la 'jug pa*), by Candrakīrti.

MMK *Treatise on the Middle Way* (*Mūlamādhyamakakārikā*), by Nāgārjuna.

MN Majjhima Nikāya. Translated by Bhikkhu Ñāṇamoli and Bhikkhu Bodhi in *The Middle-Length Discourses of the Buddha*. Boston: Wisdom Publications, 1995.

MP *Maps of the Profound: Jam-yang-shay-ba's Great Exposition of Buddhist and Non-Buddhist Views on the Nature of Reality*, by Jeffrey Hopkins. Ithaca, NY: Snow Lion Publications, 2003.

MS *The Middle Stages of Meditation II* (*Bhāvanākrama*), by Kamalaśīla. Translated by Geshe Lobsang Jordhen, Losang Chophel Gangchenpa, and Jeremy Russell. New Delhi: Tibet House, 2013.

MTC *Mādhyamaka Thought in China*, by Ming-Wood Liu. New York: E. J. Brill, 1994.

NT *The Nature of Things: Emptiness and Essence in the Geluk World*, by William Magee. Ithaca, NY: Snow Lion Publications, 2000.

OE *Opposite of Emptiness in the Middle Way Autonomy School*, by Jamyang Shay-pa. Translated by Jongbok Yi. Milwaukie, OR: UMA Institute for Tibetan Studies, 2005.

OOE *Ocean of Eloquence: Tsong kha pa's Commentary of the Yogācāra Doctrine of Mind*. Translated by Gareth Sparham. Albany: State University of New York Press, 1993.

OR *Ocean of Reasoning by rJe Tsong Khapa*. Translated by Geshe Ngawang Samten and Jay L. Garfield. New York: Oxford University Press, 2006.

P. Pāli

PP *Clear Words* (*Prasannapadā*), by Candrakīrti.

PTE "Practice and Theory of Emptiness: A Study of Jizang's *Commentary on the 'Refutation of Emptiness' of the Bailun*," by Wen-ling Jane. PhD diss., Columbia University, 2009.

PV *Commentary on the "Compendium of Reliable Cognition"* (*Pramāṇavārttika*), by Dharmakīrti.

RA *Precious Garland* (*Ratnāvalī*), by Nāgārjuna. In *Practical Ethics and Profound Emptiness: A Commentary on Nagarjuna's Precious Garland*, by Khensur Jampa Tegchok. Somerville, MA: Wisdom Publication, 2017.

RGV *Sublime Continuum* (*Ratnagotravibhāga*, *Uttaratantra*), by Maitreya.

RR *Reflections on Reality*, by Jeffrey Hopkins. Berkeley: University of California Press, 2007.

RSR *The Rice Seedling Sūtra: Buddha's Teachings on Dependent Arising*, by Geshe Yeshe Thabkhe. Translated by Joshua Cutler and Diana Cutler. Boston: Wisdom Publications, 2020.

SN Saṃyutta Nikāya. Translated by Bhikkhu Bodhi in *The Connected Discourses of the Buddha*. Boston: Wisdom Publications, 2000.

SR *Samādhirāja Sūtra*.

SRR *Self, Reality, and Reason in Tibetan Philosophy: Tsongkhapa's Quest for the Middle Way*, by Thupten Jinpa. New York: RoutledgeCurzon, 2002.

SSC *Selected Works of the Dalai Lama: Songs of Spiritual Change*, by Glenn Mullin. Ithaca, NY: Snow Lion Publications, 1985.

SV *A Study of Svātantrika*, by Donald S. Lopez Jr. Ithaca, NY: Snow Lion Publications, 1987.

T. Tibetan

TSB *Tsung-Mi and the Sinification of Buddhism*, by Peter N. Gregory. Honolulu: University of Hawai'i Press, 2002.

TT *The Two Truths in the Mādhyamika Philosophy of the Ge-luk-ba Order of Tibetan Buddhism*, by Guy Newland. Ithaca, NY: Snow Lion Publications, 1992.

Ud *Udāna*.

UT *Unique Tenets of the Middle Way Consequence School*, by Daniel Cozort. Ithaca, NY: Snow Lion Publications, 1998.

Vism *Visuddhimagga*, by Buddhaghosa. Translated by Bhikkhu Ñāṇamoli in *The Path of Purification*. Kandy: Buddhist Publication Society, 1991.

WB *The Way to Buddhahood: Instructions from a Modern Chinese Master*, by Venerable Yinshun. Somerville, MA: Wisdom Publications, 2012.

Introduction

We were received into this world at birth with kindness, and we continue to live and share with others due to kindness. But sometimes our anger and resentment obscure us from seeing the kindness around us. And that, in turn, may impair us from showing kindness.

Our attitude is the key factor. Once I visited a garden in Switzerland and people were sitting on park benches scattering seeds and bits of bread for the birds. The birds flew there without having to be called. It shows that when you show kindness to others—even animals—they will automatically come. If you are fearful and suspicious, and distance yourself from others, they refrain from approaching you and you will become isolated. So an open, more compassionate attitude toward other sentient beings is helpful for both others and ourselves.

Wherever I go I smile, so people are naturally friendly in return. Paying attention to others' well-being and having an altruistic mind is the best way to secure your own physical and mental health. Whether you believe in religion or not, being compassionate will benefit you, whereas if you think just of yourself, you are miserable. Cultivating compassion is the best way to have a happy life.

Our educational system needs to emphasize the commonalities of all beings; each of us wants happiness and to avoid suffering. No matter what people look like, where they are from, their socio-economic level, their age, or their health, we are all alike in this way. Emphasizing the differences among us breeds fear, anxiety, and suspicion. These emotions and attitudes arise in our minds, but by changing how we look at others and how we interpret situations, we can release these disturbing emotions.

In the Nālandā tradition, we emphasize reason and logic, and such analysis can help us cultivate compassion in meditation. One way to do this is to contemplate the disadvantages of the self-centered attitude—self-centeredness makes us sensitive to small slights; we interpret everything, even the smallest glance or mumbled words, in terms of ourselves; we become blind to the experiences of those around us, not recognizing that our indifference toward them leads to inequality in so many areas of life. When others believe their well-being is discounted, they become unhappy, and their unhappiness adversely influences us too. Being around unhappy people, be they friends, enemies, or strangers, makes us unhappy too.

Therefore I meditate on compassion and altruism, which are the opposite of self-preoccupation. When I wake up in morning, I recite a verse from *Engaging in the Bodhisattvas' Deeds* by the eighth-century Indian sage Śāntideva (BCA 10.55):

> For as long as space endures
> and for as long as living beings remain,
> until then may I, too, abide
> to dispel the misery of the world.

In addition, I also investigate: Where is the I? Am I my body or my mind? I'm not either of those. Even the Buddha wasn't his body, speech, or mind, so where is the Buddha? This investigation leads us to conclude that the feeling of a solid I—something that is inherently and really me—has no basis. The I exists—it is merely designated by term and concept—but we can't isolate exactly what it is separate from our bodies and minds. Thinking like this helps to reduce the strong thought of self.

People and other phenomena seem to be objective entities "out there" that are not related to our minds. They don't seem to depend on their causes or their parts—they are just "there." But if we investigate and try to find what they really are, there's nothing there; it is all mental fabrication. Buddhist philosophy and quantum physics are similar in this regard: nothing exists independent of our minds. Because things appear to be objectively existent entities, we grasp them to exist as such. Someone appears kind to us and we think they are an inherently existent friend. Another person says something we don't like and we designate them as a disagreeable person and think they will always be like that. All the strangers around us don't influence us one way or the other, so we navigate our way around them and forget that they have feelings. But if we investigate exactly who the friend or enemy is, we can't find them in their body, speech, or mind. They don't exist as self-enclosed permanent entities.

Bodhisattva practice consists of cultivating wisdom—understanding the deeper mode of existence of people and phenomena—and method—generating bodhicitta and engaging in the bodhisattva practices. From the side of wisdom, nothing exists independent of other factors, such as its causes, parts, and the mind that conceives and designates them. From the method side, compassion and altruism are the basis for virtuous actions. Wisdom and method are my main practices. If you think of these two upon awakening every day, it shapes your mind and influences how you see and experience situations the entire day.

Every day I read a portion of a text by one of the great scholar-adepts. Nāgārjuna's writings are exceptional, and those of his indirect disciple Candrakīrti are bold. Vasubandhu, Dignāga, and others are afraid to think everything is mentally designated; they fear that nothing could be pinned down if that were the case, so they rejected that belief. I feel fortunate because the idea that everything exists by being merely designated, not by having some inherent essence, is firm in my mind. I feel like a close disciple of Candrakīrti and every day I read his *Supplement to the "Treatise on the Middle Way"* and its autocommentary.

The two bodhisattva practices of method and wisdom combined are very powerful; we should practice these ourselves, then share them with others. If you just study and discuss the teachings but don't practice them, you become a hypocrite. Instead, you should be a good example for others; that is the proper way to serve sentient beings. If your speech and your actions aren't in accord, how can others trust you? Trust is the basis of harmonious and beneficial relationships.

I've heard that some psychologists say that our compassion fades as we get older and are exposed to more and more tragedy. I think if we just rely on whatever feeling or mood of discouragement arises in our minds, that could happen. But if we investigate our feelings and moods, our compassion can be sustained and enhanced. If you feel discouraged, investigate: What are the causes of this way of thinking? What are its effects? You can change your thoughts and feelings by investigating which thoughts and feelings are more realistic and more beneficial and then familiarizing yourselves with them.

Although single-pointed concentration (*sāmadhi*) is valuable, it is not the only quality to develop in our Dharma practice. Analytical meditation is essential because it cuts down all our justifications and excuses that support our self-centered attitude. We can't find one logical reason to cherish ourselves more than others and to ignore the well-being of others. All the emotions that bring us problems have no logical basis. Contemplation of dependent arising and emptiness destroys the ignorance that is the basis of selfishness.

When I first became interested in science and began to learn about it, some people warned me not to get too close to scientists because my faith in the Buddha would decrease. But I use logic and reasoning to discern what is true and what to believe. Maybe I'm half Buddhist monk and half scientist! Both Buddhists and scientists seek truth. So we can learn from scientists and scientists can learn from us Buddhists. With a deeper understanding of reality, we can then use our human intelligence to solve problems. Just wishing that our problems would disappear doesn't make that happen. We created the problems, so we must develop our knowledge and ability to solve them.

The Buddha himself told us not to accept statements with blind faith, but to investigate. We should not sit back and say, "Oh, my lama said that, so it must be true." I sometimes read the teachings of some Tibetan lamas, but when I think about what was written or spoken, I cannot accept it.

The Buddha taught according to the two truths—ultimate and conventional (veiled). Understanding the ultimate truth is the direct opposite of following ignorance. Cultivating nonattachment, ethical conduct, and altruism enables us to relate properly to the conventional world. My meditation practice is based on these two truths.

Bhikṣu Tenzin Gyatso, the Fourteenth Dalai Lama
Thekchen Choling

1 | The Two Truths

LOOKING AT A person's books tells us a lot about him or her. Sometimes the initial pages of the lamrim text are well worn, the pages in the middle less so, and the pages of the insight chapter are untouched. This person has become lazy when it comes to studying difficult topics and needs to put more energy into understanding them. Someone once told me that the subjects I teach are too difficult for the audience and asked me to teach something simpler. I replied that we need to learn and understand what we don't already know, not just review the easier material that we are familiar with. Some texts are more concise when they arrive at the section on wisdom, but the texts of the great masters explain the difficult sections in more detail.

Studying many treatises and commentaries broadens our understanding, and it is worthwhile to wait to reach a firm conclusion until we have learned and contemplated the various assertions. By doing so, we will gain an understanding based on reasoning, which will strengthen our practice and enable our meditation to be successful. Without this, we may spend years doing retreat in a secluded place and emerge only to find that our minds have not been transformed very much. So let's galvanize our joyous effort and delve into the topic of the two truths.

Introduction to the Two Truths

The topic of the two truths—veiled truths (*saṃvṛtisatya*) and ultimate truths (*paramārthasatya*)—comes up in several different contexts. In the context of the four truths, true cessations are ultimate truths, whereas the other three truths are veiled truths. In the context of dependent arising and emptiness, dependent arising principally, although not exclusively, relates to veiled truths, whereas emptinesses are ultimate truths. In the context of method and wisdom, the method aspect of the path, the collection of merit, and the form body of a buddha are related to conventional truths, whereas the wisdom aspect of the path, the collection of wisdom, and the nature truth body are related to ultimate truths.

The topic of the two truths is important for several reasons. First, it helps us to understand that the everyday functioning of people and things in the world is compatible with their emptiness of objective existence. Dependent arising and emptiness are not only compatible but also mutually reinforce each other. Emptiness does not negate veiled truths such as karma and its effects or the method side of the path. Although all phenomena lack inherent existence, maintaining excellent ethical conduct is of crucial importance and the bodhisattva conduct of engaging in compassionate action is essential for attaining awakening. In fact, cause and effect can function only in a world in which everything is empty of inherent existence.

Second, the two truths are different objects and understanding both is valuable, useful, and necessary to attain awakening. Understanding them helps us balance and combine the practice of the method aspect of the path and the wisdom aspect of the path. Although the realization of phenomena's ultimate nature—their emptiness of inherent existence—will liberate us from saṃsāra, it does not inform us as to how things interrelate and operate conventionally. If we need directions to go to Delhi, veiled truths such as a map, signposts, and a vehicle will fulfill that need, whereas ultimate truths will not. To function effectively and with compassion in the world, an understanding of both truths is essential.

Someone who remains absorbed in the direct realization of ultimate truth may be free from saṃsāra but will not have all the skills needed to function in the world, let alone to benefit others. On the other hand, those who are totally immersed in the details of veiled truths will reify situations, be distracted from learning about ultimate truth, and afflictions will easily arise in their minds. To fulfill their own and others' aims, bodhisattvas seek knowledge of both truths.

Please read this and the following chapters carefully. The way words are used in the topic of the two truths is very specific. One term can have multiple meanings depending on the context. For example, "real" and "real for the world" have different meanings. Veiled or conventional truths are not true. Emptiness is true—it is an ultimate truth—but it doesn't exist ultimately or truly. Understanding the meaning behind these words reveals many nuances that refine our understanding of emptiness and dependent arising.

The Importance of Understanding the Two Truths

As Dharma practitioners, our ultimate aim is to be of the greatest benefit possible to all sentient beings. To do this, becoming a buddha is imperative, and to accomplish that the causes to attain a buddha's two bodies—the truth body and the form body—must be created. These causes are the collection of merit and the collection of wisdom, and to fulfill these two collections, the practices of the method aspect of the path and the wisdom aspect of the path, respectively, are done. To engage in these two aspects of the path, correct understanding of the basis—the two truths—is essential. That is, we must have an understanding of the ultimate truth, the emptiness of inherent existence of all phenomena, and of dependent arising, the manner in which everything comes into being and exists dependent on other factors. This entails overcoming the two extremes of absolutism and nihilism that thwart the arising of these two understandings in our minds.

In other words, without banishing the extreme of grasping inherent existence and the extreme of believing that the law of cause and effect doesn't exist, we cannot understand emptiness and dependent arising correctly, and without that understanding, we will not correctly understand the two truths—ultimate and conventional truths. Lacking this understanding inhibits properly engaging in the method and wisdom aspects of the path, which, in turn, inhibits fulfilling the two collections. Without doing this, the causes to attain the truth body and form body of a buddha cannot be created, and thus buddhahood is not attained. This means that all the sentient beings we could benefit through displaying the awakened activities of a buddha will struggle in the ocean of saṃsāra longer. Thus, gaining the correct understanding of the two truths is of great importance.

Ultimate truths are objects found by a reasoning consciousness distinguishing the final mode of existence. Nāgārjuna says (MMK 24.8–10):

The Buddha's teaching of the Dharma
is based on two truths:
a truth of worldly convention
and an ultimate truth.

Those who do not understand
the distinction between these two truths
do not understand
the Buddha's profound teaching.

Without depending on the conventional truth,
the meaning of the ultimate cannot be taught.
Without understanding the meaning of the ultimate,
nirvāṇa is not attained.

In the first verse, Nāgārjuna emphasizes that statements in the Buddha's teachings should be understood within the context of two truths, the veiled and the ultimate. As the second verse explains, understanding the two truths and the distinction between them is important; without it we will not correctly understand the profound meaning of the Buddha's teachings. We will be unable to distinguish existents from nonexistents or to reliably establish the existence of everyday objects as well as their ultimate nature in a noncontradictory way.

As the third verse conveys, veiled truths are the means to arrive at the meaning of ultimate truth. Without depending on veiled truths, such as conceptual thought, and societal conventions, such as language, the meaning of ultimate truth cannot be taught. The very act of teaching the Dharma involves the use of concepts and language. Lacking correct instructions, we will not know what to practice and what to abandon on the method side of the path, and we will not have the slightest idea how to meditate to realize the ultimate truth. Stymied, we will be unable to attain nirvāṇa.

In learning the two truths, it is imperative to receive teachings from spiritual mentors who have the correct understanding of the two truths. Candrakīrti says (MMA 6.79–80):

Those who remain outside the master Nāgārjuna's way
have no means for attaining true peace.
They have strayed from the truths of convention and of suchness,
and because of this failure, they will not achieve liberation.

Veiled truth is the means,
while the ultimate truth is its end.
Those who fail to know the distinction between the two
will enter wrong paths through false conceptualization.

The teachings of the Yogācāra Buddhist school are not definitive. As Yogācārins see it, dependent phenomena are truly existent. Prāsaṅgikas reply that if that were true, then veiled truths would be permanent, and our world would be frozen and unchanging. Yogācārins retort: If true existence were refuted, then dependent phenomena would be nonexistent and nothing would exist. Because Yogācārins do not see dependent arising and emptiness as compatible, *they have strayed from the truths of convention and suchness*, and their proponents cannot attain liberation, let alone full awakening, until they right their views.

The second verse describes what is to be understood: veiled truths exist and function. They are necessary tools for us to use to understand emptiness, and they are the bases of emptiness. Emptiness is the ultimate nature of veiled truths; therefore we must be able to assert both in order to avoid the two extremes and have the correct view. Once we have attained the correct view, our meditation on emptiness will be effective and we will realize emptiness directly.

It is unwise to think that since veiled truths are falsities involving terms and concepts, they are a hindrance to realizing emptiness and should be ignored. Rather, they are an aid through which an understanding of ultimate truths will come about. Furthermore, veiled truths are the objects whose emptiness we realize—they are the bases of emptiness—so it is imperative that we understand them correctly.

Knowable objects (*jñeya*)—phenomena perceivable by mind—are the basis of division into the two truths. Nonexistents, such as a turtle's moustache and the objects seen in drug-induced hallucinations, are not knowable objects. All phenomena—that is, all existents—are either a veiled truth or an ultimate truth; a third truth does not exist. *The Meeting of the Father and Son Sūtra* (*Pitāputrasamāgama Sūtra*) says (TT 39):

> It is like this: The Tathāgata thoroughly understands conventionalities and ultimates. Also, knowable objects are exhausted within the two, veiled truths and ultimate truths.

The two truths are not two ways of looking at one thing. They are distinct objects that are apprehended by two different types of consciousnesses. Conventional reliable cognizers operate within the framework of language and everyday perception where we are concerned with attributes and properties of objects and describe how they interact and function. These cognizers know veiled truths. Probing awareness and ultimate analysis cognize ultimate truths, which are beyond the limits of our everyday perception and way of speaking. Probing awareness inquires, "What is the ultimate mode of existence of phenomena?" Looking beyond objects' appearance, ultimate analysis seeks objects' true mode of being, the way in which they actually exist. A conventional reliable cognizer knows the flower; a probing awareness knows that the flower does not exist from its own side.

The two truths are understood in relation to two aspects or two natures of each phenomenon. They are not two levels of objective reality, with ultimate truths superseding and negating veiled truths. Rather, all phenomena are equally empty of inherent existence and equally exist conventionally. Candrakīrti says (MMA 6.23):

> [The Buddha] said that all phenomena have two natures:
> those found by perceivers of the true and of the false.
> Objects of perceivers of the true are suchness,
> objects of perceivers of the false are veiled truths.

An object found by a direct perceiver of the true is a phenomenon that exists the way it appears; it is an *ultimate truth*. Ultimate truths are objects found by probing awareness that perceives phenomena as they actually are. They are nondualistically realized by nonconceptual, direct reliable cognizers. Since only emptinesses are true in this way, only they are ultimate truths.

An object seen by perceivers of the false—by an awareness under the influence of ignorance—is a *veiled truth*. These objects are falsities because they do not exist in the way they appear: they appear truly existent although they are not. When we say that veiled truths appear truly existent, it may sound like that false appearance is projected by the object itself; but an apple and a jet plane don't cause themselves to appear truly existent. Rather, ignorance and its latencies on our mindstreams obscure our consciousnesses so that apples, people, gravity, and so forth falsely appear truly existent to them. The latencies of ignorance are completely eradicated only at buddhahood. Even arhats' and āryas' minds that are not in meditative equipoise directly perceiving emptiness have this false appearance. However, because these beings have previously perceived emptiness directly, they know this appearance is false.

The reality—the ultimate nature—of veiled truths is concealed or veiled by ignorance. Ignorance does not establish their existence because ignorance is a wrong consciousness. They are objects dualistically realized by direct and inferential reliable cognizers that cognize them. Veiled truths are truths for ignorance because they do not exist as they appear, not because only ignorant people perceive them. Apples, people, and mental factors are examples of veiled or conventional truths; their actual mode of existence is an ultimate truth. However, truly existent apples and so forth—the conceived objects of ignorance—do not exist at all and are not veiled truths.

False veiled truths exist. They are not made up in order to communicate with ordinary foolish people who do not perceive emptiness. This is an important point, because some people deprecate veiled truths and reify ultimate truths, seeing the latter as an independent absolute unrelated to mind. In this way they fall to the two extremes of absolutism and nihilism, reifying ultimate truth and deprecating veiled truths. In fact, both truths are dependently existing phenomena; they depend on each other and on the consciousnesses that apprehend them, among other factors.

Some people mistakenly believe that veiled truths are known only by immature ordinary beings who perceive falsities, whereas emptiness is known only by āryas who know suchness. This is not the case. Ordinary beings on the paths of accumulation and preparation—and even those who have not yet entered a path—can realize emptiness inferentially. Āryas also perceive veiled truths; they must in order to engage in their daily life activities.

Buddhist Tenet Systems and the Two Truths

The topic of the two truths is common to many classical Indian philosophical traditions, both Buddhist and non-Buddhist, although how the two truths are defined differs. When we understand the order of the Buddhist tenet systems as the way for practitioners to gradually develop more profound views, the array of views concerning the two truths becomes clearer.[2] For Vaibhāṣikas, a veiled truth is a phenomenon that, when physically broken down or mentally isolated into parts, can no longer generate a consciousness knowing that object. A person and a table are examples of veiled truths. If you break the table into parts, you no longer see a table there. An ultimate truth is an object that, no matter how it is broken down physically or isolated into parts mentally, still generates the thought of that object. Directionally partless particles, temporally partless moments of mind, and unproduced space are examples of ultimate truths.

For Sautrāntikas—specifically Sautrāntika-Reasoning Proponents—a phenomenon that is ultimately able to perform a function is an ultimate truth, and a phenomenon that is not ultimately able to perform a function is a veiled truth. Unlike other Buddhist systems, they say all impermanent things—such as a person and a table—are ultimate truths because they ultimately perform a function. In this view, veiled truths are imputations—permanent phenomena such as permanent space, conceptual appearances, and true cessations.

According to Yogācārins, an ultimate truth is a phenomenon that is the final object of awareness of the path of purification. It is realized by a direct reliable cognizer that realizes it clearly without dualistic appearance; emptiness, consummate phenomena such as true cessations, and suchness are ultimate truths. All other phenomena, such as tables and persons, are veiled truths.

For Svātantrika Mādhyamikas, veiled truths are objects that are realized with dualistic appearance by their reliable cognizers, whereas ultimate truths are those realized by direct reliable cognizers by the vanishing of dualistic appearances. Chairs, tables, persons, and conceptual appearances are examples of veiled truths, while the emptiness of true existence is ultimate truth.

According to Prāsaṅgika Mādhyamikas, veiled truths—also called conventional or nominal truths—are objects found by a conventional reliable cognizer perceiving a false knowable object.

The definitions of the two truths for the Vaibhāṣikas and Sautrāntikas have to do with how or if objects function in the world. The definitions for the Yogācārins and Mādhyamikas are related to how phenomena exist, the type of cognizers that apprehend them, and how they appear to those minds.

REFLECTION

1. What are the two truths? What are some of the defining characteristics of each truth?
2. What are the benefits of understanding the two truths? What are the drawbacks of not understanding them correctly?

2 | Veiled Truths

THE DEFINITIONS OF veiled or conventional truths given by the masters of the Nālandā tradition have changed over the centuries, probably due to the concerns of people at the time. Candrakīrti emphasizes the false and illusory nature of veiled truths, not their conventional existence. In the *Supplement* he says, "[The Buddha] said that all phenomena have two natures—those found by perceivers of the true and of the false. Objects of perceivers of the true are suchness; objects of perceivers of the false are veiled truths."

Tsongkhapa in *Illumination of the Intent* says, "An object found by a conventional reliable cognizer perceiving a false knowable object is a veiled truth." In *Ocean of Reasoning* he explains veiled truths in relation to a sprout as "the entity of a sprout that is found by a conventional consciousness comprehending a knowable object that is a false, deceptive object." He maintains Candrakīrti's emphasis that veiled truths are false and deceptive, but emphasizes that they are known by conventional reliable cognizers. In this way he clarifies that veiled truths are validly existing objects; they are not nonexistent. His clarification remedies the tendency toward nihilism of earlier Tibetan masters. Emptiness and dependent arising are compatible; veiled truths exist even though they lack inherent existence. Tsongkhapa explains illusion-like existence in his *Middle Stages of the Path*, and in the *Great Treatise on the Stages of the Path*, he gives a lengthy quote from the *King of Concentration Sūtra* (*Samādhirāja Sūtra*) about the false and deceptive nature of conventionalities.[3]

Tsongkhapa's immediate disciple, Kedrup, defines veiled truth as "that with regard to which the reliable cognizer by which it is found becomes a distinguisher of conventions." Tsongkhapa's definition emphasizes veiled truths being false and deceptive as well as their being knowable objects, whereas Kedrup's definition emphasizes their being existent knowable objects perceived by conventional reliable cognizers. Kedrup explains later that "distinguisher of conventions" means "a mind that examines the qualities of falsities without questioning their deceptive appearance as inherently existent."

A few centuries later, in the tenets texts written by Tibetan masters, the false and deceptive nature of veiled truths is not emphasized, whereas establishing their validity is. Jamyang Shepa gives two definitions of veiled truth: "that which is an object found by a conventional reliable cognizer that comprehends it and that becomes a conventional reliable cognizer with regard to it," and "an object explicitly found by an awareness engaging in the terms or conventions of the world." Ngawang Palden gives the definition as "an object found by a reasoning consciousness distinguishing conventions," and Konchog Jigme Wangpo defines it as "an object that is found by a reliable cognizer distinguishing a veiling and with respect to which a reliable cognizer distinguishing a veiling becomes a reliable cognizer distinguishing a veiling." All these definitions focus on establishing the validity of veiled truths. Their cumbersome wording is due to wanting to include a Buddha's omniscient mind as a knower of veiled truths. These later writers preserve the emphasis on validity in Tsongkhapa's writings, but not his stress on veiled truths being false.

Nowadays, the extremes of both nihilism and absolutism thrive in society; thus emphasizing both the falsity and the reliability of veiled truths is needed. If we neglect to emphasize their falsity, we may slide into thinking that veiled truths are the very objects that exist exactly as our ignorance perceives them. If we neglect to emphasize that veiled truths are known by conventional reliable cognizers, we risk slipping into nihilism and negating the validity of cause and effect. Holding in mind that conventionalities are false yet exist will keep us in the Middle Way.

Why the Buddha Taught Veiled Truths

In the *Meeting of the Father and Son Sūtra*, the Buddha said (GR 361):

For the sake of engendering faith in bliss
in those beings journeying to the state of a sugata,
the Conqueror has revealed the veiled truth;
this is for the sake of helping people of the world.

To encourage people to practice the path and attain the state of a sugata, one gone to bliss, and to have faith in the goal of the path, the Buddha described it as a blissful state of omniscience. Faith, bliss, and beings who are sugatas are all veilings.

In the same sūtra, he also cautioned us to be aware of entanglements with other veiled truths (GR 362):

Beings who delight in this [surface level of truth]
revolve in cyclic existence with eight worldly concerns:
gain and loss, pleasing and unpleasing,
praise and disparagement, pleasure and pain.

When they gain something, attachment for it arises;
when they do not gain, this too causes distress;
those not spoken of here should be known likewise.
Through these eight diseases, their minds are harmed.

The "eight diseases" are the eight worldly concerns: gain and loss, disrepute and fame, blame and praise, pleasure and pain, all of which are veiled truths.[4] When we take delight in veiled truths with all of their interesting diversity and don't make effort to understand ultimate truths, we easily become enchanted with and attached to their attractive qualities. When we cannot obtain attractive objects or encounter unattractive or harmful ones, distress and anger flare up. Their attractive and ugly qualities and these pleasing and unpleasant objects are falsities, appearing truly existent although they are not. They are called "truths" only from the perspective of ignorance. Seeing them as they actually are and realizing their ultimate nature frees us from being captivated by them.

The Meaning of Saṃvṛti

"Veiled truth" and "conventional truth" are synonymous translations of the Sanskrit term *saṃvṛtisatya*. The term *saṃvṛti* has three meanings—veiled, interdependent, and conventional. These three are not definitions but general etymologies. Nevertheless, knowing the etymology helps us to understand what veiled or conventional truths are.

The **first meaning of *saṃvṛti***—veil—refers to ignorance, the veiler (*samantādvarana*) that obscures and veils the mind from knowing things as they really are. Ignorance conceals the ultimate nature of every phenomenon—its emptiness—and superimposes true existence on it instead. *Veiled truths* or *truths for a veiler* appear true to an ignorant mind. Although veiled truths in fact lack true existence, they appear truly existent. All phenomena except emptinesses are veiled truths because all appear truly existent to their principal reliable cognizers. Although emptiness appears truly existent to an inferential cognizer, it is not a veiled truth because āryas' meditative equipoise on emptiness directly and nonconceptually realizing emptiness is the principal cognizer of emptiness and does not superimpose true existence on emptiness.

Ultimate truths exist the way they appear to wisdom, whereas veiled truths are true only from the distorted viewpoint of ignorance, which veils phenomena's actual mode of existence, their empty nature. Although they are called "truths," veiled truths are not actual truths because they do not exist as they appear; they appear truly existent but are not. They are falsities (*mṛṣā*, *mithya*) because they appear one way—truly existent—although they exist in another way—empty of true existence.

"Veil" refers to the ignorance in whose perspective objects are mistakenly posited to be true—that is, to exist in the way they appear. But the consciousnesses that posit objects as existing are not ignorance; they are conventional reliable cognizers. Objects are posited as truths from the perspective of true-grasping consciousnesses, even though these objects are not true—they do not exist in the way they appear. Tsongkhapa clarifies (GR 239):

> The reason why a fact needs to be established as false to be established as a veiled truth by an instance of cognition is this: When the meaning of *truth* is understood in the context of the veiled

> truth of, for example, vases and so on, we need to bear in mind two senses of the term *truth*—one from the perspective of the subject (the cognizer) and the other in the objective sense. When one sees that their truth is not posited in the objective sense but posited as true merely from the perspective of grasping true existence, [which is] the veiler (*saṃvṛti*), one comes to recognize that without such qualification, such phenomena do not possess true existence and are instead seen to be false.

For phenomena to be established as veiled truths, they must first be understood as false because their being called "truth" is from the perspective of an ignorant mind. They are not truly existent objects in and of themselves even though the ignorant true-grasping mind apprehends them to be true. By understanding this, we will know them to be false and lacking true existence. If we don't understand that true existence is projected from the mind and instead think that it comes from the side of the object, we won't be able to see veiled truths as falsities and will instead believe that our ordinary consciousnesses perceive phenomena's ultimate nature.

The ignorance that erroneously grasps phenomena as truly existent is the ignorance that is the first of the twelve links of dependent arising.[5] This ignorance is an afflictive obscuration. As a wrong consciousness, ignorance does not establish phenomena as veiled truths. In fact, what ignorance grasps—inherently existent people, truly existent buildings and fields, and so on—doesn't exist even conventionally. They are called "truths" merely from the perspective of ignorance.

Although at present we may not be able to identify the appearance of true existence or the conceived object of true-grasping, hearing that our everyday sense consciousnesses and the objects they perceive are false stimulates us to begin to doubt our perceptions and assumptions. This doubt leads us to investigate how things actually exist, which in turn increases our interest in learning, thinking, and meditating on emptiness.

The **second meaning of *saṃvṛti***—interdependent or mutually dependent (*parasparasaṃbhavana*, T. *phan tshun rten pa*)—indicates that phenomena do not exist from their own side but exist dependent on many other factors, including the conventional reliable cognizers that know them. This is the meaning of "conventional" in the phrase "conventional existence"—

existing dependent on many factors. Many phenomena are also mutually dependent in that they are posited in relation to other phenomena. Up and down are posited in relation to each other; so are veiled truth and ultimate truth; agent, object, and action; and so on. Saying that veilings are interdependent stresses that their appearance as truly existent is false and they do not exist in the way they appear.

Ultimate truths—emptinesses—are dependent and lack inherent nature; they depend on their bases and on the conventional reliable cognizers that establish their existence. The emptiness of the plum depends on the plum, which is the basis of the emptiness of the plum, and on the conventional reliable cognizer that establishes that emptiness exists. Emptiness conventionally exists—conventional existence is the only type of existence there is. Emptiness is not a veiled truth because it is not false; it exists the way it appears to its principal cognizer.

The **third meaning of** ***saṃvṛti***—convention—refers to worldly conventions, which concerns objects expressed and means of expression. Means of expression are "object possessors"—terms and consciousnesses, both of which possess their own objects. Terms possess objects in that they refer to something. The term "apple" refers to a red, round, crunchy fruit. The visual consciousness possesses an object, such as the apple it sees. The conventional, everyday world depends on language and concepts and on ordinary nonanalytical consciousnesses that know their objects. In this context, nonanalytical consciousnesses are those that do not probe the ultimate nature of their objects, although they may engage in conventional analysis such as deciding whether an action is virtuous or nonvirtuous, or if this fruit is a tangelo or a tangerine. Conventions include mutually accepted principles and ideas of time, distance, laws of nature, cause and effect, logic, and so on.

It's important not to get confused over the meaning of "conventional"—another translation of *saṃvṛti*—when it is used in two different circumstances. When "conventional" means "veiled," as in "veiled truths," it refers to the perspective from which things are seen as true by the veiler, ignorance. But "conventional" in "conventionally existent" means that phenomena exist according to worldly conventions. Conventional existence is juxtaposed with ultimate existence. Although nothing exists ultimately, because only emptiness is found when phenomena are examined with ultimate analysis, phenomena do exist conventionally, as certified by conventional reliable cognizers.

Like the above two etymologies, "convention" is not a definition of *saṃvṛti*. Even though emptiness is the object of a term and of the consciousness perceiving it, it is not a veiled truth (conventional truth) because it exists in the way it appears to a consciousness that directly perceives it. Emptiness appears empty of true existence and is empty of true existence. Nonetheless, it exists conventionally. To exist ultimately, something would have to be found under ultimate analysis, and no phenomenon is found by ultimate analysis to be its own ultimate nature.

Impure phenomena—so-called because they arise under the influence of afflictions and karma—are veiled truths. These include our saṃsāric bodies and minds, the twelve links of dependent origination, and our environment. Many pure phenomena are also veiled truths. Produced by the accumulation of merit, they include the buddhas' enjoyment bodies, buddhas' purelands, buddhas' compassion, as well as path consciousnesses and the eightfold ārya path. These are conventional truths in that they are perceived as truly existent by a mind affected by ignorance and its latencies.

Please note that although whatever is a veiled truth necessarily appears true to a veiled consciousness, whatever appears true to a veiled consciousness is not necessarily a veiled truth. A truly existent lamp appears true to a true-grasping consciousness, but it is not a veiled truth because it does not exist. A lamp, however, is a veiled truth. Initially this may sound strange because as yet we are unable to distinguish a truly existent lamp from a lamp. We think they are the same although they are not. The former does not exist; the latter does. The more we think about this, the clearer the difference between them will become.

Although veiled truths are true from the viewpoint of ignorance, ignorance does not establish their existence. As an erroneous consciousness, ignorance cannot establish the existence of phenomena. The conceived object of ignorance—a truly existent bottle, for example—does not exist at all, but a bottle exists. It is a veiled truth, whose existence is established by a conventional reliable cognizer, a visual consciousness perceiving that bottle. Candrakīrti says in his *Commentary on the Supplement* (FEW 325):

> Ignorance grasps true existence and thus the object grasped by it does not exist even conventionally, and whatever is a veiled truth necessarily exists conventionally.

Furthermore, it is not the case that veiled truths exist only for an ignorant mind. If that were so, the entire world would cease for someone who has attained nirvāṇa. Veiled truths continue to exist after we have realized emptiness nonconceptually; āryas and buddhas also perceive them.

Understanding the evolution of afflictions helps us discern veiled truths from nonexistents. In dependence on ignorance, distorted conceptions arise. They superimpose more characteristics, such as inherent attractiveness and unattractiveness, on the inherently existent object grasped by ignorance. Responding to ignorance's false superimposition of inherent beauty and ugliness, other afflictions arise. Analytical reasoning can be used to refute the inherent existence grasped by ignorance. It can also disprove distorted conceptions and the erroneous ways that attachment, anger, and other afflictions apprehend their objects. In his *Commentary on the "Four Hundred Verses,"* Candrakīrti says (LC 3.183):

> Attachment and so forth superimpose characteristics such as attractiveness or unattractiveness only upon the inherent nature of things that ignorance has superimposed. Therefore they do not work apart from ignorance; they depend on ignorance. This is because ignorance is the main affliction.

The conceived objects of these innate afflictions can be refuted by reasoning and do not exist even conventionally. Here we must differentiate two types of objects of innate minds. The first are those that reasoning cannot refute. For example, money, which is posited by a conventional reliable cognizer, exists conventionally and cannot be refuted by reasoning. The second are those that reasoning can refute. Inherently desirable money—that is, money as it is seen by a mind filled with greed—does not exist even conventionally. In this case, the extreme allure of money is superimposed and exaggerated.

Differentiating these is important in order to discern the difference between an afflicted mind and a conventional reliable cognizer and to differentiate a nonexistent from an existent object. This is a delicate procedure, for we must be able to not only negate inherently existent objects but also establish conventionally existent ones.

REFLECTION

1. What are the three meanings of *saṃvṛti*?
2. Are veiled truths true?
3. If they are false, does that mean there is no value in learning and understanding them?

Veiled Truths and Veilings

All consciousnesses of sentient beings, except for āryas' minds of meditative equipoise directly realizing emptiness, are deceived in that phenomena appear truly existent to them although they are not. The "three types of beings"—that is, śrāvaka arhats, solitary-realizer arhats, and pure-ground bodhisattvas—have eradicated all afflictive obscurations. They know that all conditioned phenomena are empty of true existence but appear truly existent, just as a mirage in the desert is empty of water but appears to be water. A boat that appears truly existent is false. The boat exists, but the true existence superimposed on it does not.

Although worldly beings may know veiled truths, such as a person or a flower, they do not know them *as* veiled truths. To do that, they must first ascertain them as false; but without having refuted these things as true, they cannot establish with a reliable cognizer that they are falsities. In other words, to know they are false, practitioners must first realize emptiness and refute the existence of the conceived object of true-grasping—truly existent phenomena. Only then can they establish these knowable objects as falsities and as veiled truths. Although cars and people are veiled truths, a mind establishing them as existent does not necessarily know them as veiled truths.

When false things appear to the three types of beings, they recognize them as falsities and see them as like illusions—things that do not exist as they appear. From the perspective of these three types of beings, boats, feelings, and forests are "mere veilings" (mere conventionalities, *saṃvṛtimātra*). "Mere" eliminates their being truths, but that does not mean that the three types of āryas don't cognize veiled truths. Whatever is a veiled truth exists conventionally, and these liberated beings perceive conventionally existent phenomena.

Other beings who are not one of the three types of beings or buddhas possess self-grasping ignorance. Of these, ordinary beings—those who have not yet attained the path of seeing—do not directly perceive any objects as empty of true existence. Bodhisattvas on the first-to-seventh grounds perceive emptiness directly in meditative equipoise. During this time, they do not perceive veiled truths. Since veiled truths appear truly existent, they are not perceived by wisdom consciousnesses realizing the lack of true existence. As long as the awareness of emptiness has not faded in post-meditation times, they will see things as like illusions. However, since they still have self-grasping ignorance—even though it is much weaker than the ignorance of ordinary beings—they are not included in the three types of beings who perceive veiled truths as mere veilings.

As ordinary beings, we have both afflictive obscurations and cognitive obscurations. Ārya bodhisattvas below the eighth ground have eliminated some, but not all, afflictive obscurations, which include true-grasping and all other afflictions. Bodhisattvas on the pure grounds (eighth, ninth, and tenth grounds) have eliminated all afflictive obscurations and are similar to arhats in that particular regard. All ārya bodhisattvas on the ten grounds—but not buddhas—possess cognitive obscurations: the latencies of ignorance, anger, and attachment, and the appearance of true existence (dualistic perceptions) that these bring about.

During meditative equipoise on emptiness, neither the appearance of true existence nor true-grasping appear to the minds of āryas. In post-meditation, all of them (except buddhas) have the appearance of true existence and know it to be false. What they perceive in meditative equipoise and in post-meditation differs greatly. Buddhas, on the other hand, perceive both emptiness and veilings simultaneously.

Conventional truths appear falsely to the three types of beings, but they exist the way they appear to buddhas because buddhas have eliminated all obscurations from their mindstreams. The latencies of ignorance, which are cognitive obscurations, are the source of the false appearance of true existence that plagues all sentient beings. Since buddhas have eradicated these forever, phenomena no longer appear falsely to them. However, since buddhas perceive all phenomena—which includes veiled truths as sentient beings perceive them—they also know false appearances because these appear to sentient beings.

Distinctions among Veiled Truths

Knowable objects or existents can be divided into ultimate truths and veiled truths. Veiled truths are true to an ignorant mind, although when compared with ultimate truths they are false because they appear truly existent although they are not. The consciousnesses to which these false veiled truths appear are mistaken because objects appear to be truly existent to them. These consciousnesses cannot posit their false objects because truly existent objects do not exist, and their falseness can be identified and eliminated only through reasoning analyzing the ultimate and meditative equipoise on emptiness. This is said from the perspective of Mādhyamikas.

The discussion beginning with the verse below is stated from the *perspective of the world*—that is, how things appear to and are apprehended by the everyday consciousnesses of people who have not realized emptiness either inferentially or directly. These everyday conventional consciousnesses are *perceivers of falsities* because their objects appear to be truly existent although they are not. Candrakīrti says (MMA 6.24):

> Also, perceivers of falsities are of two types:
> those with clear sense faculties and those with impaired sensory faculties.
> A consciousness with an impaired sense faculty
> is considered wrong compared with a consciousness with an unimpaired sense faculty.

Worldly consciousnesses (T. *'jig rten pa'i shes pa*) are the sense and mental consciousnesses in the mindstreams of ordinary beings and āryas that perceive veiled truths. Worldly consciousnesses are of two types: those that are accurate (*tathya*, T. *yang dag*) and those that are wrong (*mithyā*, T. *log pa*). The former has clear sense faculties, the latter has impaired faculties. Here, impaired faculties are those with superficial, adventitious defects. Those consciousnesses that depend on unimpaired faculties are correct (T. *phyin ci ma log pa*) and those depending on impaired faculties are incorrect (T. *phyin ci log pa*) in relation to the world. Their objects are posited respectively as accurate or fraudulent in relation to the world. Candrakīrti says (MMA 6.25):

> Objects known by the world [and] apprehended
> by the six unimpaired sense faculties
> are correct from just [the perspective of] the world.
> The rest are posited as wrong (fraudulent) from just [the perspective of] the world.

Prāsaṅgikas negate true existence even conventionally and consider objects that appear to be truly existent to be false and mistaken. Since all veiled truths appear inherently existent although they are not, all of them are falsities. For this reason, Prāsaṅgikas do not make a distinction between accurate and fraudulent veiled truths, because all veiled truths appear deceptively to sentient beings.

However, objects can be deemed accurate or fraudulent *in relation to the world* (T. *'jig rten shes ngo la ltos te*) depending on whether a conventional reliable cognizer—a conventional consciousness with unimpaired faculties—validates or discredits them in relation to the world. For example, a pot is perceived by a conventional reliable cognizer. Because it can perform a function that accords with its appearance, it is an accurate veiled truth. The ghost seen in a hologram, on the other hand, is not able to perform a function in accord with its appearance and is a fraudulent veiled truth.

Impaired faculties prevent us from knowing everyday conventional things correctly. They may have an internal or external cause of error. *Internal causes* of error include jaundice, which causes a yellowish appearance; bad eyes that cause blurry perceptions; and drugs that cause hallucinations. *External causes* of error are, for example, a quickly turning propeller that appears as a circle, a mirror that seems to be a real face, a cave reverberating an echo, sunlight on asphalt or sand forming a mirage, as well as televisions, hologram projectors, and magicians' mantras and salves that create the appearance of things that are not there. Our location may also be an external cause of error: while riding in a car, the scenery around us appears to move, whereas in fact it is stationary and we are moving. Although these external causes of error are not within the person, they nevertheless become the cause for seeing mirages, reflections, and so on.

The causes of error of the mental faculty are wrong philosophical or psychological beliefs, false reasonings, and sleep, which causes us to believe dream objects are real. People who have learned that a permanent soul exists believe this. People who were instructed that it is proper to avenge harms inflicted on their ancestors will regard certain individuals, ethnic or religious groups, or countries as evil, thus justifying taking revenge on them. People who are told that the causes of suffering lie with their genes and neural activity in the brain will attribute their suffering to these chemical and electrical events. The notion of superior and inferior races as set forth by social Darwinism is another wrong philosophical view that has resulted in millions of deaths in the twentieth century and even today. Many afflictions arise due to incorrect beliefs that people erroneously hold as true, and many wars are fought under their influence. The ability to discern accurate and fraudulent veiled truths is not merely an intellectual endeavor; it has real implications for sentient beings' welfare.

All of the above are superficial causes of error. Reliable cognizers of ordinary people without impaired faculties know that a mirage isn't water, that the objects they see are blurry due to cataracts, and that the scenery around them is not moving when they ride in a train. As babies they may not know that the baby in the mirror isn't a real baby, but as they grow up this will become obvious to them.

Incorrect philosophical or psychological beliefs and distorted reasonings are also temporary and superficial impairments, even though ordinary worldly cognizers would not regard them as fraudulent—after all, not many ordinary people contemplate whether or not a primal substance exists. However, those whose mental faculty is not impaired by wrong philosophical or psychological beliefs, false reasonings, or sleep know that a permanent soul does not exist, nor does an external creator or a universal mind. We may learn incorrect beliefs at any time in our lives, but we can eliminate them by learning and thinking about more reasonable beliefs. The views mentioned above are acquired views that stem from superficial causes of error;[6] a conventional reasoning consciousness can disprove them. However, consciousnesses of ultimate analysis are necessary to overcome both acquired and innate views grasping true existence. Those views are not due to superficial causes of error but to a deep-seated true-grasping that has been with us since beginningless lifetimes.

As for the referents conceived by acquired and innate true-grasping, they are considered objects apprehended by unimpaired senses and are seen as accurate from the perspective of the world, even though they do not exist even conventionally. For example, when we are angry at someone, our minds grasp them as truly existent. However, truly existent enemies do not exist in the least, even though our enraged minds perceive them as very solid and existing in their own right.

Conventional reliable cognizers can discriminate between correct and incorrect consciousnesses. They know that the face in the mirror and the ghost in a hologram are unreal in relation to the world and that the red of apples and the chirping of birds are real in relation to the world. They also understand that functioning things arise from concordant causes.

Worldly Consciousnesses

Worldly consciousnesses are consciousnesses that apprehend conventionalities without analyzing whether they exist inherently or not. They are of two types:

1. Those with clear faculties. Their objects are accurate in relation to the world.
2. Those with impaired faculties that are superficial causes of error. Their objects are fraudulent in relation to the world.
   A. Sense consciousnesses associated with defective faculties.
      (1) Those with an internal cause of error: for example, jaundice, bad eyesight, or hallucinogenic drugs.
      (2) Those with an external cause of error: for example, movement, mirrors, acoustics, sunlight on asphalt. Certain medicines and mantras used by conjurers are causes of error for mental consciousnesses.
   B. Mental consciousness with impaired faculties. Their causes of error are incorrect philosophical tenets or psychological theories, false reasoning, and sleep.

The causes of error noted above are superficial and temporary in that the objects can be discerned as fraudulent in relation to the world by conventional reliable cognizers. Although the visual consciousness may see the scenery move when we are in a car, our mental conventional reliable cognizer knows that it is not moving. The visual reliable cognizers of people standing near the road can corroborate that the scenery is not moving.

Reasoning analyzing the ultimate is necessary to counteract wrong tenets that assert true existence, even though these tenets are a superficial cause of error. This reasoning is the opponent to both acquired self-grasping that holds wrong tenets and innate self-grasping that is possessed by all sentient beings. For example, as an ordinary being, Ngawang possesses innate true-grasping, just like all other beings who take rebirth under the control of afflictions and karma. One day he attends a lecture given by a philosopher espousing Sautrāntika tenets, where he is taught that all phenomena are truly existent. This sounds reasonable to him and he believes it. This is acquired true-grasping. The more Ngawang talks to his friends who believe that phenomena are truly existent and who present Ngawang with arguments to support that belief, the more confident he becomes that this view is correct. To dispel this acquired true-grasping, ultimate analysis is required, and for that someone with the correct view needs to instruct him in one or more of the Prāsaṅgika reasonings that refute true existence.

Thus it is not the case that all superficial causes of error can be counteracted by worldly consciousnesses; erroneous tenets that conceive phenomena to be inherently existent require ultimate analysis to be overcome. Similarly, it is not the case that ultimate analysis counteracts only deeper causes of error—innate true-grasping. It also opposes the wrong tenets that conceive inherent existence.

Both acquired and innate grasping of permanence can be suppressed by a reasoning consciousness that is a conventional reliable cognizer ascertaining impermanence. Eradicating these two types of grasping of permanence is more difficult and requires a yogic direct perceiver that apprehends emptiness. It is not necessary to realize emptiness with a consciousness focused on the ultimate to understand that a permanent person or a permanent universe do not exist even conventionally. However, to completely eradicate both acquired and innate grasping of permanence, we must realize emptiness directly and attain the path of seeing.

Similarly, both the acquired and innate grasping at a self-sufficient substantially existent self can be known as erroneous by a conventional reliable cognizer that has arisen through reasoning. Ultimate analysis, which investigates if something truly exists, is not necessary to know this. However, to eradicate both acquired and innate grasping of a self-sufficient substantially existent person, we must realize emptiness directly and attain the path of seeing.

ACCURATE AND FRAUDULENT OBJECTS IN RELATION TO THE WORLD

OBJECT	AFFECTED BY SUPERFICIAL CAUSES OF ERROR?	UNDERSTOOD AS FRAUDULENT BY SOMEONE WHO HASN'T UNDERSTOOD EMPTINESS?	ACCURATE IN RELATION TO THE WORLD?
Yellow flower	No	No	Yes
Scarecrow seen as a person	Yes	Yes	No
Fundamental substance asserted by non-Buddhists	Yes	Yes	No
A body that is permanent, pure, pleasurable, and self*	Yes	Yes	No
Truly existent body	No	No	Yes
Reflection of a face	Yes	Yes	No

* "Self" in this context refers to a coarse self, a self that is self-sufficient, substantially existent.

In short, an *accurate object in relation to the world* is a veiling that cannot be realized as not existing as it appears by a conventional reliable cognizer of a person who has not realized emptiness. Examples are tables, chairs, buses, combs, cats and dogs, and so forth that ordinary people without an understanding of emptiness do not see as false—as appearing to exist truly although they do not. They are objects of consciousnesses that aren't affected by a superficial cause of error. An example is an olfactory consciousness perceiving the smell of cookies baking and an auditory consciousness perceiving the sounds of a whistle.

A *fraudulent object in relation to the world* is a veiled truth that can be realized as not existing as it appears by a conventional reliable cognizer of a person who hasn't realized emptiness. That is, ordinary people can realize this object is false. Examples are the reflection of a face in a mirror, people inside a television, and drug-induced hallucinations. These things are veiled truths despite their objects being fraudulent. They are objects of a consciousness with an impaired sense faculty that is affected by an immediate cause of error, such as a visual consciousness of someone with a detached retina perceiving flashing lights that aren't there.

Thus there are two degrees of "not existing as it appears." All veiled truths are mistaken in that they do not exist as they appear: they appear truly existent although they are not. Fraudulent veiled truths, such as a mirage that appears to be water, do not exist in the way they appear, in that they appear to conventional consciousnesses with impaired faculties and they can be known as false in relation to the world.

A *correct subject in relation to the world* is a consciousness that a conventional reliable cognizer of a person who hasn't realized emptiness cannot ascertain is a wrong consciousness. An example is a mental consciousness apprehending a flower to truly exist. An *incorrect subject in relation to the world* is a consciousness that a conventional reliable cognizer of a person who hasn't realized emptiness can realize as a wrong consciousness. Examples are an auditory consciousness of an ordinary being that takes an automated voice as the voice of a human being.

REFLECTION

1. What does it mean to be accurate or fraudulent in relation to the world?
2. How does a reflection of your face in the mirror differ from your face?
3. Give some examples of cognitions that are affected by a superficial cause of error.
4. Give examples of some veiled truths that are accurate in relation to the world. Does an ordinary being perceive them without any error?

False and Mistaken

There is a deeper deceptive factor that makes all consciousnesses of sentient beings except the wisdom minds of āryas in meditative equipoise on emptiness mistaken. This culprit is the innate self-grasping ignorance and its latencies, under the influence of which all phenomena appear truly existent although they are not. Although reliable worldly consciousnesses of ordinary beings can know objects affected by superficial causes of error as fraudulent, they cannot recognize the appearance of true existence as mistaken. Only reasoning analyzing the ultimate can break through ignorance and know the appearance of true existence is mistaken. Our reliable mental cognizer knows that the people on the television screen are unreal and do not exist. But it does not examine the ultimate nature and thus does not know that although the television appears truly existent, this appearance is false. Ultimate analysis is needed to know this.

Sense consciousnesses to which persons, fruit, trees, and text messages appear truly existent are mistaken; nothing is truly existent. Nevertheless, those objects exist and are accurate conventionally; they are apprehended by conventional reliable cognizers. When we pull the corner of our eye and see two moons, or perceive a face in the mirror, a conventional reliable cognizer knows that such objects are fraudulent and the conventional consciousnesses that perceive them are erroneous. Reasoning analyzing the ultimate isn't necessary to know this.

When a conventional consciousness knows that the reflection doesn't exist as it appears and is false, does that consciousness know that the reflection of the face lacks true existence? No, it does not. There are two kinds of falsities: (1) those that can be discerned as false by conventional reliable cognizers, such as a face reflected in a mirror that our mental consciousness knows is not a face, and (2) those that must be known as false by employing ultimate analysis, such as a tree that appears to be a truly existent tree. Only wisdom analyzing the ultimate knows a truly existent tree is false because such a tree doesn't exist.

Trees and reflections both appear to conventional consciousness, and a worldly consciousness knows that the reflection of a face is false. It is fraudulent for the world—that is, for a conventional consciousness. A face in the mirror does not exist and is not a conventional truth. A tree that appears truly existent is also false, but in a different way, because a conventional consciousness cannot know it as false. Thus the tree is accurate in relation to the world—that is, it is accurate for a worldly conventional consciousness. However, it is a falsity because it appears truly existent although it is not. This conventional consciousness apprehending the tree is *mistaken* because the tree appears truly existent to it although it isn't; however, it is a correct consciousness in that it accurately knows that is a tree. There is no contradiction in that consciousness being both mistaken and accurate. There is also no contradiction in the tree being a veiled truth and a falsity.

Can a conventional consciousness refute true existence?[7] Tsongkhapa clarifies (LC 3.174):

> Reason refutes the essential or inherent existence of forms and so forth. It cannot do this ultimately [because nothing can be done ultimately in this system that refutes ultimate existence], so it must do it conventionally. For that kind of conventional consciousness, the sense consciousnesses are mistaken. Apart from that, the sensory consciousnesses are not mistaken as seen by ordinary conventional consciousnesses; thus there is no contradiction. For example, it is like the worldly convention, "Some are here; some are not here." The term "some" is the same, but no one supposes that the some who are here and the some who are not here are the same. So also, the "nonmistaken" quality of the sensory consciousnesses is posited in terms of an ordinary worldly consciousness; Mādhyamikas do not assert them to be nonmistaken.

Nevertheless, these mistaken sense consciousnesses can posit conventional truths. All phenomena except emptiness are like illusions and are falsities. Candrakīrti says (LC 3.175):

> Because ignorance obscures the nature of phenomena, we call it the veiler.

An object, such as a building, is true for the veiler, ignorance, and is a veiled truth, although it is a falsity. But what about the reflection of a face; is that a veiled truth? Tsongkhapa says in his *Middle Exposition of the Stages of the Path* (TT 133):

> Since the reflection of a face, for instance, is not accurate as a face for a worldly conventional [consciousness] of someone trained in language, it is not a veiled truth in relation to [that consciousness].

> Nonetheless, because it is an object found by a perceiver of a false knowable object—a deceptive object—it is a veiled truth.

Veiled truths are true for worldly conventional consciousnesses. The reflection of a face in a mirror is not accurate for a worldly conventional consciousness of someone who knows reflections are false. However, since it is an object found by a conventional reliable consciousness perceiving a false knowable object (this is the definition of a veiled truth)—that is, by a consciousness to which a truly existent object mistakenly appears—it is a veiled truth. The veiling consciousness in "veiled truth in relation to the world" does not grasp true existence; it is a consciousness knowing that the reflection of a face is a face. However, the veiling consciousness for veiled truths is ignorance. For that reason, the reflection of a face is a veiled truth. It has two levels of falsity: superficially it appears to be a face although it is not; on a deeper level it appears truly existent although it is not. Knowing that a reflection of a face isn't a face is not knowing its ultimate nature or its emptiness.

Emptiness is not perceived by worldly consciousnesses. It is true because it exists as it appears to the principal cognizer that knows it—a direct perceiver of emptiness. Emptiness is not a conventional truth because it is not an object found by a conventional reliable cognizer perceiving a false knowable object.

False, Mistaken, False for the World

	Discerned as false for the world by conventional cognizer	To know it, ultimate analysis is required	Appears falsely to its principal cognizer	Conventional truth	Ultimate truth
Reflection of face in a mirror	Yes	No	Yes	Yes	No
Tree	No	No	Yes	Yes	No
Emptiness	No	Yes	No	No	Yes
I	No	No	Yes	Yes	No

If this discussion of truth and falsity, reliable and unreliable, accurate and fraudulent, mistaken and erroneous, and so on leaves you confused and wondering what is the purpose of all these categories, there is meaning and purpose to it. Dividing phenomena into those that are true and those that are false reminds us that the objects we ordinary beings perceive with our senses and our mental consciousness do not exist the way they appear. In addition, when we grasp those false objects as true, our minds are wrong consciousnesses—the truly existent objects we grasp do not exist.

That can be shocking to realize, for when we're angry, how many of us are aware that the truly existent I who feels harmed and the truly existent person who is harming us do not exist? This forces us to explore how grasping things as truly existent is the source of our duḥkha and counteracting it is the path to liberation. True-grasping is a stealthy and crafty invader that occupies our minds and causes the havoc of anger, greed, jealousy, arrogance, confusion, and the rest. Thinking the people and objects grasped by true-grasping exist, we become inflamed about what is the creation of our own minds.

Discerning what is accurate from what is fraudulent from the perspective of the world stimulates us to investigate our sense perceptions. If we are called to testify in court regarding what we saw, are we sure that we saw this person and not that one? Did we hear those words, or did we just imagine we heard them? That is, did our visual and auditory consciousnesses have impaired faculties?

Going deeper, we must also check our thoughts, assumptions, and conclusions to see if our mental consciousness suffers from impaired faculties. We ask ourselves: Is my belief based on rumor or hearsay or is there factual evidence? Have I fallen prey to disinformation, or do my thoughts accord with the three criteria that affirm something as conventionally existent? These questions are important in our world where we are bombarded with contrary information.

In short, these discussions pertain to our daily lives and give us ways to check the accuracy of both our sense perceptions and our thoughts.

True and False

I (Chodron) have noticed that in our native language we accept that a word can have many different meanings depending on the context. However, when studying translations of philosophical texts, we would like a word to have the same meaning in all contexts. The words "true" and "false" as translated from Sanskrit or Tibetan are good examples of words having divergent meanings according to the circumstance or the scholar. In "ultimate truth," "truth" means something that exists the way it appears to its principal cognizer, as emptinesses do. In "veiled truths," "truth" means true for a mind influenced by ignorance. But veiled truths are falsities because they do not exist inherently the way they appear to. To arhats, pure-ground bodhisattvas, and buddhas, who have eliminated ignorance, veiled truths appear false, like illusions. These beings see veiled truths as falsities, as mere conventionalities, because they do not see them as true.

In "truly exist," "true" is understood in terms of an object's mode of existence. A truly existent phenomenon exists by its own character without being posited by thought. Although phenomena appear truly existent—they appear to exist objectively without being posited by thought—they are not. They are falsely existent. Here "false" means existing only nominally, by being merely posited by thought. Thus all phenomena, including ultimate truths, are falsely existent because they exist by being merely designated by mind. It may sound strange to say that emptiness is falsely existent, because emptiness is true in that it exists the way it appears. We must remember that here "falsely" means "nominally"; it doesn't mean erroneous or nonexistent.

In other contexts, "false" means something does not exist in the way it appears. In an example of coarse falsity, a reflection of a face is false because although a face appears, there is no face there. But when we say "veiled truths are falsities," it means that they don't exist from their own side although they appear to. Their appearance as existing from their own side is false.

When Prāsaṅgikas assert that veiled truths are false, it doesn't mean they don't conventionally exist or that they are not dependent arisings. Falsities such as a radio or a barber are dependent arisings and they conventionally exist. They're established as existent by conventional reliable cognizers, not by reasoning analyzing the ultimate. Such a reasoning consciousness can ascertain that they lack true existence, but that does not negate their conventional existence. Although this reasoning consciousness can refute the existence of an inherently existent piece of bread, it cannot refute the conventional existence of the bread that satisfies our hunger when we eat it.

REFLECTION

1. What are some of the meanings of "true"?
2. Why are veiled truths false? What is the difference between a veiled truth being false and being fraudulent? Give examples of both.
3. When we cognize a veiled truth as truly existent, is that cognition correct?

Conventional Consciousnesses

There are two types of conventional consciousnesses (T. *tha snyad pa'i shes pa*): (1) ordinary conventional consciousnesses that are not influenced by a realization of emptiness, and (2) special conventional consciousnesses that are influenced by reasoning analyzing the ultimate.

Ordinary conventional consciousnesses are mistaken with respect to their appearing objects because they appear to exist inherently although they do not. Nevertheless, an ordinary conventional consciousness can determine that an object is false when a superficial cause of error is present. For example, when we look at a propeller of a plane that is rotating quickly, it looks like a circle. An ordinary conventional consciousness can determine that this is an optical illusion and thus an erroneous perception.

A special conventional consciousness arises in the wake of the realization of emptiness. Influenced by that previous consciousness that has realized emptiness, it knows that the sense consciousnesses are mistaken and their objects are false because they appear inherently existent whereas they are not. Although a special conventional consciousness does not realize emptiness itself, it is influenced by a mind that does. For example, when an ārya arises from meditative equipoise on emptiness and sees the room, she knows its appearance as inherently existent is false and sees it as like an illusion. Similarly, compassion of the unapprehendable, the third type of compassion Candrakīrti praised in the *Supplement's* homage,[8] is influenced by a previous mind realizing emptiness and sees sentient beings as false, like illusions in that they appear truly existent although they are not.

A special conventional consciousness can perceive conventionalities that an ordinary conventional consciousness cannot. For example, emptiness itself is an ultimate truth; it is perceived by the wisdom directly realizing emptiness. The existence of emptiness is a veiled truth. After āryas arise from meditative equipoise on emptiness, a special conventional consciousness ascertains the existence of emptiness. It also knows that phenomena nominally exist and exist by mere imputation.

In conclusion, a sense consciousness that is without external and internal causes of error is mistaken with respect to the appearance of an inherently existent object, but it is not erroneous and is able to establish the conventional existence of its object. In other words, the mistaken appearance of inherent existence does not necessarily make a consciousness erroneous or prevent it from being a conventional reliable cognizer. Some worldly consciousnesses are reliable cognizers that conventionally establish trees, tables, persons, and so forth.

Conventional and Ultimate Analysis

Conventional consciousnesses accept things at face value without investigating their deeper mode of existence. When we do not analyze, flowers, people, moods, and loans appear to the mind. They function; we refer to them and communicate with other people about them without investigating how they exist—that is, whether or not they are truly existent in the way they appear. However, this does not mean that conventional consciousnesses are totally non-analytical. Tsongkhapa says (LC 3.178):

> In a sense, conventional consciousness operates in a non-inquisitive manner. It operates within the context of how a given phenomenon appears to it without asking, "Is this how the object actually exists, or does it just appear that way to my mind?" It is thus called non-analytical, but it is not the case that it is utterly non-inquisitive. It operates within the context of how things appear, how they are known to a worldly or conventional consciousness ... Therefore it is called worldly knowledge.

Conventional analysis (T. *tha snyad dpyod byed kyi rigs pa*) investigates the conventional nature and function of objects; for example, is a person permanent or changing? Is what we usually call happiness in fact happiness or is it a lesser form of suffering? Conventional analysis investigates: Does this computer have the features I need to do my work? Is this person guilty of a crime? Is light a wave or a particle? What is the difference between love and attachment? Is there a creator god? Which disease is this person suffering from and how can it be treated? All analysis that is not aimed at realizing the emptiness of inherent existence is conventional analysis. Conventional analysis and conventional consciousnesses in general exist in the mindstreams of all beings, whether or not they adhere to a specific tenet system, whether or not they meditate or realize emptiness.

Ultimate analysis (T. *don dam pa'i dpyod byed*) is not satisfied with the conventional appearance of phenomena. It investigates their deeper mode of existence to discover what they really are. Does my job inherently exist or dependently exist? Is there an I that is findable among my aggregates or completely separate from them? What is the ultimate nature of this I who is so upset?

Everything exists by being merely imputed or designated by mind. When we are not satisfied with the mere appearance of an object, such as the I, we examine: What is the person's true nature? What is the final referent of the term "I"? Who am I really? These questions involve ultimate analysis.

Reasoning analyzing the ultimate investigates the ultimate nature. It may begin with a logical syllogism and evolve into a deep exploration of the ultimate nature that eventually takes us beyond words and concepts to direct perception. Ultimate analysis unlocks the door to realize ultimate truths, the deeper nature of existence, and nirvāṇa.

3 | Ultimate Truths

VEILED TRUTHS ARE posited in relation to ultimate truths. One cannot exist without the other.

What Is an Ultimate Truth?

In *Clear Words* (*Prasannapadā* 494.1), Candrakīrti explains the etymology of the Sanskrit term *paramārthasatya*, or ultimate truth (TT 93).

> Because it is an object (*artha*, T. *don*) and is ultimate (*parama*, T. *dam*), [it is] an ultimate object (*paramārtha*). Since just that is a truth (*satya*), [it is] an ultimate truth.

An ultimate truth is an *object*—a phenomenon found by a reliable cognizer, in this case the wisdom of meditative equipoise. An ultimate truth is *ultimate* in that it is the deepest or actual mode of existence; and it is a *truth* because it is nondeceptive and exists the way it appears to its principal cognizer. The emptiness of true existence—a nonaffirming negation that is the mere absence of true existence—is the ultimate truth; it is an object found by a perceiver of a true knowable object.

One definition of ultimate truth is: an object found by a probing awareness distinguishing the final mode of existence. An ultimate truth is the object found by a probing awareness that knows phenomena as they actually are. Another definition is: an object that is nondualistically realized by a direct nonconceptual reliable cognizer that cognizes it directly. Unlike veiled truths, ultimate truths are true in that they exist in the way they appear to their principal cognizer, a yogic direct perceiver of emptiness. Emptiness lacks inherent existence and appears empty of true existence to the direct, nonconceptual reliable cognizer perceiving it. There is no sense of separation between the perceiving mind and the perceived object, emptiness. They are indistinguishable, like water poured into water.

Early Tibetan scholars discussed emptiness at great length, with some saying it is not a knowable object (an existent) and others asserting it is truly existent. Both notions are incorrect. The former misconception arose from misinterpreting a verse from Śāntideva (BCA 9.2):

> The veiled and the ultimate,
> these are asserted as the two truths.
> The ultimate is not the province of an awareness.
> Awarenesses are said to be veiled.

This verse explains the meaning of a passage in the *Meeting of the Father and Son Sūtra* (TT 106):

> The Tathāgatas see veilings as the province of the world. That which is ultimate is inexpressible, is not a knowable object, is not an object of consciousness, is not an object of thorough knowledge, is indemonstrable.

"Awareness" in the third and fourth lines of Śāntideva's verse refers to a dualistic awareness. Saying the ultimate truth is not "the province of an awareness"—that is, that it is not an object of consciousness—means that the ultimate is not an object of an awareness involved with dualistic appearances, such as sense consciousnesses or conceptual consciousnesses. Those consciousnesses are deceptive and obscure us from seeing the ultimate truth. Objects of those consciousnesses involving dualistic appearances are veiled truths, and such awarenesses are considered veiled.

An ultimate truth, on the other hand, is the principal object found by a probing awareness of āryas in meditative equipoise on emptiness. It is an object that exists as it appears to the principal mind that takes it as its object. An ultimate truth is an existent, a knowable object. Saying that the ultimate truth is *inexpressible* means that the experience of realizing emptiness cannot be adequately described by words and concepts; saying it is *indemonstrable* indicates that it cannot be directly perceived by conventional consciousnesses to which everything appears truly existent.

If emptiness were not a knowable object, many faults would arise. The Buddha would have taught emptiness without knowing it. Practicing the method aspect of the path would be unnecessary because it would not aid in realizing emptiness. There would be no deeper mode of existence, so the appearance of veiled truths would be their mode of abiding. In that case, sentient beings would have already realized the ultimate nature of phenomena. Emptiness would not be an object analyzed by āryas, so there would be no difference between an object's mode of appearance and mode of existence to common beings and āryas.

If emptiness were inexpressible in all ways, there would be no way to talk or think about it. In that case, the Buddha could not have spoken about it and the great Buddhist sages could not have written so many treatises and commentaries explaining emptiness and the methods to realize it. The centuries of debates of the Nālandā tradition would have been useless, and even reading this book and hearing teachings on emptiness would be a waste of time. But that is hardly the case. Without hearing and reflecting on teachings about emptiness, we wouldn't know how to meditate on it; meditation on emptiness isn't a matter of emptying our minds of all thoughts. We must realize the nonaffirming negation that is the opposite of what ignorance grasps.

The misconception that emptiness is truly existent came about by mistakenly thinking that since emptiness is found by āryas' wisdom of meditative equipoise, it must exist ultimately, inherently, and truly. However, being found by this wisdom is not the same as being able to bear ultimate analysis. When examining how the self exists, the self cannot be found because it cannot bear ultimate analysis. However, ultimate analysis finds the emptiness of the self. That emptiness exists, but not truly or inherently, because when emptiness itself is subjected to ultimate analysis, the emptiness of emptiness is found. Nothing—not even emptiness—can bear ultimate analysis.[9] However, emptiness is found by ultimate analysis; when phenomena's mode of existence is sought, emptiness is found. Emptiness exists.

Veiled truths and ultimate truths are known by different consciousnesses. Veiled truths—such as persons and their environments—are known by conventional reliable cognizers, sentient beings' unimpaired five sense consciousnesses and unimpaired mental consciousnesses that cognize veilings. Ultimate truths—the emptinesses of these phenomena—are perceived primarily by āryas' wisdom of meditative equipoise on emptiness.

That does not mean that ultimate truths are never cognized by ordinary beings. Ordinary beings can cognize, find, ascertain, and realize emptiness, but not directly or nonconceptually. They do so by means of an inferential cognizer—a correct, nondeceptive conception that realizes emptiness by means of a conceptual appearance of emptiness. Such a realization may occur on the path of preparation and below. By diligently meditating on the correct view, ordinary beings improve their understanding and gain direct perception of ultimate truths, at which point they become āryas.

REFLECTION

1. What is the difference between conventional analysis and ultimate analysis? When a scientist analyzes how the brain functions, which kind of analysis is it?
2. Is that the same type of analysis as when a Buddhist analyzes whether the brain is truly existent?

The Perfection of Wisdom

A verse from the *Twenty-Five-Thousand-Line Perfection of Wisdom Sūtra*, which was spoken by Rāhula,[10] is often recited before the *Heart Sūtra*. The wisdom mentioned in this verse realizes emptiness and dawns as the meaning of dependent arising.[11] It encapsulates the Madhyamaka view:[12]

> Inexpressible, inconceivable, indescribable is the perfection of wisdom;
> unborn, unceasing, the nature of space itself,
> the object of apprehension of self-realized pristine wisdom.
> To the mother of the buddhas of the three times, I pay homage.

Emptiness is *inexpressible*—it cannot be adequately expressed in words, which are sounds. When a person who has realized emptiness and someone who has studied emptiness well but hasn't realized it express the teachings on emptiness, the words they say are almost the same. Nevertheless, for listeners who have some knowledge of emptiness, there is a difference in what these two people convey. The former person's experience of emptiness cannot be expressed in words, but the listeners can intuit it.

The perfection of wisdom is *inconceivable*—conceptual consciousnesses cannot know it exactly as it is. The experience of realizing emptiness directly is very different than thinking about or imagining that experience. The way a conceptual consciousness, even an inferential realization of emptiness, knows emptiness is very different than experiencing it directly. It's like the difference between imagining a delicious meal when you're hungry and actually putting the food in your mouth and eating it.

Emptiness is also *indescribable*—it cannot be articulated by language. Emptiness as it is experienced by a yogic direct perceiver cannot be fully known or understood by words or concepts no matter how many statements are made about it or how much it is described. It goes beyond being an object of terms and conceptual minds; words cannot accurately express it and conceptual consciousnesses cannot realize it exactly as it is.

The Perfection of Wisdom sūtras mention the natural perfection of wisdom, the path perfection of wisdom, and the mother perfection of wisdom. The natural *perfection of wisdom* is indicated in the first line; it refers to emptiness itself. When a person or phenomenon is examined with ultimate analysis that searches for its actual mode of existence, an inherently existent person or object cannot be found and a conventional object cannot be seen. What is found is the emptiness of inherent existence, which is inexpressible, inconceivable, and indescribable.

Emptiness is *unborn* and *unceasing*—it has no beginning and no end. It does not arise from causes and conditions, nor does it disintegrate and cease due to causes and conditions. Emptiness is the ultimate nature of all persons and phenomena; it is a nonaffirming negation and does not fluctuate or change. In these ways it can be compared to clear, open, unconditioned *space* that is the absence of all obstruction. It is unbounded and limitless. Just as unobstructed space allows for objects to exist in it, emptiness allows for the arising and existence of all veilings. All phenomena arise within emptiness, which is their ultimate nature. They cannot exist apart from emptiness and are one nature with it. Arising and ceasing occur in the perspective of minds knowing veilings, but in the perspective of the mind of ultimate analysis, there is no arising and ceasing.

Emptiness is not nonexistent; it exists and is established by a reliable cognizer. It is the *apprehended object of self-realized wisdom*, the āryas' wisdom of meditative equipoise that directly and nonconceptually realizes emptiness. This wisdom is the only mind that can realize emptiness exactly as it is. The wisdom mind knowing emptiness is itself empty of inherent existence, so it directly knows its own ultimate nature, its emptiness of inherent existence. For this reason, the wisdom mind is called *self-realized wisdom* (*pratyātmagati*)—it is a personal direct experience of reality—and its own emptiness is its apprehended object. In this realization, there is no appearance of the subject, the wisdom mind, that realizes an object, emptiness. Rather subject and object are experienced as undifferentiated, like water poured into water.

Here words are used to describe the experience of directly realizing the emptiness of our own wisdom mind. As the preceding lines make clear, words and concepts are insufficient approximations of the experience of realizing emptiness. Nevertheless, to gain this experience, we must start by learning the words and concepts to refute inherent existence and to establish emptiness. Learning the scriptures generates the wisdom arising from learning or hearing in us. We then progress to thinking deeply about these teachings and gain the wisdom arising from reflection that clears away all doubts about the lack of inherent existence and brings definitive ascertainment of emptiness. At this point, we know that things do not exist inherently in the way they appear to—that all the inherently existent people and things that appear to us on a daily basis do not exist. This inferential realization of emptiness, when conjoined with serenity, initiates the path of preparation. This begins the path perfection of wisdom—paths (consciousnesses) in the mindstream of a bodhisattva that are explicitly conjoined with great compassion and wisdom realizing emptiness.

Now we familiarize ourselves with this inferential realization of emptiness until the veil of the conceptual appearance vanishes and emptiness is perceived directly; this occurrence marks the beginning of the path of seeing. Through repeated meditation, this realization gradually diminishes the innate self-grasping until it and all other afflictive obscurations cease. With further meditation, even the cognitive obscurations are cleansed from the mind and buddhahood is attained. This is the resultant perfection of wisdom.

"Perfection of wisdom" sometimes refers to emptiness and other times refers to the wisdom realizing emptiness. This pristine wisdom is known as the *mother of the buddhas of the three times* in that it gives birth to the omniscient minds of all buddhas who abide in the past, present, and future. Without this wisdom, it is impossible to eradicate all afflictive obscurations and cognitive obscurations and transform our minds into the minds of fully awakened buddhas. Just as we depend on our mothers who gave birth to us, all buddhas awaken to full and complete buddhahood by depending on their "mother," the perfection of wisdom.

The wisdom realizing emptiness only becomes the perfection of wisdom when it is conjoined with bodhicitta and skillful means—the six perfections that constitute the method aspect of the path. The *Jewel in the Crown Ārya Sūtra* queries (MS 33):

> What is the emptiness possessing the best of all qualities? It is that which is not divorced from generosity, ethical conduct, fortitude, joyous effort, meditative stabilization, wisdom, or skillful means.

The buddhas' magnificent qualities—the signs and marks of their bodies, the sixty qualities of their speech, the ten powers and four fearlessnesses of their minds, and their incredible courage and clarity when benefitting sentient beings—all these qualities that enable them to attain buddhahood and to ripen sentient beings' minds come from conjoining wisdom and skillful means.

When I go to Bodhgaya and sit under the bodhi tree, the place where the Buddha attained full awakening, I contemplate that this is the place where the Buddha himself meditated on emptiness with self-realized wisdom; here he directly cognized the ultimate nature of his mind. I am meditating on emptiness in the same way he did, and I have the same buddha nature that he had. I too can realize the nature of mind and attain buddhahood just as he did. With this in mind, I recite the above homage to the mother, the perfection of wisdom, and contemplate its meaning. With a sincere aspiration to generate this wisdom and attain buddhahood for the benefit of all sentient beings, I then meditate on emptiness and dependent arising.

I recommend that you do the same when you visit Bodhgaya or any other holy place. Even when in your own room or in another country, you can imagine being in Bodhgaya and practice like this.

Actual and Concordant Ultimates

To review the etymology of the Sanskrit word *paramārtha*, which is translated as "ultimate," *artha* means "object" or "purpose," and *parama* means "highest" or "supreme." The term "ultimate" has three references:

(1) The ultimate is *an object of the supreme.* Emptiness is the ultimate truth because it is the object directly realized by the supreme consciousness—the nonconceptual pristine wisdom that directly knows the ultimate.

(2) The ultimate, emptiness, is the *highest object* because it is the supreme object to be known. It is the final mode of existence of phenomena, the way in which all phenomena actually exist.

(3) *That which is concordant with the ultimate* refers to a conceptual probing awareness[13] that realizes phenomena's ultimate mode of existence. An inferential reliable cognizer of emptiness is a sublime, mundane wisdom. It is *sublime* because it realizes emptiness. It is *mundane* because it realizes emptiness indirectly, by means of a conceptual appearance. A conceptual reliable cognizer may also be an ārya's subsequent wisdom knowing emptiness that arises after meditative equipoise when an ārya teaches or reads about emptiness. It may also be an ordinary being's wisdom of hearing, thinking, or meditating that correctly realizes emptiness.

The emptiness realized by an inferential reliable cognizer of emptiness is a *concordant ultimate object.* This object and its cognizing consciousness (the subject) are *concordant ultimates* because they are similar to, but not the same as, the nonconceptual pristine wisdom and its object, which are *actual ultimates.* Śāntarakṣita says in *Ornament for the Middle* (*Madhyamakālaṃkāra*, FEW 139):

> Because of according with the ultimate,
> this is called an "ultimate."
> Actually, [the ultimate] is free from all
> collections of elaborations.

Actual and Concordant Objects and Subjects

	OBJECT	SUBJECT
Actual ultimate	Emptiness realized by a direct nonconceptual reliable cognizer of emptiness*	Āryas' pristine wisdom of meditative equipoise directly perceiving emptiness⁺
Concordant ultimate	Emptiness realized by an inferential reliable cognizer of emptiness*	Conceptual reliable cognizer of emptiness (conceptual probing awareness realizing emptiness), such as āryas' wisdom of emptiness during subsequent attainment or non-āryas' inferential realization of emptiness⁺

* Both actual and concordant objects are emptinesses, which are ultimate truths. Emptiness is the ultimate.
⁺ Both actual and concordant subjects are consciousnesses, which are veiled truths. Here they are called ultimates although they are not actual ultimates.

The two kinds of probing awarenesses (T. *rigs shes*) analyzing the ultimate—āryas' pristine wisdom of meditative equipoise nonconceptually perceiving emptiness and the conceptual probing awarenesses realizing emptiness—are not ultimates because they are consciousnesses. All consciousnesses are veiled truths. Nevertheless, they may be called ultimates because they perceive the ultimate object, emptiness. Similarly, the wisdom consciousnesses arising from hearing, thinking, and meditating that realize emptiness may be called ultimates, even though they are not actual ultimates because they are not emptinesses. These wisdom consciousnesses are impermanent veilings that may be called ultimates because they realize the actual ultimate, emptiness, and thus are the ultimate among consciousnesses. Kamalaśīla said in *Illumination of the Middle Way* (*Madhyamakāloka*, SV 138):

> All wisdoms arisen from correct hearing, [thinking, and meditation] are nonmistaken subjects. They are called ultimates because their [object] is the ultimate.

All conceptual wisdom consciousnesses knowing emptiness—from those arisen from hearing up through āryas' correct inferential realizations—are considered concordant ultimates. Wisdom arisen from hearing arises dependent on a correct syllogism that is posited by another person. Wisdom arisen from thinking or reflecting is an inferential understanding that arises in dependence on a correct syllogism by our own thought, without another person saying it to us. The wisdom arisen from meditation arises from a union of serenity and insight. Such an ultimate consciousness cognizes emptiness, not veiled truths. It may be conceptual or nonconceptual, depending on whether it cognizes emptiness by means of a conceptual appearance or not.

Both the conceptual and nonconceptual probing awarenesses realizing emptiness are free from the elaboration of grasping true existence. Āryas' wisdom of meditative equipoise that directly perceives emptiness has also eliminated the elaborations of conceptuality and of dualistic appearance, because that mind nonconceptually perceives the emptiness that is its object. In addition, that wisdom and its object are mixed like water in water. For this reason, this wisdom may be called an actual ultimate although it is not. As a consciousness, it is a veiled truth. The nonconceptual probing awareness does not do any analysis because it is a yogic direct perceiver of emptiness.

The conceptual probing awareness realizing emptiness does so through the medium of a conceptual appearance. Although emptiness appears truly existent to this mind, its apprehended object is just emptiness—it is not truly existent emptiness. If it were, this mind would be a wrong consciousness because truly existent emptiness does not exist at all. The elaborations of conceptuality and the dualistic appearance of subject and object still exist for this mind.

The objects—emptinesses—of both the conceptual and nonconceptual probing awarenesses realizing emptiness are in fact actual ultimates. However, they are called "actual" or "concordant ultimates" depending on the consciousness that realizes them. The nonaffirming negation that is the apprehended object of āryas' pristine wisdom of meditative equipoise on emptiness is free from all three elaborations—inherent existence, conceptuality (perceived by means of a conceptual appearance), and dualism (the sense of subject and object being distant and cut off). It is thus an actual ultimate and an ultimate truth. The emptiness realized by an inferential cognizer and the emptiness realized by nonconceptual wisdom are the same emptiness, but they are realized in different ways.

From the perspective of the consciousnesses cognizing emptiness being called "actual" or "concordant," an inferential probing awareness realizing emptiness is a concordant ultimate subject, and its object, emptiness, is also *called* a concordant ultimate and thus is not free from the elaborations of conceptuality and duality and is not an actual ultimate. However, this does not mean that *in fact* it is not an actual ultimate or an ultimate truth.

No matter what type of mind cognizes emptiness, emptiness is an ultimate truth. It is a nonaffirming negation that has refuted all possibilities of inherent existence; it is the ultimate nature of all phenomena. Tsongkhapa says in the *Medium Exposition on the Gradual Path* (*Lam rim 'bring ba*, DAE 433):

> Because [the object emptiness] is free from just a portion of elaborations for a conceptual probing awareness, it is not [called] the actual ultimate that is free from both elaborations. However, this is not to say that in general [the emptiness comprehended by an inferential probing awareness] is not an actual ultimate truth.

The illusion-like composites that appear to post-meditative consciousnesses are not objects of either the inferential or nonconceptual wisdom realizing emptiness. These illusion-like appearances are affirming negations in that inherent existence has previously been negated and the appearance of veiled phenomena is subsequently affirmed. The cup that appears to a yoginī's mind after she arises from meditative equipoise on emptiness is an illusion-like composite of the cup's appearance and its emptiness. This illusion-like cup may be called a concordant ultimate but, unlike the emptiness known by an inferential cognizer, it is not an ultimate truth because it is a veiling.

These illusion-like appearances may arise through the force of either the conceptual or nonconceptual probing awareness that realizes suchness, although those probing awarenesses do not cognize or establish illusion-like appearances. After someone has realized emptiness conceptually or nonconceptually, when she arises from meditation and goes about her daily activities, veiled truths appear as falsities in that they appear to exist inherently although she knows they do not. These appearances, which are veilings, are known by conventional reliable cognizers, not by probing awarenesses.

Initially it may sound strange to say that an ārya's wisdom of meditative equipoise directly realizing emptiness is *called* an actual ultimate although it is not one, because all consciousnesses are veiled truths. It may also seem odd to say that the emptiness realized by a conceptual probing awareness is concordant with the ultimate, although it is an actual ultimate truth. However, when we understand the distinctions being made here, these discriminations make sense.

In another way of categorizing the "ultimate," we may refer to the ultimate object, attainment, and practice. The ultimate object is emptiness. The ultimate attainment is nirvāṇa. The ultimate practice is the pristine wisdom of meditative equipoise.

Divisions of Emptiness

To the pristine wisdom that directly realizes emptiness, there are no divisions or categories of emptiness. However, when we speak about emptiness, we often do so in reference to an object whose emptiness we are discussing. In this way, many emptinesses can be posited in dependence on the base or object that is empty. Thus the Buddha spoke of two emptinesses: the emptiness of functioning phenomena and the emptiness of nonfunctioning (permanent) phenomena. He further distinguished four, sixteen, and eighteen emptinesses—all depending on the objects that are empty—to emphasize that all phenomena are empty.

This classification of many divisions of emptiness also indicates that emptiness is not an absolute reality that is independent and unrelated to other phenomena. An emptiness is posited in relation to a phenomenon that is empty of inherent existence; it is dependent on the conventionally existent object that lacks inherent existence. As the nature of each and every phenomenon, emptiness is here, right now; it is not a faraway, abstract reality. Being dependent, emptiness lacks inherent existence. Although we can nominally delineate countless emptinesses because there are limitless objects that are empty, to an ārya's wisdom of meditative equipoise all these emptinesses appear undifferentiated. In addition, that undifferentiated emptiness is nondual with the wisdom realizing it.

The *Twenty-Five-Thousand Line Perfection of Wisdom Sūtra* speaks of multiple divisions of emptiness. The sixteen types of emptiness (*ṣoḍaśaśūnyatā*) are as follows (GR 486):

> Subhūti, again the great vehicle of the bodhisattvas is this: Emptiness of the internal, emptiness of the external, emptiness of both internal and external, emptiness of emptiness, emptiness of the vast, emptiness of the ultimate, emptiness of the conditioned, emptiness of the unconditioned, emptiness of what is beyond extremes, emptiness of the beginningless and endless, emptiness of the unrejectable, emptiness of nature, emptiness of all phenomena, emptiness of specific characteristics, emptiness of the unapprehendable, and emptiness of the nature of non-things.

From the viewpoint of a direct perceiver of emptiness, there is no difference whatsoever among the various divisions of emptiness. Nevertheless, emptiness can be divided in terms of the phenomena that are its bases. Subdividing emptiness in this way emphasizes that all phenomena—however we may classify them and whatever similar or dissimilar characteristics they may share—have the same ultimate nature, the emptiness of inherent existence. Everything that exists conventionally—including emptiness itself—does not exist under its own power.[14]

1. The *internal* (T. *nang*) are phenomena conjoined with the continuum of a sentient being, such as the six primary consciousnesses (T. *rnam shes*) and the six sense faculties (T. *dbang po*).
2. The *external* (T. *phyi*) are the five objects—visible forms, sounds, smells, tastes, and tangible objects—that are not conjoined with consciousness.
3. The *internal and external* (T. *phyi nang gnyis ka*) are the coarse sense organs: the eyeball, ear, nose, and so forth.
4. *Emptiness* (T. *stong pa nyid*) indicates that emptiness itself also lacks inherent existence. This eliminates the thought that emptiness truly exists.
5. The *vast* (*T. chen po*) refers to the ten directions, which encompass the environment of all sentient beings.

6. The *ultimate* (T. *don dam pa*) refers to nirvāṇa, the ultimate goal of the three vehicles.
7. The *conditioned* (T. *'du byed*) are products, impermanent phenomena. Here it refers to the three realms of saṃsāra.
8. The *unconditioned* (T. *'du ma byed*) are permanent phenomena such as unconditioned space, true cessation, and nirvāṇa.
9. *What is beyond the extremes* (T. *mtha' las 'das pa*) includes all phenomena, which arise dependently and are free from the extremes of absolutism and nihilism.
10. The *beginningless and endless* (T. *thog ma dang mtha' ma med pa*) is saṃsāra because ultimately it lacks a beginning or end. However, the saṃsāra of each sentient being, although beginningless, has an end because each sentient being has the possibility to attain liberation.
11. The *unrejectable* (T. *dor ba med pa*) refers to the Mahāyāna. While someone may follow the Fundamental Vehicle because it is more suitable for them at the present moment, according to the Mahāyāna every sentient being will eventually generate bodhicitta, follow the bodhisattva path, and become fully awakened. The Mahāyāna is not something that can be turned away from or rejected forever.
12. The *ultimate nature* (T. *rang bzhin*) is the quality of being empty of inherent existence that all phenomena have had beginninglessly. This nature is not made by a creator and is itself empty of inherent existence.
13. *All phenomena* (T. *chos thams chad*) include the eighteen constituents, twelve sources, five aggregates, and so on—all permanent and impermanent phenomena.
14. *Specific characteristics* (T. *rang gi mtshan nyid*) subsume the particular characteristics of all phenomena from form to omniscience—the basis, path, and result.
15. The *unapprehendable* (T. *mi dmigs pa*) refers to the three times—past, present, and future—that cannot be apprehended as inherently existent. The present ceases the moment it arises, the past has already ceased, and the future has not yet arisen.
16. The *nature of nonthings* (T. *dngos po med pa'i ngo bo nyid*) refers to unconditioned phenomena that are permanent and are not produced by causes and conditions.

When eighteen emptinesses are identified, the following two are added:

17. *Functioning things* (T. *dngos po*) include the five aggregates and all other impermanent phenomena.
18. *Nonfunctioning things* (T. *dngos po med pa*) refers to phenomena that are not products, are permanent, and do not perform a function.

Together functioning things and nonfunctioning things account for all existents. They subsume the above sixteen classes and are added here to emphasize that all existents lack inherent existence.

When emptiness is counted as four, the four corresponding bases of emptiness are:

1. *Functioning things.*
2. *Nonfunctioning things.* These two are as above.
3. *Self-nature* (T. *rang gi ngo bo*) is the true nature of all phenomena. This indicates that ultimate reality itself lacks inherent existence and is not an independent absolute.
4. *Other-nature* (T. *gzhan gi ngo bo*) has three connotations: (1) *supreme* is ultimate reality, (2) *other than you* refers to the object of the supramundane wisdom, and (3) *transcendence* is nirvāṇa, which transcends saṃsāra.

Sometimes emptiness is classified into two, in which case its two bases may be either functioning and nonfunctioning phenomena or persons and phenomena.

Reflecting on emptiness from the perspective of the diversity of phenomena that are empty emphasizes not only the multitude of existents in the mundane and supramundane spheres but also that each and every one of these does not exist from its own side.

REFLECTION

1. What is the purpose of dividing phenomena into actual and concordant ultimates?

2. What is the purpose of divisions of emptiness when emptiness is the same to a mind that directly perceives it?

Emptiness, True Cessation, and Nirvāṇa

All Buddhist traditions agree that a true cessation is the elimination of a defilement from the mindstream of an individual by means of applying an antidote so that that obscuration can never return. However, there is a lot of discussion among proponents of various tenet systems regarding the exact nature of true cessation and its relationship with both emptiness and ultimate truth.

According to Prāsaṅgikas, the antidote that uproots all defilements is the wisdom directly and nonconceptually realizing the emptiness of inherent existence. In all three vehicles, defilements are eliminated in stages, and each stage consists of meditative equipoise on emptiness and a period of subsequent attainment when practitioners accumulate merit, adjust to the new freedom of having abolished a level of defilement, and prepare for the next stage in which another level will be overcome. To use the bodhisattva path as an example, during the uninterrupted path of each ground, the wisdom realizing emptiness is in the process of cleansing the mind of a particular level of obscuration. As soon as that obscuration has been completely overcome, that wisdom is called a liberated path; a true cessation of that level of obscuration has also been attained. When all afflictive obscurations have been eliminated, śrāvakas, solitary realizers, and bodhisattvas attain nirvāṇa. When all cognitive obscurations have been removed, bodhisattvas attain buddhahood, nonabiding nirvāṇa.

True cessations have two *objects of negation*:

(1) inherent existence, which is the object grasped by ignorance. Although inherent existence has never existed, it is called a *natural stain* (T. *rang bzhin gyi dri ma*) because our grasping inherent existence doesn't allow us to see the actual ultimate nature of the mind. Inherent existence itself is not a defilement, because it doesn't exist. However, refuting it overcomes grasping inherent existence, which is a defilement. The nonaffirming negation of inherent existence—emptiness—is permanent and is the factor of natural

purity. Natural purity is the emptiness of inherent existence of the mind that has existed beginninglessly; the ultimate nature of the mind has always been pure or free from inherent existence.

(2) the particular obscurations to be abandoned at that ground, which are existent phenomena. These defilements are *adventitious stains* (T. *glo bur gyi dri ma*)—impermanent phenomena that arise due to causes and conditions.

Corresponding to these two stains, there are two types of freedom: (1) freedom from natural stains is the emptiness of inherent existence of the mind, the ultimate nature of the mind, and (2) freedom from adventitious stains is freedom from defilements.

Considering that a true cessation is the absence of both objects of negation, is there a common locus between the two absences?

Some systems, such as the Sautrāntika and Svātantrika, assert true cessation is a conventional truth. Sautrāntikas do so because of the unique way they define a conventional truth—something that is not able to perform a function ultimately. Since a true cessation is permanent and thus unable to perform a function, Sautrāntikas consider it a conventional truth.

Svātantrikas say true cessations are conventional truths and emptiness is an ultimate truth. They define true cessation as the resultant state of freedom due to having eradicated the afflictions; true cessation is the abandonment of a level of defilement. Since defilements are conventional truths, they say their cessation must also be a conventional truth.

In contrast, Prāsaṅgikas assert that a true cessation is a quality of the mind; it is the purified aspect of the emptiness of the mind that has abandoned defilements by means of emptiness—that is, by meditation on emptiness—and abandoned defilements within emptiness—that is, by meditation on the emptiness of the defilements themselves. The purified aspect of the emptiness of the mind of an ārya who has abandoned a level of defilements is a true cessation. The purified aspect of the emptiness of the mind of an ārya who has abandoned all afflictive defilements is nirvāṇa. Thus a specific emptiness—the emptiness of the mind of an ārya who has abandoned a level of afflictions or all afflictions—is a true cessation or nirvāṇa, respectively. This combines both objects of negation: the mind is empty of inherent existence (the first object of negation above), and true cessation and nirvāṇa are the emptiness of a mind that has abandoned a level of afflictions (the second object of negation above).

Prāsaṅgikas accept true cessations as ultimate truths by distinguishing a mere cessation from a *true cessation* of a defilement. The *mere cessation* of a specific defilement is, for example, the cessation of the first moment of anger that occurs when the second moment of anger has arisen. The cessation of the first moment of anger occurs naturally, without the application of a counterforce. Another example of a mere cessation of a defilement is the cessation of anger that is brought about by meditating on fortitude or love. These and other such meditations are antidotes that temporarily subdue anger or other afflictions but do not eradicate them forever. These temporary cessations of a specific defilement are a "having ceased" (*naṣṭa*, T. *zhig pa*)—a "having happened"—of a defilement, and as such are impermanent, conditioned phenomena that are the product of a process. The mere cessation of the causes and conditions of a specific affliction produces the affliction's temporary cessation.

In the case of a mere cessation of a specific affliction—for example, our manifest resentment temporarily ceases when we contemplate love—the potential of the affliction that has temporarily ceased continues in the form of the seed of the affliction on our mindstreams. However, in the case of a true cessation, the potential for the reappearance of that affliction is cut from the root—the seed of the affliction as well as the manifest affliction have been destroyed.

A true cessation is an ultimate truth and is permanent. Are all ultimate truths emptinesses? Most Tibetan scholars say that true cessations are ultimate truths as well as emptinesses.[15] Tsongkhapa explains in *Illuminating the Intent* (GR 152–53):

> In his *Commentary on the Sixty Stanzas of Reasoning* too, Candrakīrti explains nirvāṇa to be an ultimate truth and the other three truths [out of the four] as conventional truths. *Nirvāṇa* here refers to true cessations. Furthermore ... Candrakīrti points out that the Buddha asserted that there is direct knowledge of true cessations, and this would be untenable for the Buddhist essentialists who assert direct reliable cognitions to possess as their object things with inherent characteristics. In his own tradition, Candrakīrti establishes that [true] cessation is directly known in terms of the realization of suchness by the unpolluted

> wisdom of meditative equipoise. If true cessations were conventional truths, such presentations would become utterly untenable. Furthermore, Candrakīrti proves with great effort that when a nirvāṇa is actualized, one must cognize the meaning of suchness directly.

Tsongkhapa also states (LC 3.199):

> Candrakīrti says that to attain nirvāṇa means to perceive nirvāṇa, and he says that nirvāṇa is considered a true cessation and that true cessations are ultimate truths . . . When you attain nirvāṇa, you must perceive the ultimate truth of cessation.

Here nirvāṇa refers to the true cessation of a certain level of defilements. When the mind becomes a liberated path, its emptiness is a true cessation because it is the emptiness of a mind that is free from a level of adventitious defilements. At each successive ground a bodhisattva's uninterrupted path realizing emptiness has increased power and ability to overcome ever more subtle defilements. This leads to the cessation of subtler defilements with the liberated path of that ground.[16] From the path of seeing onward, as bodhisattvas eliminate more and more defilements that prevent seeing the natural purity of the mind, the emptiness of the mind is free not only from inherent existence but also from more and more adventitious stains. That purified aspect of the emptiness of the mind is called a true cessation. When all defilements have been irrevocably eliminated, the mind becomes a buddha's wisdom truth body, and its emptiness is the nature truth body—nonabiding nirvāṇa, the ultimate true cessation.

A doubt is raised: If the purified aspect of the emptiness of the mind is nirvāṇa, since the emptiness of the mind has existed since beginningless time, nirvāṇa should also have existed beginninglessly. To resolve this, we must distinguish the emptiness of the mind that is not free from afflictions, the emptiness of the mind that is free from some level of afflictions, and the emptiness of the mind that is free from all afflictions. The emptiness of the mind that is not free from all afflictions is obscured, whereas the emptiness of the mind that is freed from all afflictions is completely purified. Although both are free from natural stains, only the latter is free from adventitious stains.

An example may help. There's a stainless steel table. Its nature is such that it cannot actually be stained. But it is covered with many layers of grime—motor oil, toxic waste, and epoxy glue. Cleaning the stainless table creates a new sort of purity that, when achieved, is right together with the original purity.

The mind and its emptiness are one nature, but nominally different. They are one nature in that one cannot exist without the other, although they are not identical. The mind is a conventional truth and its emptiness is an ultimate truth. From the perspective of emptiness being the mere absence of inherent existence, it does not change as the mind is purified. Emptiness remains the nonaffirming negation that is the absence of inherent existence of the mind. But from another perspective, because the mind is purified as it advances through the bodhisattva grounds, so is its emptiness. The emptiness of the mind of the first ground differs from the emptiness of the mind of the second ground, because their basis—the mind—has changed.

Although the object of meditation—the emptiness of all phenomena—remains the same, the mind's ability to eliminate subtler defilements increases. This is not determined by the purity of emptiness, but by the purity of the mind. This increased purity and power of mind allows for deeper levels of defilements to be purged from the mind as meditators progress from one ground to the next. Furthermore, because the bodhicitta of bodhisattvas on each subsequent ground is stronger, their meditative equipoise on emptiness has greater ability to eliminate subtler defilements.

A practitioner who directly perceives emptiness on the path of seeing and a practitioner who directly perceives emptiness on the path of meditation both realize emptiness directly, but the person on the path of meditation has greater power and ability to abandon subtler obscurations because his or her mind is freed from a layer of defilements that the person on the path of seeing has not yet abandoned.

In brief, from the perspective of the emptiness of the mind being the absence of inherent existence, it does not change as a bodhisattva progresses through the ten grounds. From another perspective, the emptiness of a mind with defilements is not nirvāṇa because the very basis upon which that emptiness is understood—that mind—has defilements. When the mind is freed from defilements, the emptiness that is one nature with it is also freed from defilements, even though that emptiness itself has not changed from being the nonaffirming negation that is the absence of inherent existence. We say emptiness is purified because its base—in this case, the mind—is purified. The purified emptiness of a mind that is free from defilements is nirvāṇa, the ultimate true cessation.

Since true cessations are the purified aspect of the emptiness of the mind and the mind is naturally pure—that is, it has always been empty of inherent existence—how can multiple true cessations be posited according to the level of the path a yogi has attained?[17] It is similar to a person who wears dirty clothes and keeps changing into cleaner and cleaner clothes. The person is the same, but how he appears changes according to his clothes. Similarly, the natural purity of the mind has always been the same, but how it appears changes as the adventitious stains are gradually removed through the force of their antidote, the wisdom realizing emptiness on the paths and grounds.

That leads to the question: Are true cessation and nirvāṇa posited in relation to the separation of defilements from the mind or in relation to the separation of defilements from the emptiness of the mind? In other words, do defilements obscure the mind or do they obscure the emptiness of the mind?

Since the mind and its emptiness are one nature, when the mind is defiled, the emptiness of the mind is also defiled. When the mind is purified of defilements, its emptiness is also purified. By realizing emptiness directly, the defilements are removed primarily from the mind. But as the mind is purified, so is its emptiness. Tsongkhapa explains in *Illuminating the Intent* (GR 153):

> Although the negation of true existence—the object of negation—with respect to any base is considered an ultimate truth, it does not necessarily follow that the object of negation of all ultimate truths does not exist among knowable objects. Nāgārjuna's *Praise of the Sphere of Reality* (*Dharmadhātustava* 1–2) says:
>
> > Homage and obeisance to the sphere of reality [emptiness];
> > when it is not thoroughly understood,
> > one wanders in the three existences
> > although it does in fact abide in all sentient beings.

> Just this is the truth body (dharmakāya)
> and the nirvāṇa that is the purity
> from having purified that which serves
> as the cause of saṃsāra.

> The [ultimate] nature of phenomena [specifically the mind] is accompanied by defilement, and when that is purified, Nāgārjuna says that this nature becomes a nirvāṇa and a truth body. There are many similar teachings that defilement is the object of negation with respect to the purified nature of phenomena. If their nature could not become free from defilement, toil [on the path] would be fruitless. Also, if the nature of phenomena can be freed from defilement, then its object of negation can exist among knowable objects . . .
>
> In general, pure and impure phenomena are qualified by this nature [the absence of inherent existence], and in this context the negations of the two selves [of persons and phenomena], for instance, are negations in the sense that the object of negation [inherent existence] simply does not occur among knowable objects. However, when the phenomena qualified by this nature are gradually purified of defilement, their nature also becomes purified. Therefore with respect to a certain phenomenon qualified by this nature, it is not sufficient for its nature to be a partial purity, it must also be purified of the adventitious defilements which accord with a particular level [of the path]. These are called true cessations.

In short, the purified aspect of the emptiness of the mind—a mind that was initially defiled but has been purified of defilements—is nirvāṇa. Is the object of negation of the emptiness of the mind that is purified of defilements existent or nonexistent? Tsongkhapa says it could be an existent phenomenon. In that case, this emptiness, which is nirvāṇa, is free from two objects of negation—inherent existence, which is nonexistent, and defilements, which exist.[18] Therefore, there is a common locus between the absence of inherent existence and the absence of adventitious stains. The emptiness of the mind has been free from the first object of negation, inherent existence, from beginningless time, although the mind hasn't realized that. As pristine wisdom repeatedly sees that natural purity, successive levels of true cessation are actualized. When the mind is free from all defilements, the adventitious stains, so is its emptiness. At that time the purified aspect of that emptiness of the mind is nirvāṇa. In the *Ocean of Reasoning*, Tsongkhapa says (OR 525):

> Here [in Prāsaṅgika], the real nature [*dharmatā*] of a mind that is the basis for [both] the abandonment of the seeds of afflictions and the vanishing of appearances of the appropriated aggregates is considered nirvāṇa.

The object of bodhisattvas' meditative equipoise is the emptiness of inherent existence. The mind as the perceiving subject and emptiness as the object being perceived are fused nondualistically during the time of meditative equipoise realizing emptiness directly. There is no sense of a subject, I, realizing an object, emptiness. There is simply nondual emptiness. "The appropriated aggregates" refers to all veilings, the appearance of which has ceased during this time of nonconceptual perception of emptiness. This occurs because for the unawakened mind, the appearance of veilings is mixed with the appearance of true existence due to the cognitive obscurations on the mind. Since true existence has been negated during meditative equipoise on emptiness, its appearance—which is a veiled truth—has also ceased during that time, so veilings do not appear to that mind; only emptiness appears. The suchness of the mind that is a final liberated path to which all appearances of veilings has ceased is also the suchness of the mind that is the basis for the cessation of all afflictions. Thus it is a nirvāṇa.

REFLECTION

1. Why is a true cessation considered emptiness?
2. What is the difference between a mere cessation and a true cessation?
3. What are the two stains and the two types of freedom?
4. Since emptiness is the natural mode of existence of our mind, can it ever really be stained? Why is it purified on the path? What is the difference

between the emptiness of an unpurified mind and a mind that is free from all afflictive obscurations?

5. How does it help your practice to understand the answers to these four questions?

Conventional and Ultimate Truths and Conventional and Ultimate Existence

The words "ultimate" and "conventional" have different meanings according to the context. When saying that emptiness is an ultimate truth, "ultimate" means that it is an object realized or found by a supreme consciousness—an ārya's pristine wisdom of meditative equipoise; it is the highest object to be known. It is a truth because it exists as it appears to its principal cognizer.

When it's said that nothing ultimately exists, "ultimately" refers to the object of negation—existence from its own side, existence by its own mode of subsistence without depending on other factors. Nothing, not even emptiness, exists in this way.

Emptiness is the ultimate mode of existence of phenomena. Here "ultimate" means the final or supreme mode of existence. Emptiness is the ultimate mode of existence, but it does not ultimately exist because it cannot bear ultimate analysis. However, when a phenomenon's final mode of existence is analyzed, emptiness is found. When ultimate analysis searches for the final mode of existence of a book, it does not find a book; it finds the emptiness of the book. When ultimate analysis searches for the final mode of existence of emptiness, the emptiness of emptiness is found. Emptiness is found and realized by ultimate analysis, but it cannot bear ultimate analysis.

Because nothing can bear ultimate analysis, Prāsaṅgikas don't assert anything ultimately. All assertions and refutations are done on the conventional level. All phenomena, even emptiness, exist conventionally. Conventional existence is the only kind of existence there is because ultimate existence is inherent existence.

When saying emptiness is true, "true" means it exists as it appears to its principal cognizer. Emptiness, true cessations, and nirvāṇa are true. They are also ultimate truths; here "truth" means the highest objects. When we say the rocking chair is a veiled truth, "truth" means true from the perspective of ignorance. Such objects are not true.

The Tibetan terms *tha snyad* (*vyavahāra*) and *kun rdzob* are translated as "conventional," although strictly speaking *tha snyad* means "nominal." Usually these terms are synonymous. In the context of saying that all phenomena exist conventionally, "conventional" refers to existing nominally, existing by mere name—that is, existing by being merely designated. Since emptiness like all other phenomena exists by being merely designated, it exists conventionally. Whatever conventionally exists does not ultimately exist; nothing is ultimately existent.

"Conventionality" (T. *kun rdzob*), "nominal truth" (T. *tha snyad bden pa*), "worldly conventional truth," and "deceptive phenomena" are synonymous with "conventional truth." Emptiness is not any of these because it is an ultimate truth. However, emptiness exists conventionally in that it has been merely designated by term and concept.

To review: Although every existent phenomenon is either a conventional truth or an ultimate truth, all phenomena exist conventionally and none exist ultimately. Conventional truths are established by the six nondefective consciousnesses, even though they falsely appear as inherently existent to these consciousnesses that are influenced by ignorance and its latencies. Conventional truths (veiled truths) exist conventionally; their existence cannot be refuted by reasoning analyzing the ultimate. However, they do not exist in the way ignorance grasps them, for ignorance superimposes inherent existence on them. Such inherently existent phenomena apprehended by an ignorant awareness are nonexistent and are refuted by reasoning analyzing the ultimate. When we are angry because someone gave us undesired feedback, the inherently existent criticism apprehended by ignorance does not exist at all. However, dependently existent feedback exists. Differentiating between the two is difficult because we are so used to apprehending inherent existence that we don't even recognize it as something other than the object we are perceiving.

The Relationship of the Two Truths

The two truths are contradictory: something that is one cannot be the other. An apple (a veiled truth) is not emptiness (an ultimate truth), although the apple is empty. The two truths are also a dichotomy because any phenomenon must be either one or the other. There is no third alternative. To show the relationship of the two truths, Nāgārjuna said (BV 67cd–68):

> Independent of the conventional
> no [ultimate] truth can be found.
> The conventional is described as emptiness;
> emptiness itself is the conventional.
> One does not occur without the other,
> just like product and impermanent thing.

The Indian sages wrote using a specific poetic form that did not allow for full explanations. For this reason, the words or phrases may need to be explained. In this verse, *the conventional is described as emptiness* means that veiled truths are described as empty of true existence. *Emptiness itself is the conventional* means that emptiness exists conventionally.

There is nothing that is both a veiled truth and an ultimate truth. The book is not its emptiness, and the emptiness of the book is not the book. Why? The book is a conditioned phenomenon and its emptiness is unconditioned, and one object cannot have two contradictory attributes. Furthermore, they are known by different types of mind: the book is known by a conventional reliable cognizer, whereas its emptiness is known by the reasoning analyzing the ultimate.

The two truths are *one nature but different isolates* (T. *ngo bo gcig, la dog pa tha dad*). They are *one nature* in that they exist at the same time and one cannot exist without the other. A book (a veiled truth) does not exist without the book's emptiness (an ultimate truth), and the emptiness of the book does not exist without the book. Even though the book's emptiness is an ultimate truth and a permanent phenomenon that is not produced, it comes into existence at the same time the book arises and it goes out of existence at the time the book ceases. This indicates that emptiness exists here and now; it is neither some independent absolute in another universe nor an abstract theory. Emptiness is our very nature and the ultimate mode of existence of everything in the universe and beyond. Remembering this is important when we reflect and meditate on emptiness. Otherwise there's the danger of grasping emptiness as another affirmative object unrelated to the here and now.

Although the book and its emptiness are one nature, they are *different isolates*, meaning that they can be isolated or differentiated by thought. They are nominally distinct and can be discussed separately. An isolate of an object refers to just that object; it is that object in both term and meaning. An object and its isolate appear the same to a conceptual cognizer. Book is the isolate of book, but blue book is not the isolate of book because a blue book is nominally distinct from a book; in addition, a blue book and a book appear differently to a conceptual consciousness. The book and its emptiness are one nature, but they appear differently to conception and are different isolates. This is the meaning of the statement in the *Heart Sūtra*, "Form is empty; emptiness is form. Form is not other than emptiness; emptiness is not other than form." Form and its emptiness are not the same. Nevertheless form is empty, and emptiness is a quality of form; it is the ultimate nature of form. Form and its emptiness cannot occur without each other. They are one nature and different isolates.

The *Sūtra Unraveling the Thought* points out four faults that would occur if a form, such as a table, and its emptiness were the same (TT 68):

1. When ordinary beings directly perceive a table, they would also directly perceive its emptiness.
2. Just as chocolate cookies give rise to afflictions in the minds of ordinary beings, the emptiness of chocolate cookies would also give rise to afflictions when cognized by ordinary beings. In that case, when meditating on the emptiness of chocolate cookies, ordinary beings could have desire in their minds because the cookies and their emptiness were one and the same.
3. It would be meaningless for a yogi to try to realize the emptiness of a table because when he perceives the table, he would automatically perceive its emptiness.
4. Just as the table has color and mass, so would its emptiness.

On the other hand, if the two truths were different natures, four faults would also arise (TT 68):

1. The wisdom realizing the emptiness of the table could not counteract the superimposition of inherent existence on the table, because a table and its emptiness would be unrelated.
2. The emptiness of the table would not be the ultimate reality of the table, because they would be unrelated. Two things that exist simultaneously but are different entities are unrelated.
3. The table would not be the basis for the nonaffirming negation that is the emptiness of the table. The nonaffirming negation that is the absence of inherent existence of the table would not be the ultimate nature of the table.
4. The omniscient Buddha could apprehend the table as inherently existent and also apprehend its emptiness because the table and its emptiness would be unrelated, like a table and a chair.

Here we see that although the two truths are not the same, they are the same nature. They are different, but they are not different natures. The two truths can be viewed as basis and attribute, with veiled truths being the basis and emptiness being their attribute. But how does this work when we refer to the emptiness of emptiness, where emptiness is the basis and its emptiness is the attribute? Since emptiness is the basis of its own emptiness, emptiness—in this context—is *called* a "veiled truth" although it is not.

In the pair, emptiness and dependent arising, emptiness correlates with ultimate truth and dependent arising correlates with veiled truth. Although emptiness and ultimate truth are synonymous, dependent arising and veiled truth are not. For example, emptiness is a dependent arising in that it is merely dependently designated, but it is not a veiled truth.

Realizing the Two Truths

As Nāgārjuna stated, "Without depending on the conventional truth, the meaning of the ultimate cannot be taught." Śāntideva agrees. In the chapter on the perfection of wisdom in his *Compendium of Trainings*, he cites extensively from various scriptures that discuss the conventional characteristics of phenomena—their causes, nature, results, function, parts, and attributes. After describing this, he concludes by saying that all phenomena lack inherent existence, indicating that understanding the dependent, conventional nature of phenomena leads to understanding that they lack inherent existence.

This occurs in several interrelated ways. First, before seriously undertaking study and meditation on emptiness, we must have a robust understanding of the law of karma and its effects as well as engage in purification of negativities and collection of merit. When we then learn the refutations of true existence, this will prevent us from falling to an ethically nihilistic position that thinks there is no virtue and no nonvirtue because everything is empty.

A firm foundation in the initial and middle stages of the path as well as in bodhicitta is also needed. These are veiled truths, and familiarizing ourselves with them ensures that we have a proper motivation for learning the meditations on emptiness.

Furthermore, dependent arising, which is correlated with veiled truths—is the "monarch" of reasons that prove emptiness. Reflecting on the dependent nature of veiled truths leads us to understand that they cannot exist independently and set themselves up. Because veiled truths depend on so many diverse factors, they do not have an inherent essence that is findable under ultimate analysis.

To learn the reasonings proving emptiness by listening to teachings and reading books requires concepts and language, which are veiled truths. The same is true when we discuss and debate the meaning of emptiness to clarify and refine our understanding of it.

Knowing an instance of a veiled truth is not the same as knowing something *as* a conventional truth. For example, the apple is an instance of a veiled truth, and we know its conventional qualities. However, that does not mean we know it *as* a veiled truth, which entails understanding that while the apple appears inherently existent to our minds, it does not exist as it appears. It is false. Our sensory consciousnesses are not capable of knowing this. To fully understand it, understanding the apple's emptiness is necessary. Only after we have ascertained that the apple is empty of inherent existence—either through an inferential cognizer or a direct perceiver—can we know that the way it appears is false. It appears true only to the veiler, ignorance. At that time, we know the apple *as* a veiled truth and gain a deeper comprehension of dependent arising.

Understanding persons and other phenomena as veiled truths that are falsities in turn helps us to understand their emptiness more deeply. When we reach the culmination of the analysis of the profound view, dependent arising and emptiness converge so that emptiness dawns as the meaning of dependent arising and dependent arising dawns as the meaning of emptiness. In this way the understanding of one truth facilitates understanding the other. Both understandings are necessary.

Awarenesses cognizing veiled truths and awarenesses realizing ultimate truths inform and enrich each other. Ārya bodhisattvas develop both types of cognizers by using their refined powers of concentration to go back and forth between them. They practice seeing the I, for example, as a dependent arising and as empty, going in and out of meditative equipoise on emptiness. This has a profound transformative effect on the mind, which prepares these bodhisattvas to attain buddhahood, at which time they will be able to directly perceive both truths simultaneously.

REFLECTION

Contemplate the following points:

1. To cognize a blanket, it is not necessary to have ascertained the Middle Way view, but to cognize the blanket *as* a veiled truth, the Middle Way view must have been previously ascertained. If this were not the case, then everyone who saw a blanket would have already realized the Middle Way view.
2. To understand the blanket as a veiled truth, we must first know it is a falsity; that it is taken as true only for a mind under the influence of ignorance. It is not true because it appears inherently existent although it is not. The way it exists and the way it appears are discordant.
3. To explicitly cognize the blanket as a falsity, we must previously have refuted its inherent existence with either an inferential or nonconceptual reliable cognizer.

4 | What Exists and the Reliable Cognizers That Know It

On an average day, we experience an array of emotions. Many times, without our choice and better judgment, we become aggravated, defensive, anxious, or insecure. We may speak harshly or even become physically violent. At those times, the people and surrounding environment appear to our minds to be 100 percent negative. To free ourselves from anger and other afflictions, we must overcome the distorted conceptions that exaggerate the positive or negative qualities of people and things. Since afflictions and distorted conceptions depend on true-grasping, the ignorance that grasps true existence must be overcome. This involves cultivating the pristine wisdom that knows ultimate reality as well as reliable conventional cognizers of the people and things we encounter.

To do this, we now turn to the topic of reliable cognizers and how to differentiate them from erroneous mental states. The various types of awareness were explained in chapter 2 of *The Foundation of Buddhist Practice*; you may want to review that as you read this chapter. Here we will focus on the Prāsaṅgika view of reliable cognizers, which differs in some respects from that of Dignāga and Dharmakīrti, which was explained in that chapter.

Appearing, Apprehending, and Grasping

In chapter 1 we discussed true and false minds and their accurate and fraudulent objects, respectively. This was explained from the viewpoint of the world—that is, not according to the Madhyamaka view but according to the perspective of people who do not know about emptiness and do not question how phenomena actually exist. The explanation in this chapter will accord with the Madhyamaka view unless otherwise noted.

Before going further, a review of terms covered in preceding volumes would be helpful.[19] According to the lower schools, the *appearing object* (*pratibhāsa-viṣaya*) is the object that appears to a consciousness. The appearing object to a sense direct perceiver is that object—for example, an apple. The appearing object to a conceptual cognizer is a conceptual appearance of the apple, which the mind confuses with an actual apple. The *apprehended object* (*muṣṭibandhaviṣaya*) of a cognizer is the main object with which the mind is concerned, the object that the mind is getting at or understands. The apple is the apprehended object for the visual consciousness seeing the apple and for the mental consciousness thinking about the apple. A visual consciousness to which the apple appears to be a plum is erroneous because the apple isn't a plum. A conceptual mental consciousness that thinks the apple is a plum is also erroneous.

A reliable cognizer is a consciousness that is nondeceptive (incontrovertible, *avisaṃvādi*) with respect to its own principal object, which is its apprehended object. The conceptual mental consciousness that knows an apple is an apple is correct; a mental consciousness thinking the apple is a plum is erroneous.

So far, so good. The above fits very comfortably with a system that asserts inherent existence. But what happens when we look at this from the Prāsaṅgika perspective that asserts phenomena lack inherent existence? The visual consciousness to which a flower appears inherently existent is a mistaken consciousness because the flower appears falsely to it. The conceptual mental consciousness that apprehends the flower as inherently existent is erroneous because an inherently existent flower does not exist. It is also mistaken because the flower appears by means of conceptual appearance.

Since this is the case, can either the visual consciousness to which inherent existence appears or the mental consciousness that grasps inherent existence be a reliable cognizer? That visual consciousness apprehends a flower and identifies it as a flower and not a pine tree, so even though it is mistaken, it is not erroneous; it is incontrovertible regarding its principal object. A visual consciousness apprehending the flower as a wad of yellow paper, on the other hand, is a wrong consciousness and is not a reliable cognizer.

Appearing refers to how an object appears to a consciousness, whereas *apprehending* and *grasping* pertain to how the mind engages with that object. Sense consciousnesses do not grasp true existence, although true existence appears to them. The conceptual mental consciousness, however, may be afflicted by grasping inherent existence. In that case, not only does an inherently existent flower appear to it, but it erroneously grasps that flower to exist inherently.

Conceptual consciousnesses are always mental consciousnesses. The sense consciousnesses don't think or conceive. After the visual consciousness sees the flower, the mental consciousness may think about the flower and grasp it as inherently existent. This conceptual mental consciousness is erroneous with respect to its apprehended object and conceived object—an inherently existent flower—because inherently existent flowers do not exist.

The English words "apprehend" and "grasp" are translations of the same Tibetan word, *'dzin*, which has different meanings according to the context. For clarity, we'll use "grasp" when the mind erroneously grasps an object to be inherently existent. Only conceptual mental consciousnesses grasp their object as inherently existent, although not all conceptual consciousnesses do. Some simply apprehend their object, even though that object appears inherently existent to it. For example, when we casually think "I," as in "I'm sitting," the conceptual mind apprehends the I but does not grasp it as inherently existent. However, when someone else wants to sit in that seat and we don't want to give it up, grasping the I as inherently existent arises, "*I'm* sitting here. This is *my* seat, and *I'm* not going to move!"

The above example shows the problems that arise from grasping the I, the aggregates, or other phenomena as inherently existent—due to this grasping, afflictions arise, and as we know, afflictions are based on the projection or exaggeration of an object's qualities. Because we're grasping the object incorrectly, we respond inappropriately, making a big deal out of something that isn't such a big deal. Our actions not only create negative karma but also act as conditions that trigger other people's afflictions. Others often respond to us inappropriately, and together we live in a world of unnecessary duḥkha.

Because phenomena appear to exist independently to a mind influenced by ignorance and the latencies of ignorance when in fact they exist dependently, these phenomena are falsities and the consciousnesses perceiving them are mistaken (*bhrānti*). All consciousnesses of sentient beings, except those of āryas in meditative equipoise that directly and nonconceptually perceive emptiness, are mistaken because their objects appear inherently existent. After they arise from meditation on emptiness and go about their daily lives, āryas' sense and mental consciousnesses are also mistaken because phenomena appear inherently existent to them. Āryas know these appearances are false and practice seeing phenomena as like illusions.

However, not all consciousnesses of sentient beings are erroneous or wrong (*viparyaya*). The olfactory consciousness can smell *kapse*—Tibetan fried bread, a treat that we eat on holidays—and accurately know it is the smell of kapse. The mental consciousness that identifies "Chokyi is coming" is a correct consciousness.

Erroneous consciousnesses are wrong with respect to their apprehended objects, or conceived objects in the case of conceptual consciousnesses. Examples are our visual consciousness mistaking one person for another, a mental consciousness grasping the body to be inherently existent, or the mind of someone who believes a false rumor or a lie. According to the Prāsaṅgika view, the four distorted conceptions associated with true duḥkha—thinking the aggregates are permanent, blissful, pure, and have a self[20]—are erroneous because permanent, blissful, and pure aggregates as well as inherently existent aggregates do not exist. Minds believing the opposite—that the aggregates are impermanent, duḥkha in nature, foul, and lack a self—are correct insofar as the mode of apprehension of their main object is not compromised by any other reliable cognizer. That is, the aggregates are in fact impermanent, foul, duḥkha in nature, and selfless as those conceptual consciousnesses apprehend them to be. However, the four correct conceptions are mistaken insofar as their objects appear to exist inherently.

Interestingly, we hardly ever consider the mind that is attached to a beautiful object or angry at someone to be erroneous. We believe those consciousnesses to be completely accurate and true, when in fact they are erroneous. Ignorance blinds us from even considering this fact, thereby compounding our saṃsāra.

REFLECTION

When you're in a public place, such as a train station, be aware of the people around you and the objects you see, hear, smell, taste, and touch.

1. Observe: Your visual consciousness sees people and your mind knows there are people and trains. True existence appears to your visual consciousness and conceptual consciousness. Both consciousnesses are mistaken regarding their appearing objects, people and trains. Nevertheless, both consciousnesses correctly apprehend and identify the people and the trains. There is no particular emotion in your mind and your actions are undisturbed.
2. Observe what happens if you then think, "That's my train. Is it leaving the station so soon? Oh no, I don't want to miss it!" At that time, the mental consciousness has grasped the I and the train as truly existent. The train now has a special and important relationship to you that will influence your happiness. Based on this grasping, you become stressed, and that is reflected in your actions as you run down the platform, pushing people aside to board the train.
3. In your daily life, observe many such events, from the ones where no true-grasping is present to the ones where the mind is overwhelmed by true-grasping that then sparks clinging attachment, resentment, jealousy, arrogance, or an array of other emotions and attitudes. Observe how true-grasping and the afflictions and attitudes that are based on it motivate your actions.

The question arises: When we cultivate the clear appearance of ourselves as a deity in tantric practice, is that an erroneous awareness? In tantra we imagine ourselves as a deity with a deity's body for a specific reason. We want to become a buddha, and the principal cause for attaining a buddha's form body in Tantrayāna is actualizing the illusory body on the completion stage. To do that, on the generation stage we must cultivate the clear appearance of ourselves as the deity and the divine identity (T. *lha'i ngar rgyal*), thinking we are the deity.[21] Although we are not presently a deity, because this view is cultivated for a particular virtuous purpose in the framework of Dharma practice, that mind is not erroneous. However, the consciousness of a person hallucinating that they are a deity is erroneous.

The mind of a meditator with strong clear appearance and divine identity is free of afflictions and meditates on the complementary nature of the two truths: the deity body appears but is empty of true existence. The deity body is empty, but it appears. Meditating in this way is very different from someone with a mental illness who thinks he is a deity. That person is not deliberately cultivating that perception with a good intention. In addition, misconceiving himself to be an inherently existent deity causes afflictions to arise in his mind, whereas afflictions do not arise in the mind of a yogi practicing clear appearance and identity dignity of the deity.

Similarly, cultivating the pure appearance of our environment as the deity's maṇḍala does not negate the conventional validity of our house as being made of bricks, stone, or wood, and cultivating the view that the people around us are deities does not negate that they are sentient beings with afflictions. Here, too, pure appearance is cultivated for the specific reason of subduing afflictions. Our imagining that we and our companions are deities and that our environment is a pureland does not make them so. If it did, when our friend is in pain with a broken leg due to a skiing accident, we could say, "You have a body made of light so it's impossible that you feel pain!" However, our friend, clutching his broken leg, would not be very happy with that reply.

In the same way, as part of establishing mindfulness of the body, we view our body as just bones and expand the appearance of bones so that it fills the entire universe. We consciously cultivate this appearance to the mental consciousness for the purpose of subduing attachment. It is not an erroneous awareness.

Similarly, seeing our spiritual mentor as a buddha is not an erroneous awareness because we are consciously cultivating this view for a virtuous reason. We know that seeing our guru in this way will make us a receptive vessel when listening to teachings or receiving Dharma instructions. However, if with an afflictive mind we project unrealistic expectations on our spiritual mentors, such as thinking they don't need to go to the doctor when they are sick because they are buddhas who manifest in bodies of light, what began as a beneficial practice has become an erroneous consciousness that in severe cases could endanger our gurus' lives.

Reliable Cognizers

To review, according to all Buddhist tenet systems, "existing" means that something is known or established by a reliable cognizer. Prāsaṅgikas define a reliable cognizer as an awareness that is incontrovertible with respect to its principal object.

In the past, so-called Mādhyamikas misunderstood the refutation of inherent existence and thought that the pristine wisdom realizing emptiness perceives phenomena's nonexistence. Furthermore, they thought conventional consciousnesses, such as the visual and auditory consciousnesses, are not reliable cognizers because Candrakīrti says in the *Supplement* (MMA 6.31a):

> In all respects worldly [consciousnesses] are not reliable cognizers.

In addition, the *King of Concentration Sūtra* says (SR 9.23):

> The eye, ear, and nose [consciousnesses] are not reliable cognizers.
> The tongue, body, and mental [consciousnesses] are also not reliable cognizers.
> If these sense [consciousnesses] were reliable cognizers,
> of what use to anyone would the ārya's path be?

These so-called Mādhyamikas then erroneously concluded: Because neither āryas' pristine wisdom nor worldly consciousnesses are reliable cognizers of phenomena, and because no other possibilities of reliable cognizers exist, phenomena are not established by reliable cognizers and therefore do not exist.

Mādhyamikas clarify these errors by explaining that the meaning of both of the above passages is that worldly consciousnesses, such as our sense consciousnesses, are not reliable with respect to emptiness, the ultimate nature. However, this does not deny the reliability of ordinary worldly consciousnesses with respect to conventional objects such as sights and sounds.

Why are our senses not reliable with respect to reality—emptiness? Sense consciousnesses know veiled truths, and veiled truths appear truly existent to them. If our senses were reliable cognizers of reality, the true existence that appears to them would be how phenomena exist. If that were so, there would be no need to realize emptiness, for our senses would already perceive phenomena's ultimate nature. In that case, we would not need to exert time and effort to train ourselves in the ārya path or to hear, think, and meditate on emptiness.

What consciousnesses are reliable cognizers of emptiness? These are inferential reliable cognizers of emptiness and āryas' pristine wisdom of meditative equipoise on emptiness. The former perceives emptiness by means of a conceptual appearance, whereas the latter perceives it directly.

Sautrāntikas say that sense reliable cognizers are nonmistaken consciousnesses. They consider consciousnesses that apprehend true existence to be nonmistaken because, according to them, phenomena exist truly. To them, it seems that Candrakīrti is saying that sense consciousnesses are erroneous and are never reliable, nondeceptive cognizers, and thus sights, sounds, and so forth do not exist because no reliable cognizer perceives them.

Asserting true existence, Sautrāntikas believe that if phenomena did not truly exist, they would not exist by their own character (*svalakṣaṇasat*) and would thus be incapable of performing functions. Since they perform functions, sense objects have their own character, and reliable cognizers correctly apprehend and establish that phenomena exist by their own character. If sense direct perceivers were not direct reliable cognizers of the existence by their own character of the five sense objects—that is, if they did not establish sense objects as truly existent—they would not be reliable cognizers of those objects.

To these assertions, Candrakīrti responds: Objects of the five senses are false in that they do not truly exist even though they appear in that way to their direct cognizers. Therefore the sense consciousnesses that establish them are not reliable with respect to the own-character (true existence) of those phenomena. Those consciousnesses are mistaken in that the five sense objects appear to exist by their own character although they do not. Sense consciousnesses are reliable simply with respect to the conventional existence of the five sense objects. They are not reliable with regard to the true existence of their objects because such own-character does not exist.

Thus Candrakīrti refutes both reliable cognizers that exist by their own character and objects that exist by their own character, although he accepts reliable cognizers and reliable objects that exist dependently. Sense consciousnesses are not reliable cognizers of emptiness because they do not perceive the ultimate nature. Also, they are not reliable cognizers of an object's own character because phenomena do not exist by their own character.

If things truly existed as they appear, that true existence would become clearer and clearer the more we searched for it. But that is not what happens; when we search for truly existent objects with ultimate analysis, truly existent objects are not found, and the objects' emptiness of true existence is found instead. For example, if a mirage were water, the closer we got to it, the clearer the perception of water would be. But the opposite happens: we discover there is no water there. This points to a disparity between how objects appear to our sense consciousnesses and how those objects actually exist. For that reason, our sense consciousnesses are said to be mistaken with respect to their appearing objects, in that their objects appear to exist truly. However, that does not mean those consciousnesses are erroneous and unreliable in general. The visual consciousness still apprehends and establishes yellow and other visible forms. Sense consciousnesses that are not erroneous regarding their apprehended object are conventional reliable cognizers.

For the lower systems, a cognizer that is mistaken regarding the mode of existence of its object does not realize that object. This is because that cognizer does not correctly apprehend the object as it actually is. However, for Prāsaṅgikas, being mistaken with respect to an object and realizing the object are not mutually exclusive. A visual consciousness seeing the yellow of a daisy is mistaken with respect to yellow's appearing truly existent, but it realizes and is a reliable cognizer of yellow. In other words, this visual consciousness is not reliable with respect to its appearing object, because yellow mistakenly appears truly existent, but it is reliable regarding its apprehended object, because it correctly knows yellow.

Each tenet system has its reasons for saying sense consciousnesses are mistaken or nonmistaken. For Sautrāntikas, as noted above, sense direct perceivers are reliable cognizers of an object's true existence, and objects exist the way they appear to those consciousnesses. Because sense direct perceivers are true and nonmistaken regarding the mode of existence of their objects, Sautrāntikas consider them ultimate consciousnesses and consider sense objects to be ultimate truths.

Yogācārins assert that sense consciousnesses are mistaken in that phenomena appear to be a different nature from the consciousness perceiving them, whereas they are not. Objects appear to be external and unrelated to the perceiving consciousness, whereas in fact they are the same nature as the consciousness perceiving them. Nevertheless, Yogācārins assert that things appear truly existent and that appearance is not mistaken because dependent phenomena are truly existent.

Although Svātantrikas negate inherent existence on the ultimate level, they assert that objects exist inherently on the conventional level. Thus they assert that sense consciousnesses are reliable regarding their inherent existence, whereas Prāsaṅgikas assert that sense consciousnesses are mistaken because sense objects appear to inherently exist although they do not. This means that all our daily perceptions and thoughts are mistaken in that their objects appear to inherently exist, whereas in fact these objects are empty of inherent existence. Knowing this is definitely humbling!

In this discussion, various notions about the object of negation become apparent. Svātantrika Mādhyamikas say the object of negation appears only to conceptual consciousness, whereas Yogācārins and Prāsaṅgika Mādhyamikas say it also appears to direct perceivers.

In short, the lower schools accept the appearance of inherent existence as nonmistaken and assert that sense and mental reliable consciousnesses are not mistaken with respect to their appearing objects because things exist inherently as they appear. Likewise the lower schools do not assert that consciousnesses grasping inherent existence are erroneous with respect to their apprehended or conceived objects because phenomena exist inherently and those consciousnesses are reliable cognizers with respect to inherently existent objects. To the lower schools, a consciousness cannot be both mistaken and a reliable cognizer with respect to the same object, whereas according to Prāsaṅgikas, a consciousness can be reliable with respect to the existence of the object and mistaken in that the object appears inherently existent.

Prāsaṅgikas refute reliable cognizers that exist by their own character and apprehended objects that exist by their own character, but they accept reliable cognizers and objects that exist dependently. A reliable cognizer and its apprehended object are established by mutual dependence. When one exists, the other does as well. In general, we ordinary sentient beings regard an object, such as a flower, as existing independently, objectively, "out there." Similarly, it seems to us that a perceiving consciousness exists independently "in here," and that when these two independent things contact each other with the help of our eye faculty, perception occurs. However, this is not the case. A reliable cognizer and a reliable object are posited in relation to each other. A consciousness is considered reliable because its apprehended object exists, and an object is considered existent because a reliable cognizer certifies it. Regarding reliable cognizers and objects of comprehension that are dependent arisings, Candrakīrti says in *Clear Words* (LC 3.167):

> [Reliable cognizers and their objects] are established through mutual dependence. When reliable cognizers exist, there are things that are the objects of comprehension. When there are things that are objects of comprehension, there are reliable cognizers. However, neither reliable cognizers nor objects of comprehension exist inherently.

To back this up, Candrakīrti asserts four reliable cognizers: direct reliable cognizers, inferential reliable cognizers, reliable cognizers based on an example, and reliable cognizers based on authoritative testimony.[22] However, his assertions about conventional reliable cognizers—awarenesses that are sources of accurate information about what does and doesn't exist and the functions of these existent objects—differs greatly from those of Dharmakīrti. Whereas Dharmakīrti believes that reliable cognizers truly exist and are correct in establishing the true existence of their objects, Candrakīrti refutes the true existence of both cognizers and their objects. Given that according to Candrakīrti all cognizers of sentient beings—except āryas' meditative equipoise on emptiness—are mistaken, how can we trust any of our conventional consciousnesses to give us accurate information on the conventional level? Does whatever our six senses apprehend exist? If not, what are the criteria for conventional existence (T. *kun rdzob tu yod, tha snyad du yod*)?

Three Criteria for Conventional Existence

To answer those questions, Tsongkhapa says (LC 3.178):

> How does one determine whether something exists conventionally? We hold that something exists conventionally (1) if

> it is known to a conventional consciousness, (2) if no other conventional reliable cognizer contradicts its being as it is thus known, and (3) if reason that accurately analyzes reality—that is, analyzes whether something inherently exists—does not contradict it. We hold that what fails to meet those criteria does not exist.

To determine what does and does not exist, Prāsaṅgikas do not rely on the incontrovertible certification of conventional direct perceivers or inferential cognizers because relying on such would necessitate their being inherently existent. Rather they first set out all objects known by conventional consciousnesses and then determine which can be discredited. Those that cannot be contradicted by either another conventional reliable cognizer or ultimate analysis are said to exist. Let's examine the three criteria for conventional existence, which is the only kind of existence there is since nothing exists ultimately.

1. It Is Known to a Conventional Consciousness

To exist conventionally, an object must be known by a conventional consciousness; it must be renowned in the world. Conventional consciousnesses, such as those used in our daily lives that see visible forms and hear sounds, function only in the context of objects appearing to them. They do not analyze their object's mode of existence to determine if it inherently exists or not. However, these consciousnesses are not totally nonanalytical, for they discern the qualities of their object. Conventional consciousnesses reflect on the groceries needed to make lunch, what medications to take at what time, and how to apply for your pension. Although they do not analyze whether the groceries are truly existent, they may analyze what food is more nutritious and economical. Conventional consciousnesses are worldly or mundane knowledge that operate within the context of things appearing to them and the names they are called in common parlance.

Conventional consciousnesses exist in the mindstreams of all sentient beings—humans, animals, ordinary being, āryas, and so forth—regardless of whether or not they have learned philosophical tenets. Not every consciousness of people who have learned tenets examines the nature of reality; they still think about washing the dishes and talking to friends. Even if two people are discussing the ultimate nature of a sprout, they still identify it and share common knowledge about it. "Known by a conventional consciousness" means an object appears to or is experienced by an ordinary consciousness. Based on that appearance or experience, we give names to these objects so we can talk about them. Thus "known to a conventional consciousness" also indicates that the object has a name that people use to refer to it so that it can be an object of discussion.

To be an object known to a conventional consciousness, an object does not need to be known by everyone. For example, the paths and stages to awakening and the law of karma and its effects are known by conventional consciousnesses, although not everyone knows about them. Similarly, the details of brain physiology and auto mechanics are not known to everyone in the world, but they are objects known to conventional consciousness because we can think about them without examining their ultimate nature.

2. It Is Not Discredited by Another Conventional Reliable Cognizer

An object known by a conventional consciousness must not be discredited by another conventional reliable cognizer. If I mistakenly think a coiled rope in the garden is a snake, either my own subsequent cognition of the object or the conventional reliable cognizer of another person who tells me to relax, that no snake is there, can discredit my first perception.

Some beliefs are undermined by conventional reliable cognizers. When we look at a mountain, we think it is the same mountain we saw yesterday. The conventional reliable cognizer of another person can discredit this. Some people believe that because their ancestors fought with the ancestors of another group hundreds of years ago, the present people in the two groups must be enemies. Conventional analysis can disprove this as well.

For something to exist conventionally not everyone must know about it and believe it exists. Physicists talk about tiny particles and mathematical equations, but not everyone must know, understand, or believe these for them to exist conventionally. Similarly, not everyone must disbelieve something for it to be nonexistent. Although some people believe that we human beings are irredeemably selfish, we are not, and although many people believe that awakening does not exist, it does. In the folktale "The Emperor's New Clothes," the emperor and all the townspeople believed the emperor was wearing lavish garments, even though their own visual consciousnesses knew he wasn't. It was only when a child's conventional reliable cognizer pointed out that he wasn't wearing anything that they realized their belief was wrong.

Some conventional consciousnesses are erroneous and others are not. The first criteria, that something is known to the world, does not mean it is established by a reliable cognizer. We commonly believe our aggregates to be permanent, pleasurable, and pure. These misconceptions and their objects are erroneous, even though they are commonly believed in the world. The conventional reliable cognizers of those who have studied philosophy can discredit the conventional consciousnesses that misapprehend permanence, pleasure, and purity and establish the correct conceptions that the aggregates are impermanent, unsatisfactory, and foul. Alternatively, the person with the wrong views may later reconsider their own conceptions and, by employing analytical wisdom, discredit them with their own conventional reliable cognizers.

Emptiness is an ultimate truth; what conventional consciousness establishes it? Emptiness is established by the conventional consciousness that knows the existence of emptiness. Analysis to determine if emptiness exists is conventional analysis, whereas analysis to determine if phenomena inherently exist constitutes ultimate analysis. A conventional reliable cognizer knows the existence of emptiness and is therefore said to know emptiness in the sense that it certifies the existence of emptiness. However, probing awareness analyzing the ultimate realizes emptiness.

Sometimes we can easily and quickly validate a cognition. Let's say we're reading an instruction booklet for a new appliance, but don't have our reading glasses. We may think we read it correctly, but to make sure we ask someone with good eyesight standing nearby. That person's conventional reliable cognizer can verify whether our understanding is correct or not. In other situations, we may not know whether another conventional reliable cognizer can discredit our cognition. Since Pluto was discovered in 1930, it has been considered the ninth planet in our solar system. But new information about Pluto has been discovered since then, and the International Astronomical Union has determined that since Pluto doesn't meet the criteria to be a full-sized planet, it is not a planet.

The acuity of society's conventional reliable cognizers increases as discoveries are made. In previous centuries, people died from unknown causes.

Now cancer, kidney disease, and so on are generally known in society, and criteria have been established to test for their existence. Although none of these criteria are foolproof and misdiagnoses occur, there are more and more conventional reliable cognizers that understand these diseases and that undermine incorrect consciousnesses that misdiagnose them.

The process of learning—as individuals and as a society—occurs through the process of generating conventional reliable cognizers. We must be flexible and ready to revise our ideas rather than lock ourselves into believing that we have found the one right answer that will apply to every situation.

REFLECTION

1. Does everything your senses cognize exist? How do you determine if your sense perceptions are accurate?
2. Is everything you think true? If other people agree with your thoughts and ideas, does that make them true? What means do you use to determine if your conceptual consciousnesses are reliable or not?
3. Does your pride sometimes inhibit checking the reliability of your sense perceptions and thoughts?
4. Does wanting to be part of a group or to win someone's approval cause you to avoid examining the reliability of your ideas and opinions? Or if you do examine them and discover they are erroneous, does arrogance inhibit you from acknowledging your mistake?

3. It Is Not Discredited by a Reasoning Analyzing the Ultimate

The third criterion to establish something as conventionally existent is that it must not be discredited by a reasoning analyzing the ultimate. This criterion is necessary because knowing the first two criteria alone does not help us understand that the inherently existent object that appears to us does not exist. Without this understanding, we will continue to think that the objects that appear to us exist as they appear, whereas they do not.

To certify an object's existence, it must not be disproved by the reasoning analyzing the ultimate. An inherently existent political party is discredited by the reasoning analyzing the ultimate, because when searched for with ultimate analysis, it is not found. Only its emptiness is found.

Ultimate analysis cannot deprecate conventionally existent objects because those are outside the purview of such a consciousness. Although reasoning analyzing the ultimate cannot contradict the existence of veiled truths, it cannot establish them either. Happiness arises from virtue conventionally. This is not discredited by either a conventional reliable cognizer or the reasoning analyzing the ultimate. An external creator is discredited by a conventional reliable cognizer, and if someone grasps an inherently existent creator, ultimate analysis disproves that.

When ignorance reifies veiled truths and grasps them as inherently existent, the inherently existent object we apprehend can be negated by ultimate analysis. The Losang grasped by someone who is very attached to him does not exist. That person grasps an inherently existent Losang who has inherently existent wonderful qualities that no one else can match. Similarly, the Losang his enemy thinks about also does not exist; an angry mind reifies Losang into an inherently existent person with inherently existent faults, and such a person does not exist. But Losang exists conventionally; he eats, plays tennis, and rides a bicycle to work. Negating his inherent existence doesn't change that.

Someone suffering from low self-esteem may think he is an inherently existent incapable and unlovable person who will always fail. This notion of such an I that exists in and of itself is damaged by reasoning analyzing the ultimate; it is not found by ultimate analysis and does not exist even conventionally. Meditation on the emptiness of the I can help this person's attitude toward himself change such that he will see that he is not an inherently existent terrible person. He has many good qualities, can cultivate even more qualities, and can have a meaningful life.

Some metaphysical objects accepted by non-Buddhists or by Buddhist essentialists can be discredited by the reasoning analyzing the ultimate and thus do not conventionally exist. For example, particles that are the building blocks of the universe are seen as inherently existent by those who assert them. Similarly, a permanent soul and a fundamental cosmic substance from which everything emerges and into which everything returns is seen by its believers as existing independent of all other factors. An independent absolute creator who created and manages the universe is also thought to exist inherently by those who believe in it.

All of these are posited on the basis of people's flawed analytical reasoning. Their proponents assert these metaphysical things based on their own type of ultimate analysis that they believe knows them to exist inherently. Because they believe these things can withstand ultimate analysis, they must accept that others can scrutinize them with ultimate analysis as well. When the Prāsaṅgikas do so with perfect reasoning, they prove that such things lack inherent existence. Prāsaṅgikas' ability to refute inherent existence means these imagined metaphysical objects are totally nonexistent and do not exist even conventionally.

Don't get confused here. As discussed above, the notion of a permanent person can be refuted by someone without an understanding of emptiness. Conventional analysis is sufficient. But if someone grasps a permanent person to exist inherently, then the understanding of emptiness is necessary to dislodge this idea.

Similarly, the foundation consciousness accepted by the Yogācāra-Scripture Proponents is posited on the basis of holding it as inherently existent. Being uncomfortable with the mental consciousness and the mere I being the carriers of karmic seeds, these Yogācārins seek a more stable basis that carries karmic seeds from one life to the next. Looking for the true referent of the term "person," they conclude that the foundation consciousness is the actual identity of the person. Their notion of the foundation consciousness arose through inquiring into the ultimate nature of the person. By refuting the inherent existence of the person, Prāsaṅgikas refute the conventional existence of an imagined foundation consciousness that exists inherently.

On the other hand, refuting the true existence of happiness arising from virtue and suffering from nonvirtue does not refute their conventional existence; it simply negates their true existence. They were never asserted on the basis of grasping them as truly existent, so refuting their true existence does not disqualify them from existing conventionally.

Similarly, when the law of karma and its effects is subjected to ultimate analysis, its existence is not refuted. Unlike a truly existent soul that cannot withstand ultimate analysis, karma and its effects are not asserted to truly exist. Therefore negating their true existence does not affect the fact that they exist conventionally. It is important not to confuse not being established by the reasoning analyzing the ultimate and being disproved by it. In this instance, both karma and its effects and a truly existent soul are not established by the reasoning analyzing the ultimate. However, a truly existent soul is disproved by that reasoning, whereas the law of karma and its effects are not.

A reasoning consciousness analyzing the ultimate damages true existence in that it negates true existence. However, it does not prove that the consciousness grasping true existence doesn't exist, because that true-grasping mind is an existent phenomenon; it exists conventionally. True-grasping itself lacks true existence; what it grasps (true existence) doesn't exist, but the consciousness grasping true existence itself exists. It is a mental factor in the miscellaneous aggregate.

The reasoning consciousness analyzing the ultimate damages true-grasping by refuting its apprehended object, true existence. This weakens true-grasping and undermines its ability to continue to exist. By repeated meditation on emptiness, the mind becomes familiar with it, so that true-grasping will eventually be eradicated completely. It's important to understand that being damaged by reasoning consciousness analyzing the ultimate doesn't mean the object doesn't exist conventionally. This is because the wisdom realizing emptiness (1) damages the persistence of a consciousness grasping true existence, but (2) does not damage the fact that a consciousness grasping true existence is established by a conventional reliable cognizer, even though that wisdom negates the true existence of the true-grasping mind.

Prāsaṅgikas posit objects known by conventional consciousnesses that are not impaired by internal or external causes of error. They negate truly existent people and things that are the conceived objects of innate self-grasping, but they assert conventionally existent people and things.

In general, Prāsaṅgikas accept things known to the world as conventionally existent. Nevertheless, not everything renowned in the world exists conventionally—even if it is believed by a large number of people for many centuries. It may still be discredited by either another conventional cognizer or the reasoning analyzing the ultimate. Although ordinary sentient beings innately feel that they inherently exist, their inherent existence can be discredited by ultimate analysis. Similarly, ordinary sentient beings may grasp their country's borders, citizens, or status in the world to exist inherently. These notions, too, can be disproven with ultimate analysis. When searched for with probing awareness, such inherently existent phenomena are nowhere to be found.

Forms and the other aggregates are truths from the perspective of ignorance, which superimposes inherent existence on them. However, they are not established by ignorance but by the six nondefective consciousnesses. Buildings, people, feelings, and so forth as they are apprehended by ignorance are refuted through reasoning and do not exist. But buildings, people, feelings, and so forth exist and are established by conventional reliable cognizers. Negating inherent existence while establishing conventional existence and the existence of veiled truths is a delicate process. It is important to understand this well; otherwise we risk falling to the extreme of nihilism, unable to establish conventional existence.

I want to tell you a story about the three criteria required to know that something exists. During an audience with a small group of American Dharma students, I questioned them about their understanding of emptiness. One man replied that he thought a mirage was a very helpful example of how to understand the Prāsaṅgikas' view of emptiness and dependent arising. On the conventional level the appearance of the mirage water is a dependently existing phenomena based on causes and conditions, whereas on the ultimate level the mirage water was unfindable.[23]

I then asked, "How do you determine what is actually an illusion and what is an existing thing that appears to be an illusion?" Another student replied by referring to the three criteria: it is known to a conventional consciousness, it is not contradicted by another conventional reliable cognizer, and it is not contradicted by a mind that accurately analyzes reality.

I was very pleased with this answer and jokingly said that I wanted to give her a pandit's hat, but I was not sure what color it should be: yellow, pink, green, or purple. She quipped perhaps it should be red, white, and blue, and all of us had a good laugh.

Nature

The word "nature" (*svabhāva*, T. *rang bzhin*) has multiple and sometimes contradictory meanings that vary according to context. Without awareness of its context, we may misunderstand its meaning, leading to confusion. For example, the *Eight Thousand Line Perfection of Wisdom Sūtra* states (NT 32):

> Subhūti, since the five aggregates are without nature, they have a nature of emptiness.

Here the nature that the aggregates lack is an inherently existent nature, which doesn't exist at all. Because they lack that nature, the aggregates have the nature of emptiness, a nature that exists. "Nature" has three very different principal meanings. We know which one is being spoken about in dependence on the context.

1. A final or ultimate nature of an object, its reality nature, emptiness (T. *rang bzhin chos nyid*). Here "nature" refers to the ultimate mode of existence of phenomena.
2. A nature that is the object of negation (T. *dgag bya'i rang bzhin*). Used in phrases such as "existing by its own nature" or "naturally existent," "nature" refers to true or inherent existence.
3. A conventional nature of an object (T. *tha snyad pa'i rang bzhin*). For example, the nature of fire is hot.

Let's look at them individually.

(1) Ultimate Nature

The first meaning of "nature" refers to the final nature of all phenomena—their emptiness or reality (T. *chos nyid*). This nature exists. In *Treatise on the Middle Way*, Nāgārjuna says (MMK 15.2cd):

> Nature itself is not fabricated and does not depend on another.

In addition to these two attributes of nature—not fabricated and not dependent on another—Nāgārjuna adds a third quality: it is immutable and lacks change. He says (MMK 15.8cd):

> Change of nature is never feasible.

Some people have misunderstood Nāgārjuna's meaning, thinking either that the nature he refers to is the object of negation or that there is no nature at all. However, Nāgārjuna is firm in describing the ultimate nature as existent and possessing three attributes.

1. Emptiness, the ultimate mode of existence of all phenomena, is *unfabricated* in that it is not produced by causes. Something that is fabricated does not exist earlier and is newly created. Emptiness is not like this. As the final nature of all phenomena, it was not produced by causes or conditions. No cause made it the ultimate mode of existence. It is unconditioned, uncreated, and permanent.
2. Emptiness *does not depend on another* in that it does not arise and cease dependent on other things. It is unlike suffering and happiness, birth and death, which depend on other factors to arise and cease. All phenomena are always empty of inherent existence whether or not the buddhas appear in or depart from the world. Whereas the buddhas' appearance and departure depend on causes and conditions, the ultimate nature of all phenomena does not.

   In addition, emptiness does not depend on another in that it does not rely on comparisons such as long and short. While long and short vary depending on each other, emptiness is always emptiness. It is not posited in dependence on a comparable phenomenon. Although a meter is long in comparison to a centimeter and short in comparison to a kilometer, emptiness does not become something else in the face of a comparable object. Emptiness does depend on another in that it depends on a positing awareness, on its parts, and so forth, but it is not dependent on another in that it does not depend on comparison.
3. Emptiness is *immutable*, unchanging. Emptiness is always emptiness. It doesn't change into conventional existence or nonexistence.

Unfabricated, not dependent on others, and immutable are qualities of emptiness, but they are not emptiness. These qualities are veiled truths. Similarly, the existence of emptiness is a veiled truth, whereas emptiness itself is an ultimate truth. Why are these qualities veiled truths when emptiness is an ultimate truth? Because they are known by a conventional consciousness.

A direct perceiver of emptiness does not know these attributes of emptiness; it knows only emptiness.

In previous times, some Tibetans thought that this triply qualified nature was the object of negation. The problem with this is that an unfabricated, independent, and unchanging nature is too narrow an object of negation; negating only that is not enough. While these are attributes of inherent existence, they are also attributes of a permanent, unitary, independent self, a much coarser object of negation. Realizing the absence of the latter does not eliminate true-grasping ignorance and release us from cyclic existence.

(2) Nonexistent Ultimate Natures

The second meaning of "nature" refers to an "ultimate" nature that does not exist. There are several nonexistent so-called ultimate natures:

1. A fabricated nature, such as the heat of fire, cannot be the ultimate nature of fire because it depends on causes and conditions and is impermanent. Although heat is the conventional nature of fire, it is not the fundamental, innermost entity of fire because it changes. It did not exist earlier but was newly created, and it is dependent on another—on causes and conditions.
2. Inherent existence, which is the unique object of negation of the Prāsaṅgikas, does not exist, has never existed, and will never exist either ultimately or conventionally. When we say all phenomena do not exist by their own nature or by their own entity, "nature" refers to inherent existence. This is the final object of negation when meditating on selflessness. This nature means "existing without depending on another factor" (T. *gzhan la rag ma las par grub pa*). Here, "another factor" does not refer to causes and conditions but to a conventional mind (T. *tha snyad pa'i shes pa*) that conceives an object and imputes a name. All phenomena—those created by causes and conditions as well as permanent phenomena—do not exist without depending on the conventional consciousness that conceives and names them and establishes their existence. As a nonexistent, inherent existence is not established by a conventional reliable cognizer.

   Even emptiness does not exist by its own nature. Saying that emptiness is unfabricated and does not depend on another does not mean that emptiness is an independent entity that can stand on its own. Although it is permanent, it depends on its parts, its basis of designation, and on the mind that conceives and designates it. Emptiness is an ultimate truth, yet like all other existents, it exists conventionally.

3. A permanent, unitary, independent self has a nonexistent nature because it is an object of negation that possesses the three attributes of unfabricated, not dependent on another, and immutable. Although such a self does not exist, it is not the final or unique object of negation in the Prāsaṅgikas' presentation of selflessness.
4. A primal substance or fundamental nature (*prakṛti*) asserted by the Sāṃkhyas. It possesses six characteristics; it is (1) the agent that acts; (2) permanent; (3) unitary (partless); (4) only an object, not a consciousness or a person; (5) pervading all animate and inanimate phenomena; and (6) unmanifest and an equilibrium of three qualities (activity, lightness, and darkness).[24]
5. A positive and independent nature such as that asserted by Dolpopa (1292–1361).[25] Combining the teachings in the Perfection of Wisdom with his own unique interpretation of the *Sūtra Unraveling the Thought* and the *Sublime Continuum*, Dolpopa taught a doctrine he called the Great Madhyamaka. In it he says that the absolute and the conventional are both empty, but in different ways. Absolute reality is a substantially existent tathāgatagarbha, complete with all the signs and marks of a fully awakened buddha; it is inherently present in all sentient beings. It is other-empty (T. *gzhan stong*) or empty of other conventional phenomena but it is not self-empty, whereas for Dolpopa, conventional phenomena are empty of self-nature (T. *rang stong*) and are as real as a rabbit's horn. The ultimate for Dolpopa is positive and independent; it is the naturally luminous clear light—the dharmakāya—an eternal, indestructible, blissful wisdom present in each and every sentient being. This wisdom is permanent and is the ultimate nature of all phenomena.

Among other criticisms of the Great Madhyamaka, a prevalent one is that asserting the ultimate nature to be positive and independent goes beyond the Buddha's emphasis on selflessness as a negation. The nature Dolpopa asserts falls in the extreme of absolutism, and his assertion that veiled phenomena do not exist at all is the extreme of nihilism.

(3) Conventional Nature

The third meaning of "nature" is "character." Although no phenomenon has a nature that is established by its own entity—that is, it does not ultimately exist—everything has its own conventional nature. This nature or character may be static or changing, big or small, beneficial or harmful, and so forth. The nature of fire is hot; the nature of earth is solid. Phenomena have their own nature (T. *rang bzhin*) or character conventionally, but do not exist by their own nature (T. *rang bzhin gyis sgrub pa*) and do not exist by their own character—that is, they do not exist inherently. They have their own entity (T. *rang gi ngo bo*) conventionally, but do not exist by their own entity (T. *rang gi ngo bos yod pa*), for if they did, they would exist inherently. For example, ordinary sentient beings often create the causes for suffering even though they seek happiness. This is a characteristic of their conventional nature (the third meaning of "nature") and is a quality of beings in cyclic existence. However, it is not their ultimate nature (the first meaning of "nature"), which is emptiness. Because they are empty of inherent existence, they do not exist by their own nature (the second meaning of "nature"). Conventional phenomena are not objects of negation, inherent existence is.

A phenomenon's ultimate nature is not its conventional nature. Fire's ultimate nature is its emptiness of inherent existence, and its conventional nature is hot and burning. A thing's ultimate nature cannot be known directly by an erroneous consciousness, especially one holding wrong views. For this reason, developing a wisdom consciousness that realizes the ultimate nature is essential, and overcoming whatever hardships we may encounter on the path is worthwhile.

REFLECTION

1. What are the three meanings of "nature"?
2. Which of the three natures exist and which does not?
3. What problems occur when we can't discern which natures exist and

which don't—for example, if we can't determine if we exist inherently or don't, or if doctors cannot determine the conventional nature of someone's illness?

Conclude that even if the topic of "nature" initially seems abstract, it is actually important in the lives of sentient beings.

Ultimate and Conventional Natures

Each existent has two natures, a conventional and an ultimate. Two of the four seals—all conditioned phenomena are impermanent and all polluted phenomena are duḥkha—describe polluted phenomena's conventional nature. The other two seals—all phenomena are empty and nirvāṇa is peace—reflect their ultimate nature, their ultimate mode of existence.

Tashi's conventional nature is that he is impermanent, under the influence of ignorance, and exists by being merely designated in dependence on his five aggregates. Conventionally, he also possesses many attributes; he is tall, works as a car mechanic, likes to read, and plays soccer. These attributes are not his inherent or ultimate nature; he is not inherently any of these. Both Tashi and his various attributes exist in relation to other factors, such as their causes and conditions and the mind that designates them. Tashi's ultimate nature is the emptiness of inherent existence. This is his deeper mode of existence, what exists beyond the level of conventional appearances.

Some people mistakenly think that Mādhyamikas say that everything has no nature. All phenomena have a conventional nature. However, they do not exist by their own nature because they are dependent on other factors. They have their own respective character, but they do not exist by their own character. Existence by its own nature and existence by its own character are synonymous, and both would entail independent existence and thus are the object of negation. In the same way, each phenomenon has a basis of designation, but it cannot be found in that basis of designation; it does not exist from the side of its basis of designation.

Phenomena have coarse and subtle conventional natures. A house being produced by causes and conditions is part of its coarse conventional nature. We do not need to realize emptiness to know this. However, to fully understand its deeper conventional nature—that the house exists by being merely designated by mind—we need to realize emptiness. After realizing emptiness, we will be able to know veiled truths as falsities and as illusion-like. Ascertaining their illusion-like nature by a reliable cognizer means that we know them *as* veiled truths.

Base and Attribute

Emptiness does not exist independent of all other phenomena. It is an attribute of the objects that are the bases of emptiness. The emptiness of the flower exists because the flower exists; the emptiness of the person exists because the person exists. When the flower arises, its emptiness comes into being, although that emptiness is not created by causes and conditions and is permanent. When the flower ceases, its emptiness no longer exists.

The flower is the base that is empty, and its emptiness is an attribute of the flower. Because the flower and its emptiness exist as base and attribute, can they be perceived by one awareness? For a buddha, yes, they can. For ordinary beings and even āryas, this is more difficult.

Let's take as an example a flower, its emptiness, and a person who is on the verge of inferentially realizing emptiness. At the beginning of a meditation session, the flower appears to the meditator, who then investigates how it exists. As she continues to analyze and cannot find an objectifiable basis for the flower, the appearance of the flower dissolves and a conceptual appearance of its emptiness appears to her mind. Although the flower does not appear, it is not contradictory for the flower (the base) to be the observed object of this consciousness and the flower's emptiness (the attribute) to be its apprehended object. This inferential wisdom is not erroneous with respect to its apprehended object, emptiness. But the emptiness perceived by an inferential cognizer is obscured by the conceptual appearance, so it is called an "imputed" or "concordant ultimate object," and the wisdom mind conceptually realizing emptiness is a concordant ultimate subject.[26]

By familiarization with the view over time, eventually the veneer of the conceptual appearance fades, all mistaken appearances of inherent existence cease, and the meditator perceives emptiness directly. That emptiness is an actual ultimate and a nonaffirming negation. The wisdom that directly perceives emptiness does not perceive the base of the emptiness—in this case the flower. In fact, the relationship of basis and attribute does not exist for that mind because it sees only emptiness. Positing the flower and its emptiness to exist as base and attribute is not done by the awareness directly knowing the ultimate nature, but by another conventional consciousness after the meditation session. The wisdom directly realizing emptiness does not know "I am realizing emptiness." Emptiness and the mind realizing it appear nondual, so there is no sense of a mind or an I that is realizing emptiness. After arising from that meditative equipoise, a conventional consciousness ascertains "I realized emptiness." When the mind is still informed by the realization of emptiness, the flower will appear like an illusion. That is, it appears inherently existent to the visual consciousness, but the mental consciousness knows it does not exist as it appears; it is empty of inherent existence.

In short, the proliferations of dualistic appearance have not been eliminated for the appearance factor of a mind realizing emptiness inferentially. However, these proliferations have been eliminated for the ascertainment factor of that inferential realization. But for a mind of meditative equipoise on emptiness, dualistic appearances neither appear nor are they ascertained.

The final or ultimate nature, emptiness, is naturally pacified. In other words, it is not the case that initially emptiness is false and later becomes true or that initially phenomena exist inherently and later become empty of inherent existence.

Conditioned phenomena, such as temples, toads, and testimonies, are not established as either of the first two meanings of "nature." Although a temple is empty of inherent existence, it is not reality or emptiness; it is a veiled truth, not an ultimate truth. Furthermore, the temple is not inherent existence, the second meaning of nature. Because conditioned phenomena are not emptiness and are not a nonexistent nature, practicing the path to realize the ultimate nature, emptiness, has meaning and purpose. If the functioning things we see around us in daily life were their own final nature—if they existed the way they appeared—there would be no reason to exert effort to perceive the deeper nature of existence. The ultimate nature would already be apparent to our sense consciousnesses, which would be unmistaken. If that were the case, eliminating our duḥkha would be impossible, for we would already perceive reality and could not develop any further wisdom.

But this is not the case. Because our ordinary six consciousnesses are deceived and a deeper nature exists, following the path to realize that nature is worthwhile. There is a purpose for practicing the method side of the path—from keeping the five precepts and monastic precepts up to and including the first five perfections. These activities create the merit that supports the cultivation of the wisdom realizing the ultimate nature.

Our purpose in learning about emptiness is to cleanse our mind of disturbing emotions and wrong views. When our understanding of emptiness is profound and is accompanied by single-pointed concentration, our mind will not be easily influenced by these afflictions. According to my own modest experience, as our understanding of reality and illusion-like appearances gradually increases, our mind becomes increasingly stable and firm. Whenever some disturbances come, instead of our thoughts and emotions being blown around like leaves in the wind, the mind remains still, like a rock. The mind is peaceful and strong because it fully understands reality in all its dimensions.

These teachings are not just interesting ideas to play with; they are the key to end our own and others' duḥkha. So please practice them as much as you can.

5 | The World of Dependent, Imputed Appearances

To understand emptiness correctly, it's especially important to study particular texts: Nāgārjuna's *Treatise on the Middle Way*, Āryadeva's *Four Hundred*, and Candrakīrti's *Supplement* are a few examples. We are afflicted beings—disturbing emotions such as anger, attachment, jealousy, and conceit arise in us in quick succession, causing us suffering and confusion and instigating us to engage in actions that harm others. Despite this, or perhaps because of this fact, we often forget to apply what we learn in these texts to our minds. However, when we do so, we discover that they accurately describe how our disturbing emotions arise, what their causes, natures, and effects are, and how to remedy them.

Understanding this, we begin to see that all our afflictions center on the notion of a self that exists under its own power. By using what we have learned through studying, we apply analysis investigating how things really exist. By doing that, we recognize that such a self, which we treasure so much and is the center of our lives, is actually a mental fabrication. At this point, the impact that studying emptiness can have on our lives becomes indisputably evident, since emptiness is the negation of this self. Therefore there is no other option than to take the teachings on emptiness to heart and relate them to our personal experience. As we do so and experience the results of practice, our conviction in the truth of the Buddha's teachings and our determination to practice them and attain liberation and full awakening becomes very strong.

The full understanding of emptiness not only enables us to gradually destroy self-grasping but also opens us to the world of dependent, imputed appearances. Gaining a correct understanding of how veilings exist and function enables us to relate to the world in a realistic and harmonious way, free from absurd and farcical expectations.

Dependent, Imputed Appearances

Sometimes when people hear the word "emptiness" they get the impression that it is nothingness. And when they hear of dependent arising or interdependence, only the appearance aspect of phenomena—their mistaken appearance of existing inherently—comes to mind. Since all tenet systems accept dependent arising, that term alone—without exploring its deeper meaning—doesn't convey the complementary nature of emptiness and dependent arising. The phrase "suchness based on dependent arising" conveys the fuller meaning of the complementary nature of the two truths. It affirms both the lack of inherent existence as well as the functioning of cause and effect in our daily lives.

Affirming dependent existence in the face of the emptiness of inherent existence does not come easily. Since beginningless time, we have been accustomed to positing things—cause and effect; agent, object, and action; and so forth—within believing them to exist by their own character. After we negate such fantasized ways of existing in meditation, positing ourselves, other people, and things in our environment as nominal conventions may be uncomfortable because we don't yet understand that they can be empty and simultaneously exist conventionally. We don't realize that these two are compatible, and we must remember that realization of emptiness negates inherent existence, not all existence whatsoever. Nominal or conventional existence is not only possible but is also the only way persons and phenomena can exist.

The Buddha affirmed conventional existence, especially when he explicitly stated that he does not argue with the world about the existence of tables, persons, thoughts, countries, technology, and so forth. In the *Chapter Showing the Three Vows Sūtra*, the Buddha says (EY 301):

> The world argues with me, I do not argue with the world. Whatever is accepted in the world as existent and nonexistent, that I also accept in that way.

Here the Buddha does not mean that he accepts everything the world says. For example, worldly people believe their bodies to be clean after they bathe, but to a yogi who has cultivated mindfulness of the body, the body is unclean no matter how much we wash it.

Similarly, the Buddha does not accept the way in which worldly beings think things exist, for they grasp them to exist inherently. The world may argue with the Buddha because what he taught goes beyond the world's ordinary views about how things exist. Nonetheless, the Buddha doesn't debate with worldly beings regarding what is established by worldly, conventional reliable cognizers. He accepts that sprouts grow from seeds, although he has a radically different perspective on the mode of existence of the seeds and sprouts.

A passage similar to the one above exists in the Pāli canon (SN 22:94):

> Monastics, I do not dispute with the world; rather, it is the world that disputes with me. A proponent of the Dhamma does not dispute with anyone in the world. Of that which the wise in the world agree does not exist, I too say that it does not exist. And of that which the wise in the world agree exist, I too say that it exists.

The Buddha then continues to say that what the wise in the world agree does not exist is five aggregates that are permanent, stable, eternal, and not subject to change. The wise in the world agree that what does exist is the five aggregates that are impermanent, duḥkha in nature, and subject to change. This sūtra shows that the Buddha both rejects metaphysical speculation as he does in the *Kaccānagotta Sutta* (SN 12:15) and accepts statements about existence that can be experienced and proven.[27]

REFLECTION

1. What did the Buddha mean when he said the world argues with him but he doesn't argue with the world?
2. Does that mean that whatever worldly people in general accept, so does the Buddha? Remember the story of the emperor with no clothes.

3. Make an example of how the world may argue with the Buddha but the Buddha is confident that his knowledge is correct.

4. How do we gain correct knowledge?

Pain and Pleasure: An Example of Dependent Existence

Each phenomenon has two interrelated natures—its dependently arisen conventional nature and its empty ultimate nature. Our experiences of pain and pleasure illustrate these two natures. Both pain and pleasure depend on causes and conditions. They are mutually dependent on each other and exist by being merely designated by term and concept; that is their conventional nature. They are also empty. There is no ultimately existent pain or pleasure; this is their ultimate nature. When Mādhyamikas say that there is no pain and no pleasure, they mean pain and pleasure have no inherently existent nature.

The pain and pleasure we experience in daily life come about dependent on many factors: external people and things, internal states of mind, and our previously created karma. For instance, I am going about my day when someone comes along and criticizes me. My previous karma has a role in causing this event. My distorted conceptions further twist the situation. How I interpret the words and describe their meaning to myself also affects my experience of it. I could think "This person is unhappy" and feel compassion, or "He is blaming me!" in which case I'll become unhappy and angry. Although this type of obvious imputation affects our experience, it is not the subtle meaning of things being merely designated. "Merely designated" means that apart from what is designated by mind, nothing exists from the side of the object.

Although pain is designated by mind, it exists. If I regard the cramping in my leg only from the angle that I am in pain, the pain seems horrible. Due to my focusing and thinking only of my pain, I perceive it to be extremely uncomfortable. But if I then accidentally hit my head on a ledge, instead of focusing only on the pain in my leg, I now feel the pain in my head, which is much worse. At that time, my leg pain seems comparatively mild and tolerable. In fact, I feel fortunate that my leg does not hurt as much as my head. It's clear that pain is relative. However, this does not deny that my leg pain is pain, even though it is now designated and experienced as mild instead of extreme.

Bodhisattvas voluntarily take rebirth and intend to remain in the saṃsāric world to benefit sentient beings. From that viewpoint they do not hurry to attain nirvāṇa. But this is not because they think saṃsāric pain is not pain. They do not think, "Oh saṃsāric pain is merely mentally designated so there is no need to free myself from it." Pain is pain, and bodhisattvas also prefer not to be in pain. But when they compare overcoming their own pain with serving others, the latter is more important to them. To serve others, bodhisattvas are willing to tolerate their own pain, which seems insignificant when compared to the duḥkha of all sentient beings.

Appearances

Since objects are apprehended by reliable cognizers, how do we account for the differences in appearances to various sentient beings? In Vasubandhu's *Commentary on the Compendium of the Mahāyāna* (*Mahāyānasaṃgrahabhāṣya*), he gives the example of a deva, a human being, and a hungry ghost who look at the same glass of fluid but see different things. Due to special karmic influences, the deva sees nectar in the glass, the human being sees water, and the hungry ghost sees pus and blood. In a similar way, we humans see filth when we see cow dung and flies see dessert! Such appearances are due to karma, not spiritual attainments.

According to the realm in which sentient beings are born, their conventional reliable cognizers apprehend things differently. In the above example, nectar is a conventionally existent object apprehended by a deva's reliable cognizer, water is a conventional object apprehended by a human's reliable cognizer, and pus and blood are objects apprehended by a hungry ghost's reliable cognizer. A human being who sees the fluid as pus and blood has an erroneous consciousness because the fluid does not function as pus and blood in the human world. In addition, other humans' reliable cognizers discredit this fluid being pus and blood.[28]

The framework within which cognizers are reliable depends on the karma of sentient beings. Due to karma, in this life we were born as human beings with human sense faculties. A nondefective visual consciousness of human beings will see water in the glass, while a defective visual consciousness will see pus and blood or nectar. If beings are born as hungry ghosts due to their previously created actions, they will have the sense faculties of that realm. The nondefective sense consciousnesses of hungry ghosts will see pus and blood, whereas consciousnesses with impaired faculties will see water or nectar. In general, ārya bodhisattvas' consciousnesses are not determined by their karma but by their accumulation of merit and wisdom.

Thus majority vote isn't the determining factor of whether a perception is erroneous or correct, it is whether an object is seen by a reliable cognizer of that realm. Majority vote is unreliable because it is possible that a large number of people hold a certain idea or have a particular perception that is erroneous. For example, many residents of a country may believe a pandemic is a hoax, but that doesn't mean no one will die from the disease. Despite many people not believing that climate change and global warming are occurring, rising sea levels and fires in the tundra are realities.

While Yogācārins use the example of the three beings seeing the fluid as three different substances to illustrate that there are no external objects, Prāsaṅgikas use it to show that things do not exist objectively, from their own side. They assert that nectar, water, and pus and blood are all external objects that exist in dependence on the minds apprehending them. The three substances are present simultaneously—one facet of the fluid is nectar, another facet is water, a third facet is pus and blood. These three are not mixed, but it is not the case that one-third of the fluid is nectar, one-third water, and one-third pus and blood, as if they were stacked one on top of the other.[29] If a god drinks the glass of nectar, the humans and hungry ghosts will then see an empty container.[30] The three substances do not exist in the mind; there is an external world that is shared to some extent. But each realm of sentient beings perceives that world differently, in dependence on their physical and mental sense faculties and their previous karma. What is true for a sentient being in one realm may not be true for another in another realm. There is no one right, objective way in which the world exists from its own side.

On the other hand, whether one sees an image of the Buddha as a statue or as an actual buddha depends on one's level of spiritual realizations. An Avalokiteśvara statue that is now in Dharamsala is said to have given the Fifth Dalai Lama many teachings and empowerments. But to us—and this includes me—it is a silent statue that doesn't say even one word. This difference is not due to the statue but to our level of spiritual realization. Although today we see a statue, when our spiritual experiences develop higher and higher, the statue could become alive and we could receive teachings from it.

For us, a table is solid, but it appears differently to tantric yogis who realize its emptiness and see all things as creations of their minds. These yogis still accept the existence of the table as an external object, but at the same time they see it as a creation or reflection of the clear light mind. When yogis with profound tantric realizations touch the table, they do not experience it as solid. Initially, we may think that contradicts the table's conventional nature as described by science, but in fact scientists tell us that there is more space than mass in a table. This being the case, why shouldn't people with deep spiritual realizations be able to perceive this?

A wall appearing solid or permeable depends on the person perceiving it. Some of the great masters of the past who had actualized deep states of concentration experienced emptiness directly and were also familiar with the illusory nature of phenomena. They were able to leave their handprints in stone or metal. In Tibet there were many examples of this that we could see. Many events that ordinary people call "magic" are understandable to those who have realized emptiness and subtle dependent arising.

Existing by Being Merely Imputed by Mind

Bhikṣuṇī Vajirā said in the *Saṃyutta Nikāya* (SN 5:10.553–54):

> Just as, with an assemblage of parts,
> the word "chariot" is used,
> so, when the aggregates exist,
> there is the convention "a being."

The *Questions of Upāli Sūtra* says (FEW 39):

> Here the various mind-pleasing blossoming flowers
> and attractive, shining, supreme golden houses
> have no [inherently existent] maker at all.

> They are posited through the power of conceptuality.
> Through the power of conceptuality the world is imputed.

Candrakīrti says in *Commentary on (Āryadeva's) "The Four Hundred"* (HSY 188):

> Those that exist only when conceptuality exists and do not exist when conceptuality does not exist are undoubtedly ascertained as not established by their own nature, like a snake imputed to a coiled rope.

Prāsaṅgikas give the example of Dechen seeing a coiled rope in a dimly lit area. Thinking that it is a snake, she is terrified. In fact, no snake is there. The fear she experiences is unnecessary—the coiled rope won't inject venom into her. The fear is a result of misapprehending the object. Even though the speckled color of the rope and its coiled shape resemble a snake, there is nothing about the rope that is a snake. The snake is merely imputed by mind. In the same way, when "I" is imputed in dependence on the mental and physical aggregates, there is nothing in or about the aggregates that is a real I. The I is merely imputed by mind. In his *Illuminating the Intent*, Tsongkhapa says (GR 186):

> A coiled rope's speckled color and coiling are similar to those of a snake, and when the rope is perceived in a dim area, the thought arises, "This is a snake." As for the rope, at that time when it is seen to be a snake, the collection and the parts of the rope are not even in the slightest way a snake. Therefore that snake is merely set up by conceptuality. In the same way, when the thought "I" arises in dependence on the [mental and physical] aggregates, nothing within the aggregates—neither the collection which is the continuum [of the earlier and later moments], nor the collection [of the parts] at one time, nor the separate parts of those [mental and physical aggregates], nor the continuum of any of the separate parts—is even in the slightest way able to be posited as an illustration of that I. Also there is not even the slightest thing that is a different entity from the aggregates that is apprehend-

> able as the I. Consequently, the I is *merely* set up by conceptuality in dependence on the aggregates; it is not established by way of its own entity.

In short, what we call "I" is composed of many factors that are not I. We apprehend I only in dependence on apprehending things that are not I—the physical and mental aggregates. When we analyze and search the continuum of moments of I, we cannot find a real I. Nor can we find the I when we search in the collection of parts that is the basis of designation of I or in each of the mental and physical aggregates individually. The I is also not findable apart from the aggregates. No matter how much we look there is no I in the aggregates or separate from them. Reflecting on this is very helpful when we are angry because someone criticized us. Search for the person who is being criticized. Ask: Who is the I that is angry? The very solid I that appears to us at that time cannot be found.

Nevertheless, I, the person, still exists because we say "I do this and that." The only way the person can exist is by being merely designated by conception. We must be careful here—after negating the inherently existent I, when we again think that the I exists because it engages in various actions, we often go right back to grasping that I as inherently existent. Why? Because we're so habituated to grasp a solid I that the moment we hear that the I still exists, we go back to thinking it exists from its own side.

In the early 1960s, while I was reflecting on the above passage, a clear understanding arose in my mind. It felt like lightning in my heart: everything I had thought was real was demolished. After that, for some weeks all the people and things I saw seemed like a magician's illusions. They appeared so real, as if they had their own inherent nature, but I knew that this was a false appearance, that in fact they didn't exist this way at all.

This experience was probably some sort of correct assumption or perhaps it was a realization of the nonexistence of a self-sufficient substantially existent person, not a valid inferential realization of emptiness. Yet its potency couldn't be denied. It increased my conviction that it was possible to attain liberation by eradicating all the afflictions forever, from the root. Since then, I meditate on emptiness every morning and recall that understanding and experience in my daily life. Just thinking or saying "I," as in "I am going to do this today," will sometimes spark the understanding that the I is empty and exists only as an appearance. Although I do not have a complete understanding of emptiness, what I do understand has had a profound impact on me.

Given that there is no snake in the rope and no person in the aggregates, what is the difference between designating "snake" on a rope and designating it on a living being with a long, tapering, cylindrical body? The rope is not a suitable basis of the designation for a snake because it cannot function as one, whereas that living being with a long, tapered, cylindrical body can. In addition, other peoples' conventional reliable cognizers see a rope there and that invalidates its being a snake. Just calling something a snake doesn't make it one. The name must fit the basis in dependence on which we impute that name.

The point here is that just as there is nothing in the rope that is a snake, there is nothing in the aggregates that is a person. The I exists by being merely designated in dependence on those aggregates by the power of conceptuality. As the sūtra quotation above states, everything exists merely by being posited through the power of conceptuality. Nothing exists from its own side. Tsongkhapa says (OR 98):

> . . . the word "merely" does not mean that no objects exist besides names or that their being cognized by reliable cognizers is precluded. On the other hand, although the phrase "things exist merely by nominal imputation" means that it is impossible that they exist without being posited by nominal convention, it does not mean that everything posited by nominal convention exists.

Understanding the meaning of "merely" in the expression "merely imputed" is crucial. "Merely" does not mean that only names exist and that no objects exist other than names. You can't eat the words "toast with butter" for breakfast! "Merely" also doesn't mean things can exist independent of any reliable cognizer apprehending them. Rather, nothing can exist without being designated by nominal convention. Nothing can exist without depending on other factors, especially the mind that conceives and imputes them.

While "merely" indicates that things do not exist without being imputed by term and concept, it does not imply that everything that is imputed exists. "Merely" precludes inherent existence, ultimate existence, true existence, existing from its own side, existing by its own character, substantial existence, and any other type of reified existence. It emphasizes that on the conventional level, things exist by being designated on a suitable basis of designation by term and concept. However, saying that the basis of designation is suitable does not mean that it has certain inherent qualities that make it suitable. Our calling a horse "grapefruit" doesn't make it one. "Suitable" simply means that it can perform the function as conceived and designated by sentient beings. Tsongkhapa says (OR 385):

> The Buddha teaches that they are merely imputed on the basis of causes and conditions through the refutation of the extremes of existence and nonexistence.

Having refuted both inherent existence and total nonexistence, the Buddha teaches that things exist by being merely designated on what has come into being by means of causes and conditions.

Svātantrikas see this differently, saying that things must have some inherent character or inherent nature that make them suitable to be designated with a particular name. Otherwise, any collection of parts could be given any name, which would be impractical and result in chaos—a flat-bottomed container used to drink tea could be called a window sill and that would make it a window sill. To prevent this, Svātantrikas say that objects exist inherently on the conventional level—there must be something in them that makes them that object. This is precisely the point that Prāsaṅgikas refute and that differentiates the two Madhyamaka systems.

Conceiving an object and designating it with a term does not mean that object exists. Santa Claus doesn't exist even though many people talk about him, and the emperor doesn't have new clothes even if all of us imagine he does. Furthermore, calling a rope a snake doesn't make it a snake, and understanding that the rope isn't a snake isn't understanding either the rope's emptiness or a snake's emptiness. Furthermore, a rope being empty of being a snake doesn't make the rope nonexistent. As we contemplate emptiness in terms of dependent arising and dependent arising in terms of emptiness, we will see that they are not contradictory and in fact are mutually complementary. All existents are both dependent and empty.

REFLECTION

1. What is similar when we erroneously impute a rope as a snake and when we correctly impute a snake's body as a snake? What differs in these two situations?
2. Is there something in your body or mind that is you?
3. What feeling do you have when you think that you exist by being merely imputed in dependence on the collection of the aggregates?
4. What makes those aggregates yours?

Conventional, Nominal Existence

In *Essence of Eloquence* and *Illuminating the Intent*, Tsongkhapa stated that there are two ways phenomena could exist: either objectively and independently or nominally and conventionally. Since we are unable to find phenomena when we search for their objective existence, the only alternative is that they exist by being merely designated or imputed by mind. They exist through the power of other factors, such as their causes and conditions, their parts, and the mind that conceives and designates them. Even though this mode of existence may be difficult to fathom, Tsongkhapa advises us to become familiar with it (OR 39):

> Since objects do not exist by their own nature, they are established as existing by the force of convention.

The *Perfection of Wisdom Sūtra in 100,000 Lines* supports this (RSR 59):

> Everything exists by the power of the world's conventions, not by ultimate existence.

"Conventional" means nominal—that is, existing merely by being posited or designated by the force of terms and concepts. Nāgārjuna says (RA 114 bcd):

> Apart from that which is conventionally designated,
> what world could there be ultimately,
> either existent or nonexistent?

"Convention" involves names, conceptual thought, and ordinary knowledge. It is neither esoteric nor mysterious; the world around us is constituted by conventionalities. The flowers and grass we see when we look out the window do not exist independently, from their own side, under their own power. They exist dependently and are posited by the power of conventions; they exist by being merely designated by name (T. *ming du btags pa tsam*).

Language functions on an everyday level and we use it to understand the world and to communicate with one another. Designation by terms and concepts occurs on this level. If we start to analyze what exactly something is—What is the ultimate referent of this name? Is this object one with or separate from its parts?—we have gone beyond the normal functions of shared language. Language and conception contain a certain vagueness. For example, we say "I planted a tree" when we actually planted a seed or a sapling. No one complains that we are lying; it is understood that sometimes we give a cause the name of its result. Similarly, when someone says, "We have arrived at the border of this country," no one says, "Is this bit of dirt on the border, or is it part of this country or that one?" We simply relate to things on the level of mere words, mere constructs, and do not go beyond them to try to find what an object really is.

Imputed by mind or designated by conception refers to a conceptual consciousness forming the idea of an object, and in the case of beings who use language, giving it a name. All beings have conceptual minds although they do not all have language. Dogs can recognize their owners; a mother dog can identify her puppies. Dogs know that if they are obedient they will be patted and given a treat, but if they jump on people they will be scolded. They bark at those they see as enemies, get jealous of other dogs, and sit beside their owner when they sense he or she is upset. All of these activities involve conceptual consciousnesses; conceptual ability doesn't lie only with those who know language or are educated. It seems that all sentient beings—even worms and spiders—have concepts in that they learn how to safely operate in their environment.

Some teachers differentiate between persons being *imputed on* or *imputed to* the mere collection of the aggregates or being *imputed in dependence on* the mere collection of the aggregates. They say that being *imputed to* the basis of designation or *imputed on* the basis of designation implies some existence from the object's side—as if the object were already existent and we just stick a label on it. On the other hand, they say being *imputed in dependence on* the basis of designation does not imply existence from the object's side; the basis of designation is present but the object doesn't exist until the object is conceived and designated in dependence on the basis of designation. Tsongkhapa uses both terms synonymously. When he wants to convey the precise meaning of the person being "merely imputed," he uses "in dependence on the aggregates," whereas at other times the same meaning can be understood without using such precise language. If the disciple's mind tends toward reification, the teacher may find it useful to emphasize that persons are merely designated *in dependence on* their respective basis of designation but are not designated *on* the basis of designation.

To exist, a phenomenon does not have to be continually and actively designated by a mind. To exist, the tree doesn't require someone to stand nearby and repeat "tree, tree." Although all phenomena and their bases of designation are designated by conception, a phenomenon and the conception designating it are not necessarily present at the same time. We may weigh a kilo of fruit at the market and impute "This is a kilo of apples." When we carry the apples home, we do not continuously think "This is a kilo of apples," yet a kilo of apples is still there. Similarly, something may not be designated at this very moment by any particular sentient being, but it still exists by being merely designated by mind. The mind that designates it may exist later or it may have existed earlier. "The capitol building will be here" imputes that building while it is still in the planning stages, and Covid-19 existed before anyone had identified that virus.

Along this line, Tibetans have a story that is similar to the Western puzzle "If a tree falls in a forest and no one is there to hear it, is there a sound?" (Hopefully you know the answer to that now!) A monk was visiting a senior lama and to clarify some doubts he asked, "The scriptures say that all phenomena are merely designated by thought. If that is so, when everyone leaves this room, who will designate the pillars that hold up the roof? Will the roof still exist if no one is here designating it?" The lama replied, "Hmmm, that's a difficult point." But after the monk left the room, the lama thought, "I'm glad the thought designating a phenomenon does not always need to be tied to that phenomenon. If it did, when the monk who designated the pillar walked out of the room, the pillar would have vanished and the roof would have collapsed on me!"

In short, saying that all phenomena are merely designated by mind is a measure of the extent to which they exist. It is not an invitation to go on a quest to discover who, when, where, how, and for how long an object was designated. Rather, it emphasizes that the existence of objects depends on consciousness; things are not self-instituting, they cannot establish their own existence from their own side or under their own power.

We cannot pinpoint one specific mind that conceives and designates an object. Nor can we identify a specific time that it was designated. Many people's minds may designate an object at different times. When a certain territory in Asia became a nation, it was called "India." The minds of the people at that time designated it. That name can be applied retroactively as well. We say the Buddha lived in India and that is correct, even though no one called that land "India" at the time of the Buddha. Similarly, bacteria existed before people designated "bacteria" or understood that some bacteria cause disease while others are helpful. One of the three conditions for existing conventionally is to be renowned in the world. However, this does not entail that the object needs to be renowned at this moment for it to exist. There is room for discoveries and inventions.

Did people die from cancer five hundred years ago? From one perspective, no one on earth knew the word "cancer" or saw a particular collection of symptoms as deserving of a name that made it into an illness. Does that mean cancer did not exist then? If someone in the sixteenth century said their relative died from cancer, no one would know what they were talking about. The name "cancer" and those symptoms being conceived as being a disease came in the twentieth century. But it would be nonsensical to say now that no one suffered from cancer centuries ago simply because we didn't have the name and concept for that disease back then. The name and concept can be retroactively applied to the collection of symptoms that existed centuries ago.

External objects are part of the process of generating a consciousness that cognizes them, but these objects cannot be found when searched for with ultimate analysis. A eucalyptus tree is the object generating a visual consciousness that knows it or the olfactory consciousness that smells it. That the tree exists in dependence on designation by name and thought doesn't mean that someone's thought has to construct it right then and there. If we had to designate everything the moment before we could perceive it, it would be very difficult to perceive anything at all because it would take a long time to have all the many thoughts necessary for a consciousness to designate an object. It would be absurd to think that a concept must be present to construct everything we see before a visual consciousness could see it.

What then does it mean that phenomena are established by concept? This indicates that without depending on consciousness, phenomena cannot set themselves up; they cannot exist by their own power. To exist, phenomena must depend on conceptuality. For example, the I exists in dependence on the body and mind, but the body and mind aren't the I, and the I isn't the body and mind. There is nothing in either the body or the mind or in the collection of the two that is the I. There is nothing in the body and mind in dependence on which the I is set up. The only way a person exists is by being merely designated by name and concept in dependence on the collection of the body and mind. There is no other way for them to exist; they are totally dependent on other factors that are not themselves, including the mind that conceives and designates them.

When contemplating this deeply, we begin to sense that the I doesn't exist from its own side, but exists dependently. When we then recognize that phenomena usually don't appear to us to depend on conceptuality—they seem to have some inherent nature that makes them that object—we have a sense of the object of negation.

We may wonder: Since the buddhas perceive everything directly and have no conceptual consciousnesses, what mind imputes the buddhas' qualities—the ten powers, the four types of self-confidence, and so on? Like everything else, the buddhas' qualities are not findable under ultimate analysis. Even the tathāgatas themselves are not findable under ultimate analysis. Although the tathāgatas and their magnificent qualities exist, they do not exist objectively, independent of everything else. The only alternative is that they exist by means of mental imputation. For that reason, it is said that everything, including the qualities of the Buddha, are merely imputed by term and thought.

But the buddhas do not have conceptual consciousnesses! Their qualities are designated by the minds of sentient beings. Although the buddhas' physical and verbal qualities are directly accessible to sentient beings, their mental qualities are indirectly inferred. However, bodhisattvas on the pure grounds have developed extraordinary qualities that, when cultivated further, will become the buddhas' qualities. Therefore they can infer the buddhas' marvelous qualities and, on that basis, designate them. The buddhas' consciousnesses know and establish their own qualities although they are not the ones designating them.

If we do not think it is possible for things to exist by being merely designated, it does not mean they do not. It indicates that our minds are not familiar with that view. As we analyze and investigate how things exist, dependent and imputed existence will become more and more plausible to us.

Not Everything That Is Imputed Exists

As said above, "merely designated" does not mean that phenomena are words or that they are not established by reliable cognizers. It means that their existence depends on being conceived and designated by mind. However, just because people—either an individual or society as a whole—have conceived and named something, doesn't mean that object necessarily exists. A thing must be designated in dependence on a suitable base, but that suitable base does not exist inherently. My calling this cup of tea "cement" won't make it function like cement! The name and defining characteristics of a thing must correspond. It is suitable for me to call a drink infused with a certain plant "tea" because our society has agreed that "tea" is a suitable name for such a phenomenon. This name is commonly known to indicate this beverage. Society hasn't agreed that "tea" is an appropriate name for a building material used to make walls and sidewalks. Nevertheless, before we agreed that "tea" refers to a certain drink, we could have decided to use that term to refer to a hard, strong construction material.

Let's say on the table I see a rectangular electronic object that has a screen upon which images appear. That object is merely designated "computer." If I do further investigation, I cannot find an independent computer in the parts of that base, in its collection of parts, or separate from the parts. Many parts are combined in a certain manner, and in dependence on that basis we call it "computer." If I take my glasses off, because of blurry eyesight I may think, "There is a flat black box on the table. I can use it to store paper." That box, like that computer, is also one hundred percent designated by mind. In both cases, an object appears to my mind. In both cases, it is designated by mind. But the computer has not ceased being a computer and become a flat box just because I think it is one and give it that name.

Why not? If I put my glasses back on and look again, my eyes perceive a computer, not a black box. In addition, if I ask someone else, she will affirm there is a computer. Even though I saw a black box and that black box was designated by my mind, that does not make that object a black box. Nor does it negate its being a computer. My previous perception of a black box can be rejected by my later perception and also by the other person's perception. So even though both the computer and the black box were designated by mind, one exists whereas the other does not.

In addition, things that are mere imputations are perceived by reliable cognizers. Someone may see a rabbit, mistake its ears for horns, and say, "That rabbit has horns!" But this does not mean that rabbits' horns exist. Another person's nondefective visual consciousness can disprove that perception.

Similarly, my mistakenly designating "farmer" on a scarecrow does not make it a farmer. Even if I insist it is a farmer and all my friends agree, it will remain a scarecrow. Why? Because the base on which the name was given can perform the function of a scarecrow, but it cannot perform the functions of a human being. Furthermore, the reliable cognizers of people with good eyesight know that object in the field is a scarecrow and not a farmer. It was designated "farmer" based on a superficial cause of error—the fact that I was standing far away and could not see the object clearly.

But what about things that are commonly accepted by society that are not disproved by our physical senses? Do they always exist? For example, it is commonly accepted in many societies that an independent, external divine being created the universe and the sentient beings in it. Does that make it so? No, it does not, because that idea is based on a superficial cause of error and can be contradicted by another conventional reliable cognizer. This reliable cognizer uses conventional reasoning to disprove the idea: something that is permanent cannot produce an effect because it cannot change. Producing an effect entails that the cause changes from what it was, and permanent phenomena by definition are not momentary by nature. Tsongkhapa said in the *Middle Treatise on the Stages of the Path* (FEW 128):

> Therefore although what is posited as existing conventionally is posited as existing through the force of nominal conventions, all that is posited through the force of nominal conventions is not asserted as existing conventionally.

The idea of a permanent creator does not need to be refuted by ultimate analysis. However, if we did ultimate analysis and realized emptiness, that would expose the faults of asserting a permanent creator. Why? Anything that is empty is dependent. Since a creator changes in the process of creation, it must depend on causes, and anything that depends on causes cannot be permanent.

Similarly, the coarse four distorted conceptions—seeing the impermanent as permanent, the foul as beautiful, what is in the nature of duḥkha as pleasant, and that which lacks a self as being a self-sufficient substantially existent person—are damaged by conventional reasoning. Candrakīrti says in *Supplement to "Treatise on the Middle Way"* (FEW 127–28):

> Entities as they are imputed by the Forders
> strongly affected by the sleep of ignorance,
> and those imputed to magical illusions, mirages, and so forth
> are just nonexistent even in the world.

"Forders" is a general term for the non-Buddhist schools in ancient India. They are so-called because just as a boat is the means to ford a river, their doctrine was viewed by society as a means to ford the ocean of saṃsāra and arrive at liberation. They imputed entities such as a permanent self, a primal substance (*prakṛti*), and so forth. In ancient India magicians would put a special substance on sticks and pebbles and cast a spell on the eyes of the audience so that the sticks and pebbles appeared to be real horses and elephants to the audience. Just as these horses and elephants, water in a mirage, and double moons reflected in water are seen as false and do not exist even for the world, so too are the objects asserted by non-Buddhist absolutists.

Things such as a permanent creator, primal substance, permanent time, and so forth are fabricated by non-Buddhists and imputed by their erroneous consciousnesses. Likewise, mirages, holograms, and doctored photos that are known as false are apprehended by wrong consciousnesses. Conventional reliable cognizers can determine that a permanent creator, the "water" in a mirage, and the ghost in a doctored photo do not exist. It is not necessary to use ultimate analysis to discredit them; either unimpaired senses or conventional reasoning is sufficient.

Conventionally existent objects are not established by ultimate analysis—ultimate analysis explores whether things ultimately exist or not. But they must not be damaged by an awareness analyzing the ultimate. It may happen that someone may agree with the commonly known name and function of an object but holds that object or idea to be inherently existent. For example, Svātantrikas enter a debate with conviction that all elements of the syllogism exist inherently. Some people may view the land they live on as inherently theirs; it is the land of their forebears to which they have an inherent connection. In these cases, the third criteria for conventional existence is applied, and since such things are discredited by reasoning analyzing the ultimate, they are shown to be nonexistent.

When we say that phenomena exist by being merely imputed, "merely" eliminates everything that is not imputed or designated by a subject, the mind. It does not eliminate a reliable cognizer being able to establish that object. That is, while things exist by being merely imputed, their existence must also be established by a reliable cognizer because some imputed things turn out to be nonexistent.

A reliable cognizer is a conceptual or direct cognizer that perceives an object and is incontrovertible—not erroneous—with respect to it. The object and its reliable cognizer are established dependently, in relationship to each other. Therefore an object is said to be simply posited by awareness in general. It exists by being designated or imputed by mind. It exists by the power of the mind. This indicates that it exists because it is established by a reliable cognizer.

Some things may be commonly known in the world but are contradicted by reliable conventional cognizers. For example, most people think that the happiness they have from having many material possessions and a good reputation is actual happiness. They believe that the bodies of those they find sexually attractive are pure and attractive. However, such notions can be refuted by reliable conventional cognizers. It is readily apparent that some wealthy or famous people are miserable, and that the insides of people's bodies are repugnant, no matter how smooth their skin is. These facts are known by reliable conventional cognizers, and they contradict the false imputations society puts on many things. Candrakīrti's *Commentary on "Sixty Stanzas of Reasoning"* says (LC 181):

> The inaccurate are those that apprehend these things in cyclic existence only as pleasurable and so forth because even conventionally these things do not have this nature. The accurate are those that apprehend these things as duḥkha and so forth because these things have such a nature conventionally.

Once a certain object is conceived and named and is commonly accepted by society, we cannot simply give it another name and think it will become something else. Calling rat poison "medicine" does not make it safe to eat! Nevertheless, objects may be called by several names, and changing the name may change our view of the object or situation. For example, difficult circumstances may be called a "problem" or an "opportunity." Both are conventionally acceptable. The term we give those circumstances will influence how we relate to them. Calling them a "problem" usually makes us feel overwhelmed, whereas seeing them as an "opportunity" may help us gather our internal resources to handle the situation productively.

REFLECTION

1. Phenomena exist by being merely imputed in dependence on their basis of designation. Does that mean that everything we impute exists? Why or why not?

2. If Sam imputes a criminal motivation on Joe's actions that appear suspicious to him, does that make Joe's actions criminal? In this day when we are exposed to so much misinformation and disinformation, how do we determine if someone's imputations are correct or not?

Mere Designation

When we hear that phenomena are "mere names" and "mere terms," we may become confused, thinking that only words exist. When we hear that "everything exists by being merely imputed," we may think that imputation is the sole cause of objects or that if something doesn't have a socially recognized name it does not exist.

Tsongkhapa explains in *Essence of Eloquence* that saying phenomena are "mere name" does not mean that only names and terms exist but objects do not exist. Our personal experience tells us that the things we contact in daily life exist. "Mere name" indicates that phenomena do not exist from their own side; they are dependent, and one of the factors they depend on is being conceived and imputed by mind.

Their dependence on name and concept does not mean that phenomena are totally nonexistent before they are imputed. They may be known by another name. Before I was ordained and given the name Tenzin Gyatso, Tenzin Gyatso did not exist. But I still existed. I was called Lhamo Dhondrup, and before my parents gave me that name, I was called a baby. Now it wouldn't be suitable to designate me as a baby, and no one calls me Lhamo Dhondrup anymore.

Some phenomena come into being only at the time they are designated. A particular person becomes president only when a group designates him or her president and a socially recognized ceremony occurs, after which she legally assumes the presidential powers and responsibilities. Before the election and inauguration, she is not the president. Similarly, if we build a house with six rooms, a particular room does not become the living room until we conceive and designate it as such. If we later change our mind, put different furniture in it, and refer to it as a bedroom, that same room becomes a bedroom.

Other phenomena come into existence after they are designated. We talk about "my future lives," but these lives do not exist now. On the other hand, they are not totally nonexistent; they will occur after some time. Still, they do exist in general—they are an existent phenomenon even though they do not exist at this moment. People want to stop climate change and promote nuclear treaties because they care about future generations although the people in future centuries do not exist now.

Some phenomena existed before the specific name for them was coined. Before doctors identified certain medical symptoms, conceived of them as a discrete disease, and imputed the name "autoimmune disease," people still suffered from such diseases. Years later with the advancement of medical science, certain symptoms were grouped together and given a name although that disease had already existed for a long time. Its present name is applied retroactively. Sometimes part of the difficulty in discerning a new disease is figuring out which symptoms should be grouped together and given that designation.

To explain this in another way, a definition and definiendum (the object that is defined) exist simultaneously. "The energy created by moving charged particles" is the definition of electricity, and "electricity" is the definiendum. Before Benjamin Franklin gave the name "electricity" to the energy created by moving charged particles, that energy existed and electricity existed, although that energy was not known as electricity. Existing as something and being known as something are not the same.

As we examine the process of imputing and knowing something, we see how relative and ambiguous language is, and we come to understand why concepts, names, and language are associated with conventional existence. They are imprecise, and what exactly they refer to can sometimes be difficult to pinpoint. Some examples illustrate this point.

We can perceive something even when we do not know its name, although we do not perceive it as being that thing. That is, I may see your mother, but not knowing that she is your mother I just see a woman. Initially, the collection of those five aggregates was the basis of designation of the designated object, "woman," but after you introduce me, that collection of five aggregates become the basis of designation of a new designated object, "Donyo's mother." Furthermore, once you tell me who she is, how I perceive her changes. Perhaps I notice your physical resemblance to her or the common expressions you both use. Those attributes were there before, but only when she was imputed as your mother do I notice them.

Babies and animals, who do not use language, have concepts and designate objects. A cat does not conceive or give the name "padded chair," but the chair appears to the cat's visual and tactile consciousnesses and the cat knows it will be soft to sit on. Similarly, a baby will perceive something made from wood that has four legs and a flat top, but does not perceive it to be a table. At minimum, the baby may associate certain characteristics with one another and have an idea of there being a discrete object there, even though he does not know exactly what it is. Before I learned what the word "chess" meant, I would see two people looking at a board with white and black squares, taking turns moving different pieces. I knew the meaning of "game" and knew they were playing a game, but I didn't know it was chess, nor did I know such a game existed.

Developmental psychologists have found that very young babies see various colors and shapes but cannot put them together and conceive of them as being a discrete object. We have to learn to select certain details out of the environment and conceive of them as an object. Anthropologists who have visited remote tribes have found that when shown a photograph of a familiar object, those people cannot identify the object in the photo. A great deal of our education, even through adulthood, involves learning how to conceptually put different things together to form an object.

A tree can appear to a baby's eye consciousness, but it does not appear as a tree. The mother's face appears to the baby and the baby recognizes it, but the face does not appear as "my mother's face" and the baby doesn't know that face as his mother's face. Yet other adults nearby know that face is the face of the baby's mother. Babies don't yet have the concepts of mother, father, family, and so forth. But I think they understand kindness although they don't yet know the word.

In some cases, the designation alters how the basis of designation functions. If a certain piece of land is called "Israel," it will function in one way, whereas if it is called "Jordan," it will function in another. Many wars are fought to determine what something will be designated. Will this dirt or sand be part of this country or that country? Many arguments may occur in the process of deciding what name to designate something. Is this person innocent or guilty? In these examples, how things are conceived and named is critically important and influences an object's function or a person's future.

In other cases, the designation does not change an object's function. A stuffy nose, sore throat, and cough don't feel better (or worse) when we impute them as "a cold." However, when we experience several symptoms that are finally imputed as this condition or that disease, we often feel relief because we now know what it is. Alternatively, we may feel afraid now that our symptoms are called by that name.

The Power of Designation

Training our mind to see things as being merely designated by term and concept challenges the mind that grasps objective existence. Throughout the day, we continuously designate the people and things we come in contact with and think about. Some of our designations are correct; they are commonly known and cannot be discredited by either a reliable conventional cognizer or reasoning analyzing the ultimate. We see a flat board supported by three or four legs on which people put objects and impute "table." Some of our designations are not correct. We hear someone's voice on the phone and think, "It's Gloria," while it is Beth instead. Although mistaken imputation may not be serious in some circumstances, in other instances it can be. A police officer patrolling a certain area of a town at night sees a person near him pull something black out of his pocket and thinks, "He has a gun," whereas the person is taking out his wallet. Such an incident happened in New York and led to the death of an innocent person. Similarly, based on a few words someone said, we may incorrectly impute his motivation and become unnecessarily angry or upset. Such situations happen frequently in human communication.

Much of our education is a process of learning concepts and terms. As infants, we have yet to develop concepts well known to adults. A baby is frightened when it hears itself cry because it does not have the concept "This is my voice" and instead imputes "terrifying sound" and grows fearful. Similarly, babies may be frightened when their parents or caregivers leave the room because they think that these people have ceased to exist and will not return. Infants don't yet have the idea that their parents continue to exist even when they cannot directly see them.

Much of our early education is learning how to select certain appearances from the vast array of sensations appearing to our sense consciousnesses and conceive of them as discrete items. Babies learn to pick out a moving object that is soft and warm to the touch, has a comforting smell, and gives them food and conceives of it as something to trust, even though they don't yet know the words "mother," "father," or "kind person." As we get older, adults teach us the names for objects in our environment and we learn how to compare and contrast their attributes. We are taught the meaning of words that pertain to race, ethnicity, and religion and learn which of these names to apply to ourselves and which to others. We then proceed to pile many meanings and imputations that are often incorrect on people designated with particular terms or having particular attributes.

Forgetting that we are the ones who impute the names and attributes on objects—especially evaluative ones such as "useless," "useful," "good," or "bad"—we then think that these attributes or objects exist from their own side, unrelated to our minds. Sometimes, even in the face of contradictory evidence, we cling to this projected character, insisting that they dwell in the object itself, unrelated to our designation.

Cultural misunderstandings easily occur when all the parties have differing imputations. In pre-1959 Tibet, sticking out one's tongue was a sign of respect given to others—it indicated that one was not going to say an evil mantra that would harm someone—and clapping hands was a way of scaring away disturbing spirits. In Western countries, sticking out one's tongue is considered rude and clapping one's hands is a sign of approval. Imagine the misunderstanding that occurred when the British troops entered Lhasa, the capital of Tibet, in the early twentieth century: Tibetans lined the roads and applauded, which caused the British to mistakenly believe the Tibetans were welcoming them. When British officials met with average Tibetans, who stuck out their tongues to indicate that they were friendly, the British thought them to be rude! What is considered good and bad manners is due to human conceptualization and imputation. However, after we impute "polite" or "impolite," we forget that these behaviors have no inherent nature of their own. Instead, we reify what they indicate and then proliferate wrong conclusions about others. This can lead not only to misunderstanding but also to hurt feelings and resented judgments.

When scientists conduct research experiments, they seek to understand particular phenomena by means of conceptualizing their characteristics and giving them names. Based on the results of certain experiments, John Dalton and others said, "There are extremely tiny coalitions of energy here that exhibit the chemical properties of an element. Let's call them atoms." Conceiving and naming those properties opened up a new area of research as scientists sought to learn the functions and properties of atoms. We also see that the more information scientists gather in their particular fields, the more the conceptual framework within which they operate changes. Realizing that atoms are not the smallest unit of mass had a profound effect on physics.

Countries exist by being merely designated. In preceding centuries, a huge area of land in South and Southeast Asia was known as the British Empire. Later it was designated "India" and "Pakistan," "Burma," "Singapore," and so on. Wars have subsequently been fought over what names to impute to these areas of land. The Indians look at an area of land in the northern part of the subcontinent that the local people call "Kashmir" and call it India; the Pakistanis look at it and impute "Pakistan." Imputing it "India" results in Indian law and terms of governance being applied; calling it "Pakistan" means a different set of laws and a different way of governance will be imposed. Unable to communicate peacefully over which name to apply to this territory, the citizens of India and Pakistan have gone to war more than once. All of this occurs due to the concepts and names generated by human minds. None of it exists in the atoms of dirt that compose that area of land.

Happiness and suffering often arise depending on how we react to terms and ideas. We may have a certain set of physical symptoms and know we are sick, but when we hear the doctor apply the word "cancer" to these symptoms, our mood changes dramatically. This is a good example of how we solidify something by giving it a particular word. Before that word is associated with our symptoms, our minds are relatively balanced, but after hearing the word "cancer," we become distressed. Projecting a variety of possible scenarios in the future, we succumb to anxiety and fear. In fact, the symptoms have not changed from before the diagnosis, but once the name was given all our associations with that name were activated. The mind proliferated all sorts of conceptualizations generated by inappropriate attention, and then various emotions arose, one after the other.

A person is that which is designated in dependence on the collection of either four or five aggregates. (If the aggregates are those in the formless realm, there are only the four mental aggregates, whereas in the other saṃsāric realms, the five aggregates include a body.) Among persons are included a child, a teacher, a chemist, a Kenyan, a Hindu, a socialist, an elephant, an artist, and so on. Regarding the collection of my five aggregates, many "persons" have been designated, not all of them at the same time. I am a Tibetan, a monk, a son, a refugee, a Buddhist, and a human being. The Tibetan, human being, child, and the son existed prior to the monk, and the refugee arose after the monk. The monk came into existence at the time I received monastic ordination. The refugee came about when I fled Tibet in March of 1959. Now I am also a senior citizen—that person didn't exist at the time the child did. And I used to be a political leader, but since I resigned my position in 2011, that designation no longer applies to me. At present these persons are one nature with my general I, but they are designated in dependence on differing moments of the aggregates. Conventionally we say there is one person who is both a Tibetan and a monk; it would be very strange to say there are multiple people here in the same body. All of these persons are particularities of the general I of this life.

If things existed inherently, a Tibetan, monk, son, human being, male, and senior citizen could not be present in relation to one collection of aggregates. There would have to be six different selves, each with different aggregates. In that case, which one would be me? Or would I become inherently different people according to the role I played at certain times? But because everything exists only nominally, many different persons can be designated in dependence on one collection of aggregates; they all function harmoniously and exist in the same continuum.

Inherent existence would be rigid, whereas existence is fluid. If I were an inherently existent child, I could never have become an adult, because my being a child would have been independent of all of factors. But because I exist nominally, I can be a child at one point in my life and an adult at another point. The change in designation would not be a problem. Are the child and the adult the same person? No, they are not, but they exist in the same continuum. Is their basis of designation the same? No, one is the collection of ten-year-old aggregates, the other is the collection of eighty-five-year-old aggregates. But both go by the name Tenzin Gyatso.

Nominal existence allows for ambiguity, although sometimes we become confused or quarrel because things can't always be pinned down in exact terms. We all know what and where Delhi is. Delhi has been inhabited since the sixth century BCE up to today. The name "Delhi" has been the same throughout the centuries, but the basis of designation of Delhi has changed greatly from a cluster of houses with a few families to the enormous collection of ancient ruins, medieval forts, and modern buildings with a population of over twenty million. If we could put the original Delhi and the present one side by side, we would not recognize that they were part of the same continuum that is called "Delhi." If Delhi existed inherently, such change and ambiguity would be impossible; there would have to be a "real" Delhi frozen in time, a place that never changed, because it could not be influenced by other factors.

If people existed inherently, it would be difficult to figure out exactly who they were. We impute "baseball player" to someone who plays baseball. When that person is sleeping, is he still a baseball player? He's not playing baseball at that time, so shouldn't we call him a sleeper and not a baseball player? Is he being arrogant in allowing others to say that the famous baseball player is eating? After all, he's not playing baseball then; he's eating just like the rest of us who can't hit a homerun or steal a base.

When I (Chodron) stayed at a kibbutz in the Negev Desert, I saw a fence in the middle of a vast expanse of land. One side was called "Israel," the other "Jordan." When the wind blew some sand grains from one side of the fence to the other, did they become part of another country? If you put two piles of sand next to each other, could we identify which country they were? Why do human beings kill one another to decide what to call sand grains? The human mind is powerful; it can create happiness and harmony as well as torment and animosity.

These examples help us to see that inherent existence does not conform to our lived experience. To function in our world, things must exist by being merely designated; there is no other way they could exist.

REFLECTION

1. Things exist by being merely designated. What does "merely" mean in this phrase?
2. If things existed inherently, why couldn't they exist dependently?
3. Give some examples of phenomena that come into being only at the time they are designated.

4. Give examples of phenomena that exist before they are given a specific designation although they don't exist as that phenomenon before they are designated.

5. How does giving a particular designation to a person change your view of them?

6 | Mind and Its Objects in the Yogācāra System

AT THE GREAT monastic universities that existed in ancient times on the Indian subcontinent, such as Nālandā in modern-day Bihar, Buddhists and non-Buddhists debated and applied critical analysis to their own and others' tenets.[31] In this chapter and the next, we'll look at some of the topics of debate between the proponents of the Yogācāra, Svātantrika Madhyamaka, and Prāsaṅgika Madhyamaka tenet systems. Doing so will help refine our understanding of the correct view of the ultimate mode of existence.

The Value of Debate and Discussion

The Buddha taught according to the spiritual inclinations, interests, and mental dispositions of the audience that was present for his teaching. A skillful teacher, he did not explain the final view of emptiness to everyone but sometimes taught a view that was more suitable for people at that time, such as the existence of a self-sufficient substantially existent person. Through acquaintance with those explanations, their minds would mature and they would gradually become suitable vessels to hear the final view of the Buddha—the emptiness of inherent existence of all persons and phenomena.

As noted previously, each Buddhist tenet system has a way of determining whether the meaning of a passage is definitive or interpretable (provisional).[32] To discover the Buddha's final view, we need to employ reasoning to analyze the different views presented in various sūtras and commentaries. Such an approach is needed not only because the Buddha made different statements according to the audience but also because he wanted us to think about his teachings and not merely follow them blindly. Only through understanding them deeply by investigating and testing them ourselves will we be able to realize the meanings they convey. Analysis is the key tool to employ for this purpose. The Buddha emphatically encouraged us to scrutinize his teachings like a goldsmith tests gold, giving us the right and liberty to critically examine his words.

With this purpose, a healthy tradition developed in which students, while continuing to admire and revere their teachers, would critically analyze the teachers' words and writings. For example, the renowned Indian master Vasubandhu had among his many disciples four who were said to excel him in specific areas of Buddhist studies. Vimuktisena's understanding of the perfection of wisdom was superior to that of Vasubandhu. He took to task his teacher's Yogācāra explanation of the Perfection of Wisdom sūtras and instead presented a Madhyamaka understanding of these sūtras. Guṇaprabha was more learned than Vasubandhu in Vinaya, while Sthiramati outshone him in Abhidharma. Dignāga excelled Vasubandhu in the study of epistemology and the theory of reliable cognition. Dignāga's student Īśvarasena was the teacher of Dharmakīrti, who himself critically analyzed his teacher's explanation of epistemology and developed his own reading of Dignāga's work.

When writing on stages and paths as explained in the *Ornament of Clear Realizations* (*Abhisamayālaṃkāra*), Tsongkhapa at times criticized Abhayākaragupta's (d. 1125) interpretation. Yet when writing his *Great Exposition of Secret Mantra* (*Ngag rim chenmo*), he highly praised Abhayākaragupta's work as one of the most authoritative sources for understanding Tantra. Therefore as the Tibetan expression says, "Retain your reverence and admiration for the person, but subject their writings to critical analysis."

Alak Damcho Tsang was a disciple of the great nineteenth-century Nyingma master Mipham. Although Alak Damcho Tsang had tremendous admiration and reverence for Mipham Rinpoche, he examined his teacher's interpretations and objected to some of them. One of Alak Damcho Tsang's students questioned, "Since Mipham Rinpoche is one of your teachers, is it appropriate that you object to his interpretations of these points?" Alak Damcho Tsang immediately responded: "He is my great teacher. But if the lama says things that are not correct, we must point them out." These examples demonstrate a healthy attitude and reflect a fundamental approach of the Buddhist tradition, as expressed in the four reliances[33] where we seek clear understanding of the meaning of the teachings and direct realization of the definitive meaning of emptiness.

It is in this spirit that debate occurs in Tibetan monasteries. Such debate develops monastics' ability to think logically and encourages them to examine their own beliefs. Although we talk about refuting others' wrong views, we may share some of those wrong views, therefore we are actually refuting our own misunderstandings. The point of debate is to discern the way things exist so that we can attain liberation and full awakening. Āryadeva comments in *The Four Hundred* (CŚ 185):

> While attached to your own position
> and disliking others' positions
> you will not approach nirvāṇa.
> Neither conduct will bring peace.

The purpose of debate is not to be victorious; we are not competing with others to prove our intelligence or to inflate our arrogance by being "right." Such attachment to our own view—even if it is the correct Middle Way view—and antagonism toward others' views is an impediment to nirvāṇa, whereas open-minded discussion and in-depth investigation of our own and others' assertions increases wisdom.

The Yogācāra System

The principal sūtras the Yogācāra system relies on are the *Descent into Laṅka* (*Laṅkavatāra Sūtra*) and the *Sūtra Unraveling the Thought* (*Saṃdhinirmocana Sūtra*). The principal Indian commentators on Yogācāra were Asaṅga and Vasubandhu for the Yogācāra-Scripture Proponents and Dignāga and Dharmakīrti for the Yogācāra-Reasoning Proponents. Asaṅga relied principally on the *Sūtra Unraveling the Thought* and explained it well in his *Compendium of Ascertainments* (*Nirṇayasaṃgraha*), *Levels of Yogic Practice* (*Yogācārabhūmi*), and other texts. Jñānagarbha, who followed the Yogācāra-Svātantrika Madhyamaka school, wrote a commentary on the

Maitreya chapter in the *Sūtra Unraveling the Thought*, as did Jangchub Dzutrul.

Yogācāra became very popular in China after Xuanzang (602–64), a Chinese Buddhist monk, scholar, translator, and pilgrim, brought many Yogācāra scriptures to China and, together with his students, translated them from Sanskrit into Chinese. Xuanzang's principal student was Kuiji (632–82), whose lineage became the prominent school.

Woncheuk (613–96), a Korean monk and student of Xuanzang, wrote a lengthy commentary on the *Sūtra Unraveling the Thought* that relied on Asaṅga's and Vasubandhu's writings. It was translated into Tibetan and is one of the main sources used to understand Yogācāra in Tibet. Tsongkhapa wrote extensively about Yogācāra in his *Essence of Eloquence: Treatise Discriminating the Interpretable and Definitive*.[34]

Yogācāra in Tibet and Yogācāra in China are not identical, and in both countries there is more than one branch of Yogācāra. Śāntarakṣita and others combined particular points of Yogācāra with Madhyamaka philosophy to form the Yogācāra-Svātantrika Madhyamaka system, which accepts mind-only conventionally and refutes a foundation consciousness. Furthermore, some other traditions in each country have adopted certain aspects of Yogācāra into their own tradition. The presentation below corresponds to the Gelug understanding of Yogācāra in Tibet.

The Yogācāra system is also called "Cittamātra." The name Cittamātra, or Mind Only, comes from the *Pratyutpanna Samādhi Sūtra*, in which the Buddha says to Bhadrapāla:[35]

> When the forms are good and clear, reflections appear. In the same manner, when bodhisattvas develop this samādhi properly, they see the tathāgatas with little difficulty. Having seen them, they ask questions and are delighted by the elucidation of those questions. After thinking, "Did these tathāgatas come from somewhere? Did I go anywhere?" they understand that the tathāgatas did not come from anywhere. Having comprehended that their own bodies also did not go anywhere, they think, "Whatever belongs to the three realms is nothing but mind (*cittamātra*). Why is that? Namely, however I conceive (*vikalpayati*), so they appear."

Calling the Yogācāra philosophy "Mind Only" does not mean that everything is the mind but that phenomena exist in dependence on the mind—that is, the mind plays a crucial role in the existence and perception of objects.

Searching for the Self contained a brief introduction to Yogācāra; now we will build on that, beginning with an overview of the basic Yogācāra tenets: the role the mind plays in cognition, the foundation consciousness and latencies laid on it, the refutation of external objects, the three natures, the three naturelesses, and the selflessness of phenomena. Then we'll examine the Madhyamaka perspectives on those topics and close with a brief discussion of the benefit of studying the Yogācāra system.

Mind and Objects of Our Experience

All Buddhists agree on the mind's foremost role in creating our experiences. In the *Connected Discourses* of the Pāli canon, the Buddha says (SN 1:62):

> The world is led around by mind;
> by mind it is dragged here and there.
> Mind is the one thing
> that has all under its control.

The Sanskrit sūtra the *Flower Ornament Sūtra* (*Avataṃsaka Sūtra*) says:

> Wishing now to understand
> all the buddhas of the three times,
> contemplate the dharmadhātu;
> all things are created by mind.

Candrakīrti makes a similar point in his *Supplement* (MMA 6.89–90):

> It is the mind that constructed the vast diversity
> of both the domain of sentient beings and their universe as well.
> The Buddha said that all beings are born of karma;
> there is no karma without the mind.

> Even though matter does exist,
> it has no status of a creator like the mind,
> so what is being denied is a creator other than the mind;
> it is not that matter is being negated.

One of the chief ways sentient beings' minds create our world, our bodies, and our experiences is through our actions, or karma. This is a common theme in all Buddhist traditions and tenet systems. In addition, some Buddhist systems assert unique views regarding the mind, especially its relationship to the external world, to conception and language, and to what extent and in what manner our minds create our world and the things in it. Some assertions of Yogācārins and Mādhyamikas are examples of this.

The Yogācāra system contains many terms and concepts that you may not be familiar with. When describing the meaning of one term, we often include terminology that hasn't already been explained but will be explained later in the chapter. In certain cases, you may have to read the whole chapter to learn the meanings of all the terms and then go back and read the chapter again, now that you know the meanings of the terms.

REFLECTION

1. Why did the Buddha give different teachings about a topic depending on his audience?
2. How do we benefit from the existence of multiple tenet systems (even though we may initially find them confusing)?

Foundation Consciousness

Both branches of Yogācāra reject a self that is independent of the physical and mental aggregates. Both assert that the I is truly existent; it is not merely imputed by term and concept, but exists by its own uncommon mode of existence. Both Yogācāra branches agree that the perceiving mind and its perceived objects arise from the same cause—latencies on the mind. The mind that can receive these latencies, nurture them, and carry them to future lives in an uninterrupted continuum is said to be the person.

The two branches differ in terms of which consciousness carries the latencies. Yogācāra-Reasoning Proponents assert that a subtle, neutral mental consciousness that exists continuously throughout the life carries the latencies and is the illustration of the person. In contrast, Yogācāra-Scripture Proponents say that the mental consciousness isn't a stable basis capable of carrying the latencies from one life to the next because it can vary between being coarse and subtle, becoming almost undetectable in some deep meditative absorptions of cessation. For this reason, the Yogācāra-Scripture Proponents, in addition to the six consciousnesses accepted by all Buddhist systems, assert two additional consciousnesses: the foundation consciousness that stores the latencies and the afflictive mentality that is self-grasping. The foundation consciousness is the illustration of the person and carries the latencies. The system of the Yogācāra-Scripture Proponents is the only system that asserts the foundation consciousness.

Asaṅga, a teacher of Yogācāra-Scripture Proponents,[36] developed a sophisticated account of dependent arising in the context of Yogācāra philosophy. Unlike proponents of other Buddhist tenet systems that assert six consciousnesses—the five sense consciousnesses and the mental consciousnesses—the Yogācāra-Scripture Proponents assert eight consciousnesses, adding the foundation consciousness (*ālayavijñāna*)—also called the "storehouse consciousness"—and the afflictive consciousness (*kliṣṭamanas*)—also called the "I consciousness." Asaṅga explains that the world of our experience arises due to subtle causal dependence involving the foundation consciousness, a separate consciousness that is the repository for all seeds and latencies. The six consciousnesses engage with the world, and with each activity they engage in, latencies are infused in the foundation consciousness.

Viewing the foundation consciousness, the afflictive consciousness generates the sense of a self-sufficient substantially existent person and grasps the person to exist in this way. Because of this grasping, afflictions arise, actions are created, and more seeds and latencies are infused in the foundation consciousness. When these mature, they manifest as both the objects we experience and the consciousnesses experiencing them. Yogācārins assert that there are no external phenomena and that the things we perceive in the world around us arise from the same latencies as the mind perceiving them. Latencies also influence how we perceive and conceive phenomena. This is the process of causal dependency they describe.

The foundation consciousness is the person because, by acting as the basis of infusion for seeds and latencies, it allows for karma created in one life to ripen in a future life; it is the person that transmigrates to the next life. The foundation consciousness is truly existent; if it weren't, it would not be a stable base on which the latencies could be placed, and its various functions would not be tenable.

The foundation consciousness directly perceives its objects. However, the way it engages with its observed objects—the latencies, the five sense objects, the five sense faculties and their physical organs, and the mental aggregates—is by not ascertaining them. It is a consciousness to which its object appears but is not ascertained. The foundation consciousness is said to "intensely know but not know," in that it knows its observed object but cannot induce a memory of it. This is similar to our visual consciousness when we're in the middle of an interesting discussion. People may walk by, they appear to our visual consciousness, but due to not ascertaining them, we have no memory of them if someone asks us later if we saw anyone.

The foundation consciousness is defined as a neutral and undefiled main mind that has a thoroughly enduring continuum and is the basis of infusion of latencies with qualification. Each part of this definition tells us something important about this mind. First, it is a *main mind*. In identifying it as a primary consciousness, Yogācārins confirm that the basis for carrying the latencies is not something material, nor is it a mental factor, abstract composite, or permanent phenomenon.

This main mind is *neutral* in the sense of not being either virtuous or nonvirtuous. All ordinary beings have a foundation consciousness, even those in the form and formless realms who have no manifest nonvirtue, as well as sentient beings whose roots of virtue have been temporarily severed and those that lack virtue. This isn't because the foundation consciousness cannot hold the latencies of virtue or nonvirtue—all latencies are neutral[37]—but because the infusing consciousness (one of the six consciousnesses) and the basis of infusion (the foundation consciousness) are both present at the same time when the latency is infused. If the foundation consciousness were virtuous, it could not be present simultaneous with a nonvirtuous infusing consciousness, and if it were nonvirtuous, it could not be present at the time a latency is infused by a virtuous consciousness.

The foundation consciousness is *undefiled* in that it is not concomitant with any afflictive obscuration, such as ignorance, anger, or attachment. A consciousness and a mental factor are concomitant when they share five similarities: the object, aspect (the way the object is known), time, empowering condition (sense faculty), and substance (the same in number). The foundation consciousness is undefiled because it is concomitant with only the five omnipresent mental factors, none of which is afflictive.[38]

It is also undefiled because it is fruitional. According to the *Treasury of Knowledge*, a fruition (*vipaka*) is a neutral phenomenon included in the continuum of a sentient being that arises from a cause that is not neutral—that is, it arises from a cause that is either virtuous or nonvirtuous. Our human five aggregates are the fruitional result of virtuous karma created in a previous life. Similarly, each rebirth has a foundation consciousness that is the fruition of latencies on the foundation consciousness of the previous life. Being undefiled, the foundation consciousness can coexist with a supramundane path consciousness, providing the continuity necessary to carry the latencies without interruption.

The foundation consciousness is an *enduring continuum*; it is always present, no matter the state of the other aggregates. This quality enables the foundation consciousness to carry the latencies from the time they are infused on it to the time they mature, often in a future life. The body cannot do that because the body does not continue to the next life, and beings in the immaterial realm do not have a body. Sense consciousnesses are not continuously present: they are interrupted during sleep and when their objects aren't present. The continuity of the mental consciousness is interrupted during the five "mindless" states: the state of gods born as unconscious beings without discrimination in the form realm, who are aware only of their birth and death;[39] meditative absorption of nondiscrimination and meditative equipoise of cessation when there is no cognitive activity except for the foundation consciousness; deep dreamless sleep; or in a faint or coma when there is no conscious activity. The afflictive mentality isn't present during āryas' meditative equipoise on emptiness.

The foundation consciousness is a *suitable basis for infusion of latencies*. It can hold the latency of an action and carry it to a later time when the latency ripens and its result is experienced. In the continuums of arhats, bodhisattvas on the three pure grounds, and buddhas—in other words, in the continuums of those who have eliminated the afflictive obscurations—the foundation consciousness cannot correctly be called a foundation consciousness because that person no longer takes rebirth in saṃsāra, and thus a foundation consciousness carrying the latencies for rebirth is no longer necessary. At buddhahood, the foundation consciousness transforms into one of the five wisdoms of the Buddha. As a consciousness that perceives many objects in the ordinary state, when purified the foundation consciousness transforms into a buddha's omniscient mind.

Dignāga, Dharmakīrti, and the Yogācāra-Reasoning Proponents view things differently: they assert that the subtle mental consciousness has a stable continuum and is therefore a suitable basis to carry the latencies from one life to the next. These Yogācārins therefore assert the six consciousnesses common to all Buddhist traditions but do not assert the foundation consciousness and afflictive consciousness. They say the subtle mental consciousness carries the latencies from one life to the next.

All Yogācārins negate external objects (*bāhyārtha*) and assert that the consciousness truly exists. The mind that carries the karmic latencies must truly exist, they say, otherwise it could not transport the latencies properly. To Yogācārins a merely designated person or a merely designated mind is not capable of carrying latencies from one life to the next.

No External Objects

In general, all Buddhist tenet systems say that a consciousness arises from three conditions: the observed-object condition (*ālambana-pratyaya*), the empowering condition (*adhipati-pratyaya*), and the immediately preceding condition (*samanantara-pratyaya*). A fourth condition is added—the cooperative condition (*sahakari-pratyaya*), which is the aggregation of the other three conditions plus the mental impulse that is the wish to have a particular cognition. For all other systems except the Yogācāra, the observed-object condition of a visual consciousness perceiving yellow is the external color yellow, the empowering condition is the eye faculty, and the immediately preceding condition is the immediately preceding moment of consciousness. These three causes exist simultaneously and give rise to the effect, the visual consciousness perceiving yellow in the next moment. Non-Yogācārins assert that these three causes precede the consciousness that is their effect and must cease for that consciousness to arise, whereas Yogācārins say that the subject and object of a cognition exist simultaneously and arise from the same cause. For Yogācārins, subject and object are one nature and different isolates. They are mutually exclusive and exist simultaneously.

Yogācārins, however, present these three conditions in a unique fashion. The observed-object condition, in this case yellow, and the visual consciousness perceiving it are not cause and effect; they exist simultaneously. They both arise from the same substantial cause, a latency on either the foundation consciousness, according to Yogācāra-Scripture Proponents, or the mental consciousness, according to Yogācāra-Reasoning Proponents. The eye sense faculty, likewise, arises from a latency on the mind.[40]

The expression "external objects" in Yogācāra refers to objects that appear distant and cut off from the perceiving consciousness—things that are "out there," unrelated to our minds. In fact, say the Yogācārins, the objects we perceive do not exist in that way. They are the same nature as the apprehending consciousness; they arise from the same latency on the mind as the consciousness that perceives them. For example, the building we see appears to be over there, unrelated to our minds; we believe that when a group of people see the building we all see the same building in the same way. According to Yogācārins, these are false appearances and the mind that sees them that way is also false, for both the building and the visual consciousness apprehending it arise from the same latency on the mind. The building each person perceives is not exactly the same because the latency on each person's mind is different.

The subject and object of a cognition are different—the building and the visual consciousness are different—but they are not different substances. They are different because the observed object—the building—is not a consciousness; they are the same substance or same nature because they arise from the same substantial cause, the latency on the mind. Yogācārins assert the existence of the form aggregate, but these forms are not external forms that are distant and cut off from the mind cognizing them, like the forms we ordinary beings perceive.

Yogācāra emphasizes sentient beings' individual experiences although it asserts common objects. For example, all the people in a room see a wooden chair. This shared or common object arises from similar latencies on the minds of the people there. It is perceived by a reliable cognizer and thus it exists. That reliable cognizer isn't necessarily my mind, because the common chair that everyone in the room sees existed before I came in the room and saw it.

When it's said that the chair arises from the same substantial cause as the mind perceiving it, that doesn't mean the chair isn't made of wood. Yogācārins accept this common perception in the world. What they refute is that according to worldly perception, the chair appears to arise and exist objectively "out there," divorced from and unrelated to the apprehending mind.

Within this commonly shared experience of the chair, each person perceives and experiences the chair individually—this is the uncommon chair. The perceptions and experiences of the uncommon chair can differ considerably. For one person, it is a beautifully crafted chair, for another it is dilapidated. The uncommon chair arises from unique latencies on each individual's mind. The uncommon chair arises simultaneously with the consciousness of the individual person that perceives it.

According to Yogācāra, if the objects we experience were external to the mind as they appear to be, then everyone would perceive them in exactly the same way. But that is hardly the case. I hear a person's voice as pleasant and soothing; you hear it as harsh. I see two children running and kicking and think they are playing; another person believes they are fighting.

The texts often use the example of a glass of fluid; this is the common object. The glass and the fluid are made of the four elements—earth, water, fire, and air—that are used by all beings; they exist by the ripening of common latencies in all of our minds. But due to uncommon latencies, humans see water, gods see nectar, and hungry ghosts see pus and blood. These differences are due to the differing latencies on the minds of beings in each realm. When the human drinks the fluid, it tastes and functions like water; when the god sips it, it tastes like delicious nectar; when the hungry ghost swallows it, it burns like fire. And if one of the three drinks the whole glass of fluid, the other two will see only an empty glass.

Contemplating that what we perceive is related to our minds and arises from latencies on our minds heightens our awareness of what latencies we infuse in our minds. When we apprehend ordinary beings, we are more aware of what aspect of the object we apprehend and emphasize. An old saying that "pickpockets see pockets" applies here. A building inspector and a realtor notice different details and see the house in different ways. The latencies on each individual's mind influence what we apprehend and how we apprehend it.

REFLECTION

1. What reason do Yogācārins give for the existence of the foundation consciousness? In what way does the idea of the foundation consciousness resemble the notion of a soul?
2. According to Yogācārins, what faults arise if we say that there is an objective world out there totally unrelated to our mind? Do you agree or disagree with their assessment?

Latencies

By Yogācārins asserting that the seemingly external objects we see are projections of our minds, they must address the question of how perception occurs and what we are cognizing. To explain this, they say that all our perceptions of the world arise as a result of latencies on our minds. Latencies are dependent phenomena that are abstract composites.[41] They are simply potentials abiding on the foundation consciousness (or on the mental consciousness, according to Yogācāra-Reasoning Proponents), and almost all ordinary beings' cognitions depend on them. Like the foundation consciousness, latencies are substantial entities—impermanent things—but they are not substantially existent in the sense of being self-sufficient, because they are known only by something else appearing.[42] The foundation consciousness and the latencies are neither substantially one nor substantially different: they are one nature but nominally different. In the Yogācāra system, latency is synonymous with seed (*bīja*) and potency (*śakti*).

In the second chapter of his *Compendium of the Mahāyāna* (*Mahāyānasaṃgraha*), Asaṅga speaks of fifteen "cognitions" or categories of dependent phenomena. These are cognitions of (1) the five sense faculties, (2) the afflictive mentality, (3) the mind constituent, (4) the six objects, (5) the six consciousnesses, (6) the continuity of saṃsāra, (7) numbering, (8) the world of the environment, (9) the four conventions (the seen, the heard, the known, and the understood), (10–11) perceptions of self and others, (12) fortunate transmigrations (humans and gods), (13) unfortunate transmigrations (hell beings, hungry ghosts, and animals), (14) death, and (15) birth. These fifteen include all dependent or other-powered phenomena—impermanent things that arise from causes and conditions, specifically different types of latencies.

Asaṅga then explains the types of latencies that produce each dependent phenomenon. The first nine—both the apprehending consciousness and apprehended object—arise from the latencies for expression or verbalization. They generate conceptual minds that designate various names. The tenth and eleventh arise from latencies for the view of self that cause the mind in which the afflictive mentality views the foundation consciousness and thinks "I." The twelfth through the fifteenth arise from latencies of the causal branches of saṃsāra, which are also called the latencies of maturation. They cause the body and other factors of a life in saṃsāra.

Here Asaṅga identifies how appearances of objects and their perceiving consciousnesses are produced. Below are two different but similar versions of the types of latencies that cause the various aspects of a perceiving consciousness. In them we also see the latencies that cause how a consciousness perceives an object and how that object appears to that perceiving consciousness.

In *Opening the Eyes of the Fortunate* (*Stong thun chen mo*),[43] Kedrup describes three aspects of a visual consciousness perceiving the color blue. Each one is associated with a different latency:

1. The aspect that perceives blue as blue. This aspect is due to our being habituated to repeatedly perceiving blue and to *latencies of a similar type* (*samakulavāsanā*). That is, in the past we perceived blue, and that perception left a latency on the mind that has the potential to produce a similar type of apprehended object and apprehending consciousness. These latencies are left primarily, but not exclusively, by the sense consciousnesses.

2. The aspect that blue exists as the referent of the term "blue." This is due to *latencies for expressions* (*abhilāpavāsanā*), which are latencies to use language, to accept conventions, and to conceptualize. This aspect comes from our having repeatedly used language, particularly the term "blue," in the past. The color blue is the referent of the term "blue," so this aspect of the cognition is accurate. These latencies are left by the mental consciousness.
3. The aspect that blue appears to exist independent of the consciousness perceiving it and the aspect that blue appears to exist by its own character as the referent of the term "blue." These two aspects arise due to the *latencies of the view of self* (*ātmadṛṣtivāsanā*). These latencies also cause an awareness in which the afflicted mentality views the foundation consciousness and thinks "I." This aspect of the mind apprehending blue is erroneous because blue does not exist separate from the consciousness perceiving it, nor does it exist by its own character as the referent of the term "blue."

Building on Kedrup's presentation, Aku Lodro Gyatso speaks of four appearances and four latencies that cause them:[44]

1. The appearance of blue as blue arises due to the *latencies of a similar type*. This is the appearance of an impermanent thing, such as blue.
2. The appearance of blue as the referent of a conceptual consciousness arises due to the *latencies for expressions*. This is a conceptual appearance, which is a permanent phenomenon.
3. The appearance of blue as existing by its own character as the referent of a term arises due to *latencies of the view of self*.[45] In other contexts this is called the *latencies of believing in existence by its own character*. Blue existing by its own character as the referent of a term is a nonexistent imaginary. Nothing exists in this way.
4. The appearance of blue as an external form, separate from the consciousness apprehending it, arises due to *latencies of the branches of cyclic existence* (*bhavāṅgavāsanā*). In other contexts, this is called the *latencies of grasping the external existence* of blue. This appearance is also false; nothing exists as an external object. This appearance, too, is a nonexistent imaginary.

Regarding a visual consciousness apprehending blue, the blue color that is seen is a dependent phenomenon arising from the latency of a similar type. Its being the referent of the term "blue" is an existent imaginary that arises due to the latency of expressions. The aspect of that visual consciousness perceiving blue and the aspect perceiving that object to be the referent of the term "blue" are correct.

However, the last two appearances are erroneous, and phenomena are empty of existing in these ways. Due to the latency of grasping external existence, blue appears to be a separate substance from the visual consciousness perceiving it. Due to the latency of believing that phenomena exist by their own character as the referent of their terms, blue does not appear to be imputed by concept as "blue" on the color blue, but instead blue appears to exist by its own character as the referent of the term "blue." Blue being an external form that is separate from the consciousness perceiving it and blue being a form that exists by its own character as the referent of names and thoughts are factors (incorrectly) imputed by conceptuality. These are nonexistent imaginaries.

Yogācārins use several examples to illustrate mind-only and no external objects. *Magicians' illusions* show that the mind can apprehend things that are not external objects. A *mirage* illustrates that a mind and mental factors can arise without there being an external object. *Dreams* show that we can experience some things being desirable and others being repugnant without any external objects being present. *Reflections* show that we experience the happy results of positive actions and the unhappy results of destructive actions without there being external objects. *Hallucinations* illustrate that the various types of consciousness can arise without external objects, and *echoes* show that the variety of expressions can be produced without external objects. The *moon reflected in water* represents an "object" created by single-pointed concentration without there being an external object, and *emanations* illustrate that bodhisattvas are born in accordance with sentient beings' dispositions. In all these examples, a consciousness perceiving an object arises without the presence of an external object. Similarly, our daily-life consciousnesses perceive various things without those things being external objects that are unrelated to the perceiving consciousness.

REFLECTION

1. Contemplate each example that Yogācārins use to illustrate mind-only and no external object.
2. Relate each example to a dependent phenomenon that exists. Doing this will give you a better understanding of the Yogācāra position and will also loosen ignorance's stubborn insistence that things exist in the way they appear.

Another question arises: If all our perceptions when we are awake are like dreams, why don't we understand that they are mind-only, just like we recognize that dreams are mind-only? Asaṅga replies that those who know the suchness of phenomena view everything that appears as mind-only—as the perceived object and perceiving consciousness arising from the same latency on the mind. But just as we don't usually recognize a dream is mind-only while we are dreaming, so too when we do not know suchness, we don't recognize that all appearances are mind-only, that there are no external objects out there that are distant and cut off.

What is the actual blue that is seen by the visual consciousness? It is "inexpressible blue." This is not an external object, existing "out there," distant and cut off from the consciousness perceiving it. It is not the consciousness apprehending blue, because if blue were a consciousness, it would have to perceive objects and it doesn't. Blue is also not nonexistent. It is the appearance-factor of the consciousness apprehending blue. That is, it is a mere appearance produced by the latencies of a similar type left on the foundation consciousness or subtle mental consciousness by a previous consciousness apprehending blue. For example, a dream car (the appearance of a car in a dream) is neither a real car nor the dreaming consciousness. It is an appearance-factor of that consciousness and this appearance-factor has arisen from the same latency as the dream consciousness.

Due to the latencies of branches of cyclic existence, blue does not appear to the consciousness of an ordinary being without the appearance of blue being an external object—that is, without imaginary blue. The object of negation—the subject and object being different entities—appears to sense consciousnesses, and all sense consciousnesses are mistaken regarding the ultimate nature of their objects.

When a conceptual consciousness designates "blue," it does so within conceiving it as the "blue that exists out there, external to consciousness." This establishes a link between blue appearing to exist by its own character as the referent of the term "blue" and blue appearing to be an external object. In this way, the negations of these two—which are the two selflessnesses of phenomena—are also linked.

To explain the special objects appearing only to buddhas, such as the signs and marks of their bodies, Jigme Damcho Gyatso (1898–1946) speaks of a fifth latency—unpolluted latencies.

7 | Nature, Natureless, and Selflessness in Yogācāra

The Three Natures

To review, according to Yogācāra, the external world is an extension of our minds, and external objects do not exist. A consciousness and its object—the perceiver and the perceived—arise simultaneously from the same substantial cause, a latency or seed on the foundation consciousness, according to Yogācāra-Scripture Proponents, or on the mental consciousness, according to the Yogācāra-Reasoning Proponents. For example, the auditory consciousness hearing music and the music itself are said to be one nature in that both are produced by the same latency. The sound's appearing to exist out there, as a separate entity from the auditory consciousness, is a false appearance that arises due to deeply ingrained latencies of ignorance that have clouded our minds since beginningless time. The sound's appearing to exist by its own character as the referent for the name and concept "sound" is also false; it arose due to the latencies of the view of self.

Yogācārins have their own interpretation of the passages in the Perfection of Wisdom sūtras, where the Buddha said that all phenomena from form to omniscience are empty of inherent existence. Asaṅga says these sūtras require interpretation because accepting "there is no form, no feeling . . . no consciousness" literally would constitute falling to the extreme of nihilism. If the inherent existence of the aggregates were negated, there would be no basis on which to establish the person because there would not be any aggregates. That would be comparable to negating dependent phenomena, and if those were negated, there would be no way to establish the consummate nature either.

Instead Yogācārins set forth the definitive and provisional teachings according to the explanation in the *Sūtra Unraveling the Thought*. This sūtra explains the Buddha's view on what exists by its own character and what does not in terms of the three natures. For the Yogācārins, existing by its own character means existing from its own side without being merely imputed by conception.

The three natures (*trisvabhāva*) can be understood in two ways: (1) they are aspects of each phenomenon, and (2) they are three categories that together encompass all phenomena as well as nonexistents.

According to the first way, each phenomenon possesses three natures. For example, the table is the *dependent nature* and it serves as the *basis*. Its existing by its own character as the referent for the word and concept "table" and its existing as an external object that is not produced from the same latency as the consciousness perceiving it are its *imaginary or imputed nature*. The table being a different substantial entity from the consciousness perceiving it is also its *imaginary nature*. The absence of those imaginary natures is its *consummate nature*.

According to the second way of understanding the three natures, they may be spoken of as three different categories: for example, the table is a dependent phenomenon, space is an imaginary, and the two emptinesses are consummate phenomena.

Imputed or imaginary natures (*parikalpita svabhāva*) are posited only by names and concepts and exist only for thought. They are factors merely imputed by concepts; they do not truly exist or exist by their own character. Imputed natures are of two types: those that exist and those that do not. Nonexistent imputed natures are neither of the two truths. Examples are a turtle's moustache, the self of persons, the self of phenomena, external objects that arise from different substantial causes than the consciousness perceiving them, the consciousnesses perceiving external objects, things existing by their own character as the referent of words and concepts about them, and the consciousnesses perceiving such nonexistent things.[46] Existent imputed natures are, for example, unconditioned space, permanent phenomena other than selflessness and emptiness, and appearances of being established by their own character as the basis of entity and attribute.[47] Existent imputed natures are conventionalities.

Dependent or other-powered natures (*paratantra svabhāva*) are functioning things and dependently arisen phenomena. They are bases of mistaken dualistic cognitions in that they are the observed objects of consciousnesses grasping a self of persons and a self of phenomena. These outer phenomena (such as forms, bodies, physical sense faculties) and inner phenomena (such as the foundation consciousness, afflictive mentality, five sense consciousnesses, and mental consciousness) are called "other-powered" because they are impermanent phenomena that do not arise through their own power, but due to the power of other causes and conditions, including their respective latencies of a similar type. Arising from the latencies of a similar type means that the resultant dependent object is similar to a dependent object that existed previously. The previous object left a latency on the mind so that the person would cognize a similar object later. For example, seeing a table in one life leaves the latency to see other objects as tables in future lives.

Dependent natures arise as results of causes and conditions. They are not produced randomly or from themselves, and they are the bases for consummate natures. They may be impure (afflictions and the five aggregates of an ordinary person) or pure (such as the signs and marks of a buddha's body, the nonconceptual wisdom of meditative equipoise realizing selflessness, and the wisdom of subsequent attainment that follows it). The wisdom of subsequent attainment is pure in that it is influenced by a direct perceiver of emptiness, but it is mistaken because things appear to be a different entity from the consciousness perceiving them. Dependent things truly exist and exist by their own character. Forms and so on truly exist as only the entity of the mind.

Many sūtras in both the Pāli and Sanskrit traditions discuss dependent objects. For example, several sūtras state, "because this exists, that arises," indicating that things arise from causes and conditions, and "because this is produced, that is produced," showing that things arise from causes and conditions that are impermanent. The phrase in the twelve links of dependent origination "due to the condition of ignorance, formative action arises" indicates that effects are produced from conditions that are potencies. This also shows that things arise from concordant causes and conditions that have the capacity to produce them. There are many kinds of potencies for phenomena, so there are multiple links of dependent origination ranging from "the arising of formative actions due to the power of ignorance" up to "the arising of old age and death due to the power of birth." "The whole great assemblage of duḥkha" expresses the lack of beginning or end of duḥkha unless we eliminate the ignorance that lies at its root. None of the tenet schools question the existence of the twelve links of dependent arising; however, they differ in terms of how the twelve links exist.

Yogācārins assert that to our ordinary perception, dependent phenomena are colored or distorted by the imaginary natures that obscure them. When the imaginary nature is known as it really is in relation to the dependent nature of phenomena, the consummate nature is realized.

Consummate or thoroughly established nature (*pariniṣpanna svabhāva*) is the suchness of phenomena and the emptiness of external objects—that is, the emptiness of dependent phenomena existing by their own character as the referents of names and concepts, and the emptiness of subject and object arising from different substantial entities. The consummate nature is the apprehended object of the pristine wisdom realizing these two emptinesses. It is called "thoroughly established" because it is one nature with the dependent phenomena that are its bases and it has been there with the object from the start. This is the ultimate nature—the selflessness of phenomena as expounded by the Yogācārins. The direct realization of the consummate nature ceases all mistaken appearances. The consummate nature exists by its own character and truly exists as the ultimate nature of all phenomena. It is so-called because it is the supreme mode of existence. Because it is permanent and does not change into something else, it is not false or unpredictable. The emptiness of a self-sufficient substantially existent person is also considered the consummate nature.

Just as attractive people in a dream appear to be external objects although they are not, so are the fifteen phenomena listed on page 142. Their imaginary nature is their appearance as external objects that are separate from the mind apprehending them. Their consummate nature is the emptiness of the attractive people and the minds apprehending them arising from different substantial entities and the emptiness of those people existing by their own character as the referents of their names.

How do uncompounded phenomena have these three natures? Although permanent phenomena don't arise from causes, they are appearance factors that appear to the mind owing to the ripening of latencies. In addition, they abide dependent on their consummate nature, which is their "basis," just as clouds abide dependent on the sky. So in this sense they can be said to be dependent phenomena. As with dependent phenomena, their imaginary nature is their appearance as external objects and as existing by their own character as the referents of their names. Similarly, their consummate nature is their emptiness of existing in either of these ways.

Yogācārins assert different types of existence for the three natures:

- Other-powered or dependent natures, such as blue and the visual consciousness perceiving it, truly exist as only the nature of mind. They ultimately exist, exist by their own character, inherently exist, and exist from their own side.[48] They have a nature that is not imputed by the proliferations of names and concepts.
- Nonexistent imaginaries, such as the flower's existing as a separate entity from the consciousness perceiving it or the flower's existing by its own character as the referent of the name "flower," do not exist at all.
- Existent imaginaries, such as unconditioned space and the flower's being the referent of terms and conceptions, don't truly exist, ultimately exist, or exist by their own character, but they do exist for a conceptual consciousness. They also exist inherently and from their own side.
- Consummate natures are the three selflessnesses, which are the nonexistence of the imaginary nature in a dependent nature. The first, the absence of a self-sufficient substantially existent person, is the selflessness of persons. The second and third—the absence of form and so forth existing by their own character as the objects of the terms and concepts of them, and the absence of form and so forth existing as a different entity from the consciousness perceiving it—are the selflessnesses of phenomena. The consummate natures truly exist, ultimately exist, exist by their own character, inherently exist, and exist from their own side.

Some dependent phenomena are imputed in the sense that they cannot be known without another object appearing to the mind—for example, a person is not known without one or more of the aggregates appearing to the mind. However, unlike imputations that don't exist by their own character, dependent and consummate phenomena exist by their own character and are not merely imputed by conception. They are referents of their terms and they exist by their own character, but they do not exist by their own character as referents of their terms.

There is discussion whether the subtle selflessness of persons—a person's lack of self-sufficient substantial existence—is a consummate nature. The lack of a self-sufficient substantially existent person is the object of an ārya's wisdom, so in this respect it is a consummate nature. However, the two selflessnesses of phenomena—which are subtler than the selflessness of persons—are the consummate nature that is the main object of meditation for bodhisattvas. If the selflessness of persons were not a consummate nature, it would have to be an imaginary because it isn't a dependent thing. However, it would sound strange to say that āryas meditated on an imaginary to attain liberation, because imaginaries are things fabricated by the conceptual mind.

In *Essence of Eloquence*, Tsongkhapa speaks of the consummate nature in terms of both the selflessness of persons and the selflessness of phenomena. Although the lack of a self-sufficient substantially existent person is not the primary consummate phenomenon, it may be included as a secondary consummate nature. This is similar to the following example: the perfection of wisdom must be a wisdom in the continuum of an ārya bodhisattva. Although the wisdom on the bodhisattva path of accumulation doesn't fit this definition, it is still considered a nominal perfection of wisdom. In the same way, the selflessness of persons isn't an actual consummate, but it can be considered a nominal consummate.

REFLECTION

1. Review the various types of latencies, aspects of phenomena, and the types of appearances. Look around and choose an object you perceive. Analyze which aspects and appearances of that object arise from which latencies.

2. What effect does it have on you to think that your environment and everything in it arise from latencies on your mindstream and do not exist as objective entities "out there"?
3. How do your assumptions and preconceptions about people, things, and situations change when you think that your perceptions of them arise due to latencies on your mindstream?

Three Types of Natureless

When the Buddha spoke the Perfection of Wisdom sūtras, he said that all phenomena are natureless. In the seventh chapter of the *Sūtra Unraveling the Thought*, the bodhisattva Paramārthasamudgata asked the Buddha: "At one time you described the four truths and everything included in them as having their own nature or character, but at another time you said they all are natureless and that they are not produced, not ceasing, quiescent from the start, and naturally passed beyond sorrow. What were you thinking when you said that?"

The Buddha praised Paramārthasamudgata for asking this question in order to benefit sentient beings. In response, he spoke of the three natures and clarified in what way each phenomenon is empty or natureless (*niḥsvabhāva*).

1. Imaginaries are *character natureless* (*laksaṇa-niḥsvabhāvatā*) because they are imputed by thought and do not exist by their own character. They lack the nature of existing by their character.
2. Dependent natures are natureless in two ways:
   - They are *production natureless* (*utpatti-niḥsvabhāvatā*) because they arise through the force of other causes and conditions. They are not produced from causes that are the same nature as themselves and do not arise randomly or causelessly. Conventionally they exist falsely, like a magician's illusions.
   - They are *ultimate natureless* (*paramārtha-niḥsvabhāvatā*) because they are not the consummate nature. They are not ultimate truths and they are not the final nature of phenomena that is perceived

by the ultimate purifying consciousnesses. Dependent natures are not objects of meditation for purifying the mind, and meditation on them is not the principal cause of attaining liberation.

3. Consummate natures are *ultimate natureless*, but in a different sense. They are the actual ultimate nature of phenomena; they are the emptiness of the two imaginary natures. The consummate nature is what is perceived by the ultimate purifying consciousness. "Ultimate" in "ultimate natureless" refers to existing in the two imaginary ways mentioned above—the subject and object of a cognition being different entities, and a phenomenon existing by its own character as the referent of words and concepts about it. Consummate natures are natureless of existing in those ways because they are ultimate truths and are the observed object to purify obscurations. Meditation on the consummate nature leads to awakening.

When involved with names and concepts, sentient beings are embroiled in the imaginary nature because they believe the projections of their minds to be real. For example, ignorance imputes or projects a self-sufficient substantially existent person and we believe we are such a person. We believe some objects to be as desirable as we project them to be and other objects to be as sinister as we imagine them to be. In short, confused sentient beings mistakenly conceive dependent phenomena to be the imaginary nature when in fact these imagined qualities are nonexistent. As a result, afflictions flourish in our minds. When we stop misperceiving dependent phenomena as the imaginary nature, we will know the consummate nature.

When he initially presented the three natures in the *Sūtra Unraveling the Thought*, the Buddha first explained the imaginary nature. Then he presented the dependent nature, phenomena's conventional character. Lastly, he described the consummate nature—the ultimate truth that is difficult to understand.

But when he later taught the three natures in terms of the path to awakening, the Buddha first presented dependent phenomena and explained that they are produced by causes and conditions. Through this he wanted people to understand that their present experiences of pleasure or pain do not arise without causes; they are produced by previously created virtuous and nonvirtuous actions. This will draw them into practicing virtue and abandoning nonvirtue because they want to experience happiness in the future, be it the happiness of a good rebirth, liberation, or full awakening. Understanding dependent natures will also help sentient beings understand true duḥkha and the true origins of duḥkha, which will lead them to aspire to be free from saṃsāra.

Then the Buddha spoke of imaginaries being character natureless. Through understanding the object of negation, people will understand the consummate nature, which is the nonexistence of the imputed nature.

The Two Selflessnesses of Phenomena

Among the Buddhist philosophical tenet systems, the first two, Vaibhāṣikas and Sautrāntikas, speak only of the selflessness of persons; they do not assert a selflessness of phenomena. The two latter systems, Yogācāra and Madhyamaka, accept the selflessness of both persons and phenomena. Although meditating on the selflessness of persons is effective in counteracting afflictions in relation to ourselves, it does not harm the ignorance that projects false ways of existing onto other phenomena. For this reason, Yogācārins and Mādhyamikas extend the understanding of selflessness to the objects we use and enjoy, such as our body, possessions, and environment. These things appear to us as if they had some kind of objective reality, and our ordinary worldview endorses this.

The two selflessnesses in the Yogācāra system differ in terms of the basis of negation and the object of negation. Regarding the selflessness of persons, the basis of negation is the person (our own self), and the object of negation is its self-sufficient substantial existence. Regarding the selflessness of phenomena, the basis of negation is all phenomena, and there are two objects of negation. The first object of negation is the subject and object of a cognition being different entities: here an object appears to be cut off and distant from the mind apprehending it, as if they were unrelated. The second object of negation is a phenomenon existing by its own character as the referent of terms and concepts about it: here, objects appear to be ready to be named and conceptualized due to their own inner structure and mode of being. Corresponding to these two objects of negation, the selflessness of phenomena has two aspects: (1) the emptiness of form and so forth existing as entities separate from the consciousnesses perceiving them, and (2) the emptiness of form and so forth existing by their own character as the referent of the term "form" and so forth.

We'll now look more closely at these two aspects of the selflessness of phenomena.

Reasonings Showing No External Objects

Asaṅga says that when practitioners know the suchness of phenomena, they view everything that appears as mind-only. But if we don't know suchness, how can we infer it? Asaṅga replies by referring to scripture and reasoning. For scripture, Asaṅga refers to the Buddha's statement in the *Sūtra on the Ten Grounds*: "These three realms are mind-only," and to a passage in the Maitreya chapter of the *Sūtra Unraveling the Thought*, where the Buddha said: "[The image that is the observed object of meditative concentration] is said to be not different [from the mind]. Why? I explain that consciousness is distinguished by its observed object being just mind-only." Similarly, the perceiving mind and perceived object of our other cognitions appear to be different things to childish beings who do not know suchness. However, they are not different, for they arise from the same substantial cause, latencies on the mind. When it's said that there are no external objects, it means that the objects of our consciousnesses are empty of existing as separate entities from their perceiving consciousnesses.

On the basis of incorrectly superimposing an external reality, we believe the attractiveness or ugliness as well as the objects themselves that possess these qualities to be unrelated to the perceiving consciousness. This leads us to be repulsed by some objects we deem ugly and attached to others, which in turn leads us to create destructive karma.

On a deeper level, Yogācārins say objects themselves—not just subjective attributes like attractiveness—are related to our minds. Although ordinary beings perceive objects as separate from the perceiving consciousness, this is based on false appearance and involves erroneous perception because things do not exist in this way. What is seen as objectively real outside of us is but a projection of our minds; both the subject and object of our cognitions arise due to the same latency on the mind.

Because the subject and object of sense consciousnesses arise from the same substantial cause, external objects do not exist. The subject and object of a consciousness are nondual in this way, and this absence of duality is the ultimate truth, the consummate nature.

Realizing that an object or a quality is not objectively real immediately decreases our attachment or aversion to the object. Understanding nonduality in this way can have an immediate impact by reducing our emotional attachment and aversion to external objects and people.

Some of the reasonings Yogācārins use to prove no external objects are outlined below. By studying Yogācāra texts by Asaṅga, Vasubandhu, and so forth, you will gain an in-depth understanding of the Yogācāra view.[49]

1. The *reasoning that the consciousnesses of different beings see the same object differently* refutes the existence of external objects because consciousnesses that apprehend external objects are mistaken with respect to their apprehended objects. The consciousnesses of ordinary sentient beings are not reliable cognizers with respect to phenomena's ultimate mode of existence because they apprehend external objects where there are none. The fact that gods, human beings, and hungry ghosts all have conventional reliable cognizers of a glass of fluid although they perceive it as nectar, water, and pus and blood, respectively, indicates that there is no external object. In the *Compendium of the Mahāyāna*, Asaṅga says (RR 542):

   > In accordance with their respective type
   > as hungry ghosts, animals, humans, and gods,
   > the thing is one [but their] minds are different.
   > Hence it is expressed that [external] objects are not established.

2. The *reasoning of discordant experiences* observes that human beings each experience the same object differently. Some see it as pleasant, others as unpleasant, and a third group as neither. If external objects existed, all these people should experience the object in the same way.
3. The *reasoning that consciousnesses perceiving objects are possible without there being external objects* gives four examples: (1) Our mental consciousness is active when we reflect on past and future objects, even though no external objects are present at that time. When we remember the argument we had with a friend yesterday, that person and the

harsh words we exchanged do not exist externally at this moment. (2) Our dream consciousness perceives dream people, dream places, and other dream objects although they are not external objects. (3) The visual consciousness of someone who has the eye disease of vitreous floaters apprehends falling hairs although there are none. (4) Yogis can perceive objects created through the power of their single-pointed concentration, such as the entire space filled with skeletons, although there are no external skeletons.

4. The *reasoning that images that are the object of meditative concentrations are not different from the mind* comes from the *Sūtra Unraveling the Thought*, where Maitreya asked the Buddha if the image that is the object of meditative concentration is different or not different from that mind. The Buddha responded that it is not different because "that consciousness is distinguished by its observed object being mind-only." That is, meditative images such as images of bones covering the earth or the foulness of the body that are cultivated in meditative equipoise are said to be mind-only, meaning that the perceiving consciousness and perceived object are not different natures or entities. This reasoning is then extended to include all knowable objects. Their being different substantial entities is a nonexistent imaginary.
5. The *reasoning that if external objects existed, either liberation would be impossible or sentient beings would be liberated without making effort* refutes external objects as follows: If external objects existed, nonconceptual pristine wisdom would not be feasible because it does not perceive external objects, and without pristine wisdom, the attainment of buddhahood would be impossible. Furthermore, if external objects existed, ordinary sentient beings would have reliable cognizers of the ultimate nature and would be liberated without having to meditate.
6. The *reasoning of no partless particles* negates the existence of the supposed building blocks of external objects—tiny directionally partless particles. If such partless particles existed, it would be impossible for them to form larger objects because (1) if they met, they would merge together and occupy the same space because they lack sides that would touch, or (2) they could never meet because meeting involves having at least two sides—one that contacts another particle and another that doesn't. However, that would contradict the assertion that they are

partless. Since such ultimate tiny building blocks do not exist, neither can larger external objects that are an aggregation of them.

REFLECTION

1. Examine the reasonings given above and reflect on the examples.
2. Are they convincing for you?
3. Whether or not you fully agree with them, by contemplating them over time, you will find new angles that enrich your understanding not only of how your own mind functions but also how many of your perceptions and conceptions are erroneous.

What about Permanent Phenomena?

There is some debate whether the emptiness of subject and object being different substantial entities applies to all phenomena, including permanent phenomena, feelings, and consciousnesses. Although many scholars say it does, my thought is that the scope of objects encompassed by the two selflessnesses of phenomena differs. All phenomena—including conceptual consciousnesses, permanent phenomena, and our internal feelings of pleasure and pain—are empty of existing by their own character as referents of terms and concepts.

However, the emptiness of subject and object being different substantial entities does not apply to conceptual consciousnesses or to internal feelings of pleasure and pain, and meditating on their not being external objects doesn't affect our attachment to them. The purpose of asserting that subject and object are not different substantial entities is to reduce our attachment to external sensory objects. But this logic doesn't work for internal feelings or conceptual consciousnesses. There seems to be something lacking in the Yogācāra presentation here.

However, meditation on the selflessness of persons is effective for eliminating attachment to internal feelings of pleasure and pain. By contemplating that there is no self-sufficient substantially existent person, we stop grasping what belongs to such persons, such as their pleasurable and painful feelings.

A question arises: The table and the consciousness perceiving it have the same nature because they arise from the same substantial cause, a latency. But how can a permanent phenomenon have the same nature as the mind that perceives it? The lack of external existence that we have been discussing refers to the objects of the senses and the sense faculties; Yogācārins do not discuss whether permanent phenomena are external. However, they assert that all phenomena are the mere nature of mind and thus have the nature of nonexternal existence—that is, they have the nature of not existing externally. Unconditioned space is "nonexternally existent in nature" because there is no external existence.

When you learn that space is the mere lack of obstructive contact, you have a conception regarding space. When space appears to this conception, does it appear as a result of a previous latency? Yes, it does. In short, all phenomena, even permanent objects and their apprehending consciousnesses, arise through the ripening of latencies on the foundation consciousness. This is true and acceptable to Yogācārins because they assert that all phenomena, including permanent phenomena, are the mere nature of mind and do not exist externally.

When Yogācārins discuss the lack of external existence, they often refer to the five sense objects not existing as a composite of external particles. Nevertheless, those objects can be perceived. Similarly, although permanent objects do not exist as a composite of external particles, they can be apprehended.

Yogācārins say a form such as a book is simply an appearance that is particular to one person's visual consciousness: that book is not apprehended by others because the book each person perceives arises from the latencies on the foundation consciousnesses of that person. According to this description, the relationship between subject and object is more subtle than we normally assume. If the book existed as a common external object and if the consciousness were totally different from it, then subject and object would be different entities and this is opposite to the Yogācāra view.[50] For them, nonduality, the emptiness of duality, means the lack of external existence.

Yogācārins say that when a book appears to different people they see different things, and this is a sign that the book lacks external existence.

Svātantrikas say that a book appearing differently to many people is a sign that it doesn't truly exist. Prāsaṅgikas say it indicates that the book does not exist inherently.

Empty of Existing by Their Own Character as Referents of Terms and Concepts

The second selflessness of phenomena for Yogācārins is that all phenomena are empty of existing by their own character as the referent of terms or thoughts. That is, there is nothing in the mode of existence of the flower that makes it the basis of the name "flower" or of any other name. In the *Compendium of the Mahāyāna* Asaṅga pointed out three unwanted consequences if the flower—or any other object—existed by its own character as the basis of its name:

1. We would know the names of objects without having to be taught, because those names would inhere in the objects themselves. If that thing with a stem, petals, pistil, and stamen were established by its own character as a flower, it wouldn't have to be designated by language as a flower. Everyone would know it was a flower without having to learn that the name "flower" referred to that object.
2. Because the name would inhere in the object, only one name could apply to a particular object. In that case, the words "flower," "daisy," and "fleur" (its French name) could not refer to the same item. Because a different meaning appears to a conceptual consciousness with each different name, each name would have to refer to a different object.
3. A name could apply to only one object. Once the thing in the vase is called "flower," no other object—for example, a daisy or a rose—could be called "flower." Furthermore, if both a daisy and a rose were established by their own character as the referent of the word "flower," they would have to be one object because one name could connote only one thing.

Due to these absurd consequences, phenomena cannot exist by their own character as the referents of terms and thoughts.

The Relation of the Two Selflessnesses of Phenomena

The *Sūtra Unraveling the Thought* presents the selflessness of phenomena as the absence of subject-object duality. The *Bodhisattva Grounds* explains the selflessness of phenomena from the viewpoint of how language and thought relate to an object: things do not exist by their own character as the referent of terms or thoughts (conceptual consciousnesses). The question arises, "What is the relationship between these two selflessnesses of phenomena?"

Many great scholars have weighed in on this, and it is not easy to understand. The two emptinesses are explained under different headings in the philosophical texts; that is one reason that they are considered different. Although they are said to be equally subtle, the emptiness of form and so forth existing by its own character as the referent of a term is easier to realize than the emptiness of subject and object being different substantial entities. Since this is the case, they are realized serially, the former first, followed by contemplation of reasonings that lead to realizing the latter.

It is easier to realize the emptiness of form and so forth existing by its own character as the referent of a term because it is easier to get a sense of how a conceptual consciousness apprehends form as existing by its own character as the referent of a term than it is to get a sense of how the subject and object of a cognition are apprehended as different entities. In other words, it's easier to identify the object of negation for the former than for the latter. Just as it is easier to hit a target that is easy to see, it is easier to realize the emptiness of an object of negation that is easy to identify.

By realizing form's emptiness of existing by its own character as the referent of term and thought, we can then ascertain that the appearance of form existing by its own character as the referent of term and thought to a conceptual consciousness does not come from the side of the form casting an aspect on the consciousness, but is due to the force of the latencies for expressions. Because form arises due to latencies, it has the nature of internal consciousness and falsely appears to exist by its own character as a referent of terms in the aspect of external form. Through understanding this, we enter into mind-only—the absence of duality between apprehending subject and apprehended object—and realize the emptiness of subject and object being different entities. This is the sequence to realize the two selflessnesses of phenomena.

To put it in another way, when we think, "This is a form," there seems to be a form existing out there, from the side of the object as the referent of the term "form." Upon further investigation we come to understand that the form does not objectively exist as the referent of name and thought; it being such a referent is imputed by name and thought. Although this sounds similar to Prāsaṅgikas' assertions, Yogācārins take it in another direction and use it to prove there are no external objects. By realizing that form doesn't exist by its own character as the referent of a conceptual consciousness apprehending form as an external object, we can realize that a sense consciousness apprehending a form that exists by its own character as the referent of a term is mistaken with respect to its appearing object. Since a sense consciousness is mistaken with respect to its appearing object, the form doesn't exist as it appears to that sense consciousness. Because the form doesn't exist as it appears to the sense consciousness apprehending it, it can't be a different substantial entity from that sense consciousness. Form and the consciousness that perceives it arise from the same latencies. In this way, one enters into mind-only.

Perhaps there is a simpler explanation of how realizing form's emptiness of existing by its own character as the referent of term and thought leads to realizing its emptiness of being a separate substantial entity from the consciousness apprehending it. This is to consider that when we give names to objects, the namer appears to be on one side and the object named on the other. There is a sense that the namer—the consciousness—and the named—the object—are different entities. In the same way, when objects appear to exist by their own character as the referent of term and thought, there is the sense that the consciousness is on one side and the object named is on the other. That is, in the activity of naming there is the sense that the subject and object are different entities. Thus when we refute objects as existing by their own character as the referents of terms and thoughts, subject and object being different entities also comes to be refuted, and in this way mind-only is realized.

In asserting that there are no external objects, Yogācārins do not say that everything is consciousness. The table is not consciousness: a table is form, whereas a consciousness is not. However, the subject and object of a cognition have an interdependent nature because both are produced by the same latency. This is the meaning of "everything is the nature of mind." A consciousness and its object are like a mirror and the image reflected in it: they are not one and the same thing, but they cannot be separated. In short, things do not pass beyond the mind, but they are not mind.

Yogācārins use the example of a dreaming consciousness and the dream objects that appear to it to illustrate the lack of external objects. The giant daisy, the miniscule planet, and the queen of Mars we dream about are not the dreaming mind, neither are they separate entities from that mind. In the same way, objects in the world around us are not the consciousnesses that perceive them, but they are not separate entities from those consciousnesses either. In both cases the perceiving consciousness and the perceived object arise from the same latency on the mind. What, then, is the difference between a dream car and an actual car? An actual car functions like a car: you can drive it. However, a dream car vanishes the moment you wake up.

According to Yogācāra tenets, āryas in meditative equipoise on emptiness perceive only emptiness—the nonexistence of subject-object duality and the nonexistence of things existing by their own character as referents of terms and concepts. After arising from meditation, in the time of subsequent attainment, they perceive things as like illusions. Although the language is similar to the Prāsaṅgikas', the meaning is different because of the difference in the object of negation.

Reflecting on Yogācārins' understanding of reality gives us the sense that the appearance we perceive of an objective external world is false. This reduces the intensity of our attachment and repulsion toward the world. For example, when I reflect that the momos—Tibetan dumplings—that taste so delicious are simply an appearance arising from latencies on the mind—that there are in fact no external momos—my attachment for them decreases. Furthermore, by understanding that each of us perceives people and the world around us in different ways, I stop expecting others to see things the way I do and become more accepting of the differing perceptions among us. Although the Yogācāra view is not the final view, it is helpful in that it loosens our clinging to sense objects, people, and so on.

Realizing the selflessness of persons—the absence of self-sufficient substantial existence of the person—destroys afflictive obscurations, according to the Yogācāra system. Realizing the two selflessnesses of phenomena eradicates cognitive obscurations and brings omniscience.

REFLECTION

1. What are the two selflessnesses of phenomena asserted by Yogācārins?
2. The Vaibhāṣika and Sautrāntika systems do not assert a selflessness of phenomena. How does it change or deepen your investigation of reality when you contemplate the selflessness of phenomena (for example, your five aggregates) in addition to selflessness of persons?

Mādhyamikas' Response to Yogācārins

Throughout the centuries, there has been much debate between proponents of the Yogācāra and Madhyamaka schools. In Tibet, these debates have drawn out some interesting points that are presented below and challenge us to investigate further. Since the Yogācāra and Madhyamaka systems developed differently in Tibet and in China, the points of difference between these two schools may not be the same. This is a topic for more research.

Definitive and Interpretable Teachings

Yogācārins claim that the first turning of the Dharma wheel is interpretable (provisional) and does not fully explain the selflessness of phenomena. The second turning of the Dharma wheel includes the Perfection of Wisdom sūtras which cannot be taken literally and require interpretation, whereas the teachings of the third Dharma wheel are definitive.

More specifically, Yogācārins say the content of the second turning of the Dharma wheel is provisional because it negates existence by its own character for all three natures, and such a negation is too broad. Yogācārins agree with the Buddha's statement in the Perfection of Wisdom sūtras that imaginaries do not exist by their own character. But when he stated that dependent natures do not exist by their own character, his meaning was that they are production natureless and ultimate natureless; and when the Buddha said that consummate natures do not exist by their own character, he meant that they are ultimate natureless. In short, Yogācārins say the Buddha's meaning was actually that dependent phenomena and consummate natures exist by their own character and truly exist, a position that accords with their own tenets.

Interestingly, in the *Sūtra Unraveling the Thought*, the Buddha said that the Perfection of Wisdom sūtras are the highest, and when he taught that all phenomena are natureless, sharp-faculty bodhisattvas would understand that he was referring to the three types of natureless as described in Yogācāra. But because modest-faculty disciples require a more literal explanation, the Buddha said he spoke of the three types of natureless again in the *Sūtra Unraveling the Thought*, this time explaining them more explicitly according to the Yogācāra tenets.

Prāsaṅgikas have a different perspective, saying that the Perfection of Wisdom sūtras may be taken literally. They accept the statement that all persons and phenomena are empty of inherent existence without making a distinction between the subjective consciousness and the objects of the external world. They affirm that non-inherent existence does not mean no existence whatsoever and say that the Yogācāra explanation is flawed because it makes unnecessary distinctions between the mode of existence of the external world and of the internal consciousness. This is so because Yogācārins negate an objective external world but affirm the true existence of consciousness. Although reflection on the Yogācāra understanding of no external objects can reduce our attachment and aversion to such objects, given that they do not extend the same argument to the internal world of experience and consciousness, they lack an effective method to overcome attachment to all things, such as inner experiences of joy, unhappiness, sadness, and pleasure.

True Existence

Yogācāra asserts that all dependent phenomena and the consummate nature are truly existent because if they didn't truly exist, they wouldn't exist at all. Furthermore, external phenomena do not exist but dependent phenomena do. An external table that doesn't arise from the same latencies as the mind perceiving it does not exist, but a dependent table that is the same nature as the consciousness perceiving it exists and is truly existent.

Yogācāra-Svātantrika Mādhyamikas agree with some Yogācāra tenets but do not accept others. They too reject an objective external world and assert that the five sense objects are the same nature as their perceiving consciousnesses. However, they do not accept the existence of a foundation consciousness but do accept six consciousnesses, as do other schools. They assert that the mental consciousness carries the latencies causing the appearance of the external world. Unlike Yogācārins, Yogācāra-Svātantrika Mādhyamikas negate the mind being truly existent, and like all other Mādhyamikas, they negate ultimate existence and true existence equally and completely for all phenomena, both perceived objects and the perceiving minds. They claim that the emptiness of subject and object being different substantial natures is the coarse selflessness of phenomena, and the emptiness of true existence of all phenomena is the subtle selflessness of phenomena.

One reason Yogācārins reject external objects is because they say if external objects existed, they would be composed of objectively real, indivisible or partless particles that are the ultimate constituents of matter. Since Yogācārins do not accept partless particles, they also reject external objects composed of them.

Mādhyamikas use a similar argument to negate the true existence of the mind. If the mind were truly existent, it would be composed of indivisible moments of consciousness, which would themselves be truly existent, self-enclosed entities independent from one another. If a moment of mind were partless, it could not be divided into a beginning, middle, and end. In that case, the end of one moment of mind could not connect with the beginning of the next moment of mind to form a continuum. If there were not a mental continuum, we would not be able to remember past events because two consecutive moments of the mindstream would be totally unrelated, just as one moment of Tom's mind and the next moment of Mary's mind are unrelated.

Mādhyamikas assert that the mind is empty of true existence because it depends on the collection of all the moments of mind that are its parts. By extending the reasoning that refutes indivisible parts to the entire external material world as well as the internal world of consciousness, Mādhyamikas undermine the basis for grasping and attachment to both external and internal phenomena.

In short, Yogācārins make a hierarchical distinction in which the reality of the external material phenomena is negated, but the reality of the truly existent internal subjective world of the mind is accepted. They draw this distinction because they assume that if something exists, it must be ultimately findable when subjected to critical analysis. When external matter turns out to be unfindable, they conclude that external matter does not exist at all; it is only an appearance. This appearance and the consciousness perceiving external phenomena arise from latencies on the foundation consciousness. Since the latencies arise due to causes, the basis from which they arise must be real. In this way, they accept consciousness to be truly existent.

From Nāgārjuna's perspective, since all phenomena exist by mere dependent designation, their existence can be accepted only in relative and relational terms. When any phenomenon—be it external or internal—is subjected to ultimate analysis searching for the true referent of its term and the essence of that phenomenon, they cannot be found. When we search for the true essence of external material objects, we cannot find anything that is ultimately the true referent of their names. Extending the same analysis to our internal world of experiences and mental states, Mādhyamikas do not find anything that is their true essence or that is the true referent of their terms. Since external objects and the internal mind both exist in terms of relational dependence and dependent designation, Mādhyamikas do not draw any ontological distinction between the reality or unreality of the external and internal worlds.

Foundation Consciousness

To review, to account for the transmission of karmic seeds and latencies from one life to the next, Yogācāra-Scripture Proponents assert a separate, truly existent foundation consciousness, in addition to the usual six consciousnesses. To substantiate this claim, they quote the *Dense Array Sūtra* (*Ghanavyūha Sūtra*), which says:[51]

> [Just as] land [is the basis of] the varieties [of all things grown],
> so the foundation consciousness [is the basis for saṃsāra and
> nirvāṇa].

In this view, the foundation consciousness is the self that truly exists. Both the foundation consciousness and the person are findable under ultimate analysis.

Prāsaṅgikas disagree, saying it is not necessary to assert a truly existent foundation consciousness to account for karma created in one life bringing its results in another. Rather than emphasizing karmic seeds as the carriers of the potency to bring results, Prāsaṅgikas assert the "having-ceased" of an action. Having-ceaseds are affirming negations that are impermanent and are carried by the mental consciousness or the mere I, both of which lack true existence.[52]

Prāsaṅgikas also refute Yogācārins' assertion that the mind is truly existent. Anything that is truly existent and has its own independent nature is not dependent on causes and conditions. Whatever does not depend on causes and conditions must be permanent; thus mind would be permanent and unchanging, which is definitely not the case.

The term *ālayavijñāna*, usually translated as "foundation consciousness," can also be translated as "mind basis-of-all." Prāsaṅgikas say that the Buddha explained a foundation consciousness as a skillful means to lead certain disciples on the path to realizing profound emptiness. However, the Buddha's intended meaning when he spoke of a "basis-of-all" was the emptiness of inherent existence. Existing everywhere and at all times, emptiness is the basis from which all phenomena arise. Being permanent, emptiness is not the cause of phenomena, yet it is still the basis for all existents in that all phenomena exist within emptiness and are inseparable from emptiness. They cannot exist without being empty.

Prāsaṅgikas say the term "basis-of-all" also indicates the mental consciousness because it is the foundation of both saṃsāra and nirvāṇa. In saṃsāra, the continuity of this non-truly existent mental consciousness goes from life to life. When the mind is completely purified and its excellent qualities fully enhanced, it becomes the omniscient mind of a buddha. In tantra, the innate clear light mind is called the "basis-of-all" for the same reason.

The Buddha's purpose for teaching a foundation consciousness was to allay the fears of those who confound emptiness with nonexistence. It is also a skillful means for leading people, who in their previous lives adhered to the idea of a permanent self or soul, on the path. Because a foundation consciousness sounds similar to what they believed in the past, they will adopt the Yogācāra view. Meditating on this will gradually mature their minds so in the future they will be more receptive to the Prāsaṅgikas' view of emptiness.

External Objects and Mind-Only

Yogācārins do not accept external objects and hold that latencies on the foundation consciousness or subtle mental consciousness are the cause of both the perceiving consciousness and perceived object. In that perspective, the consciousness and its object exist simultaneously, and thus the object is not the cause of the consciousness perceiving it; the latency is.

All other Buddhist systems except the Yogācāra and the Yogācāra-Svātantrika Madhyamaka say that sense objects, such as tables and sounds, are different natures from the consciousnesses perceiving them. Perception occurs from the assemblage of a sense faculty, sense object, and a previous moment of consciousness to produce the perceiving consciousness. The object is considered a cause of its perceiving consciousness because it causes the consciousness to be produced in its image. That is, when the aspect of the object appears to the consciousness, perception occurs. Since a cause and its effect cannot exist at the same time, the object exists an instant prior to the consciousness apprehending it. Nevertheless, in general, a pot, for example, is said to be present at the time the consciousness perceives it because there is not an intervening moment between the two. That is, the pot is present in the form of its next moment when the consciousness perceives it. Although we can say that the pot is present during both the first and second moments, it is not the exact same object because the first and second moments of the pot are different.[53]

Mādhyamikas assert that the Buddha's statement in the *Sūtra on the Ten Grounds*, "Similarly, the three realms are only mind," cannot be taken literally. The Buddha was not negating the existence of external objects but was refuting the existence of an external being, substance, or a permanent self being the creator of all existents and experiences. The *Descent into Laṅka Sūtra* says:[54]

> The person, continuum, and aggregates;
> likewise conditions and particles;
> the primal substance and Īśvara;
> I declare the creators to be mere minds.

In this passage, the Buddha says that an inherently existent person, mental continuum, mental and physical aggregates, conditions, particles, primal substance (*prakṛti*) asserted by the Sāṃkhya, or creator god (Īśvara) are not the creators of sentient beings and the world. As explained in the twelve links of dependent origination, the mind is the creator of our experience in that ignorance produces formative action, formative action produces consciousness, and so forth, showing the evolution of rebirth in saṃsāra.

In addition, mind-only indicates that between mind and matter, mind is foremost in establishing the three realms of existence. An ignorant mind produces the three realms of saṃsāra and a purified mind gives rise to nirvāṇa. Through transforming our minds—not by propitiating an external creator—peace and liberation are attained.

Three Natures

Prāsaṅgikas assert that the Buddha's *final, intended meaning* when he taught the three natures is this: The dependent nature includes all things that arise from causes and conditions. Being dependent arisings, they lack inherent existence. Inherent existence is the imaginary nature, which is falsely projected onto all dependent phenomena. The consummate nature—the final nature or mode of existence—is the emptiness of inherent existence. Here we see the difference between how Yogācārins and Prāsaṅgikas identify both the object of negation and the emptiness of all phenomena.

According to Prāsaṅgikas, the Buddha's *purpose* in teaching the three natures in the third turning of the Dharma wheel was that by understanding this teaching literally, disciples would realize that external objects existing separate from consciousness are imaginary and their true nature is nondual—that is, the object and perceiving consciousness arise from the same latency. In this way, their grasping truly existent external objects will diminish. As they meditate on this further, they will broaden the reasoning that rejects partless particles as components of external objects so that the same reasoning refutes partless moments of consciousness as components of the continuity of mind. Understanding that the mind depends on parts, they will realize that it too lacks true existence. In this way, the Buddha's purpose for teaching the three natures is to eventually lead disciples to the correct understanding of emptiness of true or inherent existence as propounded by the Prāsaṅgikas.

The logical inconsistencies of the three natures as posited by the Yogācārins are many. In *Realizing the Profound View*, we used many reasonings to disprove inherent and true existence. All these reasonings also apply here to show that the teaching on the three natures as understood by Yogācārins requires interpretation.

Summary

In summary, Yogācārins regard the following assertions as definitive based on the third Dharma wheel as explained in the *Sūtra Unraveling the Thought*, whereas Prāsaṅgikas claim they are interpretable based on the second Dharma wheel Perfection of Wisdom sūtras. In each case, we must investigate three factors: the Buddha's intended meaning, his purpose for giving that teaching, and the logical inconsistencies that follow from taking that teaching literally. In this way we will arrive at the definitive meaning of the Buddha's words. To put these succinctly:

1. There are no external objects. All phenomena are mind-only.
    - The Buddha's final, intended meaning of denying external objects is that all phenomena are posited by mind. Mind, not an external creator, is the principal creator of phenomena.
    - The Buddha's purpose in giving this teaching is to subdue attachment to objects of sight, sound, smell, taste, and touch in those sentient beings who have strong grasping and attachment to external objects.
    - The logical inconsistencies that follow from taking this teaching literally are that an unnecessary differentiation is made between the subject and object. Both subject and object should be either truly existent or non-truly existent. Neither subject nor object are truly existent because they are composed of parts and are dependently designated by term and concept.
2. There is a foundation consciousness (basis-of-all).
    - The Buddha's final, intended meaning is the emptiness of inherent existence, which is the basis or ultimate nature of all phenomena.
    - The Buddha's purpose in giving this teaching on the foundation consciousness is to allay the fears of those who confuse emptiness with nonexistence by providing a basis of transmission of karmic

seeds through the continuum of lives for those who are unable to understand the mere I as the carrier of karmic seeds and latencies.
- The logical inconsistencies that follow from taking this teaching literally are that although Yogācārins say the foundation consciousness is impermanent, by claiming it is truly existent, it seems very similar to the Sāṃkhya idea of a permanent primal substance that contains all causes.

3. All phenomena have three natures, as described in the *Sūtra Unraveling the Thought*.
    - The Buddha's final, intended meaning is that impermanent phenomena exist conventionally by being designated by terms and concepts, inherent existence is the imaginary nature, and the consummate nature is the emptiness of inherent existence.
    - The Buddha's purpose in giving this teaching is to overcome the fright of those who cannot understand that impermanent phenomena and emptiness can exist without being inherently existent.
    - The logical inconsistencies that follow from taking this teaching literally are that dependent phenomena and emptiness would exist inherently.
4. There are three final vehicles, as held by the Yogācāra-Scripture Proponents.
    - The Buddha's final, intended meaning is that there are three different vehicles that sentient beings can temporarily follow.
    - The Buddha's purpose in giving this teaching is to overcome the fear of those who cannot imagine completing a bodhisattva's collections of merit and wisdom for three countless great eons by temporarily giving them the alternative of becoming a Fundamental Vehicle arhat.
    - The logical inconsistencies that follow from taking this teaching literally are that the buddha nature would not exist in each sentient being and that not all sentient beings could become buddhas.
5. There are some beings who will never attain awakening (*icchantika*) because they lack the buddha element, as held by the Yogācāra-Scripture Proponents and propounded in the *Ornament of Mahāyāna Sūtras* (*Mahāyānasūtrālaṃkāra*).

- The Buddha's final intended meaning is that all obscurations can be eradicated because all beings have the buddha lineage. They will attain awakening upon the assembly of proper conditions.
- The Buddha's purpose for teaching this is to frighten those who are hostile toward the Mahāyāna by saying they will never attain liberation.
- The logical inconsistencies that follow from taking this teaching literally is that some obscurations are eternal and can never be eliminated. However, some scriptures such as the *Tathāgatagarbha Sūtra* and *Sūtra on the Lion's Roar of Queen Śrīmāla* (*Śrīmāladevi Sūtra*) affirm that all beings have the buddha lineage.

There are further differences between the Yogācāra and Prāsaṅgika tenets that highlight the diverse perspectives of these two systems. One involves the meaning of "to exist by its own character."

For Yogācārins, dependent phenomena and consummate phenomena exist by their own character, inherently exist, and ultimately exist. Existent imaginaries such as unconditioned space do not exist by their own character although they inherently exist. According to Prāsaṅgikas, all existents do not exist ultimately; none of them have a findable essence. Here it is helpful to understand the meaning of "existence by its own character" according to these systems.

The Meaning of Existence by Its Own Character

Yogācāra	Existence without being posited (imputed) by conception, existence without being posited in dependence on name and concept. Dependent phenomena and consummate phenomena exist by their own character. Imaginaries do not.
Svātantrika Madhyamaka	Existence without being imputed by the force of appearing to a nondefective mind. This mode of existence is rejected ultimately, but accepted conventionally.
Prāsaṅgika Madhyamaka	Existence from its own side without being merely imputed by conception; findable when sought by either conventional or ultimate analysis. Existence that does not depend on being merely imputed by term and concept. No phenomenon exists by its own character.

Yogācārins negate existence by its own character for imaginaries, but accept it conventionally for dependent and consummate natures. Svātantrikas affirm it conventionally for all phenomena, but reject it ultimately. Prāsaṅgikas negate it on all phenomena conventionally as well as ultimately.

In addition, do not get confused when Yogācāra says that dependent and consummate phenomena do not exist by their own character as the basis for terms and concepts, but they do exist by their own character. They exist by their own character, because if they didn't, they wouldn't exist at all. In other words, they have an independent essence. However, they do not exist by their own character as the basis for terms and concepts because their being the basis of terms and concepts is established only by those terms or concepts, not by their own independent character.

REFLECTION

1. Review the Yogācāra position on no external objects, foundation consciousness, three natures, three final vehicles, and the inability of some sentient beings to attain full awakening.
2. The Buddha made such statements as skillful means that correspond with the disposition, interest, and capacity of a specific audience. What was his final intended meaning of making each statement?
3. What was his purpose in making each statement? What are the logical inconsistencies if such statements were accepted as definitive? Exploring responses to these questions clarifies the Buddha's skill as a teacher. It also sharpens our ability to discern definitive and provisional teachings and increases our intelligence to discover the Buddha's actual point.

Although the Yogācāra system is not the final thought of the Buddha, exploring it can be helpful because it turns our minds to critically examine how perception operates and in what ways objects of perception exist ultimately and conventionally. In the sequence of tenet systems, Yogācāra is a bridge from Sautrāntika to Madhyamaka tenets in that it asserts a selflessness of phenomena whereas Sautrāntika does not. In addition, it challenges us to investigate more deeply how objects exist in relation to their perceiving consciousnesses, which draws us into the selflessness of phenomena. In this way, by studying and meditating according to the Yogācāra view, practitioners gradually can be led to the Madhyamaka view. In his *Essence of Eloquence*, Tsongkhapa says:

> In that way, in dependence on the mode of Mind Only, (1) the self and the mine of persons and (2) the distant and cut-off apprehended and apprehender (T. *gzung 'dzin rgyangs chad*), and so forth are realized with little difficulty as without inherent existence; when those—whose power of awareness is not small and whose effort is exceedingly great—examine that mind by whether it has a nature of one or many, they do not see an essence (T. *snying po*) ultimately, whereby they realize the mode of the Middle that has abandoned all extremes ultimately; Śāntarakṣita's *Ornament for the Middle* says:
>
> > Depending on Mind Only
> > The non-thingness of external objects will be known.
> > Depending on this [Middle Way] mode
> > That [mind] also is to be known as very selfless.

By depending on the Yogācāra system, practitioners will come to know the lack of self-sufficient substantial existence of the person; this is the subtle selflessness of persons for all non-Prāsaṅgika tenet systems. They will also realize the non-thingness—that is, the nonexistence—of external objects. According to our usual perception, there is an object "out there," distant and cut off from the subject, the perceiving mind "in here." This perception is mistaken and false. When we see a daisy, it appears to be an object out there growing in the garden, while our mind perceiving it is in here, inside us. Object and subject appear to be two distinct, unrelated entities. By meditating on the Yogācāra view that refutes the existence of external objects, we will understand that the subject and object arise from the same substantial cause—the latency on the foundation consciousness (or on the mental consciousness). This brings understanding that the subject (the perceiving mind) and object (the daisy) are mutually dependent; one cannot exist without the other. Then, when the mind is examined, it is found to be a dependent phenomenon and to lack ultimate and true existence, which is the view of the Middle Way.

A disciple with great intelligence who applies diligent effort will realize these two points without great difficulty. In this way, the Yogācāra view is a bridge to the Yogācāra-Svātantrika Madhyamaka view.

Now we will turn to the Sautrāntika-Svātantrika system and Prāsaṅgikas' response to it, which takes us a step closer to gaining the correct view of emptiness.

8 The Two Madhyamaka Schools

As a child I wanted to play a lot and was a lazy student. One of my first teachers warned my next teacher, "This boy is very naughty. Be careful or he may bully you!" My laziness lasted about thirteen years, and then two years before the geshe exams I began to study hard.

Due to the kindness of all my teachers I managed to learn. Some topics that other scholars find difficult are easy for me. This is because of familiarity with them in previous lives. Still, in this life I've had to exert effort in my practice, but this effort is joyous since my motivation is one of compassion and bodhicitta. Joy in our Dharma practice makes a huge difference. As the first Dalai Lama was actively dying, his preference was to be born in a land of suffering, not in a celestial realm. This inspires me, and thus I often pray like Śāntideva (BCA 10:55):

> For as long as space endures
> and as long as beings remain,
> so too will I abide
> to dispel the misery of the world.

With compassion for sentient beings, let's investigate the nature of reality to clear the clouds of ignorance and other defilements from our minds and, with wisdom and compassion, to be of ever greater benefit to sentient beings.

As a way of skillfully leading sentient beings to the correct view, the Buddha tailored his assertions regarding the existence of the self to the inclinations and capacities of a variety of disciples. In *Clear Words*, Candrakīrti explains (PP 357.3–4, 357.7–358.6):

> To turn away the inferior disciples who perform nonvirtuous actions from nonvirtue, the buddhas, the blessed ones, in some places designated—presented to the world—the self...
>
> Those who... perform virtuous actions, even by turning away from the nonvirtuous course of action, are not able to approach... the city of nirvāṇa, the peace that is without birth and death. To loosen the adherence to the view of a personal identity of those intermediate disciples, and to engender the desire for nirvāṇa, the buddhas, the blessed ones, who desire to show kindness to the disciples, also taught the absence of the self...
>
> To those superior disciples close to nirvāṇa, whose attachment to the self has disappeared and who are capable of immersing in the most profound truth of the meaning of the Lord of Sages' scriptures, the buddhas, having determined the specificities of [their] inclination, also taught that there is neither self nor no self.

Here Candrakīrti delineates three levels of disciples: inferior disciples who engage in many nonvirtuous actions, intermediate disciples who engage in virtuous actions but still adhere to the view of a personal identity, and superior disciples who are close to nirvāṇa. To the first group, the Buddha presents the existence of the self, without discussing the self's mode of existence, as in these verses in the Dhammapada (Dhp 160):

> The self is one's own protector,
> what other protector is there?
> By a self who is well-tamed,
> the wise obtain heaven.
>
> The self is one's own protector,
> what other protector is there?
> The self is the witness of
> one's own work and wrongdoing.

And the *King of Concentration Sūtra* says (SR 37.35):

> The nonvirtuous or virtuous action does not perish;
> what is done by the self will be experienced.
> Nor is there the transference of the actions and results,
> nor does one enjoy without a cause.

The primary concern of disciples of the first level is their own well-being in this and future lives. Thinking that there is a truly existent future self who will experience the results of their actions, these disciples are motivated to abandon misdeeds, purify negativities already created, and engage in virtuous actions. By practicing in this way, they advance to become intermediate disciples. At this point, they receive teachings that refute the existence of the self (SN 5:553, AN 4:200):

> Why now do you assume "a being"?
> Māra, that is your speculative view.
> This is a heap of sheer formations (aggregates):
> here no being is found.

> . . . the instructed ariya disciple . . . does not regard form as self, or self as possessing form, or form as in self, or self as in form.

Similarly, feelings, discriminations, miscellaneous factors, and consciousness are not to be regarded as self, the self should not be regarded as possessing the aggregates, the aggregates should not be regarded as in the self, nor the self as in the aggregates. By meditating on this presentation of selflessness, intermediate disciples negate the self of persons.

Having some insight into the selflessness of persons, these practitioners now progress to be superior disciples. The Buddha then presents the selflessness of phenomena and teaches them the subtlest view of emptiness as explained by the Prāsaṅgikas. This will enable them to attain the nirvāṇa of an arhat, and when combined with bodhicitta, this will result in buddhahood.

In the previous chapter, we clarified the Prāsaṅgika view by seeing how its assertions differ from those of the Yogācārins. In this chapter, the unique qualities of the Prāsaṅgika Madhyamaka view will be seen by contrasting it to the view of the Svātantrika Mādhyamikas, who, by asserting that on the conventional level phenomena inherently exist, still cling to inherent existence.

First, Some History

Before launching into the debate between the Svātantrika Mādhyamikas and the Prāsaṅgika Mādhyamikas regarding the object of negation and the type of reasoning used to refute it, having knowledge of the development of these two branches of Madhyamaka in Tibet will place that discussion in context.[55]

The founding master of the Madhyamaka school, Nāgārjuna, had many prominent followers such as Āryadeva, Buddhapālita, Aśvaghoṣa, Bhāvaviveka, Candrakīrti, Nāgabodhi, and Śākyamitra. Buddhapālita wrote an authoritative commentary on Nāgārjuna's *Treatise on the Middle Way* called *Buddhapālita*. Later Bhāvaviveka wrote *The Lamp of Wisdom*, a commentary on *Treatise on the Middle Way*, in which he criticized some aspects of Buddhapālita's reading of Nāgārjuna. In particular, he disagreed with Buddhapālita's extensive use of consequences to disprove incorrect assertions. Bhāvaviveka did not see himself as disagreeing with Nāgārjuna, but with Buddhapālita's interpretation of Nāgārjuna.

Later, in defense of Buddhapālita's interpretation of Nāgārjuna, Candrakīrti wrote *Clear Words*, an influential commentary on Nāgārjuna's *Treatise on the Middle Way*. Here he pointed out some philosophical differences between Buddhapālita's and Bhāvaviveka's interpretation of Nāgārjuna. One concerned when to affix "ultimately" in a refutation. A second difference concerned the subjects and other parts of a syllogism: Is it possible for two parties in a debate to have a shared perception of the subject that is ascertained by reliable cognizers and that is equally reliable and valid to both parties?

Many Buddhist scriptures and viewpoints entered Tibet and, among these, two became prominent: the epistemological approach of Dignāga and Dharmakīrti, who emphasized the importance of reliable cognizers, and the ontological approach of Nāgārjuna, who discussed emptiness (the ultimate object to be known) and conventional truths (objects that appear true to minds under the influence of ignorance). The tradition stemming from Dignāga's and Dharmakīrti's commentaries accepted the true existence of phenomena, whereas Nāgārjuna's followers refuted it. The Indian scholar-adepts Śāntarakṣita and Kamalaśīla, who were some of the first sages to bring Buddhism to Tibet, began to bring the epistemological and ontological teachings together in the Yogācāra-Svātantrika Madhyamaka tenet system, but more questions remained. Over time, the interpretations of Nāgārjuna's works by Buddhapālita, Bhāvaviveka, and Candrakīrti became influential in Tibet.

Candrakīrti is lauded in Tibet as the explicator of Nāgārjuna's view. According to contemporary scholars, his texts were not widely appreciated in India during his lifetime. They only became widely known in India in the eleventh century and in Tibet beginning in the twelfth century. Although present-day Tibetans mark the object of negation and logical approach to refuting it as the main issue on which the two Madhyamaka sub-schools disagreed, those who revived Candrakīrti's teachings in the Tibetan region early on, such as Chaba Chokyi Senge (1109–69) and Jayānanda (eleventh–twelfth centuries), focused on other issues.

These issues include: How can these two approaches enhance each other and their differences be reconciled? On what points are they incompatible? On which points are they similar? Figuring this out was one of the challenges Tibetan Buddhists faced early on, especially after Candrakīrti's texts were introduced to Tibet, and it continues to be debated today. This has given rise to questions such as: If conventional truths are mistaken, in what way do they exist? In what way are the minds cognizing them reliable? If all phenomena are empty of inherent existence and all appearances are mistaken, as Candrakīrti asserts, how can there be reliable cognizers? Can cognizers of conventional truths be reliable in any way, or can consciousnesses be reliable cognizers only with respect to inherently existent objects? Are reliable cognizers themselves inherently existent?

Questions also arose regarding the ultimate truth: It is said that emptiness is ineffable. In that case, is it perceivable? If so, by what consciousness? Can human consciousness know the ultimate or does its ineffability put it beyond the range of human consciousness? If it is not perceivable, how can it be a knowable object, an existent? Or is emptiness itself nonexistent?

Regarding the transformation process, questions arose: How does ordinary, mundane consciousness transform into a supramundane consciousness? Is this even possible if all mundane consciousnesses are mistaken?

Are mundane consciousnesses unreliable in all ways, through and through? How can a mistaken instrument ever perceive the ultimate truth, which is unmistaken and not erroneous?

Regarding the resultant buddhahood, people discussed: What is a buddha's nonabiding nirvāṇa? How can a buddha dwell in the pure sphere of emptiness with no appearance of conventionalities at all and at the same time benefit sentient beings? Since conventionalities are false, if they appear to a buddha's mind, doesn't that mean that a buddha has mistaken consciousness? Does consciousness cease at buddhahood and a buddha's awakened activities flow simply by the force of their intention?

As time went on, debates and discussions on these important points expanded. Teachers reached different conclusions on some of these points. However, all agreed that buddhas were omniscient regarding all conventional and ultimate truths and that they manifested in the worlds of sentient beings motivated by intense compassion. These topics are discussed on the debate ground and contemplated in meditation to this day. This chapter will not answer these questions but will draw you into investigating them.

No clear evidence has been found that the division of Madhyamaka into two branches existed in India. Among themselves, Indian Mādhyamikas debated which logical approach—syllogisms or consequences—were more effective in refuting others' views and establishing their own thesis. Tsongkhapa observed that a divergence regarding what constituted the object of negation lay behind the differences between Buddhapālita, who favored consequences, and Bhāvaviveka, who advocated for syllogisms.[56]

This points out another difference: how Buddhapālita and Bhāvaviveka define reliable cognizers and what they identify as a mistaken consciousness. Although these various differences between Buddhapālita and Bhāvaviveka seem to center around how to identify the object of negation, Candrakīrti did not explicitly say that when he wrote *Clear Words*. It was Tsongkhapa who pointed this out centuries later, and thereafter the Madhyamaka system was seen as having two branches, Svātantrika and Prāsaṅgika.

Differences between the Svātantrika and Prāsaṅgika Tenet Systems

The Madhyamaka tenet system is unified in its reliance on the Perfection of Wisdom sūtras. Svātantrikas and Prāsaṅgikas are both Mādhyamikas, but they differ on a number of points, the most important being the object of negation. Based on this difference, other points of disagreement arise: when to qualify a statement with "ultimately," the use of autonomous syllogisms and consequences in debate, whether two members in a debate must agree on commonly appearing objects, how to posit conventional truths, reliable cognizers and mistaken consciousness, and the presence or absence of apperception.

The debate between the Svātantrika and Prāsaṅgika position is very detailed and complex, and a general overview of the main issues is presented in this chapter. I encourage you to study the great treatises to learn more about this topic.

Possible Objects of Negation

Exploring how the two Madhyamaka schools assert the object of negation when meditating on selflessness and emptiness leads us to discuss how the two delineate what does exist. Before we get into this topic, it is helpful to know some terminology. Although remembering terminology may initially seem tedious, it will later prove helpful when we examine the assertions of the two Madhyamaka schools.

Prāsaṅgikas consider the following terms to be equivalent in meaning and assert that the following ways of existence are all hypothetical because it's impossible that anything exists in that way. Svātantrikas have different meanings for some of these terms because they assert that phenomena exist in those ways. The meaning of term 12 is according to the Prāsaṅgikas.

For Prāsaṅgikas, all these terms refer to hypothetical modes of existence that are apprehended by the innate and acquired ignorance that is the root of saṃsāra. Of the twelve links showing how we repeatedly take birth in saṃsāra, this is the first-link ignorance.[57] The pristine wisdom realizing emptiness that liberates us from saṃsāra apprehends the opposite of these erroneous modes of existence. For that reason, it has the power to eradicate the root ignorance and free us from both the afflictive and cognitive obscurations and stop saṃsāric rebirth.

It is important to note that when refuting inherent existence, we say if phenomena existed inherently, they would be permanent and independent of all other factors. However, being permanent or being independent of other factors is not the meaning of inherent existence. The mind grasping inherent existence does not also grasp phenomena as permanent or as existing independent of all other factors, because we do not innately grasp phenomena as existing in either of these ways. For example, we don't innately grasp the seed and the flower that grows from it as inherently different. When we plant the seed of a daisy, we say "I planted a daisy." That shows that we know there is a connection between the seed and the daisy, that they are not independent of each other.

The unwanted consequence of accepting inherent existence is that things would be permanent and independent of all other factors, which would render them unable to function. Because things that arise from causes and conditions function and change, they cannot exist inherently.

1. True existence (*satyasat*, T. *bden par yod pa*). Prāsaṅgika: Existence in which objects exist just as they appear—that is, they exist in their own right, with their own essence, without being merely imputed by name and concept. Svātantrika: Establishment as its own mode of abiding without being posited through the force of appearing to a nondefective awareness.
2. Ultimate existence (*paramārthasiddhi*, T. *don dam par grub pa*). Prāsaṅgika: Existence such that when the object is sought with ultimate analysis, it is found. Svātantrika: Existence by an object's own uncommon mode of subsistence without being posited by the force of appearing to a nondefective awareness.
3. Existence as its own reality (*samyaksiddhi*, T. *yang dag par grub pa*). Syn. true existence.
4. Existence as its own suchness (*tattvasiddhi*, T. *de kho na nyid du grub pa*). Syn. true existence.
5. Existence by its own character (*svalakṣaṇasiddhi*, T. *rang gi mtshan nyid kyis yod pa*). Prāsaṅgika: Existence without being merely imputed

by term and concept. Svātantrika: When the object is sought with ultimate analysis, it is findable. They assert phenomena exist by their own character conventionally.

6. Inherent existence (*svabhāvasiddhi*, T. *rang bzhin gyis grub pa*). Prāsaṅgika: Existence with its own self-powered nature able to set itself up. Svātantrika: Existence by the object's own mode of subsistence within its appearing to and being posited by a nondefective awareness. They assert phenomena inherently exist conventionally.
7. Existence from its own side (*svarūpasiddhi*, T. *rang ngos nas grub pa*). Prāsaṅgika: Existence such that the object designated is findable in its basis of designation before being imputed by conceptuality. Syn. self-instituting existence. Svātantrika: Existence that is findable by ultimate analysis. They assert phenomena exist from their own side conventionally.
8. Existence through its own power (*svairīsiddhi*, T. *rang dbang du grub pa*). Prāsaṅgika: Existence through the object's own unique mode of being, able to set itself up by its own entity. Svātantrika: They assert phenomena exist by their own power conventionally.
9. Objective existence (*visayasiddhi*, T. *yul ngos nas grub pa*, *yul steng nas grub pa*). Prāsaṅgika: Existence by its own nature without being posited through the force of conventional designations. Svātantrika: Phenomena objectively exist conventionally.
10. Existence by its own mode of subsistence (T. *rang gi sdod lugs kyi ngos nas grub pa*). Prāsaṅgika: Syn. inherent existence. Svātantrika: Phenomena exist by their own mode of subsistence conventionally.
11. Existing from the side of the basis of designation (T. *gdags gzhi' ngos nas grub pa*). Prāsaṅgika: Existing such that if the designated object is searched for, it is found either among the basis of designation, or as the collection of its parts, or as the collection of their former and later moments. Svātantrika: Phenomena exist from the side of the basis of designation conventionally.
12. Existing by being able to establish itself, self-instituting existence (T. *tshugs thub tu grub pa*). Prāsaṅgika: Not established through the force of terms and expressions, but existing in the object's basis of designation by its own entity.
13. Substantial existence (*dravyasat*, T. *rdzas su yod pa*). Prāsaṅgika: Able to

support itself without existing through the force of term and concept. Svātantrika: Certain phenomena substantially exist conventionally.[58]

Objects of Negation for Selflessness of Phenomena

	SVĀTANTRIKA	PRĀSAṄGIKA
Ultimate existence	✓	✓
Existence as its own suchness	✓	✓
Existence as its own reality	✓	✓
True existence	✓	✓
Existence by its own character[59]	Negated on the ultimate level but accepted on the conventional level	✓
Inherent existence	Negated on the ultimate level but accepted on the conventional level	✓
Existence from its own side	Negated on the ultimate level but accepted on the conventional level	✓

While both Svātantrikas and Prāsaṅgikas negate inherent existence, Svātantrikas negate it only on the ultimate level, whereas Prāsaṅgikas negate it both ultimately and conventionally. Svātantrikas follow Bhāvaviveka and accept inherent existence on the conventional level, whereas Prāsaṅgikas follow Buddhapālita and Candrakīrti and negate inherent existence across the board, both ultimately and conventionally.

The Object of Negation

Differences exist between the two Mādhyamikas in several areas, most prominently in how they assert the object of negation. This influences their assertions in other areas too—when to affix "ultimately," the existence or nonexistence of apperception, how they posit conventional truths, what constitutes the selflessness of persons and the selflessness of phenomena, and so forth. How, then, do these two systems identify the object of negation? We have covered the Prāsaṅgikas' view on this extensively in *Searching for the Self* and *Realizing the Profound View*, so in this chapter, we'll focus on how the Svātantrikas assert the object of negation.

Svātantrikas do not explicitly state their object of negation. However, by knowing their assertions about conventional existence, we can infer that the object of negation, ultimate existence, is the opposite of that. Their object of negation is also known through their example of a magician's conjuration of horses and elephants.

Kamalaśīla, in his *Illumination of the Middle Way*, says (SV 144):

> An awareness that mistakenly superimposes the opposite onto things that in reality are without entityness is called the "veiler" (*saṃvṛti*) because it obstructs [itself] from [perception of] suchness or because it veils [other awarenesses] from [perception of] suchness. As it says in the [*Descent into Laṅka*] *Sūtra*:
>
> > Things are produced conventionally;
> > ultimately they are without inherent existence.
> > That [consciousness] which is mistaken about what does not
> > inherently exist
> > is asserted to be a veiler of reality.
>
> Because [an awareness] arises from [true-grasping], all false things that [such an awareness] sees displayed by the [true-grasping as if they were truly established] are called "mere conventionalities." Moreover, that [true-grasping] arises through the maturation of beginningless latencies for error, whereby all living beings see [phenomena] displayed as if [they had] a true nature in reality. Therefore all entities of false things [that exist] through the power of those [sentient beings'] thoughts are said to only exist conventionally.

An awareness that mistakenly superimposes the opposite onto things that in reality are without entityness is the innate true-grasping that superimposes true existence and ultimate existence onto phenomena that lack them. That is, it superimposes the quality of existing by its own uncommon mode of existence without being posited by the force of appearing to a nondefective awareness—this is true existence, the object of negation in the selflessness of phenomena according to Svātantrikas. This ignorant mind obstructs itself and other awarenesses from seeing the ultimate mode of existence of persons and phenomena—the emptiness of true existence.

Because [an awareness] arises from [true-grasping], all false things that [such an awareness] sees displayed by the [true-grasping as if they were truly established] are called "mere conventionalities." True-grasping is a deeply-rooted conceptual consciousnesses in which phenomena appear to sentient beings to be truly existent. This appearance is false; because phenomena do not truly exist, they are mere conventionalities, not truly existent entities. The object of negation—true existence—does not appear to sense consciousnesses, only to thought consciousnesses. Jñānagarbha (eighth century) in his *Autocommentary on "Differentiation of the Two Truths"* says that truly existent arising and so forth do not appear when things appear to sense consciousnesses, and Kamalaśīla agrees in *Illumination of the Middle*. That the object of negation does not appear to sense consciousnesses is the basis of Svātantrikas' assertion that all the parts of a syllogism have a common appearance to all parties in a debate. Prāsaṅgikas disagree; this will be explained below.

Where does the true-grasping come from? It is beginningless and innate; it is passed from one life to the next by latencies, and in each life it causes phenomena to falsely appear to our minds as truly existent, even if our minds have not been influenced by incorrect philosophies.

Understanding how Svātantrikas assert conventional existence helps us to understand what they say doesn't exist ultimately. A conventionality has two qualities: (1) it is a phenomenon that exists by its own character—that is, it has its own uncommon mode of existence, and (2) it is posited by the force of appearing to a nondefective awareness. A nondefective awareness is either a sense or a mental consciousness that is free from superficial or deep causes of error.[60] Superficial causes of error include being in a moving vehicle, the angle of the light and other factors that produce reflections, pressing on our eye to cause the appearance of two moons, a cave that causes echoes, sleep leading to dreams, learning wrong views, and so on. Deep causes of error are innate factors such as true-grasping. To exist, an object that exists by its own character must appear to a correct awareness free from such impairments and be posited by that awareness. The people in holograms being real people, a face in the mirror being a real face, and the world being under the control of interplanetary beings do not meet the criteria for being conventional truths.

According to Svātantrikas, all phenomena exist through a combination of existing from the object's side and being posited from the subject's side. From the side of the object, things have their own character that make them what they are; from the side of the subject, things are posited by the force of appearing to a nondefective awareness. Both of those factors must be present. If something didn't exist from the object's side but were only posited from the subject's side, it would not be an existent. If just being posited from the subject's side were enough, then simply positing Santa Claus, the tooth fairy, or weapons of mass destruction in a certain place would mean those things existed. Calling a giraffe a grapefruit would make it one. Thus at the conventional level, the object must exist from its own side, inherently, with its own unique mode of existence that makes it what it is.

Existing from the subject's side means that it exists dependently, by the force of being posited by the nondefective awareness of a living being. "Posited" means it is established by a consciousness through appearing to it. Since the object exists inherently on the conventional level, the consciousness to which it appears must be unmistaken regarding its inherent existence. The nondefective awareness that posits phenomena can be either a conceptual thought or a nonconceptual perception. In both the cases, that awareness is not erroneous with regard to its apprehended object.

Ultimate existence (*paramārthasiddhi*), the object of negation, is the opposite: it is existence from the object's own side by its unique mode of being *without* being posited by the force of appearing to a nondefective awareness. Ultimate existence is equivalent to true existence (*satyasat*), existence as its own reality (*samyaksiddhi*), and existence as its own suchness (*tattvasiddhi*). They are negated both ultimately and conventionally. Conventional existence, on the other hand, is existence by being posited through the force of appearing to a nondefective awareness. On the conventional level, phenomena exist by their own character (*svalakṣaṇasiddhi*), exist inherently (*svabhāvasiddhi*), and exist from their own side (*svarūpasiddhi*).

REFLECTION

1. To understand why Svātantrikas assert that phenomena exist inherently on the conventional level, meditate on emptiness. After investigating how the I exists, you may have the sense that it lacks a findable essence; it is empty.
2. But part of your mind objects, saying that there must be something that really is you conventionally. If there weren't, then who is meditating, who creates karma, and who will experience the result of my actions?
3. Although you agree that phenomena exist by being designated, you still think there must be something from the side of the object that makes it what it is. If there weren't, then either things wouldn't exist at all or they would become whatever your thought imputes them to be. This is the appeal of the Svātantrika view: things are imputed but they must also have some degree of inherent existence conventionally.

Svātantrikas say that when searched for with ultimate analysis—analysis that investigates an object's deeper mode of existence, what an object really is—phenomena cannot be found; they do not have their own mode of subsistance and are empty of true existence. But because functioning things each have their own unique potential to bring their results, on the conventional level they must have some degree of inherent existence; otherwise any cause could produce any effect and any object could be called any name. For this reason, they assert that things exist by their own character but not *solely* by their own character, for they also need to be posited through the force of appearing to a nondefective awareness. They exist by being designated, but not solely by being designated. They must exist inherently, otherwise they would not exist. The appearance of inherent existence to the sense consciousnesses is not false, for things inherently exist on the conventional level, although on the ultimate level they do not exist inherently.

The analogy of a magic show conveys the meaning of "being posited by the force of appearing to a nondefective awareness." Although I personally haven't seen this, such magic shows must have been popular in ancient India because this example is frequently used in Buddhist texts. Each tenet system may explain this analogy slightly differently so that it demonstrates their particular tenets.

A magician applies a special salve to twigs and pebbles and also recites a mantra that casts a spell on the spectators' eyes. This causes the twigs and pebbles to appear to the spectators as real horses and elephants. The salve affects the twigs and pebbles and the mantra affects the twigs and pebbles as well as the visual faculties of the spectators and the magician. Three groups of people apprehend the appearance of horses and elephants differently.

To the spectators who have been influenced by the magician applying the salve and casting the mantra spell, the illusory horses and elephants appear vividly real: some people stand in awe of these huge animals, others are terrified of them, and some may wonder if they can purchase them to help move construction materials or if they can parade the animals at a village festival.

To the magician, the illusory horses and elephants also appear to be real animals. However, he knows that this appearance is false and that no horses and elephants are present. He neither desires to possess them nor fears them.

The third group consists of latecomers to the magic show, who know nothing about the salve and mantra and may not even know that a magician was present. Because these latecomers were not present when the spell was cast, their sense faculties are not influenced by the spell and they see only twigs and pebbles. For them, there are no signs of horses and elephants at all.

The twigs and pebbles represent phenomena without the superimposition of true existence. The *spectators* who see the horses and elephants and believe they are real represent ordinary sentient beings who have not realized emptiness and mistakenly believe the objects they perceive to be truly existent. They do not accept that the horses and elephants appear to a mistaken awareness but believe the basis of conjuring—the twigs and pebbles—to be objectively real horses and elephants. Similarly, to ordinary sentient beings who haven't realized emptiness, phenomena appear to exist objectively without being posited by appearing to an awareness. They are deceived and continue to cycle in saṃsāra because of this misconception.

The *magician* represents persons who have realized the view and āryas in the time of subsequent attainment who do not believe phenomena truly exist even though they appear to. The magician knows that the appearance of horses and elephants is due to his mistaken awareness and is a false appearances. Similarly, those who have realized the view of emptiness understand that the appearances of phenomena as existing objectively without being posited by the force of appearing to a nondefective awareness are only posited by a mistaken awareness.

The *latecomers* whose awarenesses aren't affected by salve and mantra are analogous to the ārya bodhisattvas in meditative equipoise directly perceiving emptiness and buddhas whose minds are free from both obscurations and have neither the false appearance of true existence nor true-grasping. Just as the latecomers have neither the appearance nor the conception (grasping) of horses and elephants, bodhisattvas in meditative equipoise on emptiness and buddhas have neither the appearance nor grasping of phenomena as truly existent. Buddhas have eliminated all appearances of truly existent things to their own minds. However, because they are omniscient and perceive whatever appears to sentient beings, they know the appearances of truly existent things that appear to sentient beings.

How does this analogy help us understand the Svātantrikas' assertion that ultimate existence—phenomena's existing by their own uncommon mode of existence without being posited by the force of appearing to a nondefective awareness—is the object of negation? The appearance of twigs and pebbles as horses and elephants arises in the minds of the spectators and the magician because their minds have been affected by the mantra spell. The mantra and the salve also affect the twigs and pebbles, giving them the extra, objective potential to appear as horses and elephants. Absent the effect of the salve and mantra on the twigs and pebbles and on the minds of the spectators and magician, there would be no appearance of horses and elephants. If the latecomers saw horses and elephants, theirs would be wrong consciousnesses that perceive animals where there are none.

The twigs and pebbles are an objective base for horses and elephants, but that alone isn't sufficient. They must appear to be horses and elephants to a reliable cognizer that posits them. They don't appear to be horses and elephants completely from their own side, even though they have their own uncommon mode of existence. Despite their possessing the extra, objective potential to be seen as horses and elephants due to the salve and mantra, they must also be posited as horses and elephants by appearing to a nondefective awareness. This emphasizes that to conventionally exist, two factors are necessary: the object existing by its own character or existing inherently, and its appearance to and positing by a nondefective awareness, which is either a sense or mental consciousness. If objects weren't posited by a correct awareness, they would be ultimately and truly existent, but that is the type of existence that is the object of negation when Svātantrikas meditate on the selflessness of phenomena.

REFLECTION

1. Review the analogy of how the spectators, magician, and latecomers relate to the conjured horses and elephants. How does it relate to how ordinary sentient beings, āryas in post-meditation time, āryas in meditative equipoise directly perceiving emptiness, and buddhas perceive phenomena?
2. Which of the three persons above are you?

Phenomena Exist Inherently on the Conventional Level

Bhāvaviveka did not explicitly state, "I assert inherent existence on the conventional level"; however, this can be inferred by examining passages in his texts and passages in Candrakīrti's refutation of his views.

Some of the evidence Tsongkhapa cited to show that Bhāvaviveka and Candrakīrti differed in how they defined the object of negation and that Bhāvaviveka accepted inherent existence conventionally is as follows:

- One Svātantrika text says, "Just as it appears, that is the nature," indicating that for the Svātantrikas, inherent existence appears to the sense consciousnesses and this appearance is not mistaken; it is the nature of phenomena. Since things exist inherently on the conventional level, the inherent existence appearing to the sense consciousnesses is not an object of negation.
- In *Blaze of Reasoning*, Bhāvaviveka's autocommentary on the *Heart of the Middle Way*, he says to another school's proponents who assert that consciousness is the self, that they are proving what is already

established for him: "We also actually impute the term 'self' to [the mental] consciousness conventionally" and "Because [the mental] consciousness takes rebirth, it is said to be the self" (FEW 41, n. #c).

- Bhāvaviveka's statements about commonly agreed-upon subjects and the use of autonomous syllogisms and consequences in *Lamp of (Nāgārjuna's) "Wisdom,"* his commentary on the *Treatise on the Middle Way.*
- Bhāvaviveka's statement when refuting the Yogācāra view in *Lamp of (Nāgārjuna's) "Wisdom"*: "If you say that the very nature of a construct—the mental and verbal expression 'form'—does not exist, then you are mistakenly denying things, for you are mistakenly denying mental and verbal expressions." To explain: Yogācārins say that imaginaries lack inherent existence because they are fabricated by concepts and terms and have no reality of their own. Bhāvaviveka says that if the Yogācārins are negating the inherent existence of the minds and terms that fabricate imaginaries, they are going too far—they are negating the existence of those dependent entities. This implies that he believes those dependent entities inherently exist on the conventional level.
- Candrakīrti's refutation in his *Autocommentary on the "Supplement"* where he says that in Bhāvaviveka's system, arising must be found in one of the four ways—specifically by conventionally arising from other. That is, Bhāvaviveka does not negate all four alternatives for refuting inherently existent arising (arising from self, other, both, and causelessly).
- Kamalaśīla says the *Sūtra Unraveling the Thought* establishes the definitive meaning, implying that he accepts that sūtra as a definitive sūtra. When commenting on this sūtra, Kamalaśīla also qualifies all the negations with "from the ultimate viewpoint" or "on the ultimate level," showing that he thinks the negation of inherent existence applies only on the ultimate level, not on the conventional level.

True existence, the main object of negation for Svātantrikas, is existence by its unique mode of being without being posited through the force of appearing to a nondefective awareness. It does not exist on either the conventional or ultimate level.

According to Svātantrikas, things appear to exist by their own character to sense consciousnesses, and they do exist in this way. But they also exist by being posited through the force of appearing to a nondefective awareness. Although Bhāvaviveka didn't explicitly say the object of negation—true existence and ultimate existence—don't appear to sense consciousnesses, many Tibetan scholars deduce this because he said that objects found by mistaken nonconceptual consciousnesses are not established—that they don't exist. Since he obviously holds that the subjects of syllogisms exist, he must hold that they are certified or realized by a nonmistaken consciousness.

The question then arises: What consciousnesses are nonmistaken regarding objects that are not apprehended by sense consciousnesses, such as subtle impermanence and dependent arising? It can't be conceptual consciousnesses, because they are mistaken regarding their appearing objects, conceptual appearances. Furthermore, the object of negation, true existence, appears to and is apprehended by conceptual consciousnesses. There are several views on this topic of debate, one being that yogic direct perceivers are the reliable cognizers that certify the existence of these objects.

Svātantrikas assert that impermanent phenomena depend on causes and conditions and all phenomena rely on their parts. Despite asserting that all phenomena arise dependently, they fail to understand that the appearance of inherent existence is mistaken and instead they accept it as accurate. The knowledge of the subtlest dependent arising—that phenomena exist by mere imputation—eludes them.

Although Yogācārins and Prāsaṅgikas have different objects of negation, they are similar in saying that their own object of negation appears to both sense and mental consciousnesses, and thus sense consciousnesses are mistaken. Svātantrikas, on the other hand, say the object of negation appears only to the mental consciousness and not to sense consciousnesses. Tsongkhapa explains:[61]

> Because of arising from that [consciousness grasping true existence], that which sees the display by a consciousness grasping true existence as if [objects] were truly established is a conceptual consciousness, not a sense consciousness. For Jñānagarbha's *Autocommentary on "Differentiation of the Two Truths"* explains

> that true [existence]—the object of negation—does not appear to sense consciousnesses.

Because Svātantrikas believe true existence does not appear to sense consciousnesses, they say that meditation on illusion-like appearances is done only for objects that appear to the mental consciousness. The sense that things truly exist and are findable under analysis without being posited by the force of appearing to a nondeceptive consciousness is incorrect. After ultimate analysis disproves this, things then appear as like illusions to the mental consciousness. Sense objects are seen as being illusion-like in that they appear truly existent to the conceptual consciousnesses thinking, imagining, or remembering them.

To bodhisattvas on the seventh ground and below, conventionalities that appear to the mental consciousness usually appear truly existent. Bodhisattvas on the eighth ground and above still have the appearance of true existence to their mental consciousness during times of subsequent attainment. Due to having familiarized their minds with emptiness in meditative equipoise, when phenomena appear to their mental consciousness during subsequent attainment, they are now known as false—that is, although they appear truly existent, they are known to be empty of true existence.

Conventional and Ultimate Existence

Similar to the other lower systems, Svātantrikas accept that what makes a cognizer reliable is its ability to ascertain a phenomenon that has a real nature, thus implying that they accept inherently existent phenomena. When a designated object is sought, it is found to exist in its basis of designation conventionally. If this were not so—that is, if phenomena lacked a defining nature or defining character conventionally and if they existed only by being imputed by mind—then anything could be designated anything. This chaotic situation would destroy conventional truths, making its proponents fall to the extreme of nihilism. Thus Svātantrikas assert that a person exists by its own character conventionally because it is findable among the aggregates when searched for with analytical wisdom. In *Blaze of Reasoning*, Bhāvaviveka says (FEW 41):

> We also actually impute the term "self" to [the mental] consciousness conventionally . . . because [the mental] consciousness takes rebirth, it is said that it is the self.

Similarly, all phenomena are inherently existent conventionally because they can be found when their basis of designation is analyzed. That is, if we analyze the basis of designation of an apple—its skin, pulp, seeds, and so forth—we will find something that is an apple, even though the apple depends on being posited by a nondefective awareness.

Seeing the difficulties in asserting existence by its own character, Prāsaṅgikas disagree with Svātantrikas and state that if things had even the slightest trace of inherent existence, there would be no need to impute them at all. As Buddhapālita observes in his commentary on the *Treatise on the Middle Way* (HSY 193):

> If something exists by way of its own entity, what would be the need for being posited dependently?

Thus the Prāsaṅgikas consider the Svātantrikas to be absolutists because they superimpose inherent existence on conventional objects and do not negate enough.

Furthermore, state the Prāsaṅgikas, if things existed inherently everyone would see each phenomenon's inherent nature with their sense consciousnesses and as a result would always agree on the attributes and functions of each object. This is clearly not the case. One person sees Joan as a doctor, another relates to her as a mother. One person sees Norman as handsome, while another does not. Some people say a person is guilty of a crime, others say he is innocent. The fact that phenomena lack inherent existence allows them to have different names and functions according to the situation and also means that people will not always agree on what something is and how it functions.

Because Svātantrikas assert inherent existence on the conventional level, they say an object can be found when sought in its basis of designation; a conventional consciousness looks for it and will find it. The mind seeking the designated object is an awareness analyzing a conventionality. However, according to Prāsaṅgikas, when a designated object is sought in its basis of designation, it is not found because it is totally free from inherent existence. For them, the mind seeking the designated object is a probing awareness analyzing the ultimate.

Therefore the two Madhyamaka schools have different definitions of ultimate analysis. What Prāsaṅgikas consider ultimate analysis—looking for an inherently existent object in an object—Svātantrikas consider conventional analysis, because they believe such inherent existence exists in the object. Svātantrikas say that ultimate analysis searches for an object that exists without being posited by appearing to a nondefective awareness. However, when someone searches for the person in the aggregates, she does not find an ultimately existent person, but she does find a conventional person that inherently exists. Similar to the other lower schools, Svātantrikas say that the name "person" is imputed on the aggregates and when we look in the aggregates, the person can be found. If it couldn't, it would be nonexistent, like a rabbit's horn.

Although Svātantrikas negate inherent existence ultimately, they accept it conventionally. What does it mean to accept inherent existence conventionally? Because things exist by being posited by the force of appearing to a nondefective consciousness, they exist conventionally. But ultimately, they are not inherently existent because they do not exist without being posited by the force of appearing to a nondefective awareness. According to Prāsaṅgikas, phenomena exist by being merely designated by name and concept. But for Svātantrikas, that is not sufficient. They must also appear to a nondefective awareness—that is, a mind that is reliable with respect to perceiving the inherent existence of the object. This nondefective awareness can be either a sense consciousness or mental consciousness. Appearing to a nondefective awareness means that in terms of its appearance as inherently existent, the object exists in the way it appears—that is, it appears inherently existent and it is inherently existent. Things appear inherently existent and the consciousness posits or establishes them as such. That is conventional existence according to Svātantrikas. However, if a Vaibhāṣika, for example, says that phenomena exist without being posited by the force of appearing to a nondefective awareness, that is going too far and would make phenomena ultimately existent. In other words, if they existed as their own reality, without being posited by consciousness, they would exist ultimately.

REFLECTION

1. How do Svātantrikas describe conventional existence?
2. Why do they negate inherent existence on the ultimate level?
3. Why do they accept inherent existence conventionally?

Like Prāsaṅgikas, Svātantrikas assert that to exist phenomena must be posited by term and concept, but unlike Prāsaṅgikas, Svātantrikas add another condition—they must also exist inherently. This means that conventionally the object has some inherent essence that exists from its own side such that it appears to a nondefective awareness positing it. On the other hand, Prāsaṅgikas claim that all phenomena are posited from the side of an awareness and do not exist at all from the side of the object. Although a suitable basis of designation is needed, it does not exist from its own side and there is nothing in the object that makes it what it is independent of the mind.

Someone may claim that Svātantrikas assert that all phenomena are merely designated by conceptuality. However, this is not correct because Svātantrikas say:

- All phenomena are not merely designated by conceptuality but exist from their own side.
- Although phenomena are posited by appearing to an awareness, it is not contradictory that they are not merely designated by terms and concepts and that they are also inherently existent.
- Phenomena are not merely designated by names because they exist from their own side.
- Cause, effect, and so on do not exist in the sense of being merely posited by the power of nominal conventions.

Whereas for Prāsaṅgikas, being designated by name and concept precludes true existence, for Svātantrikas it does not.

Sautrāntika-Svātantrikas assert that the object of negation does not appear to a sense consciousness and that whatever appears to sense consciousnesses that are unimpaired by superficial error exists conventionally. They do not see anything mistaken about our ordinary sense perceptions in general. What we see on a daily basis exists as it appears. Prāsaṅgikas disagree, saying our sense perceptions are mistaken in that the object of negation—inherent existence—appears to them. This is a very significant difference when we think about it.

Both Svātantrikas and Prāsaṅgikas seek to describe the basis, path, and result so that sentient beings can abandon saṃsāra and attain nirvāṇa. Although both are Mādhyamikas, they have different ways of doing this. According to Sautrāntika-Svātantrikas, objects exist "out there" and impinge on consciousness, which is "in here." They consider Prāsaṅgikas to be nihilists for asserting that objects are merely designated by mind. Prāsaṅgikas respond by saying that if ordinary consciousnesses are reliable in relation to their objects being inherently existent, Svātantrikas undercut the need to practice the path and realize ultimate truth because sentient beings' mundane consciousnesses would already know things as they are.

In the *Supplement* (6.34–36) and its autocommentary, Candrakīrti delineates four absurd consequences that would follow if what appears to our sense consciousness constitutes the conventional existence of objects. These four were explained in more depth in chapter 4 of *Realizing the Profound View*. To review:

1. An ārya's consciousness of meditative equipoise realizing emptiness, which knows things as they actually exist, would destroy phenomena because it does not perceive inherently existent phenomena. "Destroy" means something formerly existed and later ceases. In this case, if conventional phenomena existed inherently, they should appear and be established by an ārya's meditative equipoise on emptiness that knows them as they actually are. If they aren't, it would indicate that wisdom has destroyed them.
2. Veiled truths would be able to withstand ultimate analysis because their inherent existence could be found. For example, when we search for the ultimate existence of the person, if we found something that is the person, then the person could withstand ultimate analysis. However, the person is not found under ultimate analysis.
3. Ultimately established arising could not be refuted because sense consciousnesses to which things appear inherently existent would be reliable cognizers of the ultimate nature.

4. Phenomena would not be empty of their own inherent nature because they would exist as they appear. This contradicts the *Kāśyapa Chapter Sūtra* (*Kāśyapaparivarta*), where the Buddha said that ultimate truth is the emptiness of inherent existence and that form is not made empty by the realization of emptiness because form itself is empty.

For these reasons, all phenomena are empty of inherent existence, and liberation is possible only for those holding the Prāsaṅgika view. I reflect on these four absurd consequences almost daily to hone my discernment of the object of negation.

When we analyze how phenomena appear and if that appearance accords with how they exist, we find that our mind often tries to find something to grasp on to, something that really is the object. We think, "If things existed only by being merely designated, then our mind could invent anything, give it a name, and say it exists. Designation is useful, but there must be something from the side of the object that makes it what it is, otherwise there would be mass confusion in determining what an object is, what street we're on, and what city or town we're in. Things must exist by their own character."

In addition, we believe that our senses, when they are not impaired by superficial errors, are totally reliable regarding how their objects appear to exist. When we see a table, we are able to know it is a table because it has the quality of "tableness" inherent in it. The table doesn't appear to be a product of causes and conditions: it doesn't appear to exist only because its causes were present. It is simply there. There is something comforting about this view; it allows us not to challenge our sense perceptions and feel that the people and world around us are stable and predictable. But are they really? Is our understanding correct?

Prāsaṅgikas emphatically say no, that if there is even the tiniest bit of existence by its own character in an object, then it exists inherently and its intrinsic essence should be findable through ultimate analysis. However, when examined with ultimate analysis, such an essence cannot be found, and wisdom finds only its emptiness. Our unimpaired senses are reliable in terms of the conventional object—we know how to find a watermelon in the market—but they are mistaken in that the watermelon appears inherently existent although it isn't. Our unimpaired sense perception is both reliable and mistaken—reliable regarding the conventional identity of an object, but mistaken regarding its deeper mode of existence. Things still exist and function despite their false appearance, and we can still navigate our way on a daily basis despite having sense perceivers that are mistaken regarding their appearing objects.

This view makes sense to us for a while, until our old habit of feeling comfortable with grasping inherent existence returns and we find ourselves once more believing that things must have some essence from their own side. We may go back and forth like this for quite a while in meditation, until through repeated analysis, our wisdom strengthens to the point when it overpowers the grasping at inherent existence and plunges into emptiness, which brings actual peace to the mind.

REFLECTION

Since Svātantrikas assert inherent existence conventionally, they say that phenomena appear inherently existent to sentient beings' sense consciousnesses and these sense consciousnesses are reliable cognizers. Prāsaṅgikas reply that four absurd consequences arise if that is true. Contemplate these four:

1. An ārya's consciousness of meditative equipoise realizing emptiness would destroy phenomena.
2. Veiled truths could withstand ultimate analysis.
3. Ultimately established arising could not be refuted.
4. Phenomena would not be empty of their own inherent nature.

When to Affix "Ultimately"

The difference in the Svātantrikas' and Prāsaṅgikas' assertions regarding the object of negation in meditation on emptiness affects many of their other tenets—for example, when to affix "ultimately," how to posit conventional existence, the presence or absence of commonly appearing elements in a syllogism, the use of consequences and/or syllogisms to prove emptiness, and assertions regarding mistaken and erroneous cognizers, and so forth.

Some people incorrectly believe that since Svātantrika Mādhyamikas frequently add "ultimately" to the object of negation—saying "phenomena don't ultimately exist because they do not arise from self, other, both, and without causes"—and Prāsaṅgikas don't use "ultimately" as often, that this is the chief factor that differentiates them. There are cases where Prāsaṅgikas say that adding "ultimately" is important—for example, in the diamond slivers refutation. Here they assert that things do not arise "ultimately" in order to emphasize that although arising does not ultimately or inherently exist, it does exist conventionally. As Nāgārjuna said in the *Precious Garland* (RA 111):

> Similarly, this world, like a magical illusion,
> might seem to arise and disintegrate.
> But ultimately there is no arising
> or no disintegrating at all.

And Candrakīrti said in the *Supplement* (MMA 6.113):

> Just as these things—pots and so forth—do not exist in reality
> but do exist for worldly renown,
> so it is for all things.
> Thus it does not follow that they are like the child of a barren
> woman.

"Reality" means on the ultimate level, and "worldly renown" refers to conventional existence. In the verses above, Nāgārjuna and Candrakīrti speak from the Prāsaṅgika perspective: phenomena do not exist ultimately, but they do exist conventionally. The difference between Svātantrikas and Prāsaṅgikas is not whether they affix "ultimately" or "truly" to the predicate of the syllogism, but the fact that Svātantrikas accept inherent existence conventionally whereas Prāsaṅgikas do not. For this reason, Svātantrikas state that phenomena do not inherently exist on the ultimate level, but they do exist on the conventional level, whereas Prāsaṅgikas assert that phenomena do not inherently exist either ultimately or conventionally. For Prāsaṅgikas, ultimate existence, true existence, inherent existence, existing from its own side, and so forth are equivalent. Svātantrikas, however, differentiate them, refuting all ultimate existence and true existence whatsoever, but refuting inherent existence only ultimately and not conventionally.

Although Bhāvaviveka follows Nāgārjuna in rejecting ultimate existence, he accepts that phenomena are inherently existent. He maintains that although the person is dependent upon her physical and mental aggregates and is empty of true existence, in the final analysis we do find something—the mental consciousness—when we search for the true referent of the term "person." Thus Bhāvaviveka singles out the mental consciousness as the actual person that can be found under analysis. In this way, he rejects inherent existence on the ultimate level but accepts it conventionally. Candrakīrti, on the other hand, rejects inherent existence across the board.

The fact that Buddhapālita does not accept inherent existence even conventionally is evident in his works. When commenting on a passage in the *Treatise on the Middle Way*, which negates the fourfold arising—arising from self, other, both, and causelessly—Buddhapālita observes that if we subject ultimate or inherent arising to critical analysis, arising becomes untenable. Yet, since things do arise from causes and conditions, we can and must accept their existence on the conventional level. However, if phenomena existed inherently, we could simply accept that as their mode of existence; we would not need to posit them in dependence on their basis of designation. However, the fact that phenomena exist only in relation to other things means they do not exist inherently and must exist by being merely designated.

It is evident from Bhāvaviveka's writing that among the four modes of arising, he accepts arising from other, at least conventionally—that is, things arise from causes that are inherently distinct from themselves. On the other hand, Candrakīrti explicitly states in the *Supplement to "Treatise on the Middle Way"* that not only can the person not be found when searched for by reasoning analyzing the ultimate and does not inherently exist on the ultimate level, but the person also does not inherently exist on the conventional level.

For Svātantrikas, "not being posited by the force of appearing to a nondefective awareness" is the measure of ultimate existence. They assert inherent existence conventionally because they say that phenomena are not merely designated by term and concept but are posited conventionally by the force of appearing to a nondefective awareness. That is, there is something inherent about an object that makes it what it is. That inherent existence combined with being posited by mind is necessary for something to exist conventionally, according to them. It is this that the Prāsaṅgikas reject.

In short, there are two reasons why Svātantrikas say phenomena are not merely designated by thought. First, they must be established through the force of appearing to a nondefective awareness. Such an awareness is needed for things to be posited. Second, the object must inherently exist so that it can be designated as that particular object. For these reasons, Svātantrikas say phenomena *are designated by thought but are not merely designated by thought.* Only Prāsaṅgikas assert them to be merely designated by term and thought.

9 | Prāsaṅgikas' Response to Svātantrikas

Positing Conventional Phenomena

According to Prāsaṅgikas whatever is inherently existent should be able to set itself up with its own entity right with the object. But a car, for example, does not exist from its own side because it is not findable in its individual parts or in the collection of its parts. The car cannot set itself up with its own entity because the awareness of a car is cancelled when the parts are separated. If the car existed inherently, we should be able to see a car even when the car parts are scattered here and there, but we don't. A car cannot be found within its parts or completely separate from them.

Svātantrikas assert that there must be a car in the collection of parts, otherwise a car could not be found conventionally and there would be no way to posit it. This is because to posit an object, it must exist by its own character. They believe that when an imputed object such as a car is sought, it must be found in the collection or shape of parts or in the individual parts.

Prāsaṅgikas respond that the collection of parts can't be the car because if you put the parts in a pile, the collection of parts still exists but the car does not. If you say the shape of the parts is the car, that doesn't work either because the shape can't perform the function of a car.

Svātantrikas and Prāsaṅgikas both say all phenomena are posited through the force of appearing to a nondeceptive awareness, but they differ in the way they say phenomena are posited. The popular analogy used to illustrate this is seeing a mottled coiled rope in the corner of a dimly lit room. Immediately we think "snake" and designate "snake" on the rope and react with fear. However, the rope lacks the characteristics and function of a snake, so a snake is not established there. No matter how certain we may be that a snake is near us and no matter how much we may be terrified of it, there is no snake in the corner of the room.

How does positing snake on a rope differ from positing snake in dependence on the living being with a thin body that slithers along the ground? Clearly the name and concept of the rope being a snake is incorrect because the rope doesn't function as a snake and doesn't fulfill the definition of a snake.

But what about the process of designating "snake" to a mottled coiled rope and to a living being with a thin body that slithers along the ground? In both cases, the process is similar: conceptuality forms some sense data—in this case the color and shape of an object in the corner—into an object and gives it the name "snake." In both cases, there is nothing findable under ultimate analysis in the basis of designation that makes it a snake. There is nothing we can identify as a snake in either the individual parts of the rope or the collection of parts. Similarly, there is nothing we can identify as a snake in either the parts of that thin, slithering sentient being or in the collection of its parts. The skin isn't a snake, the insides aren't a snake, and its color and movement aren't a snake. When contemplating this example, we may be shocked because we believe a real snake is there, but just as a rope isn't a snake, a thin, slithering body isn't a snake. This gives us the feeling of what "merely designated" means. According to Prāsaṅgikas, all other phenomena exist in the same way, by being merely designated in dependence on a basis of designation.

Svātantrikas disagree, saying that since a consciousness apprehending a rope as a snake is erroneous, a snake perceived by that consciousness doesn't exist by its own character. But in general, since a sense consciousness perceiving a snake is nondeceptive, that snake must exist by its own character. The rope, on the other hand, is seen by a defective consciousness and also does not exist by its own character as a snake. Svātantrikas believe that to exist, an object must exist by its own character and be posited by a nondefective mind.

The debate continues as Prāsaṅgikas reply that the consciousness apprehending a rope as a snake and a consciousness apprehending a live snake as a snake are both mistaken with respect to their appearing objects in that both the rope-snake and the living snake mistakenly appear to be a snake that exists by its own character, right there in the basis of designation—which for one person is a mottled coiled rope and for another person is a thin, slithering body. However, a consciousness apprehending a rope as a snake doesn't have the support of a reliable cognizer because a rope is not renowned as a snake in the world. That supposed snake doesn't exist at all. But the thin, slithering, living body fulfills the three criteria for the conventional existence of a snake: (1) it is renowned as a snake in the world, (2) it is not discredited by another conventional reliable cognizer, and (3) it isn't damaged by a reasoning consciousness analyzing the ultimate. Therefore it exists, although it does not exist inherently.

Commonly Agreed-Upon Subjects and Autonomous Syllogisms

In the midst of studying philosophy, it can be helpful to hear stories about the sages whose works we are studying. In this light, I'd like to share one of the oral stories about Candrakīrti. Although we do not know if all the details are factual, these stories give us an idea about the interaction of various Buddhist sages in classical India. This particular story concerns Candrakīrti and Candragomin, who was a poet as well as a lay scholar-adept of the Yogācāra school.

Candrakīrti and Candragomin first met when Candrakīrti was debating and Candragomin, who was passing by, stopped to listen. When Candragomin remained standing, as was the custom when challenging someone to a debate, Candrakīrti assumed Candragomin wanted to debate him. They began talking, and when Candrakīrti learned that he was speaking to Candragomin, a famous lay scholar-adept, he asked Candragomin to accompany him in a procession. During the procession Candragomin composed a verse to Mañjuśrī, whose statue was behind Candrakīrti in the procession. Mañjuśrī was so moved that the statue turned to face Candragomin. But when Candragomin's chariot accidentally pulled ahead of Candrakīrti's, Candrakīrti thought Candragomin was filled with arrogance and challenged him to a debate to resolve which was the highest view—that of Yogācāra or Madhyamaka.

The debate, which lasted seven years, attracted a lot of attention among the populace. Since Candrakīrti couldn't win, he suspected that Candragomin had a secret debate tutor and followed him to a temple of Avalokiteśvara. From outside the temple, Candrakīrti watched a statue of the deity come to life and talk to Candragomin about the points Candrakīrti would bring up in the next debate. Candrakīrti barged into the temple, which caused Avalokiteśvara to become a statue once again. And that was the end of the debate. At a later time Candrakīrti, in a prayer to Avalokiteśvara, asked why he favored Candragomin, to which Avalokiteśvara replied, because Candrakīrti was already blessed by Mañjuśrī.

It is perplexing that Tāranātha, the famous Buddhist historian who told this story, would portray Candrakīrti in an unflattering way. Some people speculate that this stemmed from Tāranātha being a follower of Dolpopa's Great Madhyamaka, a view that Candrakīrti would have criticized had he been alive at that time.

Now, to return to our topic. Two common methodologies in debate are consequences and syllogisms. A consequence shows the faults of someone's current belief by presenting them with an absurd or contradictory result of that belief. A syllogism is a proof statement that lays out an argument why a certain position should be accepted. Although philosophical consequences and syllogisms have a specific formulation, don't think that you have to be a debater to use or understand them. We frequently use informal syllogisms and consequences in our lives when discussing issues with friends.

Take, for example, someone who asserts that the body is inherently existent because of being a dependent arising. To show him the pitfalls of this belief, we might state the consequence "the body is not a dependent arising because of existing inherently." According to the Prāsaṅgikas, upon hearing this, a sharp-faculty opponent who firmly believes that the body is a dependent arising would realize that the body cannot exist inherently since it is a dependent arising. Contradicting his belief that the body exists dependently would be sufficient to make him realize that the body isn't inherently existent.

Svātantrikas, on the other hand, would first use a consequence to dislodge the opponent's conviction that the body exists inherently. Then they would state a syllogism—"Consider the body, it is not inherently existent because it is a dependent arising"—to make the thesis clear and generate in the opponent's mind the conclusion that the body doesn't exist inherently.

In this way, one difference between Svātantrikas and Prāsaṅgikas is reflected in the methodology they use to establish emptiness. Following Nāgārjuna's example in the *Treatise on the Middle Way*, Buddhapālita and Candrakīrti predominantly use consequences (*prasaṅga*, T. *thal 'gyur*) to overcome opponents' wrong views—and their own wrong views. Their works are filled with the absurd consequences of holding various wrong views. Bhāvaviveka and his followers, on the other hand, mainly use syllogisms as their preferred form of argument. In particular, Bhāvaviveka claims that opponents' wrong views could and should be disproved using autonomous syllogisms (*svatantra-prayoga*, T. *rang rgyud kyi sbyor wa*). In analyzing Bhāvaviveka's preference for autonomous syllogisms, Tsongkhapa saw that it reflected a difference in what Bhāvaviveka posited as the object of negation.

Thus Tibetan scholars distinguish two principal camps among Nāgārjuna's followers: Svātantrika and Prāsaṅgika. The Svātantrika school (Autonomist) is so-called because it accepts autonomous syllogisms—syllogisms in which the subject, predicate, reason, and example are known by an unmistaken consciousness that also certifies their inherent existence. The Prāsaṅgika school (Consequentialists) derives its name because it predominantly uses consequences. Masters such as Jñānagarbha uphold Bhāvaviveka's position, in which, in addition to consequences, syllogisms are necessary, whereas Candrakīrti and Śāntideva follow Buddhapālita's preference for consequences. Although the difference in the names of these different Madhyamaka schools suggests that the most significant difference between them is whether they primarily rely on autonomous syllogisms or consequences when they debate, actually that is not the case. The principal point of difference between the two is that Svātantrikas accept inherent existence on the conventional level, whereas the Prāsaṅgikas do not.

Svātantrikas state that our ordinary sense perceptions are not mistaken; things appear to exist inherently and they do exist in that way. The object of negation—true existence—does not appear to sense consciousnesses; it only appears to the mental consciousness. Prāsaṅgikas claim that our sense perceptions are mistaken and things do not exist truly or inherently although they appear to. In short, Bhāvaviveka's emphasis on autonomous syllogisms derives from his belief that phenomena exist inherently. Thus the real issue that the Svātantrikas and Prāsaṅgikas differ on is not whether to use syllogisms or consequences in a debate but whether phenomena inherently exist or not.

What are autonomous syllogisms? When two parties debate, people generally assume that the subject and all the other elements of the syllogism must be commonly agreed upon and free from the influence of either side's view of how they exist. That is, both parties must have a common assumption of how the elements of the syllogism exist. Is this possible? Bhāvaviveka says it is. That is, he assumes that both parties in a debate accept that all parts of a syllogism exist by their own character and are established as existents by a reliable cognizer. On this basis, the two parties debate the thesis.

Buddhapālita and Candrakīrti, on the other hand, say that if this is done, then you have already accepted what you are trying to disprove in cases involving emptiness. In other words, if reliable cognizers of both parties in the debate apprehend the four parts of a syllogism as inherently existent, then they have already accepted inherent existence, which is precisely what that particular syllogism is designed to refute. If both parties have reliable cognizers that apprehend the parts of a syllogism as inherently existent, the parts of the syllogism would be commonly agreed upon to both the proponent and opponent of a debate. Both parties in the debate would cognize an inherently existent subject, predicate, reason, and example. In addition, the three criteria—the presence of the subject in the reason, the pervasion, and the counterpervasion—would exist objectively, so that the reason, by its own nature or inherently, would have the power to prove the thesis. Such a syllogism could not disprove inherent existence because it is founded upon the assumption that things inherently exist. Thus when Candrakīrti says, "We have no theses," he means that Prāsaṅgikas do not accept autonomous syllogisms where the elements of the proof statements are assumed to inherently exist.

Prāsaṅgika Mādhyamikas use syllogisms and accept that their purpose is to refute others' wrong theses. But they do not accept autonomous syllogisms because Prāsaṅgikas refute inherent existence. Someone who accepts autonomous syllogisms accepts that both parties agree there are reliable cognizers that are accurate in terms of establishing inherent existence. In *Clear Words*, Candrakīrti refutes this, saying that no cognizers can reliably establish inherent existence because inherent existence doesn't exist at all and can be refuted by reasoning. However, syllogisms in which the subject, predicate, reason, and so on are accepted as inherently existent cannot refute inherent existence. For this reason, Prāsaṅgikas do not accept commonly agreed upon parts of a syllogism that both parties have ascertained as inherently existent.

Although the lower systems and Prāsaṅgikas both posit form as the subject of a syllogism, there is no reliable cognizer that can establish form in a commonly agreed upon manner for both parties. Forms that are established by mistaken consciousnesses are not accepted by the lower systems, and forms that are established by nonmistaken consciousnesses are not accepted by Prāsaṅgikas. For Prāsaṅgikas, forms that are established by nonmistaken perceivers cannot be subjects of syllogisms even conventionally because such forms and all other conventional phenomena are established by mistaken conventional reliable cognizers. Only emptiness is established by a nonmistaken consciousness.

There are no commonly agreed upon objects, because if we say that a consciousness is mistaken with respect to the inherent existence of its appearing object and is a reliable cognizer, then we have already established the emptiness of inherent existence, and the lower schools would not agree with this. However, if we say that a consciousness that exists inherently and is not mistaken with respect to its appearing object is a reliable cognizer, then we have already established inherent existence and Prāsaṅgikas would not agree.

In refuting autonomous syllogisms, Prāsaṅgikas still accept the subject, predicate, reason, and example of a syllogism but not inherently existent ones, because there is no reliable cognizer that establishes these four as existing by their own character. Candrakīrti says that when two parties debate, the subject must be accepted by both parties at a level that is free from philosophical assertions. Both parties must share a notion of the subject's existence but not impute their philosophical views on it. Doing so would defeat the purpose of the debate. If from the outset the subject were commonly accepted as inherently existent, what would be the purpose of having either a syllogism or a consequence refuting inherent existence?

Candrakīrti emphasizes that there is no reliable cognizer establishing the subject of a syllogism as existing inherently. Why not? Ultimate analysis refutes inherent existence, and conventional reliable cognizers are mistaken in that objects appear to exist inherently, whereas they do not. That is, reasoning contradicts that the four elements of a syllogism exist inherently, but reasoning cannot disprove that they exist conventionally because it cannot refute nondefective conventional consciousnesses in anyone's mindstream. The parts of a syllogism, like everything else, exist nominally, but not under their own power. In the *Essence of Eloquence*, Tsongkhapa says that when essentialists and non-essentialists debate, there cannot be a commonly agreed-upon subject because the essentialists assume that any reliable cognizer of the subject would certify it as inherently existent, whereas the non-essentialists would presuppose that the subject lacks inherent existence and that any cognizer seeing it as inherently existent is mistaken. Therefore the four parts of a syllogism are not commonly agreed upon by both parties in a debate and there is no necessity that they be so.

Since there are no subjects (or other parts of a syllogism) that are commonly agreed upon by both parties of a debate, does this mean that there is no reliable reasoning at all? No, there are reliable syllogisms and consequences. According to Prāsaṅgikas, what is renowned to both parties can be used to form syllogisms and consequences without the two parties first agreeing on the ontological status of their parts.

Consequences and Syllogisms

Because Svātantrikas still seek a haven for an objective basis, they insist that the process of rational argument be more formal. They prefer to use syllogisms because organizing the parts of the syllogism in a certain way has the power to give rise to an inference. Because they believe that all conventionalities are inherently existent, both parties in the debate already have a commonly agreed-upon subject and they just debate whether the predicate is accurate or not.

Prāsaṅgikas respond that this criterion for debate is too stringent. Saying the dispute is only about the predicate and that the subject is not under dispute is too much to ask because the essentialists and non-essentialists do not agree on the ontological status of the subject. Essentialists assert an inherently existent subject, whereas Prāsaṅgikas assert a nominally existent subject. Prāsaṅgikas say it is unrealistic to think that there can be a clearcut syllogism with an undisputed subject and that after you give the predicate and reason, you simply wait for the logic to work out its rational course. This is not what happens. Therefore using a consequence is a better approach.

This does not require that the ontological status of the subject be mutually agreed upon. As long as the subject in general is accepted by the opponent, you can immediately proceed with the argument because your goal is to show inconsistency in the other's position.

Contrary to the lower schools, Prāsaṅgikas assert that it is not always necessary to employ a syllogism to help someone gain the right view. When those with sharp faculties are given a consequence, they realize the contradictions present in their wrong view and a correct understanding arises in their minds. For example, to someone who believes that the world is permanent Prāsaṅgikas say, "Consider the world, it is not a product because it is permanent." That person will feel uncomfortable because he also believes that the world is a product—it arose due to causes and conditions. However, he understands that the world couldn't be a product if it were permanent. In this way, he relinquishes his wrong view that the world is permanent and understands that it is impermanent.

To someone with more modest faculties, Prāsaṅgikas give the same consequence and follow it by a syllogism. By hearing the consequence, the person's wrong view that the world is permanent is loosened and doubt arises in their mind. Then when they hear the syllogism "Consider the world, it is impermanent because it is produced by causes," the correct understanding of the world's impermanence arises in them.

To give another example, if someone believes that phenomena are inherently existent, Prāsaṅgikas say, "The pot does not arise dependently because it inherently exists." The person who asserts inherent existence will be in a quandary because she also believes that the pot arises dependent on causes and conditions. If she has sharp faculties, this consequence alone will be sufficient for her to realize that the pot is not inherently existent. But if her faculties are more modest, Prāsaṅgikas follow this consequence with the syllogism "Consider the pot, it is not inherently existent because of being a dependent arising."[62]

Some people say that Prāsaṅgikas always use consequences, never syllogisms. This is incorrect. Depending on the person, sometimes an inference can arise in the mind by means of only a consequence; at other times both a consequence and a syllogism are needed. Prāsaṅgikas tailor their debate strategy according to the mentality of the person with whom they are speaking.

Bhāvaviveka, however, disagrees, saying that a consequence must be given first to loosen a person's wrong ideas. Then a syllogism is presented to help them gain the right view. Svātantrikas and the other lower schools may use absurd consequences, but they always follow them with a syllogism.

Svātantrikas' Main Reasonings

Both Svātantrikas and Prāsaṅgikas meditate on emptiness using a variety of reasonings. This is done to expand their understanding of emptiness and to see emptiness from several perspectives. Śāntarakṣita and Bhāvaviveka, the founders of the two branches of Svātantrika, each emphasize a particular reasoning.

Yogācāra-Svātantrikas' Main Reasoning

As the originator of the Yogācāra-Svātantrika doctrine, Śāntarakṣita expressed his preferred reasoning as the first verse of his *Ornament for the Middle Way* (SV 167):

> These things propounded by ourselves and others,
> because they lack in reality
> a nature of unity or plurality,
> do not inherently exist, like a reflection.

Written as a syllogism, this verse says: Consider these things propounded by ourselves and others, they do not inherently exist because they lack in reality a nature of unity or plurality, like a reflection. Since Śāntarakṣita says "in reality," it seems that he means things do inherently exist under ultimate analysis—that is, they do not inherently exist on the ultimate level. The inclusion of "in reality" could be taken as implying an acceptance of inherent existence on the conventional level. Dharmakīrti agrees. In *Pramāṇavārttika* he says (OE 25):

> Things upon definite investigation
> are without thingness (true existence) in reality,
> for they do not have a nature
> of being oneness or manyness.

And Āryadeva says (CŚ 344):

> When different things are examined
> none of them have oneness.
> Because there is no oneness
> there is no plurality either.

Whatever is truly existent must be either truly existent one (single) or truly existent many (plural). There are no other options for how something that is truly existent can exist because true existence means something has a fixed inherent nature. That nature must be either one thing or many things. If it is neither, then it must not be truly existent.

Although conventionally something can be one object and still have parts, this is not possible for truly existent things. If a truly existent one had parts—for example, if a truly existent table had parts—then the table and its parts would have to be identical in all aspects or the table and its parts would be different natures. If they were identical, either there would be one part because there is one table or many tables because there are many parts. Alternatively, if the table and its parts were truly different, they would be totally unrelated and wood and nails would not be parts of the table. Although the example here is a table, the object could be a consciousness or even a permanent object such as unconditioned space. You may want to refresh your memory by referring to similar arguments explained in chapters 1–3 of *Searching for the Self*.

You may also want to review chapter 2 of *The Foundation of Buddhist Practice* where syllogisms and the criteria for establishing a line of reasoning as correct are explained. In brief, according to classical Indian logic, an inference is generated by means of an accurate syllogism (*prayoga*), a statement with four parts:

1. The subject (*dharmin*) is the object being discussed. In this syllogism, the subject, *things propounded by ourselves and others*, is a broad category that contains both existent phenomena as well as nonexistents—from things asserted by other Buddhist systems, such as partless particles, to those asserted by non-Buddhist systems, such as a primal

substance, which does not exist. In our case, the subject could be a truly existent I.

2. The predicate (*sādhya dharma*) is what is to be proven about the subject—*do not truly exist.*
3. The reason (*liṅga*) is the reason that proves the thesis—*lacking in reality a nature of unity (oneness) or plurality* proves non-true existence.
4. The example (*sadṛṣṭānta*) is something that is easier to comprehend that helps us to understand the thesis. We can understand that a *reflection* is a falsity and does not truly exist.

The *thesis* of the syllogism is what is to be proven. It is formed by the subject and the predicate together—*things propounded by ourselves and others do not truly exist.*

There is a lot of debate about the form of this syllogism according to the rules by which syllogisms are made. These are complex and you will learn them later when you explore the topic of signs and reasonings.[63] Three criteria need to be satisfied for someone to gain an inferential realization of the meaning of a syllogism:

1. The *reason applies to the subject* (*pakṣadharma*) corresponds to the minor premise. This is the relationship between the subject and the reason, specifically that the reason is a property of the subject. In this syllogism the reason, lacking in reality a nature of oneness or plurality, applies to the subject, things propounded by ourselves and others. That is, all these things lack in reality being either one or a plurality. "One" or "oneness" means one thing; a plurality is many things. *In reality* means that the one and the plurality are truly existent.

Everything is either one or many. It seems that it would be easy to distinguish what is a single thing and what is a plurality until we actually start to do it. A sock is one, but is a pair one or many? Is a mala made of 108 beads one or many? Being *truly one* entails not being composed of parts because parts are many. Is there anything that is truly one indivisible unit? All impermanent things are composed of many parts.

Is there such a thing as a partless particle? If so, how could it join together with other partless particles to form a larger object without having a side that joined with a particle on its east and another side that joined with a particle on its west? Even the smallest moment of time has parts: a beginning, middle, and last part. Permanent objects also have parts: Emptiness consists of the emptiness of the person and the emptiness of phenomena. True cessation is composed of the true cessation of objects of abandonment on the path of seeing and the true cessation of objects of abandonment on the path of meditation.

Hindus believe in a creator god Īśvara who is said to be permanent and unitary. But can something that is permanent and one undivided entity create? If so, all the traits and factors that constitute Īśvara today must be exactly the same as those constituting Īśvara tomorrow. How could Īśvara create something, since creation entails the ceasing of what existed previously and the arising of something different in the future?

If there is nothing that is one or single, there can't be anything that is many because many is a collection of single items.

2. The *pervasion* (*anvayavyāpti*) corresponds to the major premise. This is the relationship between the reason and the predicate: Whatever is the reason is necessarily the predicate. Whatever lacks in reality a nature of unity or plurality necessarily does not truly exist. Since one and many are a dichotomy—that is, everything must be either one or many, there is no third possibility—whatever is not a truly existent one or many does not truly exist.

3. The *counterpervasion* (*vyatirekavyāpti*) corresponds to the contrapositive of the major premise. This is the relationship between the opposite of the predicate and the opposite of the reason: If something is not the predicate, it is necessarily not the reason. Whatever truly exists necessarily does not lack in reality a nature of unity or plurality.

Sautrāntika-Svātantrikas' Main Reasoning

As the originator of the Sautrāntika-Svātantrika school, Bhāvaviveka emphasizes a reasoning found in the third chapter of his *Essence of the Middle Way* (SV 160):

> Here, earth and so forth
> are not entities of the elements ultimately
> because of being produced
> and because of having causes, like a consciousness.

This stanza translates into the syllogism: Consider the earth and so forth, they are not entities of the elements ultimately because they are produced and because they have causes—for example, like a consciousness.

The earth and so forth refers to the subject of the syllogism, the four principal elements of earth, water, fire, and wind. The syllogism wants to prove the predicate: that the four elements are not entities of the elements ultimately. Bhāvaviveka is not denying that earth and so forth are the entities of the elements conventionally, he is denying that they are the entity of the elements ultimately. To be the entity of the elements ultimately, the elements would have to ultimately exist, which would entail their existing by their own uncommon mode of subsistence without being posited by the force of appearing to a nondefective awareness. They would have an independent essence that made them elements, an essence not dependent on consciousness. Two reasons to prove that they do not ultimately exist are given: *because they are produced* and *because they have causes*. *Like a consciousness* is the example.

The reason applies to the subject in that the four elements are produced and have causes. Just as a consciousness is produced by its causes—an observed-object condition, an empowering condition, and an immediately preceding condition—so too are the elements produced by their causes—the aggregation of the eight substantial particles (earth, water, fire, wind, form, odor, taste, and tangibility).

The pervasion is fulfilled because whatever is produced is not the entity of the elements ultimately and because whatever has causes is not the entity of the elements ultimately. Things that are produced and have causes exist dependently. They are not under their own power but depend on their causes and conditions—the three conditions mentioned above, the awareness that posits them—and their parts. This is contradictory to ultimate existence in which things exist independent of a nondefective awareness that posits them.

Similarly, the counterpervasion works: whatever is the entity of the elements ultimately is not produced and does not have causes. If something existed ultimately, it would be independent of the reliable cognizer that knows it. In fact it would exist without a reliable cognizer establishing it, and nothing exists in that way.

In short, nothing exists as the entity of the elements ultimately because nothing exists ultimately. And nothing exists ultimately because everything is posited by the force of appearing to a nondefective awareness.

REFLECTION

1. Set up the syllogism for the Yogācāra-Svātantrika's reasoning of not being one or many. Then check if the three criteria for a correct syllogism are present.
2. After you have understood the "mechanics" of the syllogism, think about it and make examples from your own experience, such as investigating if your body is one or many.
3. Do the same for the Sautrāntika-Svātantrika's reasoning, using being produced and having causes as the reason to prove that phenomena lack true existence. For the subject of the syllogism, use your car, body, or your self. This will bring the reasoning alive.

Ramifications of Differing Assertions

The table below summarizes the objects of negation and some of the key differences among the Madhyamaka schools regarding reliable cognizers.

Differences among the Madhyamaka Schools I

	YOGĀCĀRA-SVĀTANTRIKA	SAUTRĀNTIKA-SVĀTANTRIKA	PRĀSAṄGIKA
Object of negation for the coarse selflessness of persons	Permanent, unified, and independent self.	Permanent, unified, and independent self.	Self-sufficient substantially existent person.
Object of negation for the subtle selflessness of persons	Self-sufficient substantially existent person.	Self-sufficient substantially existent person.	Inherently existent person.
Object of negation for the selflessness of phenomena other than persons	True existence—existing without being posited by the force of appearing to a nondefective awareness—is the subtle self of phenomena. Form's emptiness of being a different nature from the reliable cognizer apprehending it is the coarse self of phenomena.	True existence—existing without being posited by the force of appearing to a nondefective awareness—is the self of phenomena.	Inherent existence—being findable under analysis in its basis of designation; existence with its own self-powered nature.
Afflictive obscurations	Grasping the coarse and subtle selves of persons, afflictions that arise from them, and their seeds.	Grasping the coarse and subtle selves of persons, afflictions that arise from them, and their seeds.	Grasping inherent existence of persons and phenomena, afflictions that arise from that, and their seeds.
Cognitive obscurations	Grasping subject and object being different substantial entities is coarse cognitive obscurations. Grasping true existence of phenomena and persons is subtle cognitive obscurations.	Grasping true existence of phenomena and persons.	Latencies of grasping inherent existence and the subtle dualistic appearance of inherent existence due to them.
When bodhisattvas abandon innate afflictive obscurations	At the end of the continuum of a sentient being.	At the time of attaining the eighth ground.	At the time of attaining the eighth ground.

When bodhisattvas begin to abandon cognitive obscurations	At the first ground (path of seeing).	At the first ground (path of seeing).	At the eighth ground.
When bodhisattvas abandon cognitive obscurations	At the end of the continuum of a sentient being.	At the end of the continuum of a sentient being.	At the end of the continuum of a sentient being.

Some points to note about the assertions of the tenet systems in the above table are as follows:

- Svātantrikas say the object of negation is true existence (as they define it) and self-grasping ignorance is the ignorance grasping true existence. Prāsaṅgikas say the object of negation is inherent existence and self-grasping ignorance is the ignorance grasping inherent existence. One ramification of these different views is the differing descriptions of afflictive obscurations and cognitive obscurations and their eradication on the path; another is the meaning of selflessness.
- Both the selflessness of a permanent, unified, and independent self and the selflessness of a self-sufficient substantially existent person apply to all phenomena, not only to the person. That is because all phenomena are empty of being objects used by these two kinds of nonexistent selves.
- The phrase "base of selflessness" refers to the object that is empty of a negated element. For both Svātantrika schools, the bases of both the coarse and subtle selflessness of persons is all phenomena. For Prāsaṅgikas, the base of the subtle selflessness of persons is only the person.
- The bases of the selflessness of phenomena for both Svātantrika schools is all phenomena, including persons, whereas the base of the selflessness of phenomena for the Prāsaṅgikas is all phenomena except persons.
- The objects of negation for both the selflessness of persons and the selflessness of phenomena are much subtler in the Prāsaṅgika school than in the two Svātantrika schools.
- Having adopted elements of the Yogācāra, the Yogācāra-Svātantrikas

assert a coarse and a subtle selflessness of phenomena, whereas the Sautrāntika-Svātantrikas and Prāsaṅgikas do not.

- The three Madhyamaka sub-schools have different assertions about how śrāvakas, solitary realizers, and bodhisattvas progress in the paths and grounds of their respective vehicles.
- Yogācāra-Svātantrikas say that śrāvakas realize the selflessness of a self-sufficient substantially existent person, traverse the paths of the eight approachers and abiders, overcome afflictive obscurations, and attain arhatship. In addition to the afflictive obscurations, solitary realizers also abandon the coarse cognitive obscurations—grasping subject and object as different substantial entities. Because of this, the schema of the eight approachers and abiders does not apply to solitary realizers. The obscurations abandoned by the śrāvakas and solitary realizers, as well as the selflessnesses that they realize, differ in subtlety.[64]
- Sautrāntika-Svātantrikas say śrāvakas and solitary realizers both realize the selflessness of persons but not the selflessness of phenomena, and they abandon the afflictive obscurations. They present the eight approachers and abiders for both śrāvakas and solitary realizers.
- Prāsaṅgikas say that śrāvakas and solitary realizers must realize the emptiness of inherent existence and eliminate afflictive obscurations, as they define them, to become arhats.
- Svātantrikas assert that the principal afflictive obscurations that prevent liberation center on what they call "afflictive ignorance"—the ignorance grasping a self-sufficient substantially existent person. They assert that cognitive obscurations include "unafflictive ignorance," which is the ignorance grasping true existence. Prāsaṅgikas include both types of ignorance in afflictive obscurations. Thus the unafflictive ignorance that Svātantrikas say is eliminated to become a buddha, Prāsaṅgikas say must also be eliminated to become an arhat. This, too, indicates the difference in subtlety in the two schools.
- Yogācāra-Svātantrikas say that bodhisattvas eliminate acquired afflictive obscurations and acquired cognitive obscurations when they attain the path of seeing. They simultaneously abandon progressive levels of innate afflictive obscurations and innate cognitive obscura-

tions during the path of meditation. The complete abandonment of both obscurations occurs simultaneously at buddhahood.

- Sautrāntika-Svātantrikas say that bodhisattvas eliminate acquired afflictive obscurations and acquired cognitive obscurations when they attain the path of seeing. They begin to simultaneously abandon innate afflictive obscurations and innate cognitive obscurations during the path of meditation. Bodhisattvas complete the abandonment of all innate afflictive obscurations at the beginning of the eighth ground and complete the abandonment of all innate cognitive obscurations at buddhahood.
- Prāsaṅgikas assert that bodhisattvas eliminate acquired afflictions and their seeds when they attain the path of seeing. They progressively eliminate all afflictive obscurations during the path of meditation, and all afflictive obscurations have been abandoned at the beginning of the eighth ground. The cognitive obscurations are eradicated during the three pure bodhisattva grounds, and all cognitive obscurations have been abandoned at buddhahood.

At first the details about each tenet system's objects of negation, objects of abandonment, and realizations gained may seem overwhelming, but when you become familiar with them, the differences in the three vehicles—śrāvaka, solitary realizer, and bodhisattva—become clearer. That, in addition to contemplating the benefits of bodhicitta, helps us determine which spiritual goal we aspire to attain—arhatship or buddhahood—and which vehicle to practice to accomplish it. Contemplating the differences in the tenet systems' statements concerning the object of negation challenges us to think about how persons and phenomena exist.

REFLECTION

1. If it existed, what would a self-sufficient substantially existent person be like?
2. Why is such a person nonexistent?

3. If they existed, what would truly existent phenomena be like according to Svātantrikas?
4. What would they be like according to Prāsaṅgikas?

Reliable Cognizers and Mistaken Consciousnesses

We spoke of reliable cognizers in chapter 2 of *The Foundation of Buddhist Practice*, which you may want to review. Now we will look specifically at the Svātantrika and Prāsaṅgika assertions of reliable cognizers in light of how they assert the object of negation.

As in all tenet systems, reliable cognizers are important. Being able to distinguish what exists from what doesn't and to discern a conventional truth from an ultimate truth depend on them. According to Svātantrikas, a conventional truth is an object that is realized dualistically by a conventional reliable cognizer—that is, by a direct perceiver or an inferential cognizer not affected by an internal or external cause of error. This awareness is not erroneous with respect to its apprehended object. An ultimate truth is an object found by a reliable reasoning consciousness analyzing the ultimate. An ultimate truth, such as emptiness, is realized nondualistically by an unpolluted awareness—the pristine wisdom of meditative equipoise.

According to Prāsaṅgikas, a conventional truth is an object found by a conventional reliable cognizer perceiving a false knowable object. An ultimate truth is an object with respect to which a reasoning consciousness becomes a reliable cognizer distinguishing the ultimate and which is found by that reliable cognizer.

What are the qualities of a reliable cognizer? What is the meaning of "erroneous" and "mistaken" consciousnesses? Svātantrikas state that reliable cognizers are reliable and unmistaken with respect to the inherent existence of their object. For example, a direct perceiver, such as a visual consciousness apprehending blue, is not mistaken with respect to its appearing object—inherently existent blue—because blue exists inherently the way it appears to. A conceptual reliable cognizer is not erroneous regarding the inherent existence of its apprehended and conceived objects, even though it is mistaken with respect to its appearing object because the conceptual appearance of the object appears to be mixed with the actual object. For example, a conception grasping inherently existent sound is not erroneous because inherently existent sound exists.

According to Prāsaṅgikas, all conventional reliable cognizers of sentient beings—be they direct or conceptual—are mistaken because inherent existence appears to them. Only āryas' meditative equipoise that directly perceives emptiness and the unmistaken omniscience of a buddha lack the appearance of inherent existence and are nonmistaken.[65] Sentient beings' nonmistaken consciousnesses do not apprehend conventionalities, such as forms. They do not take as existent things that are not reality, and only emptiness is reality because only emptiness exists as it appears to the principal consciousness that knows it—a direct perceiver of emptiness. Conventionalities are not established by nonmistaken consciousnesses whose object is reality. None of the four reliable cognizers (sense direct perceivers, mental direct perceivers, yogic direct perceivers, and inferential cognizers) establish inherently existent objects.

Svātantrikas say that their object of negation, true existence, does not appear to sense consciousnesses. Although inherent existence appears to sense consciousness, they don't consider that to be mistaken because they assert that conventionally, things exist inherently. In addition, Sautrāntika-Svātantrikas believe that if a sense consciousness is mistaken with respect to its appearing object, it is necessarily erroneous. Prāsaṅgikas claim that their object of negation, inherent existence, appears to both sense and mental consciousnesses—except to mental consciousnesses that directly perceive emptiness—but inherent existence does not exist either ultimately or conventionally. The consciousness to which inherently existent red appears is mistaken because red does not exist inherently as it appears to. Furthermore, if a consciousness is mistaken, it is not necessarily erroneous because a nondefective visual consciousness perceiving red is not erroneous; it correctly cognizes its apprehended object, red.

Of the two main subdivisions of the Svātantrika school, Yogācāra-Svātantrika agrees with Yogācāra in asserting that there are no external objects and that all phenomena are the same nature as the mind cognizing them because they arise from the same substantial cause, a latency on the mind. The appearance of things as separate entities from the reliable cognizer that knows them is a false appearance.

Differences among the Madhyamaka Schools II

	YOGĀCĀRA-SVĀTANTRIKA	SAUTRĀNTIKA-SVĀTANTRIKA	PRĀSAṄGIKA
Reliable cognizers	Reliable cognizers are unmistaken with respect to the inherent existence of their object.	Reliable cognizers are unmistaken with respect to the inherent existence of their object.	All reliable cognizers of sentient beings, except meditative equipoise directly realizing emptiness, are mistaken because their objects appear to inherently exist, whereas they do not.
Object of negation's appearance to sense consciousness	The coarse object of negation—form's being a different nature from the reliable cognizer apprehending it—appears to sense consciousnesses. True existence does not appear to sense consciousnesses.	The object of negation, true existence, does not appear to sense consciousnesses.	The object of negation, inherent existence, appears to sense consciousnesses.
Sense consciousnesses being mistaken and/or erroneous	A sense consciousness that is mistaken is not necessarily erroneous (e.g., the visual consciousness apprehending blue as a separate entity from its perceiving consciousness).	A sense consciousness that is mistaken is necessarily erroneous.	A sense consciousness that is mistaken is not necessarily erroneous.
Apperception	It is a reliable cognizer.	Not accepted.	Not accepted.
Accept foundation consciousness and afflicted consciousness	No	No	No
Accept external objects	No	Yes	Yes

Points to note about the assertions of the Yogācāra-Svātantrika, Sautrāntika-Svātantrika, and Prāsaṅgika in the above:

- Svātantrikas state that phenomena exist from their own side as long as they are posited by appearing to an undeceptive awareness; that is, their appearance to sense consciousness is not false. In his *Essence of Eloquence*, Tsongkhapa quotes Jñānagarbha as saying, "As things appear, that is their nature." Things appear to exist from their own side; this appearance is accurate.
- Prāsaṅgikas state that things do not exist as they appear because things appear inherently existent when in fact they are not. Inherent existence is a false appearance to both sense and mental consciousnesses. If things existed inherently as they appear, there would be no point in designating them because inherently existent phenomena do not depend on any other factors, such as being designated by term and concept. If the tree existed inherently as it appears to, that would be the tree's ultimate nature, and our sense consciousnesses would know the ultimate nature. In that case, practicing the path would be useless. If phenomena existed objectively, they would not depend on causes and conditions or parts. Crops could grow without planting seeds; a car would exist without being composed of parts such as an engine, wheels, and so on.
- Here we can see the significant difference between how Svātantrikas and Prāsaṅgikas claim phenomena exist, and by extension what the object of negation that is the opposite of that is.
- Like Yogācārins, Yogācāra-Svātantrikas also assert apperception (*svasaṃvedana*), a consciousness that is simultaneous with and nondualistically aware of the consciousness it observes and experiences. It is one nature with the consciousness it observes and functions to enable us to remember cognizing an object.[66]
- Yogācāra-Svātantrikas differ from Yogācārins in that they do not assert that the mind is truly existent. Nor do they assert a foundation consciousness (the eighth consciousness) or an afflicted consciousness (the seventh consciousness). Instead, they state that the mental consciousness carries the karmic seeds and the latencies that create the appearance of the external world. Similarly, Sautrāntika-Svātantrikas

do not accept a foundation consciousness, the afflicted consciousness, or apperception, but they accept external objects and assert that they exist by their own character conventionally.

- Yogācāra-Svātantrika Mādhyamikas such as Śāntarakṣita and Kamalaśīla believe that sense consciousnesses apprehending forms apprehend them as inherently existent. Those consciousnesses are not mistaken with respect to forms' inherent existence, because they assert inherent existence conventionally.
- Like Yogācārins, Yogācāra-Svātantrikas negate the existence of external objects that are different entities from the consciousnesses perceiving them. Sense consciousnesses are mistaken because their objects appear dualistically in that they appear to be a different entity from the consciousness apprehending them. However, regarding that part of the appearance that is the appearance of inherent existence, they are not mistaken because phenomena do exist inherently on the conventional level. Similarly, on the conventional level grasping inherent existence is not erroneous regarding its apprehended object.

The Import of These Differences

We have seen that the difference in assertions regarding the object of negation between the Svātantrikas and Prāsaṅgikas has many ramifications on the assertions these two schools make about other topics. But why is this important?

To attain full awakening, we must actualize the four bodhisattva paths in sequence. The fifth path, the Mahāyāna path of no-more-learning in which the two buddha bodies that characterize buddhahood have been attained, is a buddha path. It is our goal that will enable us to benefit all sentient beings most effectively. To attain this, we must remove the innate afflictive obscurations and cognitive obscurations by letting our minds dwell in single-pointed meditative equipoise on the emptiness of inherent existence for long periods of time on the fourth path, the path of meditation. This depends on gaining the direct, nonconceptual realization of the emptiness of inherent existence that marks the beginning of the third path, the path of seeing. To have this realization depends on first gaining the conceptual realization of the emptiness of inherent existence that is the union of serenity and insight and that marks the commencement of the second path, the path of preparation. Without having the correct view of the ultimate truth, entering this second path is not possible. The proponents of the lower schools lack this extremely refined view of the ultimate nature.

Strongly holding an incorrect or incomplete notion of emptiness, as proponents of the lower tenet schools do, impedes us from understanding the correct view conceptually, let alone realizing it directly. Similarly, people who have no idea of the meaning of the emptiness of inherent existence cannot spontaneously realize it in meditation. Before being able to realize the emptiness of inherent existence either conceptually or directly, people must first relinquish their limited tenets and gain some knowledge of the correct view.

Proponents of the lower schools may realize the selflessness of persons according to the assertions of their own school—for example, realizing the lack of a self-sufficient substantially existent person. However, they do not have the full correct view and cannot enter the path of preparation of the śrāvaka or solitary realizer vehicles, let alone the path of preparation of the bodhisattva vehicle. Although Yogācārins assert a selflessness of phenomena, it is not the emptiness of inherent existence. Although Svātantrikas negate inherent existence on the ultimate level, they accept it conventionally, and thus they too lack the correct view. Even if they attain meditative equipoise on the emptiness of true existence, according to their own definition of the emptiness of true existence, they have not realized the emptiness of true existence and inherent existence according to the Prāsaṅgika meaning of these terms. Even though they may have generated bodhicitta, serenity, samādhi, and some degree of wisdom, and even though they may meditate for eons on tantric deities, they will not be able to attain even the second bodhisattva path. Nor will they be able to abandon completely the acquired afflictions, let alone abandon the subtle innate afflictions and the cognitive obscurations and attain the full awakening of buddhahood.

To avoid taking detours in our practice and spending a lot of time meditating on a view that, although accurate in a coarse sense, is not the subtle correct view of the ultimate nature, in addition to generating bodhicitta we should put effort into understanding the highest view, the emptiness of inherent existence. Having done that, we must familiarize ourselves with it and gain the union of serenity and insight on it, followed by the direct realization of it. In that way, our journey to awakening will not be circuitous.

Conclusion

This complex discussion about the object of negation and the meaning of emptiness indicates a simple point: the way in which we perceive persons and phenomena does not accord with the way they exist. Nevertheless, our experience affirms the fact that things do exist. We touch something, we get hurt, we experience pleasure, eating satisfies our hunger, drinking water quenches our thirst, and so on. We are not disputing that phenomena exist.

In the Perfection of Wisdom sūtras, the Buddha enumerated extensive lists of phenomena: afflictive phenomena—the five aggregates, sensory sources, and so forth—as well as purified phenomena such as the thirty-seven harmonies with awakening and the five paths. What would be the purpose of doing this if he thought these things were nonexistent? If the doctrine of emptiness denied their existence, there would be no point in explaining virtuous and nonvirtuous karma, bodhicitta, or any other teaching. Because—not despite the fact that—phenomena lack inherent existence, they exist conventionally. Without being empty, phenomena could not exist; they would exist inherently, which would mean that they wouldn't depend on any other factors. That would demolish the functioning of causes and conditions. But things exist dependently, so they must lack inherent existence.

Since things do exist, why don't we leave them alone? Why should we go through such complicated arguments and analyses trying to understand their actual mode of existence? Because we seek to eliminate our own and others' duḥkha.

We must make sure that our Dharma practice is aimed at eradicating duḥkha and its causes. In the *King of Concentration Sūtra*, the Buddha says that although some people enter deep meditative absorption, it does not quell their self-grasping. In our own case, we may recite mantras and visualize deities, but by themselves these do not counter our underlying erroneous belief in inherent existence. Of course, someone who is an advanced tantric practitioner knows that the understanding of emptiness is built into deity yoga. However, for people who neglect this aspect of tantric sadhanas, their visualizing deities and reciting mantras may reinforce their grasping inherent existence instead of subduing it.

Simply wishing or praying that our self-grasping ignorance vanish does not make that happen. We must cultivate a perspective that directly opposes the way in which this erroneous consciousness grasps persons and phenomena. Only by cultivating this opposing view can we begin to diminish its force.

Please do not underestimate the importance of doing this. When we observe our own experience, we know that when strong disturbing emotions arise, they make us unhappy and impel us to act in ways that bring unhappiness to others. We know there are also occasions when such negative emotions are not manifest in us. Comparing the two states of mind—one in which a disturbing emotion is manifest and one in which it isn't—we see a big difference. When a disturbing emotion is present, underlying it is a belief that the object has a concrete, objective quality of beauty or ugliness, making it appear as inherently desirable or inherently undesirable. Corresponding to the quality we perceive in the object, we react with attachment or hostility.

However, when manifest afflictions are not present in our mind, although we may still apprehend the things around us, we don't grasp an inherent or objective quality in them. As we observe this in our own experience, we will begin to appreciate the significance of developing an understanding of emptiness. It has direct practical application in our lives by subduing our afflictions and thus our duḥkha.

REFLECTION

1. Why is studying the tenets of the other Buddhist systems important?
2. What are the disadvantages of not correctly identifying the object of negation?
3. Why is employing reasoning and logic crucial if we want to attain full awakening?

10 | Unique Explanations of the Prāsaṅgikas

STUDYING AND THINKING about emptiness requires a lot of mental energy, yet it is very stimulating and monastics often stay up late at night discussing and debating. However, I've become rather lazy of late. A political leader I got to know in Arunachal Pradesh once asked me how long I slept the previous night, and I told him I had slept nine hours and had awakened at 3 a.m. to meditate and sharpen my mind so I could better cheat people. The politician laughed and retorted that since he had slept only six hours, he obviously wasn't sufficiently well equipped to cheat people!

If we neglect to study and contemplate emptiness, we cheat ourselves, but if we debate it in pursuit of a good reputation, our corrupt motivation may make us cheat others. As we now turn to learn about Prāsaṅgikas' unique explanation, may we always check our motivation to ensure it is imbued with compassion and then arouse joyous effort to familiarize our mind with the notion of emptiness.

Prāsaṅgikas' Unique Explanations

Much of the Prāsaṅgikas' critique of the essentialists involves questioning their metaphysical postulations, such as apperception and foundation consciousness. In a world that is empty of inherent existence, such conceptual constructs are not necessary to explain the everyday functioning of things. Prāsaṅgikas do not propose an alternative metaphysical theory of reality, but instead give an account of everyday experience that is accurate within a conventional framework. Thus Prāsaṅgikas do not assert unnecessary metaphysical entities, they simply give unique explanations of conventional existence that rest on the fact that everything and everyone arises dependently and lacks inherent existence. This unique way of accounting for everyday occurrences does not require metaphysical arguments and is closer to the way that conventional language operates. In short, Prāsaṅgikas realize that conventional truths cannot be pinpointed, that language is fluid and relative, and that holding rigid concepts does not accord with reality.

Prāsaṅgikas have many assertions that are not shared by non-Buddhists or by Buddhist essentialists. These unique positions arise because Prāsaṅgikas reject inherent existence even on the conventional level, and this, in turn, affects their explanation of many conventional phenomena. The key point that differentiates Prāsaṅgikas from other tenet systems is that they establish causality and the functioning of things on the conventional level within their being empty of inherent existence. Indian masters drew out the implications of this perspective and developed uncommon explanations in comparison to those of other commentators, especially the Svātantrikas. This process of refining the implications of the Prāsaṅgika view continued in Tibet. In commenting on this, Tsongkhapa speaks of *eight prominent unique explanations* that he described in the sixth chapter of *Illuminating the Intent* (GR 276):

> From the traditions of interpreting the treatises of the noble Nāgārjuna comes this unique interpretation, whereby one can still posit all effective transactions [of the world] even though not even the tiniest particle of inherent reality exists. Based on this approach, many perfect tenets emerge that are unique compared to other commentators. What are these tenets? For now here are the principal ones:
>
> 1. Rejection of a foundation consciousness that is a different entity from the six collections of consciousness [explained in chapter 6].
> 2. Unique method of refuting apperception [explained below].
> 3. Rejection of the generation of the view of suchness in the mindstreams of others by means of autonomous syllogism. These are three negative rejections [explained in chapter 7].
> 4. Acceptance of the existence of external reality to the same

extent as one accepts the existence of consciousness [explained in chapter 6].

5. Acceptance that śrāvakas and solitary realizers realize the selflessness (emptiness of inherent existence) of phenomena [explained below, in chapter 10 of *Searching for the Self*, and in chapter 14 of *Realizing the Profound View*].
6. Acceptance that self-grasping of phenomena is an affliction [explained below].
7. Acceptance that "having-ceased" (*naṣṭa*)—a functioning thing's state of having ceased—is a conditioned thing [explained below].
8. Because of the seventh point, a unique way of defining the three times [explained below].

These eight unique tenets are rooted in the Prāsaṅgikas' rejection of inherent existence. They should not be confused with another list of eight found in Gyaltsab's *Notes on Eight Crucial Points Taken as a Record of the Teaching of Tsongkhapa*, in which Gyaltsab explains four negative theses and four positive theses in terms of the basis, path, and result—these are the *eight crucial or difficult points*:

1. Rejection of foundation consciousness even on the conventional level [explained in chapter 6].
2. Rejection of inherent existence even on the conventional level; phenomena do not exist by their own character even conventionally [explained in chapters 4 and 7].
3. Acceptance of external objects. The first three pertain to the basis [explained in chapter 6].
4. Rejection of autonomous syllogisms as a means for realizing suchness [explained in chapter 7].
5. Rejection of apperception [explained below].
6. Unique account of the two obscurations: self-grasping is an afflictive obscuration and its latencies are cognitive obscurations [explained below].
7. Acceptance that śrāvaka and solitary realizer arhats realize the emptiness of inherent existence. These four pertain to the path [explained

below, in chapter 10 of *Searching for the Self*, and in chapter 14 of *Realizing the Profound View*].

8. A unique view on how the Buddha knows conventional reality; the Buddha knows all phenomena simultaneously. This pertains to the result.

What makes the eight explanations unique is that Prāsaṅgikas identify inherent existence as the object of negation. Although the Vaibhāṣikas also refute apperception, only the Prāsaṅgikas refute it by refuting inherent existence. Although the Sautrāntika-Svātantrikas also assert external objects and refute the existence of a foundation consciousness, only the Prāsaṅgikas do so based on refuting inherent existence.

A number of the Prāsaṅgikas' unique explanations have been discussed in previous chapters, and some of those may be summarized below. Yet to be discussed are the refutation of apperception, having-ceaseds being functioning things, and the three times being functioning things. A few other unique points are also explained below.

Understanding the unique Prāsaṅgika tenets is not always easy, but it is worthwhile. Here it is helpful to recall a Tibetan saying: One should avoid teaching a text in two ways—like a crow making a nest and like an old man eating. A crow patches together all sorts of dissimilar things in a messy way to make a nest, and an old man with few teeth chews the soft foods and swallows the hard ones whole. So while the material in the tenet systems may be new or challenging, we should persevere, trying to understand it without either putting bits together in a haphazard manner, accepting it unquestioned, or avoiding the hard parts.

Apperception

According to the Buddhist tenet systems that accept apperception (*svasaṃvedana*), it is a consciousness that is nondual with another consciousness and perceives that other consciousness while that consciousness is perceiving its object. Apperception functions to enable us to remember perceiving the object, while the perceiving consciousness itself enables us to remember the object. Apperception is the "knower of the knower." In the case of a visual consciousness seeing blue, the visual consciousness perceives blue while the apperception that is one nature with that visual consciousness directly and nondually perceives that visual consciousness and knows that it perceives blue.

Apperception should not be confused with introspective awareness. Apperception is a nondual cognizer of another consciousness. It is simultaneous with the consciousness that it is perceiving, whereas introspective awareness looks either at an immediately preceding moment of mind or at an aspect of mind. Apperception enables memory of having perceived the object, while introspective awareness monitors the mind to see if it has fallen under the influence of afflictions.

Sautrāntika-Reasoning Proponents, Yogācārins, and Yogācāra-Svātantrika Mādhyamikas assert apperception, whereas the other systems refute it. According to those who accept it, the existence of apperception can be established because we remember not just the object but also the experience of perceiving it. That is, memory has two parts: One is memory of the known object—the color blue, for example. The other is memory of the perceiver, the visual consciousness that perceived blue. When we say "I saw blue," "I saw" indicates memory of the perceiving consciousness and "blue" indicates memory of the perceived object. Since we remember the experience of perceiving blue, there must be a consciousness that perceived the visual consciousness perceiving blue, because without it we could not remember the subjective experience of seeing blue. That consciousness is apperception. It is an unmistaken direct perceiver that is simultaneous with the main consciousness itself. It knows the main consciousness nondually: the subject apperception and the object it apprehends—the visual consciousness apprehending blue—do not appear as different natures. In this way, apperception easily fits in with the Yogācāra tenet of the nonduality of subject (apperception) and object (visual consciousness).

The systems that assert apperception claim that it is one nature with the consciousness it knows, although it has a different object and a different empowering condition (*adhipati-pratyaya*). The object of the visual consciousness seeing blue is blue; its empowering condition is the visual sense faculty. The object of the apperception accompanying that visual consciousness is the visual consciousness perceiving blue, and its empowering condition is a previous moment of consciousness. According to Yogācārins, the visual consciousness seeing blue is mistaken because it apprehends blue to be an external object, but the apperception apprehending that visual consciousness is a reliable cognizer that knows its object without error.

Furthermore, Yogācārins assert that apperception can prove the true existence of the mind because apperception, which is a reliable cognizer, establishes the mind as truly existent. Since Yogācārins state that the external world is illusory and the substantial cause of form and so forth is latencies on the mind, they must find some way to account for causality, such as a seed growing to become a plant, a karmic action producing its effects, and practicing the path as the cause to attain awakening. The only thing left on which they can establish causality and the orderliness of existence is the mind, so the mind must be truly existent. Apperception verifies the true existence of the mind.

Prāsaṅgikas take a different stance by asserting that apperception is not necessary to remember perceiving an object. For example, there is no need to assert apperception—such as a consciousness that perceives and is one nature with a visual consciousness seeing blue—in order to remember the experience of seeing blue. This is so because when we remember the object—blue—we automatically remember seeing blue; these two are linked. By recalling the perceived object, we automatically know that there was a mind that perceived it. Candrakīrti says (MMA 6.74–75):

> If apperception were established
> it would still be illogical for memory to recall [a former consciousness];
> because [the previous consciousness and the present memory] would be [inherently] other, it would be like the recollection of someone with no prior knowledge.
> This reasoning precludes any relation [between them].
>
> Because for me this memory is not [inherently] other
> than that [consciousness] that experienced the object,
> one remembers, "I saw [this earlier]."
> This is also the way of worldly conventions.

Apperception is superfluous and unnecessary to explain how memory occurs. Because apperception is asserted to exist inherently, it must be either inherently one with or inherently different from the memory it produces of having perceived the object. Since we have already refuted effects arising from inherently existent causes by the reasoning of the diamond slivers,[67] we know that apperception does not exist on the ultimate level. And on the conventional level, apperception is not needed to explain how memory works—the visual consciousness perceiving blue is the cause of the memory of having perceived blue. (The example of the visual consciousness will be used in this section, but what is said can apply to any sense or mental consciousness cognizing an object.)

Prāsaṅgikas refute the existence of apperception, saying that to exist a phenomenon must be certified by a reliable cognizer. What reliable cognizer could possibly certify apperception? It could not be a conventional reliable cognizer because that would have to be another instance of apperception that perceives the first instance of apperception that knows the visual consciousness perceiving blue. That instance of apperception would have to be certified by another instance of apperception, and so on ad infinitum. Infinite regression makes this argument untenable.

Those who assert apperception claim it is a separate cognizer from the visual consciousness; they also say that it is one nature with the visual consciousness that it cognizes. However, two separate cognizers cannot be one nature.

Furthermore, although apperception is asserted to be nondual with the main consciousness it perceives, this is not possible. Just as a knife cannot cut itself and an acrobat cannot sit on his own shoulders, a consciousness cannot know itself. The *Descent into Lanka Sūtra* states (GR 358):

> Just as the blade of a sword
> does not cut itself, and just as
> the tip of a nail does not touch itself,
> the apperception of mind is the same.

The agent and object of any action are different. In the action of perception, the visual consciousness (the agent) perceives an object other than itself. Thus there cannot be another consciousness such as apperception that not only is part of the visual consciousness but also perceives that consciousness.

No matter how we look at it, apperception cannot be established by a conventional reliable cognizer—neither a direct perceiver nor an inference. That means it would have to be established by an ultimate reliable cognizer, in which case it would exist ultimately. If that were so, both the visual consciousness apprehending blue and the apperception apprehending that visual consciousness would be ultimately or truly existent. As we saw in the refutation of diamond slivers, two truly existent things would be totally different and unrelated.

Those who assert apperception as well as true existence and ultimate existence see the cause—in this case the visual consciousness seeing blue—and the result—a consciousness that remembers seeing blue—as truly existent. If this were the case, either the visual consciousness seeing blue was apprehended by apperception at the time it occurred or the memory of this consciousness was produced by a later consciousness. The first option—that the visual consciousness seeing blue was apprehended by apperception—has already been dismissed because a mind cannot perceive itself. One and the same mind cannot be both cognizing subject and the cognized object, just as a knife cannot cut itself.

The second option—that memory is produced by a later consciousness—evokes the question, Does the memory arise from itself, other, both, or causelessly, as in Candrakīrti's diamond slivers refutation? To establish a connection between a truly existent cause and a truly existent result, some people assert apperception. However, Prāsaṅgikas retort that if the two consciousnesses—today's experience of seeing blue and tomorrow's memory of having perceived blue—were inherently other, then all the faults discussed when refuting arising from other in the diamond slivers reasoning would occur. The later consciousness that remembers the visual consciousness perceiving blue would have no relationship to that visual consciousness at all. The two would be completely distinct from each other. If someone says that the remembering consciousness could still apprehend that visual consciousness, then the consciousness of another person that is equally different than the visual consciousness could also apprehend it. Then Fran could remember Pat's experience of seeing blue.

Prāsaṅgikas assert that the process of remembering occurs conventionally; there is no need to assert some truly existent entity to establish it. They explain that memory is established on the level of worldly conventions. There is no need to assert apperception or truly existent consciousnesses.

Simply remembering the object of a previous cognition is sufficient for us to remember having cognized the object. To make sense of our everyday experience of remembering having seen or experienced something, it is not necessary to postulate a metaphysical entity such as apperception.

In the conventions of the world, we say "I saw blue" without thinking that the present I that remembers seeing blue is the same I that saw blue last week. Nor do we think that the blue we saw before is inherently the same blue that we now remember seeing. In ordinary life we don't do this kind of analysis or make these differences, so there's no need to posit apperception to explain memory. Simply by remembering the perceived object, the perceiving mind is automatically established.

REFLECTION

1. Do you think apperception exists? Do you think remembering an object and remembering cognizing it rely on two different processes? Or when you remember the object, do you naturally remember cognizing it?
2. How do Prāsaṅgikas refute its existence? Do you agree with their reasons?

Having-Ceased

Almost all Buddhists say that a functioning thing abides, ages, and disintegrates or ceases simultaneously. What does this mean? The *arising* of a sprout occurs while the sprout is being produced; it exists at the time of the sprout's causes. The sprout hasn't attained its entity at that time. The *having arisen* of the sprout is its being something that did not exist before, although each moment of the sprout is something new that didn't exist before.

The *abiding* of a functioning thing is its similarity to what existed before or to what will exist after. At the first moment of smoke, for example, the smoke abides, but it is not similar to its immediately preceding cause, the fire. However, it is similar to the second and third moments of the smoke.

The *aging* of a functioning thing is its being something different from what it was in the previous moment, and its *ceasing* is its not lasting for another moment. Ceasing is a quality of the present object, its not enduring after "its own time," the time in which it was present.

Relating this to karma, after an action (karma) has been done, it has ceased. From that moment until the moment immediately before the result appears, the action is not there. How, then, does that karma give rise to its result? This topic is a thorny one that has drawn the attention of Buddhist philosophers throughout the ages. Some Vaibhāṣikas assert a factor of "acquisition" (*prāpti*), which is itself an abstract factor that enables karmic seeds to attach to the mindstream of the person who did the action. Other Vaibhāṣikas assert a factor of non-wastage of actions (*avipraṇāśa*), which is like an IOU ensuring that the potential of an action exists and will go from one life to the next until it ripens as the result. According to them, acquisition and non-wastage inherently exist, as does the person who creates an action and experiences its result. Sarvāstivādins say that physical and verbal actions are imperceptible forms that continue to exist and are capable of producing results.

Sautrāntikas introduce the notion of karmic seeds, which Yogācārins and Mādhyamikas also accept. Sautrāntikas and Svātantrika Mādhyamikas assert the mental continuum to be the carrier of the karmic seeds. When an action is created, the seeds are placed on the mindstream, which holds them until they ripen. Yogācārins expand on the notion of seeds and latencies, saying that karmic seeds influence sentient beings' rebirth, experiences, habits, and which environment they are reborn into, whereas other latencies are the substantial cause for a cognition and the object cognized.

Yogācāra-Scripture Proponents assert a foundation consciousness—a stable, neutral consciousness that goes from life to life and is the storehouse for all karmic seeds and other latencies. Sautrāntikas, Yogācāra-Reasoning Proponents, and Svātantrikas assert a mental continuum (*cittasaṃtāna*) on which the seeds of the karmic actions have been placed. The karmic seed is the result of the action, and through the continuity of this karmic seed the potency to experience results is carried until all cooperative conditions have come together and the seed ripens as the karmic result.

Prāsaṅgikas claim that all these assertions involve grasping inherent existence, because their proponents assert something findable that is the person and the carrier of the karmic seeds. The proponents of those views also assert that the karmic action exists inherently, as does its disintegrating; karmic seeds and latencies too are inherently existent. Prāsaṅgikas alone assert that karmic actions, their seeds, and so forth lack inherent existence. They arise and cease conventionally, not inherently.

Positing "having-ceased" (*naṣṭa*) enables Prāsaṅgikas to explain how an action or karma brings its results and at the same time to maintain that nothing exists inherently. Candrakīrti says complex theories and metaphysical assertions such as a foundation consciousness are not required to explain how something continues. For example, in common language we say that someone who has trained in a certain activity—be it typing, drawing, or high-jumping—has skill in it. She can do this activity. Where does this skill or capacity reside? Prāsaṅgikas say it does not have to reside somewhere findable, so we don't need to postulate a foundation consciousness or pinpoint the mental consciousness or anything else in the person that possesses that skill. What, then, connects the cause with the result—the past skill with future moments of doing the same action? That is the having-ceased.

There is not a clear English word that accurately conveys the meaning of *naṣṭa*, or *zhig pa* in Tibetan, so we created a word, "having-ceased," which is a noun. A having-ceased is an abstract composite—an impermanent phenomenon that is neither form nor consciousness. Whether we speak of it in terms of actions or objects, a having-ceased is the state of something's having ceased after being produced; it is an event, an action's or object's not having endured. The action no longer exists, and its having-ceased is its having disintegrated. We may speak of the having-ceased of a sprout after the sprout has ceased either by dying or transforming into a plant. We may also speak of the having-ceased of an act of generosity or an act of lying. These actions arise and disintegrate, and when they have ceased, their having-ceased is what remains. Their having-ceased is the continuity of their ceasing; thus the having-ceased of an action is caused by the having-ceased of that action's causes. That is, the having-ceased of the causes of an object produces the having-ceased of the object itself. For example, the having-ceased of the fuel produces the having-ceased of the fire. The fuel's having run out produces the fire's extinguishment. In the same way, food and water being used up in a certain locale produces the having-ceased of the living beings there; it is the cause of their death.

A having-ceased is an affirmating negation, which is very different from a nonexistent. For example, Mahatma Gandhi has ceased, but that doesn't mean he never existed. Gandhi's having-ceased is different from the nonexistence of a rabbit's horn; Gandhi did exist and ceased, while a rabbit's horn never existed and never ceased. The fact that Gandhi lived and ceased is important; it had a major impact on the world.

What is here now is related to what was before, but they are not the same. For conditioned things, to be is to be continuously disintegrating. The having-ceased of things in the past gives shape to what exists now. Who we are is influenced by choices we made in the past and by the having-ceaseds of those decisions. Although the past is not occurring now, the fact that it happened and ceased influences what exists and the circumstances we face in the present. The condition of having ceased is an existent phenomenon.

All tenet systems accept that having-ceaseds exist, but the essentialists—except the Vaibhāṣikas—say that they are permanent. When Vaibhāṣikas say that a having-ceased is a functioning thing, however, their meaning is different than when the Prāsaṅgikas say it. All systems accept that the factor of disintegration is impermanent. The having arisen, abiding, and disintegrating of all functional things exist simultaneously. While a thing is disintegrating, it still exists—when the plant is dying, there is still a plant—but once it has ceased, it is no longer there. For the non-Vaibhāṣika essentialists, having-ceased is the nonexistence or absence of the thing after it has disintegrated. It is something's having completely ceased, and therefore they say it is permanent because there is nothing we can point to as being an example of that object's having-ceased. Because the having-ceased cannot be found in the object itself, nor in a later moment of the thing that has ceased, they conclude that a having-ceased is a nonaffirming negation that is the absence of the action or object that has ceased. Being a mere absence, a having-ceased is permanent, they say.

According to the Prāsaṅgikas, while a thing—let's say a sprout—is arising, it is not present, because if it were present, it would not need to arise. When the sprout exists, it is already ceasing, so its ceasing is simultaneous with the sprout. The disintegration of the sprout is its act of ceasing, and this is an attribute of the sprout that is present. The sprout's having-ceased is subsequent to the sprout. Just as arising, abiding, and ceasing are conditioned events, so too the having-ceased of the sprout is a conditioned thing.

Karma (an action) doesn't exist at the time of its cause; after its cause, it has arisen. The having-ceased of an action doesn't exist at the time of the action; it arises subsequent to the action. Here we see a series of cause and effect. If the having-ceased were permanent, as the lower schools assert, then it could not arise from an action and could not lead to the karmic result of that action. Birth is the condition for aging and death. If birth had not ceased, that would not be the case. Fortifying the argument that a having-ceased is a functioning thing, Āryadeva says in the *Four Hundred* that the arising of a result causes the having-ceased of its causes (CŚ 352):

> Since the effect destroys the cause,
> that which does not exist will not be produced.

Effects are functioning things; they are products and are impermanent. For an effect to arise, its cause must cease. Since a having-ceased is produced upon the disintegration of its cause, it must be a functioning thing. Thus Prāsaṅgikas say that a having-ceased is an affirming negation that can give rise to an effect. Candrakīrti gives the example of someone who dies of starvation, saying that the lack of food is the cause of his death. Similarly, the exhaustion of fuel is the cause for the flame of a lamp to go out. This indicates that although a having-ceased is an absence of something that once existed, that doesn't mean it has no causal efficacy. The lack of something that once existed can be a cause for the arising of something else.

For this reason, Prāsaṅgikas state that since a having-ceased is a result of an action, it too is a functioning thing. It is produced by the action and it too disintegrates, producing a having-ceased of the having-ceased. Tsongkhapa says in *Illuminating the Intent* (GR 284):

> That which has disintegrated (a having-ceased) is not a mere elimination, but implies a conditioned thing that involves an elimination of that [phenomenon].

A having-ceased is not the nonexistence of a sprout, but its having-ceased after it existed. This differentiates a having-ceased, which is an affirming negation, from the emptiness of inherent existence or the nonexistence of a turtle's moustache, which are nonaffirming negations. Inherent existence and a turtle's moustache never existed, therefore they cannot cease and produce a having-ceased.

Furthermore, contrary to the essentialists' insistence that there must be something that *is* a having-ceased, Prāsaṅgikas say a having-ceased is posited in dependence on the object's having disintegrated. Since it exists merely nominally, nothing needs to be pinpointed as being the having-ceased of a thing.

Let's relate this discussion of having-ceased specifically to karma. The ceasing of a karmic action brings about the having-ceased of that action. The continuum of that having-ceased has the capacity to produce a result.

The having-ceased exists as the continuum of a similar type as the action. It is not separate from the action. That an action gives rise to a having-ceased means that the action has not become totally nonexistent; its having-ceased remains. This emphasizes that the fact of the action's existing and then ceasing is important. This is not the same as the action never having occurred at all. In this way, the merely imputed phenomenon of a having-ceased has the potential of our actions to bring results even after many lifetimes.

The present moment of a karmic action is a cause of its having-ceased, which exists as the continuation of that action. The completion of an action occurs while the action abides. After the completion of an action, its having-ceased comes into being. Because functioning things are momentary and do not last, they automatically disintegrate, producing a having-ceased. A having-ceased of an action preserves the potential of that action to bring its result when the cooperative causes come together. For instance, Tom encourages and gives support to a friend who is feeling down. This action ceases, leaving its having-ceased. This having-ceased also disintegrates, producing another having-ceased, and this continues until, in the future, the person who is the continuity of Tom is in a situation where he needs encouragement and a friend is nearby. The friend who is nearby is the cooperative condition for the having-ceased of Tom's previous action bearing its result, and the person who is the continuity of Tom experiences the happiness of receiving support from a friend.

A karmic seed and a having-ceased of an action are not the same. A having-ceased is an affirming negation—an absence that affirms something—while a karmic seed is an affirmative phenomenon. In this case, the having-ceased affirms that an action occurred but negates that the action is happening now. A having-ceased and a karmic seed produce the results of an action. A karmic seed is a potency; a having-ceased is not a potency, but it has potency. Having-ceaseds exist in relation to all functioning things. After the apple disintegrates, its having-ceased remains. However, we don't speak of the apple leaving a karmic seed. Seeds and latencies are spoken of only in relation to things that have to do with the mind, and karma originates with the mind. As mentioned above, a latency can also connect one moment of manifest anger to another, carrying the potency of the anger during the periods of time when the anger is not manifest. Similarly, a latency connects one moment of manifest visual consciousness to a future moment—for example, when we are sleeping and the visual consciousness is not operating.

By asserting having-ceaseds, Prāsaṅgikas have no need for the conceptual inventions of the essentialists, such as Vaibhāṣikas' postulating a nonwastage or an acquisition. Similarly, there is no need to assert a foundation consciousness, as the Yogācāra-Scripture Proponents do. Without inherently existent karmic seeds, there is no need for a foundation consciousness that carries them from one life to the next. Also, there is no need to assert that the mental consciousness is the person who carries the karmic seeds, as the Svātantrikas do. Since the having-ceaseds will ripen and influence a person's future experience, an inherently existent mental consciousness that carries the karmic seeds serves no purpose.

REFLECTION

1. What is a having-ceased?
2. What is an affirmating negation and why are having-ceaseds among them?
3. Is a broken glass a having-ceased?
4. What are examples of having-ceaseds?

The Three Times

We often speak of the past, present, and future, but what are they? Candrakīrti in his *Commentary on (Āryadeva's) "Four Hundred"* says (UT 221):

> The past is what has passed beyond just this [present time]. The present has been produced but has not ceased. The future is what has not come [into being] at the present time.

The present is primary, and the past and future are posited in relation to it. The past is established in relation to a thing's having been produced and having ceased. The future is posited in relation to the potential of something to exist but its not yet having been produced.

Even though the present is what exists now, we cannot speak of it except in relation to the past and the future. Saying the present has arisen puts it in relation to the past; saying it has not yet ceased places it in relation to the future. Candrakīrti says (UT 229):

> Those three times also are interdependent because each does not exist without depending on the [other] two.

Although we hear many people talk about "being in the present," the present is not an inherently existent, isolated moment unrelated to the past and future. "Living in the present" does not mean we deny the past and future or pretend that they do not exist. We live in the present because it is the only time to live. We cannot live in the past or in the future because neither of them is happening now. However, it is to our advantage to be aware of the past and future and the chain of causality that links the three times.

Buddhist tenet systems other than the Prāsaṅgika assert that in general the past and future are permanent. They are the absence of the present thing, either because, in the case of the future object, all of its conditions have not come together, or because, in the case of the past, it has arisen and then ceased. According to these systems, only the present is real; the past and future are only abstract constructs based on the present and are thus permanent. The Prāsaṅgikas, however, assert that the past and future are impermanent and thus are functioning things. In saying this, they emphasize the relativity of the notion of temporal periods. As mentioned above, the past and future are defined in relation to the present, and the present is defined in relation to past and future.

By saying that the three times are impermanent functioning things, Prāsaṅgikas convey the idea that apart from the temporal stages of actual phenomena—their past, present, and future—we cannot talk about time as an inherently real container. The moment we speak about time, we presuppose a framework,[68] and all our concepts about time are relative to that framework. Some people presuppose truly existent time that exists independent of any frame of reference. On this basis, they then construe time as permanent and unchanging. However, the idea of both permanent time and truly existent time are untenable because time is dependent on and measured in terms of the change of functioning things. Negating the inherent existence of all phenomena, Prāsaṅgikas base their understanding of time and of the past, present, and future on nominal existence. For this reason, they say that the three times are conditioned, impermanent, functioning things. Time is not a preestablished framework in which events occur, but something that is posited in relation to the change that conditioned phenomena undergo.

Although the present has priority over the past and future in terms of its being more imminent, when we probe deeper into the nature of time and examine the present, inquiring where and when it exists, the present becomes unfindable. We cannot find a discrete temporal stage that is the present, independent of the past and the future. There are no partless moments of time. Let's take the present moment of time—the present moment consists of parts—an initial part, a middle part, and an end part. Of these three, the middle part is the present, and with respect to it, the first part is past and the last part is future. Likewise, that middle part that is the present has three parts, an initial, middle, and end part, of which the middle is present and the other two are past or future. Following this line of reasoning, it becomes clear that we cannot pinpoint exactly when the present is.

Although we can never pinpoint one moment as the real present, without the present, the concepts of past and future would not make sense. Therefore we must conclude that these conventions of past, present, and future operate within a relative framework and that we cannot expect to ground our concept of time in some objective, identifiable basis. Furthermore, time exists only in relation to the things that exist in time. Time is not an absolute, independent entity that acts as a backdrop in which everything occurs. Rather, time is an interval measured and imputed in dependence on the change occurring in the continuum of objects.

Some terminology will help us understand the Buddhist concept of time. Please remember that this terminology is used in a philosophical context that may not always correspond to our everyday usage of the words. Here, we'll speak of the three times of a sprout.

- The future sprout (T. *myu gu ma 'ongs pa*) is defined as "a [factor of] nonarising of the sprout due to the temporary noncompletion of its conditions, even though the causes for its arising exist." The future sprout occurs first. That is, while the sprout arises and before the sprout has arisen, the future sprout exists. The future sprout is not a fully formed sprout in another dimension that is waiting to pop into the present as science fiction movies might have us imagine. Rather it's a factor of the not having arisen of the sprout. That means that the main cause of the sprout—the seed—exists but all the cooperative conditions—water, fertilizer, correct temperature, and so forth—have not come together, so the sprout has not yet arisen.
- The present sprout (T. *myu gu da ltar*) is the sprout that has arisen but has not ceased and is neither a having-ceased nor a future of another thing. After the future sprout, the present sprout occurs.
- The past sprout (T. *myu gu 'das pa*) is a factor of having-ceased of the sprout that has already arisen. After the present sprout has ceased, the past sprout exists; it is the sprout that has arisen and has ceased. The sprout's having-ceased is the past sprout.

To summarize, the sprout itself is the present sprout, its having-ceased is its past, and its not yet coming into being due to incomplete conditions, although the main cause exists, is the future sprout. The future sprout, present sprout, and past sprout are in a continuum. Because the reference point is the sprout, first its future exists, then its present, and finally its past.

The future sprout and the past sprout are both affirming negations. An affirming negation has a factor of eliminating one thing and affirming an affirmative or positive phenomenon. The having-ceased of the sprout, which is the past sprout, eliminates a sprout's not having disintegrated and implies that the having-ceased of a sprout occurs in dependence on the sprout. A future sprout eliminates a sprout's having arisen and implies that all the conditions for the sprout are not yet assembled.

The phrase "is neither a having-ceased nor a future of another thing" in the definition of a present sprout indicates that neither the future sprout nor the past sprout exists in the present. However, *in their own time* they are present—that is, the present of the having-ceased sprout is the having-ceased sprout's factor of having arisen but not having ceased. This factor is something different than the having-ceased sprout. The present of the future sprout is its factor of having arisen and not having ceased—that is, the future sprout has arisen but hasn't ceased. That factor, too, is something different from the future sprout. In short, just as the sprout has a past, present, and future, the future sprout and the past sprout—which are also functioning things—have a past, present, and future.

The action of the arising of the result and the action of the ceasing of the cause are simultaneous. At the time the seed is ceasing, the sprout is arising. Does the sprout exist at this time? No, it doesn't, because its cause—the seed—exists, and a cause and its effect cannot exist simultaneously. If the sprout had already attained its entity—that is, if the sprout had already come into being—there would be no reason for it to arise again. However, the future sprout exists, and when the conditions for its arising are complete, the sprout will attain its entity.

How can the sprout perform the function of arising if it doesn't yet exist? In a nominally existent world, the result doesn't have to be present in order to arise, whereas this must be the case if inherent existence were the norm. If everything existed inherently, the agents of the functions of arising and ceasing should be present because everything would have its own independent entity that did not depend on anything else. But if things already existed in that way—if the result existed at the time of its cause—either it would be unnecessary for it to arise or, if it did arise, it would continuously arise without stopping.[69]

Once the seed has ceased, the sprout exists. The having-ceased of the seed exists at the same time as the sprout. Without the having-ceased of the seed, the sprout would not exist.

The Three Times in Relation to a Specific Object

The following set of terms takes the sprout as the reference point and then establishes what came before it (the past *in relation to* the sprout), what exists at the time of the sprout (the sprout itself), and what happens after the sprout has arisen and ceased (the future *in relation to* the sprout).

- The future in relation to the sprout (T. *myu gu'i ma 'ongs pa*) is the result of the sprout, which comes after the time of the sprout.
- The present in relation to the sprout (T. *myu gu'i da ltar*) is the time the sprout exists.
- The past in relation to the sprout (T. *myu gu'i 'das pa*) is what happened before the sprout came into existence.

Here three different temporal stages are posited from the perspective of the sprout: first the past in relation to the sprout exists, then the present in relation to the sprout, and finally the future in relation to the sprout. This is the opposite sequence of the future, present, and past sprout explained above, in which the future sprout exists first, then the present sprout, and later on the past sprout.

According to the philosophical usage of terms, all functioning things *exist in general*, but that does not mean that they exist in the present. The child that we were does not exist now, but he or she exists in general. If he or she were not an existent phenomenon, we never would have been a child. Tomorrow's lunch does not exist now, but it exists (we hope!). Our future buddhahood exists, but not at this moment. The fact that something does not exist in the present does not mean it is totally nonexistent. If our future buddhahood did not exist at all, there would be no purpose in practicing the path because our buddhahood would be nonexistent. Our future buddhahood is an existent phenomenon in general, although it does not exist at this very moment. Therefore creating the causes to attain it is definitely worthwhile.

Nāgārjuna presents an analysis of time in chapter 19 of *Treatise on the Middle Way*, and Āryadeva refutes truly existent time in chapter 11 of *The Four Hundred*. When first reading these texts, the vocabulary and subtle lines of arguments may be baffling. However, thinking about the three times challenges our ideas of how and when things exist. It makes us look more closely at the connection of causes to their effects. Most of all, it helps us to see that the three times exist by being merely designated. They lack true existence, yet they function so that causes are created and their results arise after they cease. However, when they cease, things do not become totally nonexistent in that their having-ceased remains. In the case of karma, this having-ceased produces results as well. In other words, the fact that things happened in the past or that something existed and then ceased influences our lives. World War II does not exist now, but its having existed and then ceased has a profound effect on our present world. The fact that the future buddha you will become exists influences the choices and decisions you make in this life.

As a closing note on this topic, if you grew up with science fiction movies you may have the idea of time machines that are able to take you back to the past where you will be among the people and environment of the past as if they were now occurring in the present. A time machine could also fast forward you to the future where you would be among the people and environment of the future as though they were actually existing now. You may have some sort of expectation that when scientific technology is able to go faster than the speed of light, you may be able to travel to the past or future. Along the same line, you may think that remembering a past life or seeing a future one with supernormal powers means that they are occurring now, but on another plane that your present consciousness cannot see.

All of these ideas are based on a substantialist view of the three times. The past has arisen and already ceased; it does not exist now. The future has not yet arisen because its conditions have not assembled even though the main cause for it exists; it, too, does not exist now. The people you knew in the past no longer exist and the people you will know in the future do not yet exist. The situations you encountered in the past do not exist now, although their having-ceaseds remain. The situations you will encounter in the future are still fluid and depend upon the particular confluence of causes and conditions that come together. All these things exist by being merely imputed, although we cannot pinpoint exactly what they are.

REFLECTION

1. Does the person you were yesterday (the past person) exist now?

2. Does that person exist in general?

3. Do you sometimes get stuck dwelling on the past, even to the extent of getting emotional about people you knew or events that occurred years ago but are no longer present?

4. Do future events exist now? Do they exist in general?

5. What does living in the present mean?

Self-Grasping of Phenomena Is an Affliction

In both Tsongkhapa's list of eight unique explanations and Gyaltsab's lists of eight crucial points, we find Prāsaṅgikas' acceptance that the self-grasping of phenomena is an affliction. This is related to their assertion that both afflictive and unafflictive ignorance are afflictions and afflictive obscurations. The lower systems speak of "afflictive ignorance" (T. *nyon mongs can gyi ma rig pa*) and "unafflictive ignorance" (T. *nyon mongs can ma yin pa'i ma rig pa*), whereas Prāsaṅgikas do not. Because Prāsaṅgikas assert the ignorance grasping inherent existence as the root of saṃsāra and they reject inherent existence even conventionally, they have a unique presentation of ignorance and the afflictions. We need to bear this in mind as we examine the specific meaning of these terms in different contexts.

According to Vaibhāṣikas and Sautrāntikas, afflictive ignorance and the three poisons that spring from it are obscurations that prevent liberation. Afflictive ignorance refers to grasping a self-sufficient substantially existent person as well as all other coarser forms of ignorance. Unafflictive ignorance refers to not knowing things that are far away in distance or time, the subtle qualities of the Buddha, and subtle facets of the law of karma and its effects. The commentaries on the *Treasury of Knowledge* say that Maudgalyāyana did not know where his mother had been reborn, despite his being the Buddha's foremost disciple in the superknowledges. His lack of knowledge was due to unafflictive ignorance. Arhats have eliminated afflictive ignorance and are free of saṃsāra, but the Buddha has also overcome unafflictive ignorance, which accounts for his all-knowing.

Yogācārins and Svātantrikas define afflictive ignorance like the Vaibhāṣikas. Eliminating grasping a self-sufficient substantially existent person through realizing the lack of such a person entails realizing the selflessness of persons and leads to liberation from saṃsāra. Both these schools consider grasping a self of phenomena to be unafflictive ignorance and a cognitive obscuration. As we have seen, Yogācārins and Svātantrikas have their unique ways of defining self-grasping of phenomena. Yogācāra-Scripture Proponents assert it is grasping subject and object as being different substantial entities and grasping phenomena as existing by their own character as the referent of term and concept. They consider such grasping to be unafflictive ignorance. Svātantrikas assert grasping the self of phenomena to be grasping true existence; this is what they say is unafflictive ignorance.[70] The emptiness of their respective objects of negation is the selflessness of phenomena as defined by each school and realizing that emptiness leads to buddhahood.

Buddhapālita, a Prāsaṅgika, defines the object of negation in the śrāvaka scriptures as "all phenomena are devoid of self-existence," self-existence being existence with an essence. Refuting that is a full understanding of selflessness. The person is empty of existing with an essence, and realizing the selflessness of the person correctly and fully entails realizing that the aggregates are also empty of existing with an essence. Thus grasping the self-existence of phenomena must be an affliction since its absence is what śrāvakas realize to attain liberation.

In short, the tenet schools from Vaibhāṣika up to and including Svātantrika Madhyamaka assert afflictive ignorance to be grasping a self-sufficient substantially existent person. According to them, this ignorance is the first of the twelve links of dependent origination. None of these schools consider grasping inherent existence to be an affliction, let alone the root of saṃsāra, because they believe inherent existence is the reality of how persons and phenomena exist.

Prāsaṅgikas, on the other hand, assert that grasping inherent existence of both persons and phenomena is the root of saṃsāra and grasping inherent existence of the I in particular is first-link ignorance. They do not differentiate between afflictive and unafflictive ignorance because all self-grasping ignorance is afflictive and perpetuates saṃsāra. It is eradicated by realization of the emptiness of inherent existence of persons and phenomena.

The lower schools consider arhats to be practitioners who have realized the coarse selflessness of persons and have eliminated grasping a self-sufficient substantially existent person. According to Prāsaṅgikas, such practitioners are not actual arhats because they haven't realized the emptiness of the subtlest object of negation—inherent existence. They still manifest a subtle kind of afflictive craving, but not in the way explained in Abhidharma texts. Abhidharma texts state that craving is based on grasping a self-sufficient substantially existent person, which is afflictive ignorance. However, according to the Prāsaṅgikas, the craving of these so-called arhats is afflictive because it is supported by grasping inherent existence, which these practitioners have not eliminated. These practitioners who grasp inherent existence have both afflictive obscurations and cognitive obscurations, despite their realization of the lack of a self-sufficient substantially existent person.

In addition to the above meaning, the terms "afflictive ignorance" and "unafflictive ignorance" have another meaning that is found in Prāsaṅgika literature. Here "afflictive ignorance" indicates grasping inherent existence and "unafflictive ignorance" refers to the latencies of ignorance that are cognitive obscurations. In this context unafflictive ignorance is not actual ignorance, despite its name. Prāsaṅgikas are very clear that if it is ignorance, it is afflictive and is an afflictive obscuration. Latencies are not consciousness, whereas ignorance is, and there is no common locus between ignorance and cognitive obscurations. Genuine arhats have realized the emptiness of inherent existence and have eliminated afflictions and all afflictive obscurations. However, Fundamental Vehicle arhats have not begun to remove the unafflictive ignorance that is a cognitive obscuration.

Prāsaṅgikas give as examples of the unafflictive ignorance possessed by these arhats their inability to perceive the very subtle aspects of karma and its effects and their inability to fully understand the qualities of the buddhas.

Śrāvakas and Solitary Realizers Realize the Selflessness of Phenomena

Because of the difference in how Prāsaṅgika and the lower schools identify the object of negation and afflictive obscurations, they also differ in their assertions regarding the selflessness that arhats have realized.[71] As noted previously, all the non-Prāsaṅgika schools—as represented in the two *Knowledges*—say that the lack of a self-sufficient substantially existent person is the subtle selflessness realized by arhats. Prāsaṅgikas consider this a coarse selflessness, the subtlest being the emptiness of inherent existence. Since arhats have eliminated all afflictive obscurations, and grasping the inherent existence of persons and phenomena is an afflictive obscuration, Prāsaṅgikas assert that Fundamental Vehicle arhats must have realized the same emptiness of inherent existence as ārya bodhisattvas and buddhas. They say this because, as Nāgārjuna and Candrakīrti both mentioned, as long as there is grasping the inherent existence of the aggregates, there will be grasping an inherently existent I. Therefore there is no difference in subtlety between the two selflessnesses—of persons and phenomena—both are the emptiness of inherent existence. Thus arhats must have realized these in order to eliminate afflictive obscurations.

Furthermore, the *Sūtra on the Ten Grounds* says that first-ground bodhisattvas outshine śrāvaka and solitary realizer arhats by way of lineage but not by way of wisdom. Since first-ground bodhisattvas have realized the emptiness of inherent existence of persons and phenomena, yet do not yet outshine arhats in terms of wisdom, the Fundamental Vehicle arhats must have realized the two subtle selflessnesses. Furthermore, the "three types of beings" who have eradicated all afflictive obscurations are the śrāvaka arhats, solitary-realizer arhats, and pure-ground bodhisattvas.

Thus those accepted as arhats according to the two *Knowledges* are not arhats according to the Prāsaṅgikas because they have realized only the coarse selflessness of persons. In fact, they are not even āryas because they have not realized the emptiness of inherent existence, the subtle selflessness of persons and phenomena. Although these practitioners have some realization, they still have the self-grasping of persons and phenomena and have yet to abandon afflictive obscurations. Here again we see the far-reaching implications of how the various systems assert the object of negation.

However, practitioners can definitely attain arhatship through practicing the Fundamental Vehicle, so all śrāvaka and solitary-realizer āryas have realized the emptiness of inherent existence of persons and phenomena.

Subtle Afflictions

To review, Prāsaṅgikas identify self-grasping ignorance, the root of saṃsāra, differently than the lower schools. Because of this, their identification of the afflictions that are based on this ignorance also differs.

The lower schools state that all afflictions arise on the basis of grasping a self-sufficient substantially existent person, whereas Prāsaṅgikas say there are two levels of afflictions: coarse and subtle. Coarse afflictions are induced primarily by grasping a self-sufficient substantially existent person, and subtle afflictions are induced primarily by grasping inherent existence. Prāsaṅgikas assert that an arhat has realized the emptiness of inherent existence and thus has eliminated both levels of afflictions. The lower schools do not agree because they do not consider grasping inherent existence to be an affliction or the root of all other afflictions; in fact, they say it is known by a reliable cognizer because phenomena inherently exist. Thus the lower schools, but not the Prāsaṅgikas, consider people who have counteracted grasping a self-sufficient substantially existent person to be arhats.

The subtle afflictions asserted by the Prāsaṅgikas are not considered afflictive by the lower tenet systems. Because they assert that phenomena exist inherently, the Buddhist essentialists do not assert attachment, anger, and so forth that are induced by grasping inherent existence. For Svātantrikas, the appearance of inherent beauty in a thing isn't a false appearance. Things are beautiful from their own side, and the mind that is drawn to them is a reliable cognizer of their attractiveness; it is not attachment. Similarly, Yogācārins may grasp some foods as being inherently delicious, their good taste being established by a reliable consciousness—even though they say the delicious taste arises from the same substantial cause as the gustatory consciousness perceiving it. They do not recognize that subtle attachment—attachment induced by grasping inherent existence—is present. However, they do recognize coarse attachment that is based on grasping a self-sufficient substantially existent person and see that attachment as an object to be abandoned. They do not call this level of afflictions coarse like the Prāsaṅgikas do, because they do not classify afflictions into coarse and subtle.

Āryadeva explains how afflictions such as attachment and anger are based on true-grasping (CŚ 135):

As the tactile sense faculty [pervades] the body,
confusion resides in all [afflictions].
By overcoming confusion
one will also overcome all afflictions.

Candrakīrti's commentary on this verse explains (GR 241):

> "Confusion" refers to ignorance, for it apprehends things as real; as such, it operates by way of exaggeration superimposing truly existent natures upon things. Attachment and so on also operate by thoroughly attributing qualities of attractiveness or unattractiveness upon the nature of things imputed by confusion, and as such, they do not operate independently of delusion. Furthermore, they are contingent on delusion in that delusion is the primary factor.

Confusion (*moha*) means ignorance (*avidyā*), specifically the ignorance grasping true existence. It superimposes and apprehends objects as being truly existent. Attachment and other afflictions superimpose truly existent qualities such as beautiful and ugly, desirable and undesirable, on the things that confusion has imputed as truly existent. In this way, attachment and other afflictions don't operate separately from confusion; they depend on confusion, in which they are rooted.

Returning to Āryadeva's verse, just as there is no basis for the other four sense faculties—visual, auditory, olfactory, or gustatory—separate from the body, all afflictions are based on confusion and do not function without it. When ignorance is destroyed, afflictions are also destroyed.

In *Illuminating the Intent*, Tsongkhapa speaks of afflictions that have specific objects and aspects (T. *dmigs rnam chan*) and those that do not. Although it is not explicitly stated, he is making the distinction between coarse afflictions that are underlain by grasping a self-sufficient substantially existent person and subtle afflictions that are supported by grasping inherent existence. According to the Prāsaṅgika presentation, coarse afflictions are those presented in the *Treasury of Knowledge* and *Compendium of Knowledge*. They have objects and aspects that are different from those of the ignorance grasping a self-sufficient substantially existent person.

Subtle afflictions, on the other hand, do not have objects and aspects that are distinct from those of ignorance. Tsongkhapa explains (GR 241–42):

> Attachment and aversion operate on the basis of superimposing inherently existent qualities of attractiveness and unattractiveness . . . Since afflictions such as attachment are concomitant with confusion, their focal object is the same as that of confusion. This means attachment and aversion are defined by their aspects of attraction toward an object and repulsion from an object induced by the two types of inappropriate attention. So states of mind with aspects of wanting or not wanting induced by grasping [a] self-sufficient substantially existent person alone are not defined here as attachment and aversion.

Inappropriate attention includes distorted conceptions and incorrect mentation that superimpose truly existent attractiveness or unattractiveness of objects. It is based on ignorance grasping true existence and induces attachment, aversion, and other afflictions that are concomitant with ignorance. Being concomitant (T. *mtsungs ldan*) with ignorance means that when attachment or other afflictions are manifest in the mind, they are present in the same mental state and they share five factors in common with the true-grasping ignorance that is also in that mental state: they have the same object, the same empowering condition, the same aspect (appearance), the same entity, and they exist at the same time.[72] For example, in a mental consciousness desiring kaptse, the attachment and the ignorance concomitant with it have the same focal object—kaptse—a fried-dough treat eaten on special occasions (you could substitute chocolate if you prefer). Attachment has the aspect of grasping it as inherently delicious and desirable and clings to it; it wants to possess and not be separated from the kaptse that is delicious from its own side.

That attachment grasps the kaptse as inherently desirable does not mean that subtle attachment is a form of ignorance—the attachment and confusion are distinct mental factors, although they exist concomitantly with the same primary consciousness. Attachment grasps true existence due to the presence of ignorance, not by its own power. Ignorance grasps true existence and subtle attachment grasps the object as inherently desirable and attractive, not by its own power but because ignorance is operating.

Candrakīrti's commentary to Āryadeva's *Four Hundred* speaks of afflictions that are concomitant with ignorance and that depend on ignorance. If these two phrases—"concomitant with ignorance" and "depend on ignorance"—were synonymous, there would be no need to have two phrases. Thus they must refer to different types of afflictions.

Afflictions that are inseparable from ignorance in that they are *concomitant with ignorance* are called "subtle afflictions" by Prāsaṅgikas. Afflictions that *are dependent on ignorance* are the coarse afflictions that arise depending on the ignorance grasping a self-sufficient substantially existent person. These afflictions are not concomitant with that ignorance. All Buddhist schools recognize coarse afflictions as afflictions. Realizing the lack of a self-sufficient substantially existent person can suppress coarse afflictions but cannot eliminate them from the root. Only meditating with the meditative equipoise that directly and nonconceptually realizes emptiness can eradicate these. However, only Prāsaṅgikas identify subtle afflictions. Subtle afflictions are also removed by directly realizing and familiarizing oneself with the emptiness of inherent existence over time. They have been completely eradicated by arhats, pure-ground bodhisattvas, and buddhas.

The Meaning of Pratyakṣa

In *The Foundation of Buddhist Practice*, we noted a few unique Prāsaṅgika positions regarding direct perceivers (*pratyakṣa*). There are still more. Sautrāntikas say that a direct perceiver has three characteristics: (1) it is a nonconceptual consciousness; (2) it is unmistaken regarding its appearing object, an inherently existent thing; and (3) it arises and engages in its object by depending on a sense or mental faculty.

Candrakīrti, who differs with Dharmakīrti on several important points, disagrees with these characteristics, and asserts some unique tenets: (1) A conceptual consciousness can be a direct perceiver. Here "direct" means not relying on a logical sign or reason. In this case, an inferential cognizer of emptiness that has arisen in dependence on a correct reason is not a direct perceiver; however, the mental consciousness remembering the emptiness cognized by this inferential cognizer that arises subsequently is a direct perceiver because it does not rely on a reason to cognize its object, emptiness. (2) Sense consciousnesses are mistaken with respect to their appearing objects because those objects appear to be inherently existent although they are not.

Another difference between Sautrāntikas and Prāsaṅgikas is that the latter have a unique meaning for *pratyakṣa*. This word could be translated into Tibetan as both *mngon sum*, which usually means "direct perceiver," and *mngon gyur pa*, which is a manifest object. When speaking of the object—a table—and the visual consciousness that directly perceives it, the table is the manifest object (*pratyakṣa*). The visual consciousness that directly perceives it is not an actual *pratyakṣa* (direct perceiver) but is imputed as such because its cause, the table, is a *pratyakṣa* (manifest object). This is similar to calling a fire that burns wood a "wood fire": the name of the consciousness is given depending on its object, so the consciousness is called *pratyakṣa* because its object is a *pratyakṣa*.

Sautrāntikas say that an actual *pratyakṣa* (direct perceiver) is an unmistaken, nonconceptual consciousness. They do this based on a sūtra quotation, "A visual consciousness knows blue, but without thinking 'blue.'" Prāsaṅgikas differ; their etymology for the word is that *prati* means "before" and *akṣa* means "eyes." *Pratyakṣa* is the actual object that is manifest—or "before the eyes"—of a consciousness. It is the object perceived by the consciousness. Directly perceiving consciousnesses are merely called *pratyakṣa* because they apprehend a manifest object.

A consciousness can itself be a manifest object (*pratyakṣa*) when it is the manifest object of another consciousness. For example, when a visual consciousness apprehending blue is later remembered by a remembering mental consciousness, it is the manifest object of that remembering consciousness. Thus blue is a manifest object to the visual consciousness apprehending blue. Here the visual consciousness apprehending blue is imputed as a *pratyakṣa* or direct perceiver. Later, when the mental consciousness remembers seeing blue, the previous visual consciousness apprehending blue is a manifest object and the mental consciousness remembering it is imputed as a *pratyakṣa*, a direct perceiver. It's helpful to recall that for Prāsaṅgikas some conceptual consciousnesses, such as remembering consciousnesses, are considered direct mental perceivers (*pratyakṣa*) because they apprehend their object without depending on a reason. Similarly, since "direct" in "direct perceiver" means without depending on a reason, the mental consciousness remembering emptiness subsequent to an inferential realization of emptiness is a direct perceiver.

In an even broader way, whatever is a knowable object is an actual manifest object with respect to a consciousness that clearly—that is, directly—realizes it. Ngawang Palden explains (UT 271):

> Whatever is an established base (T. *gzhi grub*) is necessarily an actual manifest object (*pratyakṣa*, T. *mngon gyur pa*) in relation to an awareness that clearly realizes it, and with regard to whatever consciousness is a reliable directly perceiving consciousness with respect to an object, that consciousness is necessarily an imputed directly perceiving consciousness (*pratyakṣa*, T. *mngon sum*) in relation to that object.

Summary

In *Searching for the Self*, we began our discussion of the ultimate nature of phenomena with an overview of the tenets of various philosophical tenet systems, and in *Realizing the Profound View*, we learned the methods taught by the tenet systems for realizing the ultimate nature. Let's return to this topic to illustrate how studying tenets leads to the gradual penetration of the correct view.

A question that comes in the mind of almost everyone at one time or another in their life is "Who am I?" Throughout human history, many philosophies and religions proposed answers to this question. One idea is that the person is an independent entity that is entirely different from the aggregates. While the body and mind are made of many components and change constantly, the person is a permanent, unitary, independent self that does not depend on causes and conditions and therefore is unchanging. This view of the soul or ātman, which is prominent among non-Buddhists, cannot hold up to analytical reasoning, as we saw in previous chapters.

Still, as human beings we are continuously involved in discriminating attractive and desirable objects from ugly and undesirable ones. This discrimination is done in relation to the self—what I like and what I do not like. But what is this self? The Buddhist essentialists say that the self is like an employer that bosses the employees around; the I is a controller, a ruler that directs and controls the body and mind. This notion of a self also has many logical inconsistencies and can be negated by reasoning. The meditation on selflessness done at the initial stage of Dharma practice negates this kind of self, which is the self referred to in the four truths. The selflessness of this self-sufficient substantially existent person is shared in common among all Buddhist tenet systems, except the Vātsiputrīya, a branch of the Vaibhāṣika. Through reasoning and meditation, the notion of a self that exists above the aggregates and controls them is seen as false, and the realization that such a self does not exist dawns in the mind. Realizing this level of selflessness does not put us at risk of falling to nihilism because it is evident that the person exists in dependence on the aggregates. This negation of the self enables practitioners to engage in the bodhisattva conduct—the method side of the path—without doubting the existence of the person.

As our understanding of selflessness becomes stronger, we will expand it to include the aggregates. Our five aggregates—body, feelings, discrimination, miscellaneous factors, and primary consciousnesses—seem to exist objectively, and we attribute characteristics to them—good, bad, correct, incorrect, pleasant, unpleasant, and so forth. If these characteristics existed from the side of the object, the fact that different people see things in very different ways would be inexplicable. For example, there are many different perspectives from which to view a particular woman, depending on who is observing her. To some she is a mother, to another she is a daughter. Some people see her as a project manager, others as a neighbor. None of these characteristics is due to her having an essential attribute unique to herself. Rather it depends on the relationship. Depending on which attribute of a person we focus on, she will appear differently to us. This leads us to understand that we normally perceive things to exist "out there," as if our mind does not influence what they are. In this way, we are led to the Yogācāra view, which claims that the objects we perceive are related to our mind; they arise from the same latency on the foundation consciousness as the consciousness that perceives them. Recognizing this undermines the solidity of our strong emotional reactions. This is a powerful tool to dismantle our emotional reactions to external people and things.

The investigations of quantum physics encounter a similar difficulty in pinpointing a solid ground for external reality. As a result, many physicists say that the existence of external objects is related to the mind. For example, since light involves movement, there needs to be a point it moves toward and a person observing this.

Vasubandhu critiques the notion of partless particles, saying particles always have directional parts, which enable these tiny particles to join together to form larger objects.[73] Unlike the Vaibhāṣikas and Sautrāntikas, who assert an external world composed of partless particles,[74] Yogācārins say our perception of the material world depends on the mind and perceptual processes. In this way, they propose the nonduality of perceiving subject and perceived object. Although an external world appears to us, it is in fact a function of our perception and the latencies on the foundation consciousness.

Yogācārins negate the existence of external objects, whereas they assert the true existence of mind. This view is less "troublesome" than the Madhyamaka view for some people because Yogācārins accept that consciousness truly exists. If the Yogācāra understanding of emptiness is more suited and beneficial to you, focus on it. Some mahāsiddhas (great adepts) who hold the Yogācāra view practice highest yoga tantra.

Mādhyamikas challenge the Yogācārins' assertion that consciousness is truly existent, saying, "Just as you deconstruct the external world to show there are no partless particles, the same analysis should be applied to mind because mind is a continuum consisting of parts. If we dissect moments of consciousness, we see they have temporal parts—a beginning, middle, and end.[75] Thus a real, truly existent mind cannot be pinpointed." In this way, Mādhyamikas challenge Yogācārins' claim that external and internal objects have different levels of reality. Mādhyamikas assert that just as the external world does not exist independently, so too the inner world of mind does not exist independently.

Among Mādhyamikas, we find two positions. Svātantrikas say that there is no difference in the existential status of a mind and its object—both lack true existence. Nevertheless, they still hold to there being some objective validity to our perception of the world. Thus they negate inherent existence on the ultimate level, but accept it on the conventional level. That is, when examined by ultimate analysis, there is nothing findable on the ultimate level, but they accord some objective reality to all phenomena on the conventional level. Phenomena cannot be merely imputed, they say, because then anything could be imputed as anything, bringing chaos to our shared existence. Bhāvaviveka, Śāntarakṣita, Jñānagarbha, and others agree that the meaning of the Perfection of Wisdom sūtras is that there is no inherent existence on the ultimate level. However, at the level of perception what we see is correct and there is no need to negate it. In his autocommentary on the *Heart of Middle Way*, Bhāvaviveka asserts inherent existence on the conventional level when he says, "We accept the mental consciousness to be the true referent of the term 'person.'" Furthermore, Śāntarakṣita accepts apperception, stating it establishes the validity of reliable cognizers. This suggests he accepts inherent existence conventionally as well.

Candrakīrti rejects inherent existence both ultimately and conventionally. In addition, he says that all cognizers of sentient beings, aside from āryas' meditative equipoise on emptiness, are mistaken because phenomena appear inherently existent to them. There is not one atom that exists inherently and there is not one moment of ordinary consciousness that is not distorted by false perception. For some people this view may feel destabilizing and uncomfortable because they teeter toward nihilism. If you are one of these people, know that some Buddhist sages share your concern. Do not push yourself to accept a view that would lead you to the nihilistic extreme. Even Tsongkhapa was not initially able to establish conventional phenomena in the face of their lack of inherent existence. In his early work *Golden Garland* (*Legs bshad gser phreng*), he says that since not even one atom possesses inherent existence, conventional existence is not real and is accepted only for the sake of others. This shows he veered toward nihilism and did not fully understand dependent arising at that time in his life.

But after he accumulated merit, purified negativities, and continued his meditation practice, his view changed and he wrote *Praise to Dependent Arising* and *Three Principal Aspects of the Path*, in which he explains that as long as the infallibility of dependent arising and emptiness remain incompatible in our mind, we have not yet fully understood the intent of the Buddha. On the other hand, when these two understandings mutually reinforce each other, our analysis is complete. In the *Great Treatise*, he says that although it is difficult to posit cause and effect in a world that is empty of inherent existence, those learned in the Madhyamaka should uphold that dependent arising and emptiness are complementary.

If the Madhyamaka view confounds you, it is better to work on understanding coarse selflessness for now, because that way you will face no danger of nihilism. I once heard someone who knew the Dharma well say, "Buddha's teachings are beautiful, but if you push hard, there is nothing." This shows that, in fact, his understanding was not correct. Mere existence and inherent existence are difficult to distinguish. I teach the Prāsaṅgika view, but sometimes I, too, find my understanding is actually Svātantrika.

After we negate inherent existence, it may seem as if there is nothing. However, things do exist—dependently but not inherently. In the *Three Principal Aspects of the Path*, Tsongkhapa explains that by contemplating the infallibility of cause and effect, when the very perception of effects arising dependent on causes induces the understanding of emptiness, and when contemplating emptiness induces understanding of dependent arising, then our analysis of the correct view is complete.[76] This is the meaning of Nāgārjuna's statement that whatever arises dependently is empty and whatever is dependently designated is the Middle Way.

The correct meaning of emptiness must be understood in terms of dependent arising. Maintaining the functioning of things is difficult after rejecting inherent existence. When we try to account for the everyday functioning of things, it is important not to fall to the extreme of nihilism. Our everyday experiences affirm that dream people and actual people are different. Their difference is not in terms of their ultimate nature, because both are empty of inherent existence. But if nothing from the side of the object is inherently existent, how can we distinguish a dream person and an actual person? Here we must rely on the three criteria that establish something as conventionally existent: it is known in the world, it is not contradicted by another conventional reliable cognizer, and it is not contradicted by a reliable cognizer of the ultimate.[77] In the case of a dream person, its existence as an actual person is refuted by another conventional reliable cognizer. When we wake up, our own conventional reliable cognizer knows the dream person is not an actual person. After all, it vanished as soon as we awoke!

Encouragement

The correct view is not easy to ascertain. It takes time, interest, and perseverance on our part to develop it. In addition, we must study, reflect, and meditate on emptiness under the guidance of a qualified spiritual mentor who accurately teaches us the Madhyamaka view and how to meditate on it. The compassionate help of others who provide us with the four requisites—food, clothing, shelter, and medicine—is also important, as are many other conditions. Although finding all the suitable conditions for realizing emptiness is rare, we must use whatever situation we find ourselves in now to learn about and investigate the ultimate nature. Doing this is extremely worthwhile and important for our own and others' well-being.

The great sages explain the most difficult passages and topics in their texts; these explanations are weighty and require analysis and contemplation on our part. Don't be discouraged; the study and practice of the Dharma takes years and lifetimes. Even if you learn just one page a day, after a hundred days you will have learned one hundred pages. If you continue without giving up, you will reach your goal. Change is possible when you make continuous effort. I can say this from my modest personal experience. You will become like the great ārya bodhisattvas on the sixth ground, whom Candrakīrti praises (MMA 6.224):

> Thus illuminated by the rays of wisdom's light,
> the bodhisattva sees as clearly as a gooseberry on his open palm
> that the three realms in their entirety are unborn from their very start,
> and through the force of conventional truth, he journeys to cessation.

Through the rays of profound wisdom light arising from analysis and from stable meditative equipoise on emptiness, these bodhisattvas clearly see that all persons and phenomena in the three realms of saṃsāra are unborn—they are empty of inherent existence—by their very nature. These bodhisattvas obtain the true cessations of each and every grade of afflictions to be abandoned by the path as well as the cognitive obscurations that prevent omniscience. In addition, by practicing the bodhisattva deeds in the conventional, illusion-like world, they accumulate the vast merit and wisdom that together lead to full awakening.

11 | Insight

AN INTELLECTUAL UNDERSTANDING of reality is necessary and helpful, but it does not have sufficient power to undermine the innate self-grasping ignorance that has been with our mindstreams since beginningless time or to destroy the afflictions rooted in that grasping. The correct understanding of emptiness—of our self as well as everything we interact with in the environment—must be profoundly integrated into our very being through deep insight into and personal experience of the ultimate truth, emptiness. To attain that level of integration requires direct experience of insight into emptiness derived through profound analysis and sustained by unfluctuating concentration.

Insight is included in the higher training in wisdom, which depends on the higher training in concentration. Both trainings are based on the higher training in ethical conduct. *The Heap of Jewels Sūtra* (*Ratnakūṭa Sūtra*) says (MS 26):

> Single-pointed concentration is achieved by adhering to ethical conduct. With the achievement of single-pointed concentration, then meditate on wisdom. Wisdom helps you to attain a pure pristine awareness. Through pure pristine awareness your ethical conduct is perfected.

The three higher trainings are taught in a specific order and when we begin training we are advised to practice them in that order. But as we grow more proficient in all three, they come to support and enhance one another. To perfect one of the higher trainings, all three must be accomplished.

Some people become attached to the bliss of concentration and do not advance to cultivate wisdom. Others mistake deep states of concentration for liberation; they too do not develop the wisdom of emptiness that frees us from saṃsāra. *The King of Concentration Sūtra* says (MS 16):

> Even if you meditate with single-pointed concentration
> you will not destroy the misconception of the self
> and your afflictions will disturb you again;
> this is like Udrak's single-pointed meditation.
> When the selflessness of phenomena is examined discretely,
> and meditations are performed on the basis of that analysis,
> that is the cause of attaining the resultant liberation;
> no other cause can bring peace.

Udrak was a renunciant who meditated single-pointedly for prolonged periods of time, so much so that his hair and beard grew extremely long. A mouse made a cozy nest in his beard and lived there happily. One day Udrak arose from his deep concentration, chased the mouse away, and went to town to collect food. When he was sitting by the wayside a passerby disrespected him and Udrak became enraged. Unfortunately he is an exemplar of someone who has attained a refined state of meditative absorption that suppressed the coarse afflictions, but lacked the wisdom realizing selflessness. As a result, not only was he far from liberation but he also reacted like an ordinary person in response to a small slight. The only cause that can bring the peace of nirvāṇa is the realization of the emptiness of inherent existence of all persons and phenomena.

Prerequisites for Training in Insight

Serenity is an attainment shared by Buddhists and non-Buddhists alike. However, Buddhists accomplish it based on refuge in the Three Jewels with the aim of attaining liberation or full awakening.

To unite serenity and insight, we must train in both stabilizing and analytic meditation. In general, insight is of different kinds. Mundane insight is, for example, contemplating the grossness of the first dhyāna and peacefulness of the second dhyāna so that the mind will want to attain the second dhyāna. In this chapter, insight will be presented in the context of meditation on selflessness—insight that will take us beyond saṃsāra. Training in insight is accomplished on the basis of serenity. What are serenity and insight? *The Cloud of Jewels Sūtra* explains (MS 22):

> Serenity meditation is a single-pointed mind;
> insight makes specific analysis of the ultimate.

Insight meditation is cultivated on a firm foundation of the preceding steps of the path. Prior to learning about emptiness, beginners need to be properly prepared through having learned and reflected on the four truths and the aspiration to be free from saṃsāra. A firm conviction in the law of karma and its effects is also crucial.

Kamalaśīla emphasizes that when we are serious about training in serenity and insight, we must ensure the prerequisites are in place. The common prerequisites for both are (MS 19):

> (1) Living in a conducive environment, (2) limiting your desires and practicing contentment, (3) not being involved in too many activities, (4) maintaining pure ethical conduct, and (5) fully eliminating attachment and all other kinds of conceptual thoughts.
>
> A *conducive environment* should be known by these five characteristics: providing easy access to food and clothes, being free of harmful beings and enemies, being free from disease, living near good friends who maintain ethical conduct and share similar views, and being visited by few people in the daytime and with little noise at night.
>
> *Limiting your desires* refers to not being excessively attached to many or good clothes, such as monastic robes, and so forth. The *practice of contentment* means always being satisfied with even little things, like inferior monastic robes, and so forth. *Not being involved in many activities* refers to giving up ordinary activities like business, avoiding too close association with householders and monastics, and totally abandoning [worldly] practices [such as] medicine and astrology.

> Being mindful of the various defects of attachment in this life and future lives helps eliminate misconceptions in this regard [such as thinking you will never separate from objects of attachment].

In short, we must live a simple lifestyle, maintain good ethical conduct, and avoid chasing after possessions and wealth, praise and approval, a good reputation, and sense pleasures, which fill our mind with a plethora of distracting thoughts. An extremely ascetic lifestyle in which we deliberately inflict pain or starvation on the body is also inappropriate and unhelpful. Living in a secluded place doesn't mean staying alone and isolating ourselves from all others. There's nothing particularly virtuous in that; even spiders who live in the snow do that. As practitioners who seek to cultivate serenity and insight, it's important to be with practitioners who share the same views and who abide in good ethical conduct.

Kamalaśīla summarized the prerequisites for insight into three: (1) reliance on a qualified spiritual mentor, (2) broad learning of the teachings on emptiness, and (3) reflection on those teachings to establish their meaning. In the *Middle Stages of Meditation*, he says: (MS 20–21):

> What are the prerequisites of insight? They are relying on holy persons, seriously seeking extensive instruction, and proper contemplation.
>
> What type of holy person should you rely on? One who has heard many [teachings], who expresses himself clearly, who is endowed with compassion and able to withstand hardship.
>
> What is meant by seriously seeking extensive instruction? This is to listen seriously with respect to the definitive and interpretable meaning of the twelve branches of the Buddha's teachings. The *Sūtra Unraveling the Thought* says: "Not listening to superior beings' teachings as you wish is an obstacle to insight." The same sūtra says, "Insight arises from its cause, correct view, which in turn arises from listening and contemplation." The *Questions of Nārāyana Sūtra* says, "Through the experience of listening [to teachings] you gain wisdom, and with wisdom afflictions are thoroughly pacified."

> What is meant by proper contemplation? It is properly establishing the definitive and interpretable sūtras. When bodhisattvas are free from doubt, they can meditate single-pointedly. Otherwise, if doubt and indecision beset them, they will be like a person at a crossroads uncertain which path to follow.
>
> Yogis should at all times avoid fish, meat, and so forth, should eat with moderation, and avoid foods that are not conducive to good health.

Studying emptiness and cultivating insight under the guidance of a qualified spiritual mentor are essential to gain the correct understanding of emptiness and how to meditate on it. Such a spiritual mentor is not only knowledgeable and wise but also compassionate and willing to undergo hardship in teaching the Dharma. For us to receive benefit from listening to teachings, we must put them into practice to effect change in ourselves. Merely gathering information will not bring realizations. Thus we must have the correct motivation and willingness to practice with joyous effort.

After gaining the correct view of emptiness, we must employ stabilizing and analytical meditation to generate the union of serenity and insight on emptiness.[78] If we cling to wrong views or lack the correct view of emptiness, it will be impossible to accomplish insight.

Uniting serenity and insight so that they help each other is necessary to attain the various paths and grounds of all three vehicles. The process for almost everyone is gradual and, depending on the extent of our practice in previous lives and the latencies left on our mindstreams, it requires time. It is similar to winning a medal at the Olympics: a recipient of a gold medal began the journey by learning to walk as an infant, not by immediately putting on skis, riding a snowboard, entering swimming races, or doing quadruple twists.

Kamalaśīla also described the preparatory practices for meditation sessions on serenity or insight (MS 21–22):

> When meditating, first complete all the preparatory practices. Go to the toilet, and in a pleasant location free of disturbing noise think, "I will lead all sentient beings to the state of awakening." Then manifest great compassion, the thought wishing to liberate

> all sentient beings, and pay homage to all the buddhas and bodhisattvas in the ten directions by touching the five limbs of the body to the ground (two knees, two hands, and head). Place the image of the buddhas and bodhisattvas, such as a painting, in front of you, and make as many offerings and praises as possible. Confess your misdeeds and rejoice in the merit of all beings.
>
> Then, sit in the full vajra posture of Vairocana or the half-vajra posture on a comfortable cushion. The eyes should not be too widely open or too tightly closed, but lightly focused on the tip of the nose. Do not bend the body forward or backward. Keep it straight and turn your attention inward. Rest the shoulders in their natural position and do not tilt the head back, forward, or to either side. The nose should be in line with the navel, and the teeth and lips should rest in their natural state with the tongue touching the upper palate. Breathe gently and softly without making any noise, without deep breathing, and without uneven breaths. Inhale and exhale naturally, slowly, and with awareness.

Then cultivate a proper motivation. Those following the Śrāvaka and Solitary Realizer Vehicles generate the motivation to attain liberation; those following the Bodhisattva Vehicle cultivate bodhicitta, the aspiration to attain full awakening in order to benefit all sentient beings.

REFLECTION

1. What are the common prerequisites for both serenity and insight?
2. Why is it necessary to have all of them?
3. What are the prerequisites for insight? What are the drawbacks of lacking each one?
4. Is it easy to get very excited about meditation with serenity and insight and think that the prerequisites can be glossed over? What are the results of doing this?

Divisions of Insight

The many types of insight fall into two main categories: mundane and supramundane. The former is practiced by ordinary beings; the latter leads to liberation and full awakening.

Mundane insight is used to attain deeper states of concentration by analyzing the grossness of the lower levels and the peacefulness of higher levels.[79] After attaining serenity, meditators reflect on the grossness of the desire realm—for example, having a body made of flesh that ages and falls ill—and the peacefulness of the first dhyāna—long life and absence of illness. Through this, meditators encourage themselves to deepen their concentration and attain the first dhyāna. Later, by contemplating the grossness of the first dhyāna and the peacefulness of the second, they meditate to attain the second dhyāna, and so on up through the fourth dhyāna. To attain the four formless absorptions, meditators contemplate the benefits of the next object of meditation. This type of insight into peacefulness and grossness is mundane because it leads only to higher levels of meditative absorption, not to liberation. It is practiced and attained by Buddhists and non-Buddhists alike. *Supramundane insight* focuses on the emptiness of inherent existence and leads to nirvāṇa. It is practiced only by Buddhists.

Insight may also be classified into insights cultivated by āryas and those cultivated by common beings. Regarding insights cultivated by common beings, there is the fourfold insight, the insight of the three approaches, and the insight of six examinations.

The fourfold insight is spoken of in the *Sūtra Unraveling the Thought*, *Śrāvaka Grounds*, and other texts. The four are differentiated by increasingly subtle levels of analysis while abiding in the inner tranquility of serenity:

- Differentiation observes the diversity of phenomena

  1. Coarse differentiation: with *investigation*, meditators discern the diversity of phenomena in which they investigate three characteristics of phenomena: (1) objects of meditation that purify behavior, (2) skillful objects of the learned, and (3) objects purifying afflictions.[80]
  2. Subtle differentiation: with *full investigation*, they employ conceptual attention together with the wisdom knowing the

diversity of phenomena and the wisdom knowing their true nature to know the characteristics of those three types of objects.

- Full differentiation observes how phenomena exist

3. Coarse full differentiation: with *analysis,* meditators analyze the ultimate nature of these three types of objects.
4. Subtle full differentiation: with *full analysis* they correctly analyze them and intensely discern the mode of being of all phenomena, their emptiness.

Through the fourfold insight meditators understand both the conventional and ultimate nature of phenomena. Asaṅga's *Compendium of Knowledge* contains more information on this topic.

Insight of the three approaches is taught in the *Sūtra Unraveling the Thought* and lays out three ways in which insight may engage with an object.

1. Insight *arisen from a sign* (*nimitta-mayī*)—that is, a conceptual appearance—alone brings to mind the object of meditation that we have been instructed in but does not contemplate, reflect, analyze, or inquire into it. For example, we observe by means of a conceptual appearance the selflessness we have already ascertained but we don't delve into its meaning further at this time.
2. Insight *arisen from thorough examination* (*paryeṣaṇā-mayī*) involves reflecting on and closely analyzing the object to ascertain what has not been previously realized by a wisdom consciousness.
3. Insight *arisen from discerning discrimination* (*pratyavekṣaṇā-mayī*), or individual investigation, analyzes the meaning and discerns an object's individual characteristics in a way that accords with what a previous wisdom consciousness has already established; we continue to analyze a meaning that we have ascertained through thorough examination.

These three correlate with the wisdoms arising from studying, thinking, and meditating. The first insight is cultivated in relation to what we have learned and studied. It includes the insight generated on the general notion of selflessness that we have gained based on our studies. With the second insight, we investigate selflessness, gaining a definitive understanding through analysis of its details. With the third, we focus on that which was understood by the previous two forms of insight, deeply familiarizing our mind with selflessness so that an understanding of it will arise automatically in our mind.

These three ways in which insight engages with the object can be used in the six examinations of objects:

1. Examination of the *meaning* of terms and words is done to understand their meaning.
2. Examination of *things* or *facts* involves, for example, determining if the six sources are internal or external.
3. Examination of *characteristics* investigates the specific and general characteristics as well as the shared and unshared characteristics of the objects of the four establishments of mindfulness.
4. Examination of *classes* regards different classes of phenomena—for example, examining the class of virtuous objects to see their good qualities and advantages, and examining the class of nonvirtuous objects to determine their drawbacks and disadvantages.
5. Examination of the *three times* examines what existed in the past, what exists at present, and what will exist in the future. It also contemplates that the past, present, and future are designated in dependence on each other and do not exist from their own side.
6. Examination of the *four principles* or laws of nature contemplates reality, dependence, function, and evidence.[81]
   - Examining *reality* investigates (1) realities commonly known in the world, such as water's being wet—this nature cannot be understood by reasoning, it is just the way the object is; (2) inconceivable realities, such as the Buddha's abilities; and (3) the abiding reality, emptiness.
   - Examining *dependence* investigates how results arise from their causes: in terms of causal dependence, a result depends on its cause, but in terms of mutual dependence, a cause is conceptually designated as a cause dependent on its result. Examining dependence also involves investigating the conventional, the ultimate, and their instances.

- Examining *function* entails investigating phenomena to determine their individual functions—for example, fire performs the function of burning. This also involves examining the functioning of the circle of three—agent, object, and action.
- Examining *evidence* involves investigating if something exists and can be established by any of the three reliable cognizers: direct perceivers, inferential cognizers, or reliable scripture.[82]

The above six objects are subsumed into three objects to be understood by yogis: (1) *examination of meaning* investigates the meaning of utterances, (2) *examinations of things* and *of specific characteristics* analyzes the diverse knowable objects, and (3) *examination of general characteristics, classes, time, and principles* investigates the actual way phenomena exist.

The three approaches and the six examinations can be included in the fourfold insight. Furthermore, the four types of mental engagement (*manaskāra*) explained in the context of cultivating serenity—forceful, interrupted, uninterrupted, and spontaneous—are also practiced when generating insight.[83] This is so because when engaging in the analysis required for insight, we encounter similar challenges as when we were previously meditating to generate serenity, although they are not as strong now. For example, we may be reluctant to analyze and need tight focus to get us going.

Although serenity and insight focus on many of the same objects, they differ in how they do so. Insight investigates these objects, inquiring into their details and viewing them in depth, whereas serenity gathers all the details together into one object and then rests the mind single-pointedly on that object.

This is a brief description of the various types of insight. You can learn more about them by studying the treatises under the guidance of a knowledgeable spiritual mentor and practicing the teachings. This description of the classification of insight may initially seem complex, but with time we will become familiar with it. Even having general knowledge of these categories enables us to see that insight is not a simple type of meditation that can be mastered in a short period of time. It has many facets and differing degrees of depth, and it covers a broad range of objects. In this way, insight purifies and develops our mind.

Avoid Going Astray

In the remainder of this chapter, we will focus on supramundane insight. Finding the correct view of emptiness and the proper understanding of insight requires learning, reflection, and meditation. Wrong views concerning emptiness and insight abound. For example, by not identifying the object of negation correctly and mistakenly negating existence as well as inherent existence, some people think that meditation on emptiness means focusing on nonexistence.

Other people believe insight entails remaining single-pointedly in a nonconceptual state of suspension. They think that because all conceptions grasp inherent existence, abandoning all thoughts whatsoever is the path to liberation. Analysis is not necessary, for it just creates more conceptions. All one must do in meditation is use single-pointed concentration to prevent the mind from scattering to inherently existent objects. In addition, since the method aspect of the path—compassion, generosity, and so forth—involves thought, these practices lead to cyclic existence and therefore should be given up.

Thinking like this has many pitfalls. Such people forsake both the method and wisdom aspects of the path. They abandon the wisdom realizing emptiness and fall to the extreme of nihilism by believing that not perceiving inherently existent objects indicates that phenomena do not exist at all. They eschew the method aspect of the path by thinking that bodhisattvas' conduct is rooted in conceptions of inherent existence. In this way, they abandon the path to liberation and the path to awakening.

Another way to go astray is by attaining a form or formless meditative absorption and confusing that with liberation. This occurs through attachment to the bliss of samādhi. Alternatively, meditators may have cultivated the insight of grossness and peacefulness and proudly believe they are free from saṃsāra. But that insight is mundane insight, so these practitioners will continue to take rebirth in saṃsāra. They have yet to understand the importance of realizing emptiness to destroy the obscurations that bind us to saṃsāra.

How do we avoid going astray? First, we must correctly identify self-grasping ignorance, the root of cyclic existence, and its conceived object, inherent existence. Then, applying the refutations found in the definitive texts by Nāgārjuna, Candrakīrti, and so on, we analyze whether phenomena exist in the way they appear to ignorance. Only by indisputably proving to ourselves that the object ignorance holds—inherent existence—does not and cannot exist can we generate the wisdom realizing the emptiness of inherent existence. Since the object of this wisdom (emptiness) directly contradicts the object of ignorance (inherent existence), such wisdom completely overcomes ignorance. Through constant familiarization with this emptiness, we will eradicate even the seeds of ignorance so that ignorance can never arise in our minds again.

Dispelling ignorance through analytical meditation differs from avoiding any perception of inherently existent objects, which simply evades the issue. For example, if we are afraid that our car has been stolen, not thinking about it or distracting ourselves by getting something to eat doesn't dispel our anxiety. Only by going to where we parked and seeing if the car is there will we be able to reach a definitive conclusion.

Gaining insight into emptiness isn't about simply suppressing the appearance of inherent existence. The appearance of the self of persons and the self of phenomena are not the object of negation. These appearances exist, although the two selves do not. Meditation on emptiness entails negating what has never existed—inherent existence. By doing that, grasping inherent existence and the appearance of inherent existence are gradually eroded.

This point is subtle. The inherent existence of the pine tree does not exist, but the appearance of an inherently existent pine tree exists. It appears to the visual consciousness perceiving the pine tree, making that visual consciousness mistaken because its apprehended object appears inherently existent although it is not. Despite being mistaken, however, this visual consciousness is a reliable cognizer with respect to the pine tree because it can correctly identify the pine tree and enjoy its beauty.

Simply suppressing the appearance of inherently existent objects does not cut our self-grasping. We may enjoy meditating in a state without the distracting appearances or conceptions of inherent existence, but that is like having an itchy rash and temporarily ignoring and suppressing awareness of that sensation. As soon as that itchy sensation arises in our awareness again, our mind is agitated and we run around trying to find something to make the itch go away. Stopping the cause of the itch—like properly identifying the object of negation and negating it—is the actual solution. For that, analysis is necessary. *The Play of Mañjuśrī Sūtra* (*Mañjuśrīvikrīḍita Sūtra*) affirms (LC 334):

> "Daughter, how are bodhisattvas victorious in battle?"
> "Mañjuśrī, when they analyze, they do not observe any [inherently existent] phenomena."

For ordinary beings, emptiness is a slightly obscure phenomenon—it can be known through an inferential cognizer, but not direct perceiver. If emptiness were an evident or manifest object to our sense consciousnesses, everyone could directly perceive it. In that case, we would not need to study, reflect, and meditatively analyze phenomena's ultimate mode of existence.

In addition, if emptiness were evident to ordinary beings' perceptions, we ordinary beings would already be āryas, and our consciousness that knows emptiness would be a nonconceptual yogic direct perceiver of emptiness. Since this is not the case, emptiness must be an obscure phenomenon to ordinary beings. Thus there is no choice but to approach the ultimate truth through the medium of analysis, language, and thought. Our initial understanding of emptiness will inevitably have conception as an integral part of that experience. After all, teachings describing how to meditate are given using words and concepts. The next step is to gain an inferential realization of emptiness, which is also conceptual.

This is followed by uniting serenity and insight with emptiness as the object. As the realization of emptiness continues to deepen, gradually the conceptual appearance is worn away until emptiness is perceived directly. The difference between inferential and direct realization of emptiness is likened to wearing a mitten when touching a crystal and touching it with bare hands. In the first, we have a rough notion of its shape, but with the second, we will know its shape, texture, and temperature through direct experience. The wearing away of the conceptual appearance of emptiness occurs gradually with continued meditation. Joyous effort is necessary because we have been habituated with grasping inherent existence since beginningless time. When emptiness is perceived directly, the meditator becomes an ārya and begins the process of eliminating the root cause of saṃsāra. In short, while our ultimate goal is to go beyond conceptual knowledge of emptiness to direct perception, the way to do that begins with using conceptual consciousnesses.

Some people wonder, Doesn't conceptual analysis of emptiness simply create more impediments to direct realization? As discussed previously, not all thoughts are conceptions of inherent existence. For example, the correct understanding that inherent existence does not exist is not a conception of inherent existence. To the contrary, it opposes the concept of inherent existence. Although during meditative equipoise directly perceiving emptiness the mind is completely nonconceptual, in post-meditation time conceptions that are not conceptions of inherent existence can be useful on the path. When we first hear teachings on emptiness and reflect on them, we use thought. In addition, thought is active when we discuss and debate emptiness, teach it to others, and when the great masters write about it. In these instances, conceptual minds are useful on the path.

Furthermore, not all analytical meditation is conceptual. Analytical inquiry can be pursued nonconceptually as well, and yogis on the paths of seeing and meditation employ nonconceptual analysis when they meditate on emptiness. Even early on the path, analysis is not necessarily an intellectual endeavor. It involves deep investigation of the mind and of the nature of reality, the kind of investigation that brings an inner shift in our perspective and new spiritual experiences.

Bringing conceptual elaborations of inherent existence to an end is done by deconstructing grasping inherent existence. This grasping is a conceptual mind. Using inquiry and reasoning, we dismantle the identity and concept of an object until the very identity and concept of that thing become untenable. This understanding could be considered nonconceptual in the sense that it lacks the conceptualization of inherent existence. This is what Candrakīrti means by "silencing verbal elaborations," which is also referred to as "noble silence." In short, although the initial understandings of emptiness are conceptual, further meditation will release the conceptual appearance of emptiness and bring direct realization.

Someone may ask, "Since discerning discrimination (*pratyavekṣaṇā*) of the meaning of emptiness is conceptual, how can it lead to nonconceptual wisdom since conceptual and nonconceptual consciousnesses are contradictory? Don't conceptual minds produce more conceptions, not direct perceivers?" In the *Kāśyapa Chapter Sūtra*,[84] the Buddha gave the analogy of a fire started by rubbing two sticks together, which then consumes the sticks. In the same way, correct discerning discrimination will lead to an ārya's nonconceptual wisdom. Similarly, correct conceptual realization of emptiness can produce nonconceptual direct wisdom, which in turn consumes all conceptions. This occurs because that discerning discrimination is an undistorted conception and a reliable cognizer. Although an ordinary being is not similar to an ārya in many respects, an ārya can arise from an ordinary being. If it were the case that a cause and its effect could not have any dissimilarities, then a round red apple could not arise from a small oblong black seed. Similarly, we would never be able to generate unpolluted consciousnesses because all our current consciousnesses as ordinary beings are polluted. However, it is precisely by using reasoning to analyze the conceived object of self-grasping that we will come to directly realize that it does not exist.

Another person questions, "But the scriptures themselves say that emptiness is inconceivable and is beyond awareness, so what is the use of doing analysis?" Knowing the purpose and meaning of such statements in the scriptures is important. The purpose is to counteract the conceit of people who think they know ultimate reality just because they are learned, proficient in debate, or adept in talking about emptiness. The meaning of "ultimate truth is inconceivable" is that it cannot be directly experienced by those who are not āryas; any concepts ordinary beings have about ultimate truth are nowhere near the actual experience of directly perceiving it with an ārya's self-realized pristine wisdom.

Some people think that once someone has attained the correct view, all of their meditations must be nonconceptual meditation on emptiness. This is not the case, for they also meditate on the defects of saṃsāra, compassion, bodhicitta, and so forth, which involve conceptions. Furthermore, nonconceptual can also mean being free from discursive thought; in other words, remaining single-pointedly on the object of meditation without thinking it is this and it is that. A person on the path of preparation has gained a concentration that is the union of serenity and insight. This concentration is free from discursive thought, but it is still a conceptual realization of emptiness although the layer of conception at this point is very thin.

Some people think that before entering into meditation on emptiness with serenity, simply remembering the view is sufficient. If this were the case, meditation on emptiness would involve only stabilizing meditation. However, since the concentration that is a union of serenity and insight necessitates both stabilizing and analytical meditation, the latter must also be present. Having only stabilizing meditation or only analytical meditation is insufficient to produce this union.

When our concentration is strong, we may have many wonderful experiences and appearances: The coarse appearance of subject and object may vanish, the mind may be very clear, or objects may appear insubstantial like rainbows or may even disappear. However, these do not indicate insight into emptiness, nor are they examples of illusion-like appearances. Just because something appears intangible to us, it doesn't mean that we have realized its emptiness of inherent existence; the lack of tangibility and the lack of inherent existence are not the same. If they were, then seeing a rainbow would constitute knowing its emptiness. In that case, refuting the object of ignorance would not be necessary. Illusion-like appearances occur to a person who has previously realized, but has not forgotten, the correct view.

The Necessity of Both Stabilizing and Analytical Meditation

Although some people say "I am practicing serenity (*śamatha, samatha*)" or "I am practicing insight (*vipaśyanā, vipassanā*)," these two are experiences or realizations gained by principally practicing stabilizing and analytical meditations, respectively. Training in these two types of meditation gradually leads to expertise in serenity and insight.

Serenity and insight are not differentiated in terms of their observed object. It is not the case that we develop serenity on one object—for example, the image of the Buddha or the breath—and then continue doing the same type of meditation but shift the object to selflessness to develop insight. Rather, serenity is primarily stabilizing meditation and insight is primarily analytical meditation. Serenity may be developed on a variety of objects—the conventional nature of the mind, an image of the Buddha, oneself as a deity, emptiness, love, a *nimitta* or sign,[85] and so on. Attaining serenity with emptiness as its object is neither insight nor the union of serenity and insight, because the distinguishing quality of the union of serenity and insight on emptiness is that analytical meditation on emptiness can induce special pliancy and serenity on emptiness. That is, the union of serenity and insight occurs when both physical and mental pliancy arise through the power of analysis.

In serenity meditation, analysis is done at the beginning of a meditation session to discern the meditation object properly and set the mind on it. If we want to cultivate serenity on the impermanent nature of our body, we must first examine its changing nature. Otherwise, if we just have a rough idea that our body is impermanent and focus on that, our mind will concentrate on that fuzzy idea, but not on impermanence. After clearly discerning the meditation object—in this case, impermanence—we do stabilizing meditation to develop serenity because at that point continuing analysis would disturb the mind's ability to focus one-pointedly.

The *Sūtra Unraveling the Thought* and many other texts recommend attaining serenity prior to cultivating insight because the one-pointedness of serenity is necessary to develop the one-pointedness of insight united with serenity. Insight is cultivated through analytical meditation that finds the correct view of emptiness. The *Sūtra Unraveling the Thought* (LC 340) says:

> [Maitreya]: Bhagavan, from what causes do serenity and insight arise?
>
> The Buddha: Maitreya, they arise from the cause of pure ethical conduct and from the cause of an authentic view based on study and reflection . . . Failure to study willingly the instructions of āryas is a hindrance to insight.

Keeping pure ethical conduct strengthens our mindfulness and introspective awareness. On that basis, we study the texts and listen to teachings on the correct view of emptiness, for example. This is followed by analysis using many lines of reasoning and reinforced with scriptural quotations to clarify the correct view. Once we have correctly determined the view through study and reflection, repeated engagement with analytical meditation makes our understanding more precise and firm.

A practitioner with a good understanding of emptiness may focus her mind on emptiness with stabilizing meditation, but stabilizing meditation alone will not lead to insight. To keep her understanding of emptiness fresh and to deepen it, she must frequently reflect on the points and refutations leading to that understanding, and for this analytical meditation is essential.

After having a deep experience of a meditation topic one time, simply remembering that experience and trying to recreate it is not sufficient to advance our meditation. We must repeatedly engage in analysis to reaffirm and reinvigorate our ascertainment of emptiness, be it conceptual or non-conceptual. The *Cloud of Jewels Sūtra* (*Ratnamegha Sūtra*, LC 343) says:

> Those who are skilled in [abandoning] faults take up the practice of meditation on emptiness to be free from all elaborations [of inherent existence]. Through much meditation on emptiness, their minds spread everywhere. When they search for the nature of the place where the mind is happy, they realize that it is empty. When they search for what the mind is, they realize that it is empty. When they search everywhere for the nature of the mind that knows that [emptiness], they realize that it is empty. By realizing this, they enter signless yoga.

Although the higher training in concentration is usually actualized before the higher training in wisdom and the perfection of meditative stability is attained before the perfection of wisdom, analytical meditation is needed both before attaining serenity and afterward. The great sages such as Bhāvaviveka, Candrakīrti, Śāntideva, and Kamalaśīla all agree on this.

However, if only analytical meditation is done after serenity has been attained, serenity will degenerate. It needs to be reinforced by stabilizing meditation. Familiarity with both stabilizing and analytic meditation on emptiness is required. This is done by alternating them in order to maintain the view of emptiness that we ascertained, to integrate it with our mindstreams, and to attain the union of serenity and insight.

A mind meditating with serenity observes the meditation object single-pointedly. A mind engaged in insight meditation discerns and investigates the nature of the object and the object's specific attributes. A meditator may cultivate serenity with the conventional nature of the mind as the meditation object, but when doing insight meditation on the mind, she selects an attribute of the mind—for example, its emptiness—and penetrates it deeply with analysis to correctly ascertain it.

Passages in some sūtras say that if one holds the idea that phenomena are empty, one is involved in grasping true existence. These passages are not referring to the discerning discrimination of emptiness, but to minds that grasp emptiness to be truly existent. A difference exists between a correct conception thinking "this is empty" and a conception of true existence that grasps emptiness as existing in and of itself. In *The Great Treatise on Insight*, Tsongkhapa says (LC 347):

> Similarly, the statements [in sūtras] that the mind should not remain on anything from form to omniscience [mean that] it is not appropriate to hold that those [phenomena] truly exist as places for the mind to remain. Otherwise, since even things such as the six perfections are spoken of in that way, it would mean that the mind must not remain even on them.

REFLECTION

1. Some meditators seek to attain the dhyānas and formless absorptions but aren't interested in learning about or meditating on emptiness. What are the results of their practice?
2. Is emptiness the same as nothingness?
3. Is gaining an inferential understanding of emptiness necessary or is it better to clear all thoughts from the mind and abide in a nonconceptual state? What are the results of each?

Uniting Serenity and Insight

Kamalaśīla emphasized that all virtuous qualities, be they mundane or supramundane, depend on the cultivation and attainment of serenity and insight (MS 15):

> The *Sūtra Unraveling the Thought* (*Saṃdhinirmocana Sūtra*) says, "O Maitreya, you must know that all the virtuous Dharmas

> of śrāvakas, bodhisattvas, and tathāgatas, whether worldly or transcendental, are the fruits of serenity meditation and insight."

After gaining familiarity and experience with the lamrim, focus on gaining the correct view of emptiness. Meditate on the selflessness of persons, specifically the I, and when you have some understanding of that, meditate on the selflessness of phenomena, in particular the aggregates. Then employ stabilizing meditation with mindfulness and introspective awareness so that you can hold emptiness in mind without falling prey to laxity or restlessness. When you have a "good" meditation session, don't push yourself to continue. Avoid making your meditation sessions too long, because laxity and restlessness will arise easily in a tired mind. Do four sessions daily, one in each of the four times: pre-dawn, morning, afternoon, and evening. In the breaktimes, practice seeing things as like illusions—they do not exist as they appear; they appear to exist inherently, whereas they do not.

If your mind is properly involved in the meditation, the time of the meditation session will seem to pass quickly and your need for sleep will decrease. But if you feel like a long time has passed in a session when it hasn't, your mind may not have properly grasped the object of meditation.

To refine your meditation and clarify your understanding of emptiness, consult a wise spiritual mentor. When you have found the definitive view of emptiness, you will have ascertained through analysis that the person and that which belongs to the person—the aggregates—do not exist inherently. After finding the view, refresh and deepen your understanding through repeated analysis. Continually examine how the I and the aggregates appear and how they actually exist. Be aware of the difference between the two.

Either before or after gaining the correct view, cultivate and attain serenity. To review, a definition of *serenity* is a concentration (*samādhi*) held by pliancy, in which the mind is able to remain stabilized on its object as long as desired and which came about depending on the nine stages of sustained attention. This concentration has four characteristics. (1) It is *nondiscursive*[86] in that it lacks distracting thoughts and mental chatter. At this time the breath and thought processes become very subtle and hard to detect. (2) It has *mental clarity* like a bright, clear sky. (3) It is *mentally vivid*, like the limpidity of water in a clear cup in the sun, such that we can't tell it is there. (4) It is capable of perceiving the *subtle*.

Although a concentration with these four characteristics is wonderful, we should not be overly enamored with it, for it is not equivalent to insight into emptiness. The object may be other than emptiness, the meditation on the correct view may lack all four characteristics because serenity has not yet been attained, or a practitioner may have attained serenity and a correct understanding of emptiness but not yet gained insight on emptiness. The determining factors for having attained insight on emptiness are having refuted the object of negation and single-pointedly remaining on that emptiness without laxity or restlessness and with pliancy being induced by the power of analytic meditation.

A definition of *insight* is a wisdom (*prajñā*) that discriminates with discernment (T. *so sor rtog pa*) its object by being held by a bliss of pliancy induced by the power of analyzing its object within serenity.[87]

Before attaining serenity, practicing stabilizing and analytic meditation alternately in one session disturbs the mind's tranquility. For this reason, practice stabilizing meditation and attain serenity first, before alternating stabilizing and analytical meditation in one session.

The attainment of mental and physical pliancy induced by stabilizing meditation is the mark of having attained serenity. At this point stabilizing meditation can induce pliancy and serenity, but analytical meditation cannot. The attainment of pliancy and serenity induced by the power of analytical meditation is the measure of having attained insight, which is also the union of serenity and insight. Until that time, stabilizing and analytical meditations subtly interfere with each other, and there is a similitude of insight, but not actual insight. Ratnākaraśānti in *Instructions for the Perfection of Wisdom* (*Prajñāpāramitā Upadeśa*, LC 354) says:

> Thus [the attainment of insight] lies in the attainment of physical and mental pliancy... As you have strong interest in the object of internal concentration, you will carry out analytical discrimination. Until you develop physical and mental pliancy, this mental engagement is a similitude of insight. When [pliancy] develops, that mental engagement is insight.

After attaining serenity, to cultivate the ability of analysis to bring the stability of nondiscursiveness, pliancy, and serenity, begin your sessions by employing analytical meditation to discern emptiness. At the conclusion of analysis, place the mind on emptiness with stabilizing meditation. Analysis ensures that your ascertainment of emptiness remains correct and vibrant, and stabilizing meditation ensures that your mind remains clear and stable on emptiness. If your concentration falters, do more stabilizing meditation. Within one meditation session, practice analytical and stabilizing meditations alternately.

An analogy is learning to ride a bicycle. At the beginning, we must diligently concentrate to stay on the bicycle. We can't afford to look at other things but must remain focused on what we're doing. Strengthening stabilizing meditation to develop serenity is like this. When we can ride proficiently, we practice a few stunts, but doing so causes us to lose our effortless concentration and we fall off the bicycle. This resembles the way analysis initially disturbs serenity's stability on the object. With more practice, we can perform stunts without losing our concentration or falling off the bicycle. This is comparable to analysis inducing pliancy and the attainment of insight. In the same vein, Tsongkhapa advises (LC 3.351):

> Alternate between stabilizing meditation—which stays [with that conclusion] without scattering—and analysis with discriminating wisdom. At that time, if stability decreases due to excessive analytical meditation, do more stabilizing meditation and restore stability. As stability increases under the influence of extensive stabilizing meditation, if you lose interest in analysis and thus fail to analyze, then your ascertainment of reality will not become firm and powerful. In the absence of firm and powerful ascertainment of reality, you will not do even the slightest damage to the countervailing superimpositions that grasp the existence of the two selves (the self of persons and the self of phenomena). Therefore cultivate a balance of serenity and insight by doing extensive analytical meditation.

Having previously attained serenity, do analytical meditation and again go through the nine stages of sustained attention and develop the four mental engagements—forceful, interrupted, uninterrupted, and spontaneous. At the conclusion of the ninth stage, when the fourth mental engagement is attained, analysis itself induces pliancy and a special serenity. This is insight, and the union of serenity and insight is attained. When the meditation object is emptiness, the practitioner enters the path of preparation. Asaṅga's *Śrāvakas' Grounds* says (LC 3.358):

> Having fully achieved concentration, apply yourself to the higher wisdom—the differentiation of phenomena. At that time, you naturally and effortlessly enter the path of differentiating phenomena. Because the path of serenity is unencumbered by striving, insight is pure, clean, comes after serenity, and is fully suffused with delight. Therefore serenity and insight combine and are balanced. This is called the path of union of serenity and insight.

This is called "union" because previously analytical and stabilizing meditations interfered with each other. They were not simultaneous and were practiced separately. Now, without needing to stop analytical meditation to stabilize in serenity, the analytical meditation of discrimination induces pliancy and serenity. Analysis is now insight, and stability at the end of analysis is a special serenity on emptiness. Now insight and serenity operate together and are united and balanced. The union of serenity and insight is a state arisen from meditation.

We should not think of the union of serenity and insight as a little fish of analysis swimming in the still water of serenity. That analogy applies before the two are united, when analysis and stability are two distinct factors. After serenity and insight are united, the two occur in one consciousness, with the stability aspect being serenity and the analytical aspect being insight. The two mutually enhance each other, making the mind that is the union of serenity and insight extremely powerful.

The union of serenity and insight on emptiness is simultaneous with a yogi's entry into the path of preparation. At this time, emptiness still appears via a conceptual appearance, however slight, so the concentration is a similitude of nonconceptual wisdom. By continuous meditation, the conceptual appearance of emptiness becomes thinner until it finally vanishes and the person has direct, nonconceptual perception of emptiness. At this time she enters the path of seeing and becomes an ārya.

Some contemporary Theravāda meditation masters emphasize cultivating serenity first, others stress developing insight first, and still others say that practicing the four establishments of mindfulness aids in the cultivation of both simultaneously. Still, to unite them, we must avoid the inactivity that comes by overemphasizing stabilizing meditation and avoid the disturbance to concentration from overemphasizing analysis. As the twentieth-century Sri Lankan master Soma Thera said when speaking of this union:[88]

> Here, the development of penetrative insight (*vipassanā*) combines with that of tranquilizing concentration (*samatha*), and each functions in a way that does not outstrip the other. Both gain uniformity of force. Through the overdoing of analysis there could be agitation. And indolence creeps in through too much tranquility . . . In the sense of yoking (*yuganandhatthena*) and of not letting [either] become overwhelming, contemplative balance is reached.

Is it possible to gain insight before attaining serenity? Previously we were advised to cultivate serenity before insight. But Asaṅga stated in the *Compendium of Knowledge*, "Depending on insight, serenity is accomplished." Here Asaṅga is referring to the serenity of the actual first dhyāna, not the serenity of the preparatory stages to this dhyāna. The insight referred to here is that of meditating on grossness and peacefulness, which is developed during the preparatory stages to the actual first dhyāna. Depending on that insight of grossness and peacefulness, the serenity of the preparatory stages is upgraded and the first dhyāna is attained.

Thus Asaṅga's statement does not contradict the fact that in the Perfection Vehicle, serenity must precede insight. The reason is that analytical meditation, which is the core of meditation on the correct view, cannot bring physical and mental pliancy before serenity has been attained.

REFLECTION

1. What is the definition of serenity? What are the four characteristics of serenity?

2. What is the definition of insight? Why is it important in insight meditation that the bliss of pliancy is induced by analysis? How does that differ from the bliss of pliancy of serenity?

3. Is the object of the union of serenity and insight always emptiness, or may it be other objects?

4. How does the union of serenity and insight fit into the path to awakening and the five paths in particular?

Skillful Means and Wisdom in Post-Meditation Time

What we do in the break times between meditation sessions on emptiness has a strong influence on the next meditation session. Thus maintaining our mindfulness on bodhicitta and emptiness between sessions is important.

At the conclusion of a meditation session on emptiness and before standing up think, "All phenomena do not exist from their own side or with their own ultimate essence. They are dependent on other factors. Because they are empty, they can function. Sentient beings' actions bring their corresponding results. Not seeing this, ordinary sentient beings attribute a mode of existence to phenomena that they do not have. They become confused, attached, and angry, and constantly create the causes for more duḥkha even though they want happiness. Having the fortune of a precious human life, I must fulfill the collections of merit and wisdom to become a buddha and show them the way to higher rebirths and awakening."

In the break times between meditation sessions, purify destructive karma and accumulate merit by engaging in the seven-limb prayer and other practices motivated by bodhicitta. Seal these practices by seeing the agent, object, and action as mutually dependent and as illusion-like. Seeing things as like illusions does not mean to regard them as totally nonexistent, but to view them as not existing inherently although they appear to exist that way. The appearance of people and phenomena as inherently existent is a false appearance. Conditioned phenomena exist dependent on causes and conditions, and all phenomena exist dependent on parts and on being designated by mind.

Seeing things in this way imbues all the meritorious practices we do with wisdom. This helps us avoid "afflictive faith" and "afflictive compassion"—faith, compassion, and other virtuous mental states that are based on grasping true existence. Such faith sees the Three Jewels as truly existent, and afflicted compassion views sentient beings as well as their duḥkha as existing from their own side. Although these are still virtuous mental states, they are polluted by ignorance. For this reason, it is important to incorporate an understanding of emptiness in all our daily activities so that our virtuous attitudes will be powerful and unpolluted.

Based on realizing emptiness inferentially or nonconceptually in meditation sessions, while the mind is still informed by emptiness in the break times, illusion-like appearances naturally arise.[89] Meditation on emptiness isn't done only to negate true existence but also to experience everything as illusion-like during the rest of our lives. This is important to do for several reasons: it prevents falling to the extreme of nihilism, enables bodhisattvas to benefit sentient beings, reduces the possibility of afflictions arising, increases renunciation and compassion, reminds us that afflictions can be eliminated, and enables us to practice skillful means complemented by wisdom. Let's look at these benefits more closely.

Reflecting on the illusion-like nature of phenomena after meditating on their emptiness prevents falling to the extreme of nihilism. While phenomena do not inherently exist, they do exist. Although they appear to exist inherently, that appearance is false. They are like illusions in that there is a discrepancy between their mode of existence and mode of appearance. They appear to exist inherently, whereas they exist dependently, nominally.

Śrāvakas and solitary realizers strive to attain liberation as quickly as possible and thus put great energy into meditative equipoise on emptiness, whereas bodhisattvas seek full awakening, which also requires the extensive collection of merit. To create this great store of merit that will fuel their attainment of full awakening, bodhisattvas must live and function in the world and not remain absorbed in meditative equipoise on emptiness or in their own nirvāṇa. Seeing things in the world as like illusions enables bodhisattvas to reflect on their activities in a proper way while at the same time benefit sentient beings. In addition, seeing the things around them as like illusions helps to prepare them to manifest many illusion-like bodies to benefit sentient beings.

During our daily activities, viewing the people, objects, ideas, and actions we encounter as truly existent causes afflictions to arise. Viewing everyone and everything as like illusions helps to overcome this true-grasping and thus prevents afflictions from arising. However, it does not interfere with generating virtuous mental states.

Sentient beings' duḥkha appears truly existent although it is not. Seeing sentient beings trapped in saṃsāra due to ignorance sparks compassion within us, and we wish these illusion-like sentient beings to be free from their illusion-like duḥkha. This is the way to cultivate the compassion observing the unapprehendable, the third type of compassion Candrakīrti mentioned in his *Supplement*.[90] By not apprehending sentient beings as truly existent, bodhisattvas with this compassion know these illusory-like sentient beings are drowning in duḥkha because they do not see phenomena's empty ultimate nature and their illusion-like conventional nature. They also know that self-grasping can be eradicated, and they have strong compassion wishing to liberate illusion-like sentient beings from their illusion-like saṃsāric duḥkha and its origins. The *Compendium of All Phenomena Sūtra* (*Sarvadharmasaṃgraha Sūtra*) says (MS 38):

> Just as a magician endeavors to free illusory beings,
> but knowing they are illusions
> he is not attached to them,
> likewise, a master of perfect awakening (the Buddha)
> knows that the three worlds are like an illusion.
> He puts on armor to do battle for living beings,
> but knows living beings are like illusions.

Wisdom and Skillful Means

Kyabje Ling Rinpoche was my senior tutor and the preceptor who gave me the bhikṣu vow. When I was young, I was afraid of him. He didn't smile much and often had a stern face. He initially was very strict with me, but later we gradually became extremely close. He was the primary one who taught me the great Sūtrayāna and Vajrayāna treatises, and I am very grateful to him. A few years before he passed away, I related my experience of emptiness to him and he was very pleased. He also praised me and said that

I will soon become a space yogi. The term "space yogi" comes in one of the Seventh Dalai Lama's songs of experience (SSC):

> Just as a cloud disperses in the autumn sky,
> in the vision of my mind as being inseparably one with emptiness,
> all experiences and perceptions dissolve;
> I, an unborn yogi of space.

Ling Rinpoche encouraged me to continue my practice of meditation on emptiness and bodhicitta, implying that if I put effort into meditating on emptiness, I should be able to directly realize it in this life.

The realization of emptiness by the union of serenity and insight will make a qualitative difference in our lives. Our minds will experience greater and greater freedom as the clinging and attachment that breed dissatisfaction are reduced. Our feeling of connection with sentient beings and care for their well-being will expand. Realizing emptiness enables bodhisattvas to engage deeply with sentient beings in the world, but with a light touch. Their minds do not get discouraged or despondent, fearful or agitated. They continue meditating, deepening their realization of emptiness as well as their understanding of dependent arising—especially the law of karma and effects—so that they can establish subtle conventional truths in the aftermath of their realization of emptiness. Their wisdom overcomes apathy and stimulates active and joyful engagement working for the temporary and ultimate welfare of sentient beings. Candrakīrti lauds the abilities of sixth-ground bodhisattvas (MMA 6.225):

> Though their minds may rest continuously in cessation,
> they also generate compassion for beings bereft of protection.
> Advancing further, they will also outshine through their wisdom
> all those born from the Buddha's speech and the middle buddhas.

Although their minds continuously abide in clear light, they do not forget the duḥkha of sentient beings and enhance their compassion and activities to benefit those bereft of protection. They act in the domain of saṃsāra while their minds abide in the sphere of nirvāṇa. As they progress on the path, they will outshine all śrāvakas (those who hear and teach the Buddha's word) and middle buddhas (solitary realizers) due to their intelligence and wisdom that realize emptiness with many different reasonings. In short, their dazzling wisdom and heartfelt compassion work in tandem.

To practice like these bodhisattvas, practice generosity, ethical conduct, fortitude, and so forth in your daily life. Rather than pollute your mind by seeing these practices as truly existent, bring forth the wisdom seeing them as like illusions. In this way, skillful means and wisdom complement each other. For example, before giving material gifts, protection, encouragement, or Dharma teachings to others, be mindful that yourself as the person who is giving, the action of giving, and the recipient all lack true existence, yet appear like illusions. Similarly, the person who lives ethically, the action of observing ethical conduct, and the sentient beings with whom ethical conduct is being practiced are empty of true existence but exist dependently, appearing like illusions.

This reflection is also done when dedicating the merit after completing any virtuous activity. Contemplate: I as the person who creates the merit, the merit itself, and the awakening for which it is dedicated appear truly existent although they are not. I am aware of their illusion-like existence.

Conversely, skillful means complements wisdom. This is done by reflecting on the plight of sentient beings, arousing compassion for them, and generating bodhicitta before meditating on emptiness. When moved by bodhicitta, our motivation to realize emptiness is strong, and that increases our effort and mindfulness. After meditating on emptiness, we then close the session with a strong dedication, for example by reciting the "Extraordinary Aspiration of the Practice of Samantabhadra" or the "Lamrim Dedication" at the end of the *Great Treatise*.

People who lack the correct view, as well as those following the śrāvakas' path or the solitary realizers' path, cannot attain buddhahood. Those lacking the correct view cling tightly to a doctrine of inherent existence and cannot realize emptiness. Without the wisdom realizing emptiness, they cannot purify their minds completely, even if they do many ascetic practices and compassionate acts that benefit others. Although śrāvakas and solitary realizers have correct wisdom, they lack the skillful means and the great compassion that lead to bodhicitta. Without bodhicitta—the aspiration to attain buddhahood to benefit sentient beings—buddhahood cannot be attained. These arhats are content to remain in nirvāṇa.

As their faculties develop, people may change paths. Those who have incorrect views may gain the correct view as set forth by the Buddha. Śrāvakas and solitary realizers may cultivate great compassion and bodhicitta and follow the bodhisattva path. Bodhisattvas possess skillful means, so they do not aspire to remain in the peace of nirvāṇa as the śrāvakas and solitary realizers do, but to attain nonabiding nirvāṇa—the full awakening of buddhahood. By combining wisdom and skillful means, they fulfill the two collections and attain the four bodies of a Buddha. The *Vimalakīrtinirdeśa Sūtra* clarifies (MS 9):

> What is bondage and what is liberation for bodhisattvas? Clinging to life in the world without skillful means is bondage for bodhisattvas. Living in the world with skillful means is liberation. Clinging to life in the world without wisdom is bondage for bodhisattvas. Living in the world with wisdom is liberation. Wisdom not embraced by skillful means is bondage. Wisdom embraced by skillful means is liberation. Skillful means not embraced by wisdom is bondage. Skillful means embraced by wisdom is liberation.

For bodhisattvas, skillful means that lack wisdom binds them in saṃsāra, unable to be of the greatest benefit to all beings because their minds are still obscured by defilements. Wisdom lacking skillful means keeps them in an arhat's nirvāṇa, unable to fulfill their deepest aspiration to benefit all beings most effectively. Therefore bodhisattvas put energy into cultivating both skillful means and wisdom, in order to fulfill the collections of merit and wisdom, and to attain the form body and truth body of a buddha.

Some people mistakenly believe that only the practice of wisdom is necessary for full awakening. If we look at the life of the Buddha himself, we see that he practiced both wisdom and skillful means for many eons in order to complete all the causes necessary to attain buddhahood. The *Space Treasure Sūtra* (*Gaganagañja Sūtra*) tells us (MS 36):

> Because of their knowledge of wisdom bodhisattvas eliminate all afflictions. Because of their knowledge of skillful means they do not abandon sentient beings.

The *Sūtra Unraveling the Thought* says (MS 36–37):

> I do not predict supreme, true, perfect awakening for one who is not concerned with the welfare of sentient beings and who is not concerned with realizing the nature of all composite phenomena.

Kamalaśīla states in the *Middle Stages of Meditation* (MS 38):

> Based on the bodhisattvas' practice of wisdom and skillful means it is said, "Their activities remain in saṃsāra, but their thoughts abide in nirvāṇa."

So many benefits come from integrating skillful means and pristine wisdom. Coarse afflictions will be undermined and your mind will be happy—you will even have good dreams. You will abide with mental peace, enjoy good health, and get along better with others. You don't need to spend a lot of money to do this, and undergoing great hardship is not required. The happiness received from these practices is not short-lived but will endure for lifetimes.

As your practice deepens, you will be able to attain the superknowledges, such as recalling past lives, knowing the karma of others, and having insight into the future. Your mind will become very flexible and you will be able to engage in many activities and projects that benefit sentient beings and protect them from harm. Ripening many sentient beings' minds, you will lead them on the path to full awakening. Pristine wisdom will grow in your mindstream and you will directly and nonconceptually realize suchness. You will fulfill the two collections, and by continued, progressive meditation, you'll eradicate all afflictive obscurations and cognitive obscurations from your mind, making your life extremely meaningful by actualizing the four bodies of a buddha.

Don't set a timeline for when you will attain awakening. That is unrealistic and will just cause frustration. Worldly things too take time to resolve. Attaining awakening is not an easy task, so meditate continuously and with great delight over a long period of time. Candrakīrti said the following in praise of the sixth ground bodhisattvas; it applies to pure-ground bodhisattvas as well (MMA 6.226):

> And like a monarch of swans soaring ahead of other accomplished swans,
> with white wings of conventional and ultimate truths spread wide,
> propelled by the powerful winds of virtue, the bodhisattva will
> cruise to the excellent far shore, the oceanic qualities of the conquerors.

The two wings are the stages of the vast path dealing with conventional truths and the stages of the profound path that teaches ultimate truths. With these practices and realizations integrated in their minds and powered by their great collection of merit, these bodhisattvas will sail across the swamp of saṃsāra to the far shore of full awakening imbued with the magnificent qualities of a mind that is totally purified and effortlessly manifests in diverse forms to benefit sentient beings.

Those of us who aspire to attain the same result should practice with two wings—the vast and profound paths of method and wisdom—just as these great ārya bodhisattvas do. We should not be content with practicing a path that lacks both of these and emphasizes only the happiness of this life. Nor should we practice an incomplete path, like a bird with an injured wing. Having found the complete and correct path taught by the Buddha and an excellent spiritual mentor to teach and guide us, let's joyfully persevere until we reach the path's end and can be the greatest benefit to all sentient beings.

REFLECTION

1. Why is it necessary to practice insight together with bodhicitta and the skillful means of the six perfections?
2. Why is clinging to life in the world without skillful means bondage for bodhisattvas? Imagine being a bodhisattva who realizes emptiness but does not practice the perfections. Can they fulfill their bodhicitta aspirations?
3. Why is clinging to life in the world without wisdom bondage for bodhisattvas? How would the lack of wisdom inhibit their bodhisattva aspirations?

4. Imagine the uneasiness a bodhisattva would experience lacking either skillful means or wisdom.

Wise Advice for Uniting Serenity and Insight

Late in his life, Tsongkhapa composed a short text called "Vajra Lines on the View [of Emptiness]." Here he gives advice on how to practice as our understanding and experience of emptiness traverses four stages: the initial stage, the stage of cultivating serenity and insight on emptiness, the stage of meditating on emptiness after attaining serenity, and the stage of directly realizing emptiness.

1. As a beginner cultivating some experience of emptiness, do not contemplate any affirmative phenomena after negating inherent existence. Although phenomena are both empty and exist dependently, at this time stay with the mere nonaffirming negation of inherent existence.
2. When cultivating both serenity and insight on emptiness, maintain balance between the single-pointedness of serenity and the analytic process to realize emptiness. Avoid overemphasizing single-pointedness and neglecting the analysis that is so crucial to experience the correct view.
3. After attaining serenity, unite serenity and insight such that the probing awareness analyzing emptiness gives rise to the mental and physical pliancy that leads to serenity. This is the union of serenity and insight on emptiness in which analysis does not disturb the tranquility of meditative absorption and the tranquility of meditative absorption does not impede probing awareness.
4. When emptiness is realized directly and nonconceptually, the subject (the wisdom mind) and its object (emptiness) become nondual, like water poured into water. This mind is pure experience of emptiness; it does not think, "I have realized emptiness," and no veilings appear to it.

In highest yoga tantra, the realization of emptiness is developed in a slightly different way. First, as above, analysis is employed to gain the correct view of emptiness. This is a conceptual consciousness. Then, during meditation, it is not necessary to cultivate serenity and then insight in that order. Rather, yogis engage in tantric meditations that enable them to make manifest an increasingly subtle mind that is conjoined with great bliss. Since this meditating mind is so subtle, there is no need for further analysis; the mind's absorption into emptiness leads to the union of serenity and insight on emptiness.

12 | Insight in Chinese Buddhism and the Pāli Tradition

Buddhism in China: Serenity and Insight in Tiantai

China and East Asia are home to many Buddhist traditions. Among them is Tiantai, whose founder Zhiyi (538–97) explained the practice of serenity and insight in his voluminous treatise *Great Serenity and Insight* (*Mo-ho chih-kuan*).

Tiantai speaks of three truths: (1) The provisional or conventional truth refers to causality, conditionality, and dependent arising. The study of the conventional includes the study of the five aggregates and so forth. (2) The ultimate truth is emptiness, the lack of inherent self-nature of all phenomena. (3) The highest truth is the Middle Way—phenomena being both empty of self-nature and existing conventionally. This constitutes the full realization of buddhahood.

Insight practice has three steps. The first is to enter emptiness from the conventional. As ordinary beings, all our experiences involve the conventional world, so at the beginning we learn how to use conventional truths to realize emptiness. The second step is the reverse. Once we have conceptually understood emptiness, we must know how to establish the existence of the conventional world from the standpoint of emptiness and how to return to the conventional world with this new understanding of the ultimate truth. The third step is to balance the conventional and ultimate perspectives; this is the truth of the Middle Way, the highest truth. In this way, Zhiyi's Tiantai is faithful to Nāgārjuna's Madhyamaka.

Practitioners who cultivate serenity and insight progress sequentially (EBM 189):

> [Practitioners who cultivate serenity and insight] . . . realize that, in every case, all phenomena arise from the mind and, due to the falseness and insubstantiality of causes and conditions, they are empty. Because they realize that they are empty, they are unable to apprehend any existence in the names and characteristics linked to any phenomenon.

When transiting from the contemplation of conventional truth to the contemplation of emptiness, the ultimate truth, practitioners perceive neither the fruit of buddhahood nor the suffering sentient beings they want to liberate.

If someone stays in this contemplation of the unconditioned and has a direct realization of emptiness, he will follow the śrāvakas' and solitary realizers' paths to arhatship. This is because he becomes so entranced with emptiness, to the exclusion of the compassion side of the path, that he loses interest in full awakening. To express this in another way, having put too much emphasis on personal liberation, he does not perceive the buddha nature and lacks the motivation to attain buddhahood.

Bodhisattvas, on the other hand, engage in all the bodhisattva activities and do not become attached to the unconditioned. After meditating on emptiness, bodhisattvas go from the contemplation of the truth of emptiness to the contemplation of conventional truth. They realize that although the nature of the mind is empty, all phenomena in the conventional world still function. All these conventional phenomena are like magical illusions. Although they lack any fixed inherent reality, conventionally they have different characteristics that are perceived by the six senses. Through such contemplation, bodhisattvas understand that within the sphere of emptiness they can cultivate all the other bodhisattva practices. They can understand the myriad different dispositions of sentient beings and can teach them whichever among the incalculable number of different practices are most suited for those particular sentient beings. In this way bodhisattvas benefit sentient beings in all six realms of saṃsāra. This is wisdom characterized by skillful means adapted to conditions; it comes from moving from contemplation of the truth of emptiness to contemplation of conventional truth.

When meditators stay in this contemplation, they perceive the buddha nature, but not yet with full comprehension. This is because they have put too much emphasis on wisdom and have not yet entered into the fully correct and complete contemplation. Zhiyi explains (EBM 193):

> If one completely comprehends that the nature of the mind is neither true nor false, and if one puts to rest the mind that takes truth and falseness as objective conditions, this constitutes correctness.
>
> If one truly contemplates the nature of mind as neither empty nor conventionally existent while still not refuting those phenomena that are either empty or conventionally existent, and if one is able to realize this sort of complete illumination, then in the very nature of mind one attains a penetrating understanding of the Middle Way and attains perfect illumination of the two truths.
>
> If one is able to perceive the Middle Way and the two truths in one's own mind, one perceives the Middle Way and the two truths in all phenomena but still does not grasp at either the Middle Way or the two truths. This is because no definite and fixed [essential] nature can be found in them. This constitutes the correct contemplation of the Middle Way. This is set forth in a verse from *Treatise on the Middle Way* (24.18):
>
> > That which is dependent arising
> > is explained to be emptiness.
> > That, being a dependent designation,
> > is itself the Middle Way.

This verse explains the Middle Way as well as the two provisional contemplations on conventional truth and the truth of emptiness. When bodhisattvas abide in this contemplation of the Middle Way, their meditative concentration and wisdom are equal and balanced; they perceive the buddha nature completely and are established in the Mahāyāna. These bodhisattvas will be able to manifest many bodies that go to the buddha lands and make offerings to the buddhas of the ten directions and many bodies that go to teach and guide the six classes of sentient beings and lead them to awakening. They perfect the six perfections and receive and maintain the Dharma treasury of all buddhas. Ascending through the bodhisattva grounds, they become the companions of Mañjuśrī and Samantabhadra. They quickly attain full awakening, the truth body and form body, and enact the twelve deeds of a wheel-turning buddha. The *Lotus Sūtra* states that they "carry on the endeavors of the Tathāgata."

Buddhism in China: Serenity and Insight in Chan/Zen

The Chinese word Chan was originally *Chan-na*, the Chinese pronunciation of the Sanskrit word *dhyāna* (P. *jhāna*). When Chan spread to Japan in the twelfth century, the Japanese pronunciation was *Zen*.

To understand the Chan approach to serenity and insight, it's helpful to know the historical origin of this tradition. The Chan practice began one day when the Buddha was preparing to teach on Vulture Peak. Instead of speaking a sūtra, he looked at the assembly and held up a flower that had been offered to him. Nobody understood why the Buddha did this without saying a word, except for Mahākāśyapa, who smiled with understanding. Through his own meditative experience, Mahākāśyapa had understood the hidden meaning of the Buddha's gesture. The Buddha then declared, "I possess the true eye of the Dharma, the profound mind of nirvāṇa, the reality that transcends all forms, the supreme and subtle teaching inexpressible by words and speech. This mind seal outside of scriptures, I now transmit to Mahākāśyapa."

In this way, Mahākāśyapa received a special transmission from the Buddha and became the first Chan patriarch. This special transmission of the mind, which is beyond words, was passed on in a single lineage to the twenty-eighth patriarch, the Indian meditation master Bodhidharma. He went to China in the early sixth century and continued the lineage there. Over time this became the five houses of Chan in China. Currently, two sub-branches of Chan exist: Linji (J. Rinzai, K. Imje) and Caodong (J. Soto, K. Chodong), both of which developed in the ninth century and were founded by Linji Yixuan (d. 866) and Dongshan Liangjie (807–869), respectively. In Japan the two houses of Zen are characterized by Caodong (Soto), focusing more on "just sitting," and Linji (Rinzai), using *koans*—

puzzling statements that challenge us to go beyond the limits of our conceptual mind—and *huatous*—questions that confront the nature of our very being—both of which help us investigate the nature of the mind. However, in Chinese Buddhism, the masters of both sects are not restricted to these specific methods and are free to utilize methods from other Chan sects.

At its essence Chan meditation aims for the unification of serenity and insight. Chan practitioners engage in stabilizing meditation to develop strong focus and stability of mind to cultivate serenity. They engage in analytical meditation involving contemplation and investigation to bring about wisdom and cultivate insight. In traditional serenity practice, mindfulness is established on the breath, making the mind clear and sharp. With this concentrated mind, you notice the subtle characteristics of the breath. Further examining these characteristics is analytical meditation, which develops insight and wisdom. With consistent practice of both serenity and insight in one meditation session, unification of the two will occur.

This practice of combining stabilizing and analytical meditation can be applied to any activity, such as eating. Eating mindfully, being fully aware of the different flavors and textures, is analytical meditation. Doing this with a focused and undistracted mind is stabilizing meditation. This way of practicing stabilizing and analytical meditation can be done in all activities: brushing our teeth, walking, doing chores, and so forth. In principle, serenity and insight can be united in any activity.

Meditating this way when working is an important part of Chan practice. There are many Chan stories and koans that stem from dialogues between master and disciple that occur while doing manual work—planting trees, working in the field, cleaning the kitchen, and so on. Silent sitting meditation is also crucial in Chan. Practitioners aim to conjoin sitting and working meditation so that eventually no difference is seen between the two.

Another important meditation in Chan is the meditation of "no-thought" or "no-mind," the mind of no-thought. Every thought in the mind before we become awakened is a thought under the influence of self-grasping; when self-grasping is present, afflictions easily arise. The ultimate state, the mind of a buddha, is the mind of no-thought: all afflictive thoughts, all wrong views, all self-grasping are absent. This is the goal of Chan. The mind of no-thought is not a mind that is idle or blank; it is a mind free of attachment and afflictions, a mind that sees phenomena exactly as they are. This mind is free from all layers of conceptual veils and biases that obscure the unawakened mind. The cessation of conceptual fabrications reveals the mind of no-thought; it is the mind of a buddha. Reality is experienced as it is—this is true-suchness (*tathatā*), the way phenomena exist.

Over hundreds of years starting with the arrival of Bodhidharma in the fifth century, the Chinese Chan masters have developed particular Chan meditation forms—for example, the "silent illumination" or "just sitting" method, which is the preferred practice of Caodong (Soto) Chan. Here practitioners simply sit and empty the mind. They must be very careful to empty the mind in the proper way so that awareness is fully present, but all extraneous or afflictive thought has been released and there is no clinging to anything at all. This is a direct path to the mind of no-thought.

Other well-known Chan methods developed by the early Chan masters are the koan and huatou methods mentioned above. *Koan* comes from the Chinese word "gong an," and refers to a question or dialogue that doesn't seem to make any sense—for example, "What is your original face before your parents gave birth to you?" "Who is dragging this corpse around?" and "What is the sound of one hand clapping?" Practitioners are to investigate the koans, but not in an intellectual way because there are no logical, rational answers to the koans. These stories or questions appear to be nonsense to us due to our self-grasping, our afflictive way of looking at phenomena that obscures their reality. For people who are awakened, koans are not nonsensical; they understand where the question comes from and the purpose it serves. There are no fixed or correct answers to the koans. Practitioners use the question to force the mind into a corner where all conceptual thought becomes useless. At the same time, concentration deepens as they continue to investigate the koan. At some point, practitioners break through the veil of ignorance. The koan method has helped many Chan masters attain awakening.

Huatou means "beginning of a word/thought." In this method, a practitioner starts by holding a phrase in the mind—for example, "Amituofo" (Amitābha Buddha) or "Who am I?" Unlike the koan method, where practitioners investigate and try to resolve the question, with huatous they observe the origin of thoughts that arise in the mind. Before I say "Amituofo," this thought does not exist in my mind. After I say that, a thought has arisen. Before there was no thought, now there is thought; where does that thought come from? Seek in the mind the origin of that thought—where and how that thought arises. This is very subtle practice; the ordinary mind is too coarse, and at first practitioners get nowhere. Absorption in deep concentration with a very subtle and refined mind is needed to notice the origin of a thought. Through this investigation, the barrier between thought and no-thought is broken down; practitioners realize nonduality and attain awakening.[91]

In Chinese Buddhism, although the koan and huatou methods are associated more with the Linji school and the just-sitting method is more prominent in Caodong, good Chan masters examine each student individually and adopt whatever method is most appropriate to lead him or her on the path. In Japan, however, it seems to be more fixed: Rinzai practitioners contemplate koans and Soto practitioners just sit.

Although some previous Chan practitioners did not emphasize scriptural study, this was not the case with most Chan schools. Bodhidharma, the founder of Chan in China, taught the *Descent into Laṅka Sūtra* to seal or confirm one's insights. The early Chan masters in India and China relied on the Perfection of Wisdom sūtras and especially the *Diamond Sūtra*. As time went on and the tathāgatagarbha doctrine was introduced in China, some of its ideas were adopted by Chan masters. The *Śūraṃgama Sūtra* (*Shoulengyan jing*), translated into Chinese by the Central Asian monk Pāramiti in 705, is one of the main sūtras prominently referenced in the Chan school. Nowadays, some Chinese Chan practitioners and many Korean Seon practitioners study Madhyamaka. Most Chan masters do not reject scriptures or study, as some people mistakenly think. Some are very knowledgeable in the sūtras.

Pāli Tradition: Serenity and Insight

In the *In Tandem Sutta* (*Yuganaddha Sutta*, AN 4.170), Ānanda speaks of four ways through which practitioners may attain arhatship. The way that a particular individual practices depends on their faculties and the guidance of their teacher.[92]

1. Insight preceded by serenity. These meditators first practice serenity and, based on gaining a still and undistracted mind, they cultivate

insight by contemplating the three characteristics. By doing so, the supramundane path arises.

2. Serenity preceded by insight. These practitioners first cultivate insight by contemplating the three characteristics and then develop serenity. In this way, they generate the supramundane path.
3. Serenity and insight cultivated in tandem. These meditators cultivate serenity and insight together by alternating them. They attain the first dhyāna, and after emerging from it examine its constituents with insight, seeing them as impermanent, in the nature of duḥkha and not a self. They then attain the second dhyāna, and after emerging from it similarly examine its mental factors, aggregates, and so on in light of the three characteristics. They alternate the cultivation of concentration and insight in this manner with the other meditative absorptions until they actualize stream-entry.
4. Settling restlessness concerning the Dharma. Some practitioners' minds are seized by agitation and restlessness regarding the Dharma. When these obstacles are stilled and the mind settles down and becomes unified and concentrated, the supramundane path arises. What is this mental agitation? According to the canonical exegetic text, *Paṭisambhidāmagga*, it is the ten corruptions of insight (P. *vipassanā-upakkilesa*). Practitioners have remarkable experiences in their meditation, such as experiences of illumination, knowledge, rapturous happiness, serenity, bliss, resolution, exertion, assurance, equanimity, and attachment.[93] They respond to the first nine experiences with the tenth—attachment. Forgetting to contemplate the impermanence of these remarkable experiences, they overestimate their attainment, cease to practice correctly, and fall prey to attachment.

   The ten corruptions of insight do not arise in āryas or in people who lack good ethical conduct or are meditating in an improper way. They only arise in people who are practicing correctly but are beginners in insight and thus easily excited by new experiences. Because the ten imperfections of insight block further development, they need to be eliminated.

Another interpretation of this agitation could be mental restlessness produced by eagerness to realize the Dharma. In some cases this can precipitate realization of the truth, as seems to have been the case with Bāhiya Dārucīriya (Ud 1.10). Bāhiya was a non-Buddhist ascetic practicing in an area on the west coast of India. Honored and respected by others, Bāhiya began to think that perhaps he was an arhat. Noticing this, a deva told him that he was nowhere near that attainment and further told him that the true arhat in the world was the Buddha, living at Sāvatthi. Bāhiya traveled across India intent on meeting the Buddha. Encountering the Buddha on his alms round, he pleaded with the Buddha for instructions. The Buddha gave him a very brief teaching. As soon as the Buddha completed the teaching, Bāhiya attained arhatship on the spot. His persistence in searching for the Buddha paid off, because shortly after that, he was attacked by a cow and died.

Each of these four ways lead to stream-entry and to the eventual overcoming of all fetters, underlying tendencies, and pollutants. Everyone who has attained liberation has done so in one of these four ways.

Pāli Tradition: Insight into the Meditative Absorptions

The Buddha also explained how insight can be developed on the basis of the dhyānas. In the *Greater Discourse to Mālunkyāputta* he says (MN 64:9):

> And what, Ānanda, is the path, the way to the abandoning of the five lower fetters? Here, with seclusion from objects of attachment, with the abandoning of nonvirtuous states, with the complete tranquilization of physical inertia, quite secluded from sensual pleasures, secluded from nonvirtuous states, a monastic enters upon and abides in the first jhāna, which is accompanied by investigation and analysis, with joy and bliss born of seclusion.
>
> Whatever exists therein of material form, feeling, discrimination, miscellaneous factors, and consciousness, he sees those states as impermanent, as dukkha, as a disease, as a tumor, as a barb, as a calamity, as an affliction, as alien, as disintegrating, as void, as not self. He turns his mind away from those states and directs it toward the deathless element thus: "This is the peaceful, this is the sublime; that is, the stilling of all formations, the relinquishing of all attachments, the destruction of craving,

> dispassion, cessation, nibbāna." Standing upon that, he attains the destruction of the pollutants.

The first paragraph resembles the standard passage describing someone who has attained serenity and is now attaining the first dhyāna. Initially, the practitioner must have "seclusion from objects of attachment." But physical separation from objects of attachment is not sufficient; he must also have lessened his attachment to them so that his mind is not obsessed and enslaved by craving for them. Then he abandons nonvirtuous states—that is, he subdues the five hindrances that interfere with concentration: sensual desire, malice, lethargy and sleepiness, restlessness and regret, and doubt. By completely calming physical inertia, the body and mind are made serviceable. Entering and abiding in the first dhyāna, all five absorption factors are present in his mind—investigation (*vitarka*, *vitakka*), analysis (*vicāra*), joy (*prīti*, *pīti*), bliss (*sukha*), and one-pointedness (*ekāgratā*, *ekaggatā*).

The second paragraph introduces insight meditation. Now the meditator develops insight by examining the very dhyāna in which his mind was single-pointedly absorbed. If the sūtra is read literally, it seems that the person begins insight meditation within the dhyāna. But the commentary explains that insight meditation is not done within a dhyāna because when meditating in a state of dhyāna, the mind is fixed immovably on one object only. Analysis is difficult to do because it involves considering one object after another and regarding one object from different viewpoints. Thus the commentary says that the meditator dwells for some time in the first dhyāna, stabilizing and deepening it. After that, he comes out of the dhyāṇa, but his mind is still influenced by the force of the dhyāna; the impression of the dhyāna is still strong and vivid in his mind.

Then he looks into the dhyānic consciousness and analyzes its various components into form, feeling, discrimination, miscellaneous factors, and consciousness. The body in which the dhyānic consciousness dwells is included in the form aggregate. When meditating on a *kasiṇa* (S. *kṛtsna*), the sign (P. *nimitta*) is considered a form object and is included in the form aggregate. Bliss is a predominant feeling in the first dhyāna. Discrimination discerns the meditation object—the nimitta, one of the four immeasurables, and so forth. The mental factors of investigation, analysis, joy, and one-pointedness are miscellaneous factors, as are the mental factors of mindfulness, concentration, and so forth that are active in dhyāna. The mental consciousness is included in the consciousness aggregate.

Previously the dhyāna experience appeared to be one unified experience. However, upon dissecting it into its various components and clearly identifying and examining those components, the perception of the dhyāna shifts and the meditator recognizes it as a compounded, conditioned phenomenon. It is made from and consists of the five aggregates and is nothing more than a compound of certain aspects of the five aggregates. It is not one whole, self-sufficient thing.

The meditator then investigates this compound of the five aggregates in terms of the three characteristics, seeing each component as impermanent, unsatisfactory in nature, and selfless. In the passage above, the Buddha describes eleven ways that the meditator views the aggregates with insight. "Impermanent" and "disintegrating" point to the characteristic of impermanence; "suffering, a disease, a tumor, a barb, a calamity, and an affliction" indicate the characteristic of duḥkha; "alien," "void," and "not self" refer to the characteristic of selflessness. This must be a powerful meditation because in the dhyānic state the meditator experiences a bliss and peace that he had never known as a desire-realm being. Now, upon further examination, he realizes that this experience is not a realization of the ultimate. It is not to be clung to because it is impermanent, unsatisfactory, and empty of substantial reality. As he continues to meditate, he expands this new understanding that arose from insight and arrives at deeper insight knowledge.

At some point, the meditator becomes completely disenchanted with the five aggregates and begins to turn away from them, seeking that which is not disintegrating and not impermanent—the unconditioned—which is blissful and secure. With insight knowledge he directs his attention toward what exists beyond the five aggregates—the unconditioned, the deathless. He has heard it extolled as peaceful and sublime—it is the stilling of all conditioned things, the giving up of all attachments, the abandonment of craving, the freedom from clinging, cessation, and nirvāṇa.

When the meditator's mind reaches the peak of insight knowledge and insight wisdom, it spontaneously turns away from conditioned phenomena to penetrate the deathless, seeing it with clear vision. The mind has now reached the ārya path, the supramundane path with nirvāṇa as its object.[94]

At this point, if the meditator's mind remains firm and can hold the direct vision of nirvāṇa, he can attain arhatship—the destruction of all pollutants—by eradicating all ten fetters in one fell swoop. This is difficult, however, because a subtle delight can easily arise. This delight is not ordinary craving. According to the commentary, it is a subtle attachment to serenity and insight. This is what is meant by "desire for the Dharma" and "delight in the Dharma." This subtle attachment to serenity and insight corrupts the experience of nirvāṇa and blocks the full eradication of all defilements. Instead of becoming an arhat, the meditator destroys the five lower fetters—view of a personal identity, doubt, view holding bad ethics and modes of conduct as supreme, sensual desire, and malice—and becomes a nonreturner. When his human life ends, he is no longer born in the desire realm and will spontaneously be reborn in the form or formless realm where he will attain arhatship.[95]

The sūtra continues with the same description of cultivating insight knowledge and then turning the mind to penetrate the deathless on the basis of the second, third, and fourth dhyānas, as well as on the basis of the formless realm absorptions of the base of infinite space, the base of infinite consciousness, and the base of nothingness. However, if the meditator enters a formless absorption and later emerges from it to analyze its components with insight, he does so in terms of only four aggregates. This is because formless-realm beings lack a material body and have only the four mental aggregates. Although this meditator is still a human being and has a material body, he does not perceive it while in the formless realm absorptions. The peak of saṃsāra—the base of neither-discrimination-nor-nondiscrimination—is not mentioned as a basis for this meditation because it is too rarified. The consciousness and mental factors present in this attainment are so subtle that the meditator cannot discern them with enough clarity to contemplate them in terms of the three characteristics.

REFLECTION

1. Consider that the consciousness of the first dhyāna involves all five aggregates: it dwells in the body and focuses on a kasiṇa, which is form; bliss is feeling; discrimination discerns the meditation object; the mental factors

of investigation, analysis, joy, and one-pointedness are miscellaneous factors; and the mental consciousness is consciousness.

2. Examine one of your mental states, analyzing it as above, and become aware that it involves the five aggregates and is nothing beyond those five. It has no essence of its own and is not mine, I, or my self.

In summary, all four dhyānas and three of the formless absorptions can be used as a basis to realize the three characteristics and penetrate nirvāṇa. If the first dhyāna is not strong enough to act as a basis to eradicate all five fetters at once, the meditator could enter a deeper level of samādhi until she finds one that is suitable, so that her insight into the three characteristics and penetration of nirvāṇa is strong enough to cut off the five fetters. The process is the same no matter which samādhi is used: First the meditator dwells in that samādhi for a period of time, infusing her mind with that experience. Then she leaves the samādhi and begins insight meditation, analyzing the factors of that samādhi in terms of the five aggregates. Then she reflects on the five aggregates present during that samādhi as impermanent, unsatisfactory, and empty of a substantial self. Being disenchanted with conditioned phenomena such as the aggregates, she turns her mind to the unconditioned, initially because she heard it was peaceful and sublime. At the point her wisdom has acquired sufficient power, she penetrates through conditioned phenomena and directly realizes nirvāṇa, the unconditioned, the deathless. If she can maintain her realization firmly, she will eradicate all ten fetters at once. If, because of subtle attachment to serenity or insight, she is not able to do this, she will instead eradicate the first five fetters and become a nonreturner.

In the *Discourse to the Man from Aṭṭhakanāgara*, Ānanda presents an approach to insight that resembles the one above with certain modifications. In this sūtra, the householder Dasama asks if there is a method whereby a monastic who practices diligently and earnestly can go from being unliberated to being liberated and can go from being with pollutants to being unpolluted. Ānanda responds (MN 52.4):

> Here, householder, quite secluded from sensual pleasures, secluded from nonvirtuous states, a monastic enters and abides in the first jhāna, which is accompanied by investigation and analysis, with joy and bliss born of seclusion. He considers this and understands it thus: "This first jhāna is conditioned and intentionally produced. But whatever is conditioned and intentionally produced is impermanent, subject to cessation."

As with the method explained in the *Greater Discourse to Mālunkyāputta*, this meditator has attained the first dhyāna. Based on reducing craving for sensual pleasures and suppressing the five hindrances, she attains the first dhyāna with its five dhyānic factors. With her mind absorbed one-pointedly in this state of concentration, she gains stability in it. After a while, she emerges from the dhyāna to analyze it with insight. Her mind is not in an entirely ordinary state and is still imbued with the flavor of the dhyāna. Unlike in the method taught to Mālunkyāputta where the first dhyāna was dissected into its constituent five aggregates and each aggregate investigated individually, here the dhyāna is taken as a whole and seen as conditioned and intentionally produced.

The first dhyāna is "conditioned," meaning it was mentally conditioned and mentally fabricated; it is also "intentionally produced," indicating that the mental factor of intention is prominent. Without examination, it could seem that the dhyāna is a unitary, substantial thing. Because of the great joy and bliss experienced in that state, it is easy to become attached to it, and if the meditator then viewed the dhyāna as an independent entity, she could easily misinterpret it to be a permanent self. In fact, many meditators at the Buddha's time and afterward have mistaken the mind in deep states of meditative absorption to be a self-existing self or soul, or to be Brahmā or God. Thus caught in craving for bliss and in clinging to wrong views, the meditator is far from liberation.

The examination that Ānanda proposes not only prevents and counteracts this but also leads to wisdom and liberation. A dhyāna, like any other thing in saṃsāra, is conditioned. It was created through the effort of the mind. Intention played a chief role in this, for without the intention to attain dhyāna, the person would not have gone about generating the antidotes to the five hindrances and cultivating the five factors of the first dhyāna. The meditator thus reflects on the many various causes and conditions—the antidotes to the five hindrances, mindfulness, concentration, the five dhyānic factors, and so forth—that she had to cultivate to fulfill her intention to attain the first dhyāna.

After meditating deeply on the fact that the first dhyāna came about due to causes and conditions, the meditator recalls that whatever is mentally fabricated and intentionally produced is impermanent and subject to ceasing. It cannot be any other way, because something that arises through causes and conditions ceases when those causes and conditions cease. From there the meditator may directly begin to reflect that because it is dependent, conditioned, and impermanent, it is not a self. Or she may first reflect that something that is impermanent and dependent on polluted conditions is unsatisfactory and therefore cannot be a self.

Ānanda continues, saying that if the meditator can hold with firm insight the impermanence of this conditioned and intentionally produced dhyāna, it is possible that she will attain arhatship, the destruction of the pollutants. Here it appears that a meditator whose aptitude is ripe and mature can go directly from the state of an ordinary being to arhatship. However, if subtle liking and attachment for serenity or insight arise and the meditator cannot free herself from that, the clarity and power of the insight is impaired and it cannot cut through all ten fetters at once. As a result, instead of becoming an arhat, she overcomes the five lower fetters and becomes a nonreturner. Ānanda then explains the same process in terms of the second, third, and fourth dhyānas.

Ānanda continues by describing the same analysis and procedure to develop insight in terms of the four immeasurable states (MN 52.8):

> Again, a monastic abides pervading one quarter with a mind imbued with loving-kindness, likewise the second, likewise the third, likewise the fourth; so above, below, around, and everywhere, and to all as to himself, he abides pervading the all-encompassing world with a mind imbued with loving-kindness, abundant, exalted, immeasurable, without hostility and without malice. He considers this and understands it thus: "This liberation of mind through loving-kindness is conditioned and

> intentionally produced. But whatever is conditioned and intentionally produced is impermanent, subject to cessation."

The meditator mentioned in the above passage is one who has cultivated loving-kindness for a long time. Having gone through the steps that involve thought and reflection, she has subdued anger and resentment. Having extended loving-kindness in a gradual way to the beings in different directions and different realms, she can abide single-pointedly in the experience of loving-kindness that radiates to all beings equally. This level of concentration corresponds to one or another of the dhyānas. That is, immeasurable loving-kindness is a dhyānic-like state of concentration in which the meditator is fully immersed. Having mastered this concentration and become stable in it, she then emerges from it and investigates it as conditioned and intentionally produced. Then she reflects that whatever is mentally fabricated and intentionally produced is impermanent and subject to cessation. If she is steady in this and is able to sustain this insight clearly, she will directly realize the eradication of the pollutants. But if the power and clarity of insight are impaired due to subtle attachment to the experience, she will become a nonreturner.

The same analysis and way of meditation is then explained in terms of the other three immeasurables—immeasurable compassion, empathic joy, and equanimity—and the first three formless absorptions.

In this sūtra there are eleven states that could be taken as the object of analysis on which to cultivate insight—the four dhyānas, the four immeasurable states, and the first three formless absorptions. A meditator using any of these distinguishes them by their various factors and then contemplates that those factors are conditioned, they in turn condition other things, and they are produced by intention. Because individuals' aptitudes, prior level of development, and capabilities vary, each person will need a different degree of strength and depth of concentration to develop insight and for that insight to be effective in uprooting the fetters.

Pāli Tradition: The Supramundane Path

Some people think that serenity and insight are two types of meditation and that either one or the other can be done. Although a teacher may instruct a disciple to emphasize one over the other in the initial stages of training, to attain the supramundane path both must be cultivated. When the disciple's practice is mature, serenity and insight are brought into harmony so that both are present, supporting each other. Insight needs the focus of samādhi to be powerful, and samādhi needs the penetration of insight to be effective. When the two are united, the mind remains steady and tranquil on the meditation object and wisdom sees deeply into the nature of phenomena.

When the mind is tranquil and insight is deep and clear, penetration by direct knowledge occurs and the supramundane path of the āryas arises. In the *Discourse on the Great Sixfold Base*, the Buddha says (MN 149.10):

> He fully understands by direct knowledge those things that should be fully understood by direct knowledge. He abandons by direct knowledge those things that should be abandoned by direct knowledge. He fully develops by direct knowledge those things that should be developed by direct knowledge. He realizes by direct knowledge those things that should be actualized by direct knowledge.

Describing the fulfillment of the eightfold path and the realization of the four truths, these lines sum up the entire practice of the higher teachings. Each line applies to the function of one of the four truths. The five aggregates subject to clinging are fully understood by direct knowledge: The specific nature of each aggregate, including its specific characteristics, causes, conditions, and results, and the way it interacts with other factors is understood. Its general characteristics, such as the three characteristics that it shares with other conditioned phenomena, are also known. Wrong views and erroneous perceptions regarding each aggregate are eliminated.

Ignorance and craving for existence in saṃsāra are abandoned by direct knowledge: attachment, anger, and confusion, and the pollutants of sensual desire, craving for existence, and ignorance are vanquished.

In this sūtra, the Buddha advises disciples who have already developed the path to a high extent to develop serenity and insight—concentration and wisdom—by direct knowledge. To a less well-developed audience, the Buddha instructs the cultivation of the thirty-seven harmonies with awakening and the eightfold path.

Higher knowledge (P. *vijjā*), which is the sublime knowledge that arises at the end of the path, and liberation (P. *vimutti*), a conditioned event that brings nirvāṇa, are realized by direct knowledge. What is to be developed is higher knowledge, as expressed in the third sentence, and what is to be actualized is liberation, which is conveyed in the fourth sentence.

In this way the four functions regarding the four truths occur: duḥkha is understood, its origin is abandoned, its cessation is actualized, and the path is cultivated. These four activities occur simultaneously at the time of the supramundane path. The ancient Buddhist sages compared the supramundane path to an oil lamp simultaneously burning the wick, consuming the oil, dispelling the darkness, and radiating light. In the supramundane path, serenity and insight arise together simultaneously and in a balanced way, with serenity being right concentration and insight being right view.

Nirvāṇa is not an object of insight wisdom, which understands the five aggregates by knowing the three characteristics. Insight wisdom understands the mundane—the conditioned world of the five aggregates—whereas supramundane wisdom reaches beyond the conditioned to know nirvāṇa, the unconditioned, the deathless. This is known when the mind sees beyond the five aggregates. When meditators first realize nirvāṇa, they also experience true knowledge and gain the initial level of liberation—stream-entry—the result of developing the path.

The Buddha is adamant that true knowledge and full understanding of the four truths are essential for liberation (SN 56:32):

> If anyone should speak thus: "Without having made the breakthrough to the truth of dukkha as it really is, without having made the breakthrough to the truth of the origin of dukkha as it really is, without having made the breakthrough to the truth of the cessation of dukkha as it really is, without having made the breakthrough to the truth of the path leading to the cessation of dukkha as it really is, I will completely make an end to dukkha"—this is impossible.

He then continued by saying that anyone who has made these breakthroughs can make an end to all duḥkha. When the supramundane path is attained with stream-entry, the three lower fetters—view of a personal identity, doubt, and view holding bad ethics and modes of conduct as supreme—are removed. With the attainment of once-returner, sensual desire and malice are significantly weakened. When the stage of nonreturner is attained, the five lower fetters are eliminated, including sensual desire and malice; when all ten fetters and three pollutants are forever abandoned, one becomes an arhat.[96]

At the time of realizing nirvāṇa, the eight mental factors comprising the āryan eightfold path arise simultaneously. Right view sees nirvāṇa, and right intention directs the mind to nirvāṇa. Right speech, right action, and right livelihood counteract their opposites, allowing meditation to continue without hindrances. Right effort enthuses the mind realizing nirvāṇa, right mindfulness focuses on the unconditioned, and right concentration unifies the mind as it remains absorbed on nirvāṇa.

13 | The Diversity of Chinese Buddhist Schools

CHINESE BUDDHISM IS the elder sibling of Tibetan Buddhism since the Dharma spread to China several centuries before it was introduced into Tibet. In general, in Central and East Asia Mahāyāna Buddhism is prominent, so most scriptures and many practices are shared among the various Buddhist traditions in this area. However, divergence in interpretation of the scriptures and the emphasis on what and how to practice naturally occur. To look at this more closely, we'll briefly examine the major Buddhist traditions that arose in China. Some of these spread to Korea, Japan, and Vietnam as well. We'll then explore the main philosophical traditions in East and Southeast Asia and the principal practice traditions as well. To conclude, we'll learn of the Buddhist revival that took place in China in the nineteenth and twentieth centuries and continues to influence Chinese Buddhism in East Asia and other countries as well.

Chinese Buddhist Traditions

Buddhism came to China in the first century CE, about six centuries before it entered Tibet. It came first via the Silk Road—from Central Asian lands where Buddhism flourished—and later by sea from India and Sri Lanka. The first reference to a Buddhist monastery in China stems from the second century; this is also when Buddhist texts began to be translated into Chinese. Many of the early translations employed Taoist terminology, which led to some misunderstanding of Buddhist thought. Fortunately, this was corrected by the fifth century when more standardized translation terms were settled. The early fifth century also marked the translation of many Vinaya texts, which enabled the Saṅgha to develop.

As in other countries, Buddhism in China consists of a diversity of traditions, with some views and practices held in common and some unique to each tradition. Some traditions are differentiated based on their philosophical tenets, others on their manner of practice, others on the principal texts they follow. There is some overlap in the scriptures some traditions rely on, and over time elements of one tradition or philosophical system have been incorporated into others. Thus there is a richness in Chinese Buddhism that reflects the vastness of the Chinese canon and the vastness of the Buddha's skillful means of guiding disciples.

The Chinese canon is extensive, containing an array of scriptures from both the Sanskrit and Pāli traditions, as well as treatises and commentaries from many early Indian schools. The first sūtra, *Sūtra of Forty-Two Chapters*, was translated with the arrival of two Central Asian monks in 67 CE, the first monks to appear in official Chinese historical records, although there is evidence that some form of Buddhism had already been in China among some of the royalty as well as the common people before that.

For centuries Chinese emperors sponsored translation teams so that a wealth of Buddhist treatises and commentaries from India and Central Asia could be translated into Chinese.[97] While the majority of translations into Chinese occurred in the early centuries beginning in roughly 200 CE, there continued to be an active interest in and translation of valuable Buddhist scriptures into the Sung and Ming dynasties. In the early twentieth century translations were made of Buddhist scriptures prominent in other countries.

Because Buddhism came to China comparatively early, four of the five *nikāyas* found in the Pāli tradition are found in the Chinese canon, where they are known as *āgamas*. The Chinese canon also contains a plethora of Mahāyāna and Indian commentaries as well as a few tantras. Many early Abhidharma texts, including the *Mahāvibhāṣā* and Abhidharma texts by Saṅghabhadra—whose Sanskrit originals are no longer extant—can be found in the Chinese canon.

It is generally said that there are eight Mahāyāna schools and two Fundamental Vehicle schools in Chinese Buddhism. In Buddhist institutes in present-day Taiwan, students acquire a general understanding of all ten schools, although Pureland and Chan are the most widely practiced. The eight Mahāyāna schools are Chan, Pureland, Tiantai, Huayan, Three Treatise, Mind Only, Esoteric, and Vinaya.

1. Chan (J. Zen, K. Seon, V. Thien)

Chan was briefly explained in the previous chapter and will be explored more below.

2. Pureland School (C. Jingtu, J. Jodo, K. Jungto)

The Pureland tradition in China is based on three main sūtras: (1) the *Smaller Sūtra Displaying the Land of Bliss* (*Sukhāvatīvyūha Sūtra*, T. *Bde ba can gyi bkod pa'i mdo*, C. *Wuliangshou jing*), also called the *Amitābha Sūtra*, was translated several times into Chinese, the most popular being the one translated by the Central Asian monk-scholar Kumārajīva in 402; (2) the *Larger Sūtra Displaying the Land of Bliss* (*Sukhāvatīvyūha Sūtra*, T. *Bde ba can gyi bkod pa'i mdo*, C. *Wuliangshou jing*) was also translated several times, the most popular being the translation by the Sogdian monk Saṅghavarman in 252; and (3) the *Sūtra on the Meditation on Amitāyus* (*Amitāyurdhyāna Sūtra*, C. *Guan wuliangshoufo jing*), translated by Kālayaśas between 424 and 442. No Sanskrit original of the third text has been found.

Pureland as commonly practiced emphasizes chanting the name of Amitābha Buddha or another buddha and making fervent prayers to be reborn in that buddha's pureland. However, there is much more to this practice—including ethical conduct, renunciation of saṃsāra, bodhicitta, and the cultivation of wisdom—that is not widely taught. Once born in the pureland, one is never again born in saṃsāra and has all conducive circumstances to practice the Dharma and attain full awakening. The pureland can also be viewed as the pure nature of our own minds. Prominent Pureland masters are Huiyuan (334–416), Tanluan, Daochuo, Shandao, and Cimin. Honen brought the Pureland teachings to Japan in the late twelfth century, where they became popular.

After the ninth century, Pureland practice was integrated into several other Chinese schools, and today many Chinese monasteries practice both Chan and Pureland. The Pureland practice is also found in Tibetan Buddhism.

3. Tiantai (J. Tendai)

Tiantai was founded by Huisi (515–576), and his disciple Zhiyi (538–597) established its major principles. Zhiyi saw the Buddha as a skillful teacher who taught according to the disposition of the disciples. He classified the Buddha's teachings into four doctrines and established a gradual progression of practice from the easier to the most profound. Tiantai finds the ultimate teachings in the *Lotus Sūtra* (*Saddharmapuṇḍarīka*), the *Mahāparinirvāṇa Sūtra* (henceforth the *Nirvāṇa Sūtra*), and Nāgārjuna's *Great Perfection of Wisdom Treatise* (*Mahāprajñāpāramitā Upadeśa*, C. *Dazhidulun*; hereafter *Treatise on Wisdom*). The latter text is a huge volume covering many topics; it is not found in the Tibetan canon. Tiantai balances study and practice and is closely related to the Chan and Pureland schools.

4. Huayan (Flower Ornament School, J. Kegon, K. Hwaeom)

The Huayan school is based on the *Flower Ornament Sūtra* (*Avataṃsaka Sūtra*), which was translated into Chinese in 420 by Buddhabhadra. Dushun (557–640) was the first Huayan master; Zhiyan, Facang, Chengguan, and Zongmi were also great Huayan masters. Huayan emphasizes the interdependence of all people and phenomena and the interpenetration of their worlds. The individual affects the world, and the world affects the individual. The profound Huayan philosophy also emphasizes the bodhisattvas' activities in the world to benefit all beings. The Huayan and the Tiantai traditions set forth their own ways of organizing the sūtras and their themes as well as describing the Buddha's method of teaching and leading disciples.

5. Three Treatise School (C. Sanlun, K. Samnon)

This is the Madhyamaka school, founded by the great Indian translator Kumārajīva (334–413). Originally from Kucha, an ancient Central Asian kingdom that is now part of China's Xinjiang Province, he was said to be fluent in more than twelve languages. The three treatises that are the source of its name are the *Treatise on the Middle Way* and the *Twelve Gate Treatise* by Nāgārjuna and *The Hundred* by Āryadeva. Nāgārjuna's *Treatise on Wisdom* is often added as the fourth principal text of the Sanlun. This text is a line-by-line commentary on the *Twenty-Five-Thousand Stanza Perfection of Wisdom Sūtra*. As in Tibet, the Madhyamaka system relies on the Perfection of Wisdom sūtras and follows the *Akṣayamati Sūtra* in saying that these sūtras reveal the definitive view. The Sanlun school contains the essence of the Madhyamaka view as well as its reasonings.

Kumārajīva stopped the then-prevalent use of Taoist and Confucian terms when translating Buddhist texts. His priority was conveying the meaning rather than translating texts literally, and as a result his translations remained more popular than more exact translations such as those by Xuanzang. Some Chinese and Western scholars have said that Kumārajīva edited and abbreviated his translations. However, when compared with earlier versions in Indic languages of the same texts, his translations are very accurate.[98]

Jizang (549–623), a prominent Sanlun master, wrote extensive commentaries on the three treatises and many Dharma texts. Chinese Madhyamaka does not contain the debates that developed in Tibetan Madhyamaka. As such, for academic and philosophical purposes, Sanlun represents a valuable interpretation of early Madhyamaka.

Although the Madhyamaka school did not persist as a separate school past the Tang dynasty (618–907), its ideas were incorporated into the indigenous Chinese schools. Madhyamaka philosophy is still taught and studied in Chinese and Korean monasteries and universities today, and many practitioners meditate on it.

6. Yogācāra (Mind Only, Cittamātra, C. Weishi, J. Hosso, K. Yushikhak)

The Yogācāra school is based on the *Sūtra Unraveling the Thought*, the *Yogācārabhūmi Śāstra*, the *Vijñaptimātratāsiddhi Śāstra*, the *Explanation on the Collection of Mahāyāna Abhidharma* (*Mahāyāna Abhidharma Samuccayavyākhyā*), and other treatises by Maitreya, Asaṅga, and Vasubandhu. As with the Sanlun school (Madhyamaka), Mind Only did not remain a distinct school in China past the Tang dynasty, but its philosophy influenced the emerging indigenous Chinese schools and is widely studied and followed by Chinese practitioners of many traditions today.

7. Esoteric School (Vajrayāna, C. Mi Zong, Zhenyan, J. Shingon, K. Keumgangsang, Milgyo)

The Esoteric school was begun by the arrival of three Indian tantric masters, Śubhakarasiṃha (637–735), Vajrabodhi, and Amoghavajra, who together translated most of the Vajrayāna texts in the Chinese canon.

Śubhakarasiṃha brought the *Caryā Tantra* (*garbhakośadhātu* teaching), and Vajrabodhi brought *Yoga Tantra* (*vajradhātu* teaching). The *Vairocana Tantra*, *Diamond Apex Sūtra*, and *Susiddhi Tantra*—all Yoga Tantra texts—were practiced.

This early Chinese Vajrayāna was popular in the Tang dynasty, but almost disappeared after the persecution of Buddhism toward the end of that dynasty. Some groups practiced Vajrayāna during the Jin dynasty (1115–1234). After the Mongol emperor Kublai Khan conquered Tibet, he was converted to Buddhism by the Sakya master Drogon Chogyal Phagpa and brought Tibetan Vajrayāna to China, where it received royal patronage and became popular during the Yuan dynasty (1271–1368). To distinguish it from traditional Chinese Buddhism, it was called Lamaism in Chinese; this is not a continuation of the earlier Esoteric Buddhism from the Tang dynasty.

Tibetan Buddhism was suppressed in the Ming dynasty but was revived and became popular and had royal patronage with emperors of the Qing dynasty (1636–1912), the last dynasty of China. Kukai (774–835) brought Vajrayāna to Japan, where it is still extant.

The Chinese usually think of the Esoteric school in terms of teachings that are kept private or secret between the teacher and disciple. Interestingly, the *Śūraṃgama Sūtra* is considered a tantric sūtra in the Chinese Tripiṭaka, although no one considers it a secret practice. This sūtra contains the longest mantra in the Chinese canon and describes the wonderful benefits one derives from chanting it. Before Buddha presented the mantra, he explained an elaborate way of setting up a maṇḍala, a sacred space for tantric rituals. Basic tantric practices such as chanting mantra have always been popular throughout Chinese Buddhism; they are not considered esoteric and have been integrated into traditional Chinese Buddhism. Chanting the Great Compassion Mantra, the Śūraṃgama mantra, Medicine Buddha mantras, and the Amitābha Buddha's mantra are some examples that have been incorporated into the daily liturgy of every Buddhist monastery. Some simpler forms of setting up maṇḍalas are regularly used in Buddhist ceremonies.

8. Vinaya School (C. Lu, J. Ritsu Shu, K. Yul Jong)

Based on the *Dharmaguptaka Vinaya*, which was translated into Chinese by Buddhayaśas in 412, Daoxuan (596–667) founded the Vinaya school. Ever since the Tang emperor Zhongzong issued an edict in 709 saying that all monasteries in China must follow the Dharmaguptaka Vinaya, this Vinaya has been followed by practitioners of all Chinese traditions. Four other Vinayas from ancient India were also translated into Chinese, and Chinese Buddhists also consult these on specific points that the Dharmaguptaka Vinaya treats cursorily. Although Vinaya in general is in common with the Fundamental Vehicle, this school is considered a Mahāyāna school because there are elements in the Dharmaguptaka Vinaya that lean practitioners toward Mahāyāna ideas. For example, the closing dedication of the *poṣadha* ceremony, the fortnight purification and restoration of precepts, says, "I have recited the *Prātimokṣa Sūtra* and the assembly's poṣadha is concluded. I now dedicate all the merit of reciting the *Prātimokṣa Sūtra* so that all sentient beings may attain buddhahood."

The bodhisattva ethical code is included in the Vinaya school, and when the three-platform ordination is given in China, the novice and full monastic ordinations and the bodhisattva precepts are bestowed.

The two Fundamental Vehicle schools are the Satyasiddhi school and the Knowledge school.

1. Satyasiddhi School (C. Chengshizong, J. Jojitsu-ron)

This school is based on the *Treatise on Establishing the Truth* (*Satyasiddhi Śāstra*), an Abhidharma-style text that discusses emptiness, among other topics. Attributed to the third- and fourth-century Indian scholar Harivarman, who studied both the Fundamental and Mahāyāna traditions, this text was translated into Chinese by Kumārajīva in 412. Some scholars say Satyasiddhi is a Fundamental Vehicle school that stems from the Sautrāntika school in India; others say it bridges the Fundamental Vehicle and the Mahāyāna by presenting some Mahāyāna ideas such as the two truths and the selflessness of both persons and phenomena. Kumārajīva initially saw this text as a way to expose people to the idea of emptiness before introducing them to the Madhyamaka presentation. Although initially Satyasiddhi was popular, once some masters considered it to be a Fundamental Vehicle school, its popularity waned.

The *Satyasiddhi Śāstra* asserts that phenomena are empty and unreal. To attain nirvāṇa, attachment must be abandoned, and this happens in three steps. (1) Since all beings and things exist due to causes and conditions and are given temporary names, they are empty. Thus being attached to a self that is only a name is useless. (2) The five sense objects and the elements (dharmas) are analyzed into smaller and smaller units until it is seen that they, too, are empty and unreal. (3) Although grasping both the self and phenomena have been eliminated at this point, there may still be grasping to the idea of emptiness as something real. This grasping, too, needs to cease, and when it does, the person enters nirvāṇa.

In China, the goal of this path seems to have been arhatship, but in Japan the Jojitsu school relied on the *Lotus Sūtra* and other Mahāyāna sūtras and said that Satyasiddhi practice can result in a buddha's dharmakāya and form body.

2. Knowledge School (Kośa or Abhidharma School, C. Jushe, J. Kushe, K. Kosa Non)

This school was based on the *Treasury of Knowledge* (C. *Jushe lun*) by Vasubandhu and was introduced into China by Xuanzang. Once popular in the "golden age of Buddhism" during the Tang dynasty, this school is small now. Prior to the introduction of the *Treasury of Knowledge* into China, many people studied the āgamas and Abhidharma literature such as the *Mahāvibhāṣā Śāstra* (C. *Dapiposha lun*) and the seven Sarvāstivāda Abhidharma texts. After the *Treasury of Knowledge* was introduced and translated into Chinese, those interested in the Fundamental Vehicle focused more on it than on the individual Abhidharma texts. In modern times, it does not exist as a separate school, but Chinese scholars and practitioners still study the āgamas and Abhidharma philosophy. Some teachings from the *Treasury of Knowledge* have been integrated into Tiantai as the teachings of the śrāvaka path.

Vasubandhu's *Explanation of the "Treasury of Knowledge"* (*Abhidharmakośabhāṣya*) was translated into Chinese and together with Nāgārjuna's *Treatise on Wisdom* it serves as a popular source for definitions and quotations in Chinese Buddhist glossaries and dictionaries.

* * * * *

Chan, Pureland, and Huayan—all of which speak of the tathāgatagarbha—were more successful in China than the philosophical schools of Sanlun (Madhyamaka) and Yogācāra for several reasons. First, they were indigenous Chinese traditions, not Indian transplants, and thus they had adapted the Buddhism received from India to fit Chinese culture and way of thinking. They fulfilled the Chinese proclivity and liking for harmony. Old notions and new ideas were not contradictory but could fit in well together. The indigenous traditions were concerned more with the practical matter of attaining awakening than with the reasoning and debate that proved the philosophical view, and the array of indigenous traditions offered a variety of approaches. Those who valued education and study of the scriptures could satisfy their interests, those who favored direct experience had that option, and those who were more devotional and felt uplifted by faith could practice according to that approach.

The above brief descriptions of the prominent schools are a general introduction to Buddhism in China. Centuries ago all ten traditions were active and had many practitioners. Over the years, different schools of thought formed within a school; other minor schools existed for some time and then disappeared or merged with other schools. Some of the ten schools are no longer separate schools but still have a strong influence on Chinese Buddhism. For example, in Taiwan there are only a few monasteries from the Vinaya school, but the Vinaya continues to flourish in Taiwan, Korea, and Vietnam. The well-known and respected monk Hongyi (1880–1942) was instrumental in the revival of the Vinaya school, as he was devoted to the modern study and clarification of texts from past Vinaya masters. All Chinese Buddhist monastics follow the Dharmaguptaka Vinaya and the bodhisattva ethical code.

Other traditions, such as Chan and Pureland, became more vibrant and popular. Many contemporary monasteries practice Chan and Pureland together. Some traditions, such as the Satyasiddhi, have declined. The Knowledge or Abhidharma tradition doesn't exist as a distinct practice tradition, but Chinese Buddhists still study the Abhidharma and the āgamas. In recent years some Western Theravāda monastics who are very knowledgeable in the Pāli tradition have been studying the āgamas and comparing them with the Pāli nikāyas. Meanwhile the Yogācāra and Sanlun (Madhyamaka) traditions, together with the Tathāgatagarbha, have become the major philosophical systems in Chinese Buddhism. Their philosophies and tenets have influenced the other traditions.

China was a land with a very rich culture and sophisticated intelligentsia prior to Buddhism's arrival there. Everywhere the Buddhadharma goes, it is influenced by the culture, climate, government structure, economics, and so forth of the area. These factors and their influence cannot be ignored. Although Chinese masters always relied on the Buddha's sūtras and Indian treatises when teaching, there was also the need to adapt Buddhism to Chinese mentality. Chinese culture values harmonizing various elements more than discerning and debating their distinctive characteristics, so the dialectical approach of ancient India did not suit the Chinese people well and thus did not take hold in China. Because of such conditions and the fact that each place has access to different sūtras, people may prefer different philosophical approaches. Thus Buddha's ability to match the teaching to the capacity and interests of the audience is indicative of his skillful wisdom that guides sentient beings. In this way, the true essence of the Dharma is preserved to this day.

Buddhism also influences the culture, language, art, and other aspects of each land where it takes root, and it did so in China as well. Although Taoist terms were used to translate Buddhist terms and concepts when Buddhism first came to China—much as Christian terms were used when Buddhism first came to the West—Dao An (312–85) initiated the movement to reject using Taoist and Confucian terminology to translate Buddhist concepts, and Kumārajīva firmly established the practice of using Buddhist terms to explain Buddhism. This resulted in introducing a huge number of new words and concepts into the Chinese lexicon and thought.

During the Tang and following dynasties, almost all educated people needed to be acquainted with some Buddhist verbiage to be considered intellectual. Buddhism brought on new forms of prose, painting, sculpting, and even drama, especially to act out Buddhist stories to commoners. Many of the most important calligraphy artists created works from Buddhist texts. The relationship of Chinese monks with emperors and the priest-patron connection (C. *tanyue guanxi*) between Chinese emperors and Tibetan lamas during the Yuan and Qing dynasties influenced government.

Indigenous Chinese Schools

Buddhism is not static; new commentaries and translations constantly draw out the meaning of the teachings to make them understandable for different groups of people. As we look at the Buddhist schools that evolved in China itself—Huayan, Tiantai, Pureland, and Chan—we see that each of these was influenced by three philosophical schools—Yogācāra, Madhyamaka, and Tathāgatagarbha—and each centered around the teachings of one or another group of Mahāyāna sūtras. In the next two chapters we'll see how the three philosophical schools developed in China, with successive generations raising new points and unpacking their profound meanings even more.

The Chinese inherited a vast collection of Buddhist material—sūtras, treatises, and commentaries. Arranging this material in an orderly way so that students would understand how diverse instructions fit into the grand scheme of the path to awakening was the work of many Chinese masters during the Sui dynasty (581–618) and Tang dynasty. These schemas (C. *pan jiao*) served many purposes: they organized the material into a coherent doctrinal framework, legitimized the claims of various groups to have the supreme or final teaching of the Buddha, and provided a map of the path to awakening for practitioners to follow. Although the result is different, this process is similar to the way Tibetans used the schema of tenet systems to organize and understand the various teachings that came to Tibet.

These various schemas are based on the idea that the Buddha was a skillful teacher who explained the Dharma according to the various dispositions of his many disciples. Nāgārjuna says in the first chapter of the *Treatise on Wisdom* that the Buddha taught using many skillful means. In this light, he explains four kinds of teaching (*siddhānta*)[99] given by the Buddha:

1. The conventional teaching employs ordinary ways of expression to communicate effectively with listeners. It emphasizes explaining phenomena in terms of causality.
2. The appropriate teaching for the audience is given by knowing the dispositions and interests of the listeners. Just as different medicines are prescribed according to the disease to treat, the Buddha adapted

the teaching to the capacity of the listeners, giving different teachings according to disciples' faculties and particular needs.

3. Teachings about counteractive measures are given to remedy specific afflictions.
4. The ultimate or definitive teaching is the teaching of the highest, perfect truth.

Huayan's Presentation

Fazang (643–712), the third of the five Huayan patriarchs, espoused a fivefold classification of the Buddha's teachings that can be subsumed into three:

1. Fazang explained that the *gradual teachings* are so-called because (TSB 137) "the understanding and practice within them lie within words and explanations; the stages [of the bodhisattva path] are sequential; cause and effect follow from one another; and one proceeds from the subtle to the manifest." The teaching of the Fundamental Vehicle and the elementary and advanced teachings of the Mahāyāna are included in the gradual teachings.
2. In the *sudden teachings* (TSB 137), "all words and explanations are suddenly cut off, the nature of the truth is suddenly revealed, understanding and practice are suddenly perfected, and buddhahood [is attained] upon the nonarising of a single moment of thought." The sudden teachings are identified with Vimalakīrti's silence in the *Vimalakīrti Sūtra* after thirty-one bodhisattvas explain their understanding of nonduality and Mañjuśrī tells them that the truth is ineffable and cannot be experienced by words and concepts. Later on, Chan teachings became associated with the sudden teachings.
3. The *perfect teaching* is the Huayan teaching. It is unique and foremost of all the Buddha's teachings because he taught the *Flower Ornament Sūtra* while absorbed in the samādhi of oceanic reflection. The ocean is a metaphor for the Buddha's awakened mind in which all phenomena are reflected and perceived at once. In his *Reflections on the Dharmadhā*, Fazang says (TSB 155):

> It is like the reflection of the four divisions [of a great army] on a vast ocean. Although the reflected images differ in kind, they appear simultaneously on [the surface of] the ocean in their proper order. Even though the appearance of the images is manifold, the water [that reflects them] remains undisturbed. The images are indistinguishable from the water, and yet [the water] is calm and clear. The water is indistinguishable from the images, and yet [the images] are multifarious . . . it is also described as "oceanic" because its various reflections multiply endlessly and their limit is impossible to fathom. To investigate one of them thoroughly is to pursue the infinite, for in any one of them, all the rest vividly appear at the same time. For this reason, it is said to be "oceanic." It is called "reflections" because all the images appear simultaneously within it without distinction of past and present. The myriad diverse kinds [of images] penetrate each other without obstruction . . . Even though myriads of images arise in profusion, it remains empty and unperturbed.

All phenomena lack self-nature and yet arise dependent on one another. Each thing is part of the harmonious whole. Each thing is influenced by the whole of which it is a part, and the whole is influenced by each of its many parts. This interdependence and interpenetration of all phenomena is expressed by the metaphor of Indra's net—an infinite net extending in all directions—representing the universe. At each intersection of the threads is a jewel. Each jewel both reflects every other jewel and is reflected by every other jewel, infinitely. In the same way, every phenomenon in the universe is related to every other phenomenon without obstruction.

The fifth Huayan patriarch, Zongmi (780–841), was also a Chan practitioner. In his *Inquiry into the Origin of Man* (*Yuan ren lun*), he classified the Buddha's teachings into three categories:

1. Hidden intent that sets forth the appearances of phenomena that are based on the nature. The six realms of rebirth are appearances of the true nature. They arise only because sentient beings are confused about

their nature. These teachings are called "of hidden intent" because the Buddha did not reveal the true nature in them.

2. Hidden intent that negates the appearances of phenomena in order to reveal the nature. These are the teachings given in the Perfection of Wisdom sūtras and the Madhyamaka treatises. Zongmi considers these provisional teachings because they do not reveal the Buddha's ultimate intent. In *Chan Preface* he says (TSB 211):

> According to the true ultimate meaning, since afflictive thoughts are originally empty, there is nothing that can be negated. All phenomena, being without defilement, are originally the true nature, and its marvelous functioning-in-accord-with-conditions is not only never interrupted but also cannot be negated. It is only because a class of sentient beings clings to unreal appearances of phenomena, obscures their true nature, and has difficulty attaining profound awakening that the Buddha provisionally negated everything without distinguishing between good and bad, tainted and pure, or the nature and its appearance of phenomena.

3. Direct revelation that the mind is the nature. These teachings directly indicate that one's very own mind is the true nature (inherent, pure awareness) and explain the tathāgatagarbha (ultimate source of all pure and impure phenomena), or knowing. What is this knowing? Zongmi says (TSB 217):

> This teaching propounds that all sentient beings without exception have the empty, tranquil, true-mind. From time without beginning, it is the intrinsically pure, effulgent, unobscured, clear, and bright ever-present knowing (C. *chang zhi*). It abides forever and will never perish in the infinite future. It is termed "buddha essence"; it is also termed "tathāgatagarbha" and "mind ground" [*xin di*]. This knowing is not wisdom, because knowing is possessed by ordinary beings and sages, while wisdom is had only by the

latter. It is also not discrimination, but it is the underlying ground of knowing that is always present in sentient beings.

Fazang and Zongmi are both Huayan patriarchs, but from the difference in their schema we see a difference in their view. Fazang saw the Huayan teaching of interpenetration to be the highest teaching, whereas Zongmi considers the tathāgatagarbha doctrine as supreme.

Tiantai's Systematic Presentation

Unless we understand the full range of expedient means the Buddha used, we might think the content of various sūtras are in conflict. However, if we understand that the Buddha's primary purpose is to lead all sentient beings to full awakening, we will find no contradiction or inconsistency. This is the basis on which the Tiantai masters formed a system that organizes all the Buddha's sūtras within one framework, thus eliminating conflict. The great Tiantai master Zhiyi (538–97 CE) systematized the various Buddhist teachings that arrived in China into four doctrines, from the basic to the most profound:

1. The Tripiṭaka doctrine or the doctrine of birth and cessation (saṃsāra and nirvāṇa) explains causality—karma and its effects—and the path that śrāvakas and solitary realizers practice to attain nirvāṇa.
2. The common doctrine or the doctrine without birth (or cessation) pertains to practitioners of all three vehicles and includes the teaching that all persons and phenomena are empty of self-existence. They exist dependently; their appearance of existing independently is false, like an illusion. This takes one beyond the duality of existence and nonexistence and beyond the duality of saṃsāra and nirvāṇa.
3. The specific or limitless doctrine is for bodhisattvas who learn how to transcend the dualities of saṃsāra and nirvāṇa, self and selflessness, and who also learn how to use these doctrines to awaken sentient beings. Understanding emptiness, bodhisattvas compassionately enter the saṃsāric world to benefit sentient beings. They learn the limitless dispositions and interests of sentient beings and the limitless Dharma teachings to impart to them. All these are temporary or provisional

means: they are Dharma methods that are to be used and then discarded when leading sentient beings to awakening.

4. The perfect doctrine that explains the ultimate purpose of the Buddha's appearance. That is the teaching on the one vehicle as imparted in the *Lotus Sūtra*.

By understanding these four and knowing in which of them a particular topic belongs, practitioners understand the layout and way to practice the teachings.

Zhiyi described five stages in which the Buddha revealed the Dharma:

1. The Huayan stage is the Buddha's first teaching upon attaining buddhahood. Given for advanced bodhisattvas who are ready to immediately receive the most profound teachings, it emphasizes the *Flower Ornament Sūtra* and primarily expounds the Perfect doctrine with some of the Specific doctrine.
2. The Āgama stage was directed primarily for disciples who have an ingrained culture of seeking personal liberation quickly from the duḥkha of the mundane world. These teachings emphasize the Fundamental Vehicle sūtras and expound in detail the path to free sentient beings from afflictions and defilements, teachings that are essential for all vehicles.
3. The Vaipulya stage includes most "mixed" Mahāyāna sūtras. "Mixed" means the scripture is definitely a Mahāyāna scripture but may contain some āgama/śrāvaka teachings.[100] When his disciples' faculties had matured, the Buddha, with the intention of helping mundane beings and śrāvakas to transition from the Fundamental Vehicle to the Mahāyāna, taught sūtras such as the *Vimalakīrti Sūtra*. These sūtras may contain teachings of all four doctrines or any combination of them but primarily expound the Common, Specific, and Perfect doctrines.
4. The Prajñā stage refers primarily to the Perfection of Wisdom sūtras, the subject of Nāgārjuna's Madhyamaka. Its intended audience are novice or advanced bodhisattvas, so the Buddha expounds the bodhisattva teachings, especially those on emptiness and the cultivation of wisdom. The *Diamond Sūtra* is a classic example, which begins with

the question "How shall good men and good women, having generated bodhicitta, tame and stabilize their minds?" These sūtras primarily teach the Perfect doctrine but will include elements of the Common and Specific doctrines as necessary.

5. The Lotus-Parinirvāṇa stage teaches primarily the *Lotus Sūtra*, which reveals the Buddha's true intention of one final vehicle without speaking of buddha nature, and the *Nirvāṇa Sūtra*, which expounds on the buddha nature and reviews all the Buddha's teachings, including the āgamas, in light of one final vehicle. The four truths and thirty-seven harmonies are explained in Mahāyāna terms as part of the Perfect doctrine, emphasizing that all teachings of the Buddha are part of this one vehicle—that even when the Buddha taught the practices leading to arhatship, his intention was to lead all beings to the bodhisattva path and to full buddhahood.

By understanding this framework, Zhiyi says we will not see the Buddha's various teachings as contradictory and will understand that the Buddha does not follow hard and fast rules when teaching disciples. When a disciple is ready, the Buddha gives her the teachings appropriate for her present way of thinking. Understanding this, the Chinese are not so concerned with which schools have the one right doctrine because they know that the Buddha gave various teachings according to the audience's capacity.

Zhiyi propounded Middle Way Buddha Essence (*buddhagarbha*, C. *fo xin*)[101] and used a system of three contemplations on three aspects of the truth to describe it. This system is not contradictory to the two-truth system or conventional and ultimate truths established by Nāgārjuna, who is revered as the founder of the Tiantai school. Rather it is a skillful teaching method to lead sentient beings to awakening. The three aspects of the truth are the provisional or conventional, emptiness, and the Middle Way.

These three are not separate from each other and are unified in the Middle Way. To attain Middle Way Buddha Essence, practitioners engage the threefold contemplation, initially meditating on these three aspects of the truth sequentially, but at advanced levels perceiving them simultaneously. Bodhisattvas and mahāsattvas must integrate the realization of emptiness with all compassionate activities done to benefit sentient beings in the world. The fully integrated realization of emptiness, conventional existence, and the Middle Way is buddhahood.

REFLECTION

1. Give some examples of how Chinese culture and Tibetan culture influenced the indigenous Buddhist traditions and the way Buddhism was taught in those places.
2. How do you think the culture in the country where you reside influences and will influence the way Buddhism is taught there?
3. What is the pure teaching of the Buddha? How do we preserve it as well as the essence of the Buddhadharma while adapting its external manifestations to new cultures?
4. What factors in the culture and minds of the people where you live could bring the degeneration of the Buddhadharma?

Sudden and Gradual Teachings

Throughout the centuries, Buddhist practitioners have debated whether awakening is arrived at gradually or suddenly, and teachings exist that support each position. Zongmi described two types of sudden teachings: one for beings of high faculties, the other as a method of exposition. The Buddha gave the *first type of sudden teachings* for higher-faculty disciples when he spontaneously and directly revealed the true Dharma to unawakened beings who immediately attained awakening. Here "awakening" refers not to the path of no-more-learning of any of the three vehicles—not to arhatship or buddhahood—but to the first direct perception of reality. For Zongmi, this means that practitioners have the first experience of seeing that their own true nature is—and always has been—the same as the nature of all the buddhas. They see that the functioning of their minds with its thoughts and objects is simply an expression of, or the play of, their inherently awakened true-mind (C. *zhen xin*).

Although practitioners have an experience of awakening at this time, they are not yet fully awakened. They must still remove all afflictions, karmic seeds, and other conditioning affiliated with a mind in saṃsāra from beginningless time. This is done through gradual practice. The situation resembles the sun and the frost: the sun may rise suddenly, but the frost melts gradually. The experience of sudden awakening harms practitioners' primordial ignorance but it does not eliminate all defilements. These are overcome through gradual cultivation after the initial, sudden experience of awakening. One experience of seeing that they are buddhas does not enable them to act like or to be buddhas from then on. The gradual elimination of defilements and the integration of that experience of awakening are necessary and cannot be rushed.

The sudden teaching for those of high faculties correlates with the scriptures expounding the tathāgatagarbha, such as part of the *Flower Ornament*, *Śūraṃgama*, *Dense Array* (*Ghanavyūha*), *Lion's Roar of Queen Śrīmālā* (*Śrīmālādevī Siṃhanāda*), and *Tathāgatagarbha* sūtras. This teaching was not taught at a set time in the Buddha's life but was given only when highest-faculty disciples were present.

The *second type of sudden teaching* is based on another part of the *Flower Ornament Sūtra*—the teachings on the interpenetration and interdependence of all phenomena and the universe being contained in a mote of dust. It was taught just after the Buddha attained awakening to an audience of bodhisattvas who had high faculties as a result of practice done in previous lives.

The sudden teachings are not the same as the highest teachings. The highest teachings can be approached in two ways, either gradually through consistent development or suddenly through a direct experience of reality. High-faculty disciples are suited for the sudden teachings, whereas middle- and low-faculty disciples fare better with the gradual approach. The Buddha leads the latter progressively to understand the ultimate meaning. This is the approach revealed in the *Lotus Sūtra* and *Nirvāṇa Sūtra*. Here disciples begin by learning how to create the causes for fortunate rebirth through abandoning nonvirtue and creating virtue. Then the Buddha teaches them how to eliminate defilements, and after that he expounds the Yogācāra view that negates external objects. Then he teaches the Madhyamaka, and at the end the Tathāgatagarbha doctrine.

According to Zongmi, an initial experience of awakening is essential, no matter whether it comes suddenly or gradually. Further progress must be built on the foundation of an awakening experience. Zongmi outlined the path to awakening in ten stages; the initial experience of awakening is the first of the ten stages (TSB 201):[102]

1. Sudden awakening. Practitioners meet a spiritual mentor who guides them to have insight into the inherently awakened true nature of the mind. Due to this experience, they gain faith in suchness[103] (ultimate reality) and in the Three Jewels and begin their return to inherent awakening.
2. Resolving to attain awakening. Practitioners generate compassion and wisdom, and with bodhicitta make vows to benefit all sentient beings by becoming buddhas.
3. Cultivating the five practices. They now engage in the practices of generosity, ethical conduct, fortitude, joyous effort, and meditative insight (serenity insight).
4. Spiritual development. They further cultivate the compassion, wisdom, and vows generated on the second stage.
5. Emptiness of self. They realize there is no self-sufficient substantially existent person and counteract attachment to the self.
6. Emptiness of phenomena. Practitioners realize that all phenomena lack self-nature and abandon attachment to phenomena.
7. Mastery of form. Realizing that what they perceive is a manifestation of their own mind, they gain mastery over these perceived objects.
8. Mastery of mind. Now mastery is gained over the mind, the perceiving subject.
9. Freedom from thought. They become fully cognizant of the ultimate origin of all afflictive thoughts and know that the true nature of the mind is eternal.
10. Attainment of buddhahood. Practitioners know that since the mind's essence is free from thought, there are actually no divisions in the stages of the path to awakening. From the beginning, they have been undifferentiated and have been the same as inherent awakening, which is also one and indivisible. In this way, they are brought back full circle to their original awakened nature, which has been present

> all along. They see that all the stages they have traversed on the way to awakening are just a manifestation of their own mind, whose basic nature is forever pure, awakened, and unsullied by the defilements that appear to shroud it.

These ten stages counteract saṃsāra, which, like awakening, depends on the one-mind (C. *ixin*), the ultimate source of all the pure and impure phenomena that constitute saṃsāra and nirvāṇa. The one-mind of the *Awakening of Faith* is synonymous with the one true dharmadhātu of the *Flower Ornament Sūtra*. As the basis of saṃsāra and nirvāṇa, the one-mind is the same as the tathāgatagarbha and is itself beyond all these dualities. It is also the basis from which all pure and impure phenomena arise. Impure phenomena are those producing saṃsāra; pure phenomena are those developed through Dharma practice that cease the evolution of saṃsāra and lead practitioners back to their original source—the one-mind, original awakening.

The one-mind is both the basis for saṃsāra and nirvāṇa and the object on which practitioners develop insight. The one-mind has two aspects. The first is suchness, that which is neither born nor dies. This aspect is permanent. The second aspect is impermanent—the mind that is subject to birth and death. This is the foundation consciousness where the tathāgatagarbha and that which is subject to birth and death are mixed in such a way that they are neither one nor separate. The foundation consciousness also has two aspects, one that is awakened and gives rise to pure phenomena, the other that is unawakened and produces impure phenomena.

The defilements that obscure the awakened one-mind of suchness are manifestations of that mind that arise due to various conditions. Saṃsāra comes about due to afflictive thoughts that differentiate phenomena. When practitioners halt these afflictive thoughts, the appearances of external phenomena stop as does the creation of karma.

REFLECTION

1. What is the correct way of understanding sudden and gradual awakening according to Chan? What is the incorrect way?
2. Why does it take time, effort, repeated practice, and familiarity to

transform our mind from nonvirtue to virtue and to gain the Buddha's exceptional qualities?

Chan: True-Suchness and Buddha Essence

Chan has been influenced by Madhyamaka, Yogācāra, and Tathāgatagarbha. The branches of Chan that are well known today stem from the sixth Chan patriarch, Huineng (638–713), the author of the *Platform Sūtra*, whose awakening was rooted in Madhyamaka. Huineng was from a poor family, and as a woodcutter he took the wood to the marketplace to sell. There he heard someone chanting a phrase from the *Diamond Sūtra* and had his first awakening. The fifth patriarch then taught him the *Diamond Sūtra*, and at the line "The mind arises from the state of nonabiding," Huineng reached great awakening. The explanation of nonabiding, found in the Perfection of Wisdom sūtras, is a key point in Chan, as are the explanations of no form, meaning that practitioners should not be attached to anything; no thought, which refers to observing their thoughts without clinging to them; and no mind, meaning neither craving nor rejecting.

Chan seeks to directly understand the nature of the mind, the buddha nature. Buddha nature is viewed in an affirmative way, as one's own original or primordial pure nature, also called "true-self" and "original awakening." The idea of original awakening has its source in *Awakening of Faith in the Mahāyāna* (*Mahāyānaśraddhotpāda Śāstra*), where the tathāgatagarbha refers to the one-mind (true-mind) that is the primordially pure awareness[104] that gives rise to saṃsāra. Just as the water of the ocean is still water, even when the wind stirs it up and forms waves, the primordially pure awareness of the one-mind is the ultimate nature, despite sentient beings existing in saṃsāra.

Ultimate reality is an affirmative phenomenon that already abides in sentient beings' continuums; it is the nature of wisdom. Chan practitioners employ the understanding of emptiness to free the mind from discursive thoughts. Some Chan masters bring in the idea of tathāgatagarbha, which focuses on buddha nature and true-self. They then say the ultimate suchness—the tathatā or suchness of the mind—is the tathāgatagarbha, not emptiness. Emptiness and suchness are not synonymous as they are in Madhyamaka philosophy. However, Chan masters who adhere to the Madhyamaka view say that talking about true-self and buddha nature is a skillful method suited for disciples who still grasp the I. The ultimate truth to be realized is beyond such concepts, and clinging to the existence of a buddha nature that is the self is a hindrance to full awakening.

Śrāvaka and solitary-realizer arhats realize emptiness but not buddha essence. For that reason, they prefer to abide in nirvāṇa and do not feel the wish or need to complete the bodhisattva path.

Buddha essence is the potential to become a buddha. It is unborn and undying; it is not produced and cannot be destroyed. Buddha essence means the "knowing"—the pure consciousness that is present before the mind begins to conceptualize and spew forth its endless preferences, opinions, biases, and ideas. It is fundamental awareness, not the content of a cognition. According to the *Śūraṃgama Sūtra*, knowing precedes conscious analysis, designation, and conceptualization. While the eight consciousnesses arise and cease, fundamental awareness is said to be permanent. Here "permanent" means ever-present; it does not mean constant and unchanging, and the fundamental or pure mind (C. *qingjing xin*) is not a permanent self as asserted by non-Buddhists. Rather, it is not born and does not die like the body; it is neither male nor female; it is not this nationality or that one; it is neither wise nor foolish. It is not inside or outside of the body. It is not physical and does not exist anywhere in space.[105]

The pure mind has karmic latencies, although they are not an inherent part of that mind. The mind is like a pure, beautiful pearl, while karmic latencies and afflictions are like the mud in which it lies. As long as the mud of afflictions and karma cover the pearl of the buddha nature—the pure mind—suffering will continue. But at the moment of first seeing awakening, enough mud has been wiped off to see the pearl and know that it is unpolluted. However, because the mind is so habituated to afflictions and karma, it takes a long time to free it from these defilements. Therefore practitioners must continue to cultivate the path and wisdom over time to reach final awakening.

The mind is not impure and thus cannot be made pure. It is not affected by the transitory conditions that affect our body and superficial mental states. It is empty because it lacks characteristics. This mind is not a self or soul because grasping a self involves a mass of dualistic discriminations that think "I am this" or "I am that." In the *Śūraṃgama Sūtra*, the Buddha says:[106]

> All you good people! I have often said that all phenomena with physical form, all phenomena of mind, the conditions under which they arise, as well as the phenomena that interact with the mind and all other conditioned phenomena, are mere manifestations of true-mind. Your bodies and your minds appear within the wondrous light of the true essence of that wondrous mind. How is it that you all have lost track of the wondrous nature of the fundamental, marvelously perfect, wondrously understanding and resplendent mind, so that your understanding of it is confused?

Simple pure awareness free from all conception is the ultimate state of mind in which to abide. Dharma practice entails letting go of all thoughts, keeping the mind in emptiness, and just focusing on pure awareness, being present. This is directly experiencing Middle Way reality, which is a mind free from all conceptions, ideas, afflictions, and illusions. Being free from conceptions does not deny the value of all conceptions but involves accepting that conceptions are provisional and limited.

There is a Chan saying, "The mind of no mind is the ultimate mind." This is what Nāgārjuna is referring to when he teaches the emptiness of inherent existence in the *Treatise on the Middle Way*. Nirvāṇa and saṃsāra are both empty; they are both designations and concepts. Nirvāṇa is a teaching to help you go beyond saṃsāra. Once you see the delusion of saṃsāra, there is no need to talk about nirvāṇa.

Chan does not use the phrase "object of negation," but it is not an unfamiliar concept. The world is illusion-like and not to be taken as real. Meditation on dependent arising and the four establishments of mindfulness are methods to realize that phenomena are not real. What is real? The buddha essence, true-suchness, the attainment of buddhahood.

But in another way, ultimate reality transcends the ideas of real and unreal. We talk about buddha essence, pure mind, and pure awareness with the understanding that ultimately those are still characterizations that we need to dispense with. Ultimately there is no real and unreal. These terms and ideas are not the actual things.

The mind may ignorantly grasp the buddha essence, imagining it to be something pure that is always there, something we can hold on to. Such conceptualization makes the grasping mind feel comfortable. But in fact that is merely grasping buddha essence as truly existent. We must turn to Nāgārjuna and his teachings on emptiness to free our minds from this delusional grasping.

On a conventional or provisional level, "real" refers to what is not associated with ignorance: the four truths are real, nirvāṇa is real, the āryan eightfold path and the six perfections are real. They are real in that they are like rafts helping us to cross the ocean of saṃsāra and arrive at the shore of nirvāṇa. Once we have reached the other shore, we do not need to carry the raft with us. Thus at buddhahood, the discriminations of "real" and "unreal" are not necessary, although for the purpose of teaching sentient beings, buddhas use these devices.

The ordinary mind is like muddy water, without clarity or wisdom, buffeted around as we react to the ever-changing flow of sense objects we contact each day. Once we awaken and purify our mind, it will return to its original state of purity. Then we will be able to go anywhere and come in contact with anything, but our mind will remain steady.

There are two forms of Chan practice: gradual cultivation and sudden awakening. Gradual cultivation is the path of the six perfections. Three countless great eons plus one hundred small eons are necessary to create the merit and wisdom to awaken in this way, whereas the path of sudden awakening is much quicker. But do not think that because it is quicker it is easy. Sudden awakening requires seeing that this mind of an ordinary being is the mind of a buddha. It is awakening to our true nature, which is originally pure. The *Flower Garland Sūtra* speaks of the possibility of sudden awakening:[107]

> By always loving to observe/contemplate the nonduality of all phenomena, this is possible: at the moment of bringing forth the [bodhi] mind, one achieves a buddha's awakening [*saṃbodhi*] [and] understands the true nature of all phenomena, [one is] replete in the wisdom body, awakened without relying on others.

After gaining an initial experience of the buddha essence, we must still practice to remove obscurations from our minds. The gradual cultivation is equal in importance to sudden awakening. Sudden awakening may come from the culmination of prior gradual cultivation, although a person of sharp faculties may not need many preliminaries. Even after sudden awakening, gradual cultivation is practiced, but now with an awakened perspective. In this case, the gradual cultivation and sudden awakening have combined to become one single practice. As such, the gradual and sudden approaches are not in conflict and complement each other.

Practices such as sitting meditation, chanting, and making offerings are valuable practices, although they remain preliminary work. By engaging in these merit-making practices, eventually the original nature will manifest and we will awaken.

When the mind suffers from deluded thoughts, sleepiness, boredom, and so on, using the method of gradual cultivation to counteract these problems is helpful. When they have stopped, simply focus on the awareness. Whether we follow sudden awakening or gradual cultivation, both are of benefit. Both require persistence, faith, and great vows on our part.

Chan meditation evolves progressively. We begin with focusing on and counting the breath. But when we get to the meditation on no mind, various approaches can be used, such as Caodong's just sitting, Middle Way Reality, mindfulness of breathing, koans, and huatou. A Chan master may prescribe one of the above methods or several of them for a particular disciple. All of them bring the experience of pure awareness. Thoughts come and go, sounds enter our field of awareness and depart. We still notice them, but as soon as we do, we release them; we do not cling to, develop, or follow them. In that way, they do not disturb pure awareness.

The *Śūraṃgama Sūtra* tells us that awakening occurs when the afflictive mind takes a rest and does not cling to the past, present, or future. The *Diamond Sūtra* says that the past mind, the present mind, and the future mind cannot be grasped. The past is gone, so we cannot hold on to it; it is useless to ruminate about it. The future has yet to come, so there is nothing there to cling to. The present mind arises and ceases in each split second, so it, too, cannot be grasped. The mind abides by not abiding. We let the mind be without abiding, without clinging to the past, present, or future. In this way, we will eventually realize the mind of the Buddha, our original nature.

This very place becomes a pureland, and we transform from an ordinary being into a sage.

Whenever thoughts are in the mind, there is naturally a subject and an object—the one that is aware and that which one is aware of—but with practice the thoughts subside. They diminish, and then there will be periods of time when no thoughts arise. There seems to be just pure awareness. This is similar to a state of nonduality because the meditator thinks there is no subject or object. However, the actual experience of nonduality is very difficult to attain. Even after years of practice, there will be periods when a practitioner may think, "My mind is empty. Just pure awareness." But in the next moment, he realizes that subtle thought is still going on and he did not recognize it. But because his mind is not clinging to coarse thoughts, the mind naturally becomes more and more refined, clearer and more aware. In the quiescence of the mind, the mind can recognize more and more subtle thoughts and release them, until eventually it arrives at the state of nonduality.

"Freedom from conceptions" indicates freedom from clinging, freedom from grasping things as real. It does not mean getting rid of all thoughts, be they good or bad, and dwelling in a state of samādhi. Even in the second dhyāna and above, when the meditators have relinquished investigation and analysis, they still have conceptions: the conception of samādhi and the conception of the joy and bliss of that samādhi. These conceptions may not be verbal, but they are still ideas and objects of attachment. The mind clings to them, mistakenly thinking they are real. This is not the state of nonduality.

Beings who lack understanding of emptiness but dwell in states of deep samādhi still have the sense of I; they cling to the self and are not beyond conception and clinging. Chan masters use several ways to free their disciples from grasping a self. Some masters instruct their students to first practice the four establishments of mindfulness to release at least the coarser grasping of self. The Middle Way Reality method then makes them aware of more refined clinging—even clinging to the Dharma or to the idea of nirvāṇa. Ultimately practitioners reach a point where all duality is shattered. Training in koan and huatou practice is another method used to penetrate the beginningless ignorance that shrouds the self.

Chan: Moderation and Extremes

Tibetans refer to the great debate at Samye (792–794) as a decisive point in their Buddhist history. As recounted by Tibetan historians, the Chinese abbot Hva Shang Mahāyāna[108] asserted that all thoughts are distractions to be abandoned on the path. Just as clouds, be they black or white, obscure the sky, so too do thoughts, be they constructive or destructive, obscure the true nature. Thus the entire method side of the path was unnecessary because it involved thought. One simply had to empty the mind of all thought whatsoever to attain nirvāṇa. Kamalaśīla refuted this, saying that constructive thoughts and practices on the method side of the path are imperative for the collection of merit, and that emptiness must first be approached by means of thought before it can be realized nondualistically.

Another topic of this debate was whether awakening occurred suddenly, as stated by Hva Shang, or gradually, as asserted by Indian Buddhists. Here, too, Kamalaśīla's argument prevailed, and as a result, Tibetans turned toward India rather than China as the principal source for Buddhist scriptures and ideas.

Interestingly, a similar debate was going on in China during the late eighth and early ninth centuries. Among the many Chan lineages at that time, the Gongzhou lineage advocated nondiscrimination. These monks did away with Buddhist rites such as ordination and repentance ceremonies and Dharma activities such as reciting scriptures and studying sūtras because these involved conceptions and thus discrimination. Zongmi firmly criticized these views as lacking an ethical basis and deprecating the necessary practice of virtuous activities. As seen from his ten-stage outline of the path above, Zongmi highly valued the method aspect of the path, seeing the gradual accumulation of merit as an essential support for the development of wisdom. Although Zongmi agreed that awakening was beyond words and conceptions, he believed that Chan was not and should not be disengaged from the philosophical traditions of Buddhism that employ words and concepts to lead sentient beings to the truth.

In *Chan Preface*, Zongmi says that there is no contradiction between the scriptures studied by scholars and the practices taught by Chan patriarchs because they all come from the Buddha. As time went on, this unity of scriptures and practice was lost on the Chinese. Because some Buddhists became so attached to words, Bodhidharma taught in a "mind-to-mind" transmission to balance the scale and help practitioners understand the actual point of the Dharma. Over time, however, people failed to see what Bodhidharma did as skillful means and thought that the teachings in the sūtras and treatises were separate from the Chan teachings.

Zongmi disagreed and was concerned that some Chan sects were not practicing properly because they dismissed sūtra study. Scholars "do not realize that the cultivation and realization [they discuss] are truly the fundamental concerns of Chan," and Chan practitioners "do not realize that the mind and the Buddha are truly the fundamental meaning of the scriptures and treatises." Zongmi tried to show these monks that what Chan patriarchs transmitted by mind was the same as the meaning expressed in the scriptures.

In building this bridge, Zongmi mollified the critics who said that Chan lacked a basis in the scriptures and tried to neutralize the extreme view of certain Chan practitioners who said that Chan awakening was totally distinct from Buddhist scriptures. To those who didn't take sūtra study seriously, Zongmi explained that practitioners can learn valuable Dharma from the scriptures, which would provide accurate measuring points of a meditator's progress. Likewise, meditators' realizations could be verified by comparing them to the Buddha's statements in the scriptures. Thus Zongmi encouraged people to both study the scriptures and meditate to practice a path that combines both samādhi and wisdom.

Not all Chan sects disparaged sūtra study, although the words in which Chan is often expressed may give this wrong impression. Many great Chan masters were aware of this misinterpretation and acted upon it in their teachings. Zongmi is one example of this.

Pureland

The Amitābha practice was done in ancient India beginning around the second century. It centers around three principal sūtras, as mentioned above. In the *Descent to Lanka Sūtra*, the Buddha establishes Nāgārjuna as a Pureland practitioner by saying that having attained the first bodhisattva ground, he will be born in Sukhāvatī, Amitābha's Pureland.

The Pureland tradition has an illustrious lineage in India and well as

China. Nāgārjuna spoke of the pureland in his *Daśabhūmika Śāstra*; Vasubandhu wrote about the pureland in his *Treatise on Birth in the Pureland* (*Jingtu lun*) and *Commentary on the Amitāyus Sūtra* (*Amitāyussūtropadeśa*), and Sthiramati (c. 510–70) mentioned it in his *Ratnagotravibhāga*.

The Pureland tradition became immensely popular and spread widely in China, Japan, Korea, and Vietnam. Later Pureland masters considered Huiyuan (334–417) the first Pureland patriarch in China. He set up the White Lotus Society and instructed his disciples to visualize and meditate on Amitābha to gain samādhi and to focus on the vision of Amitābha to be born in Sukhāvatī. Huiyuan practiced many of the contemplations from the *Sūtra on the Meditation on Amitāyus* and had in-depth discussions with Kumārajīva on wisdom. About two hundred years later, in the Tang dynasty, chanting "Amitābha" became the most favored practice of Pureland Buddhists due to the influence of several Pureland masters. Still, many of the masters knew the scriptures well. Later on, the idea that one only needs to chant "Amitābha" without any need to learn or practice anything else became popular. This way of practicing Pureland is criticized by other Buddhists, although it enabled common people with little education to engage in the practice, cultivate compassion, and feel close to Amitābha.

Pureland was practiced in several Buddhist traditions in China, and masters from these traditions, such as Jizang and Zhiyi, wrote commentaries on the Pureland sūtras. Throughout the centuries there have been practitioners who chant the names of Medicine Buddha or Maitreya, wishing to be born in their purelands. They are also considered Pureland practitioners, though they are a minority among Pureland practitioners.

Another great master of this practice was Tanluan (476–542), whose teacher was the Indian master Bodhiruci (sixth century). Bodhiruci used the recitation of dhāraṇī (mantra) to develop meditative concentration and advocated the practice of *nianfo*—literally "mindfulness or recollection of the Buddha," in this case Amitābha Buddha. In Tanluan's early writings, nianfo referred to meditation recollecting Amitābha and his qualities with the mental consciousness. However, over the centuries, it came to refer to the verbal recitation of Amitābha's name.

Nian has three meanings: (1) meditation or concentration, in this case, meditation and concentration on Amitābha; (2) one thought or the time of one thought; and (3) verbal recitation, where *shi nian* was seen as ten recitations (ten moments). Nowadays most Pureland masters emphasize that while verbal recitation is good, it isn't sufficient, and ethical conduct, compassion, and meditation on Amitābha is important.

Tanluan's teachings on the Amitābha practice gradually began to incline toward the perspective of other power—that is, as ordinary beings in saṃsāra, we cannot attain nirvāṇa by our own efforts alone; the merit and qualities gained through nianfo and faith in Amitābha are important. Birth in the pureland is made possible by Amitābha's vows, and awakening is dependent on the power of his blessings and inspiration.

Tanluan said that even people who had created great negative karma could be born in Sukhāvatī because all sentient beings have the buddha nature and thus could experience the bliss of the pureland. However, he did not go so far as to say those who deprecate the Dharma could be born there.

Many great bodhisattvas and masters aspired for rebirth in Amitābha's pureland. Mañjuśrī is said to have vowed to see Amitābha at the time of death. The fifth-century Yogācāra master Aśvaghoṣa, to whom *Awakening of Faith* is attributed, also saw recitation of the Buddha's name as an excellent method. Daochuo emphasized the other-power practice because beings in these degenerate times needed to entrust themselves completely to Amitābha's power, and his disciple Shandao (613–681) stressed the importance of reciting Amitābha's name continuously. While other practices such as meditation, ethical conduct, sūtra recitation, making offerings, and study were of great value, recitation of Amitābha's name was important for birth in the pureland.

The Tiantai master Zhiyi wrote a commentary on the sixteen contemplations of Amitābha. Although well known for their Dharma treatises and scriptural talks, many later Tiantai masters have turned to nianfo for their meditative practice.

Some Chan masters also advocated the practice of Pureland, including Baizhang, renowned for formulating rules of Chan monasteries. Of these, Yongming Yanshou (904–976), a patriarch of the Fayan House of Chan and also regarded by many as a Pureland patriarch, is perhaps the most famous for combining Chan and Pureland practices into a single practice. He wrote extensively on both traditions.

Other well-respected Chinese masters also practiced and taught this method of recollection of the Buddha. Hanshan Deqing (1546–1623) wrote

The Record of Dream Wanderings, in which he explained the Amitābha practice and emphasized its compatibility with Chan. Ouyi Zhixu (1599–1655) was a great practitioner, learned in Vinaya and Tiantai philosophy. He initially practiced Chan but later turned to Pureland practice and wrote a commentary on the *Amitābha Sūtra* from the Yogācāra perspective. His commentary served as a bridge between Chan and Pureland, showing how they could be practiced together.

Pureland became very popular in Japan, especially under the guidance of Honen (1133–1212) and his disciple Shinran. It also spread to Korea, Vietnam, and now to Western countries.

The Pureland practice can be understood on two levels: the transcendental and the ordinary, depending on the faculties and disposition of the disciple. Those who practice on an ordinary level and recite Amitābha Buddha's name believe the pureland to be an external place and do not understand that it is created by mind and that the mind is buddha. They relate to Amitābha as a child does to his or her mother, calling out to him for compassion and protection.

Those who practice Pureland on the transcendental level of inner truth see Amitābha and the pureland as innate features of their own pure minds. Knowing that the pureland is created by mind, they use the Amitābha Buddha's name, which is innate in their minds and is the creation of the mind, as a focal point to help them remember this deeper truth. For these practitioners who aim for full awakening, meditating on Amitābha and reciting his name transform the ordinary, afflictive mind into the self-nature true-mind; that is, it enables them to realize the buddha nature—their original face—emptiness. The wisdom that does this is called the original wisdom; it knows that all phenomena arise dependently, have no self-nature, and are therefore empty.

14 | Yogācāra and Tathāgatagarbha in China

Three Principal Philosophical Traditions in China

Throughout history Chinese masters have created schema to understand how the various teachings of the Buddha are related to one another. Taixu, an early twentieth-century Chinese master who advocated the reform and modernization of Buddhism, developed a threefold schema to classify the Mahāyāna philosophical systems present in Chinese Buddhism: Yogācāra, Tathāgatagarbha, and Madhyamaka. All three philosophical systems originated in India. Although Yogācāra and Madhyamaka were initially separate Chinese schools, Tathāgatagarbha was not. However, its philosophy has had a profound influence on the indigenous Chinese Buddhist schools, especially Huayen, Tiantai, Pureland, and Tantra. Taixu's disciple Yinshun, a well-known Buddhist scholar, made use of this schema extensively in his writings, making it widely known and adopted.

Each of these three doctrinal systems relies on specific sūtras as the basis of its view, and each claim that those sūtras possess the complete view of the Buddha. Although Yinshun seems to favor the Madhyamaka view, he states that he presents each view according to its scriptures, not according to later scholars, and leaves it to each person to exercise their wisdom to discern which view is definitive and which is provisional. In doing so, he emphasizes the importance of the Buddha's skillful means and noncontradictory approach to guiding people of different dispositions and interests.

All three systems share the same important concerns: establishing the efficacy of karma and its effects and explaining how rebirth in saṃsāra occurs as a dependent process; explaining the ultimate nature of phenomena, the realization of which leads to the elimination of the afflictions; and describing the path of practice that brings liberation and full awakening.

Mahāyāna Buddhism was prominent in both China and Tibet, and the two canons shared many of the same sūtras, Indian treatises, and commentaries. The views of Yogācāra, Madhyamaka, and Tathāgatagarbha spread to both Tibet and China and strongly influenced the development of the indigenous Buddhist traditions in both countries. In addition to these similarities, differences also exist. To list a few among many, Buddhism entered China several centuries before it spread to Tibet. This influenced the scriptures that were brought into each country. Tantra was not widespread in India when many Buddhist scriptures were taken to China, so these practices did not take hold strongly in China, as they did in Tibet. The āgamas and many scriptures of the initial eighteen schools were prevalent in India when Buddhism first came to China, whereas some of those schools had died out by the time Buddhism came to Tibet intact. In addition, the culture and climate of the two lands are different, and these factors influence how the Buddhist ideas from India are understood and how Vinaya is practiced.

With the background of the previous chapters on Yogācāra, Madhyamaka, and Tathāgatagarbha in Tibet, let's now look at these philosophical systems in China and how they were assimilated into the indigenous Chinese traditions.

Yogācāra

The Yogācāra (Weishi) philosophy[109] came to China in three waves. The first began in 508 with the arrival of the Indian masters Ratnamati, Bodhiruci, and Buddhaśānta. Their system was based on Buddhaśānta's translation of Vasubandhu's *Commentary on the Ten Grounds* (*Daśabhūmikabhāsya*), a text that later became prominent in the Huayan school.

The second wave was based on the translation of Asaṅga's *Compendium on the Mahāyāna* (*Mahāyānasaṃgraha*) done by the prolific translator and Indian master Paramārtha (499–569). The Chinese were fascinated with Yogācāra's notion of the foundation consciousness. However, Yogācāra's idea that a defiled consciousness was at the heart of each sentient being clashed with the preexisting idea in Chinese culture that the core of sentient beings is good. So when the Indian Yogācāra master Paramārtha came to China, as a skillful means to make Yogācāra more compatible with the Chinese view of the goodness of human nature, he taught that there are nine consciousnesses. The ninth consciousness that he added is an undefiled consciousness (*amala vijñāna*), which is a purified version of the foundation consciousness. Paramārtha taught that the original form of consciousness is pure, but due to past karma stored in the foundation consciousness, the primordially pure mind (*citta prakṛti parśuddha*) is defiled. However, when sentient beings practice the Dharma, the defilements are purified, and the pure mind that has been there all along can be seen. Because of this emphasis on primordial purity and buddha nature, this view of Yogācāra became popular in China.

The third wave was headed by the great translator Xuanzang (596–664) and his disciple Kuiji (632–682). Studying at Nālandā Monastery for many years, Xuanzang delved into Vasubandhu's *Thirty Stanzas on Consciousness-Only* (*Triṃśikāvijñaptimātratā*) and its commentaries and *Twenty Stanzas on Consciousness-Only* (*Viṃśatikā*). Upon returning to China, Xuanzang translated many of these scriptures. Thinking that his disciples might become confused by the diversity of ideas, he consolidated the commentaries into one major commentary by using Dharmapāla's *Commentary on (Vasubandhu's) Thirty Stanzas on Consciousness-Only* as the basis and adding portions of nine other Indian commentaries. This became Xuanzang's *Treatise on the Establishment of the Doctrine of Consciousness-Only* (C. *Chengweishi lun*), which is the primary Chinese text on Yogācāra. Regarded as the pinnacle of Yogācāra thought in China, as many as two dozen Chinese commentaries have been written on it. Xuanzang's Yogācāra tradition also relies on the *Sūtra Unraveling the Thought*, the *Yogācārabhūmi*, and *Compendium on the Mahāyāna*. This Yogācāra literature has sparked sophisticated philosophical analysis for centuries.[110]

Xuanzang was an exceptional person who dedicated his life to the Dharma and risked the dangers of traveling overland to India to learn the Buddha's teachings and bring scriptures back to China. Remaining in India and Central Asia for seventeen years, he brought 657 texts from India to China and translated seventy-four of them himself, including the *Sūtra Unraveling the Thought*, the Perfection of Wisdom sūtras, and the massive *Abhidharma*

Mahāvibhāṣā Śāstra. He had over three thousand disciples, the two main ones being Kuiji and Woncheuk (613–696). Kuiji was the principal master who transmitted Yogācāra doctrine in China, writing four commentaries on *Establishment of Consciousness-Only*.

Korean by birth, Woncheuk (C. Yuance, T. Wen tshegs) was a great scholar who synthesized Paramārtha and Xuanzang's views. Relying on the *Lotus Sūtra* and *Flower Ornament Sūtra*, he asserted one final vehicle and said that all sentient beings could attain awakening. A pilgrim took his *Commentary on the "Sūtra Unraveling the Thought"* to the Dunhuang area, and from there it was taken to Tibet, where it was translated into Tibetan between 815 and 824. When composing *Essence of Eloquence*, Tsongkhapa referred to this commentary, calling it the *Chinese Great Commentary*.[111] Through it, he learned of the writings of Bodhiruci, Dharmapāla, Paramārtha, and Xuanzang, whom he mentions in his other works on Yogācāra. Influenced by Woncheuk's textual outlines with subsections, Tsongkhapa began to outline texts, thus initiating the widespread Tibetan practice of making detailed outlines for texts.

While the Chinese and Tibetan canons share some Indian Yogācāra scriptures in common, several works are found in the Chinese canon that are absent from the Tibetan canon. Among these are the *Xianyang shengjiao lun*, a comprehensive work by Asaṅga; Dharmapāla's commentary on Vasubandhu's *Twenty Stanzas*; and Xuanzang's *Treatise on the Establishment of the Doctrine of Consciousness-Only*.

During the time of Xuanzang and Kuiji, Yogācāra was immensely popular and overshadowed studies based on previous Yogācāra texts. But it faced persecution in the Tang dynasty,[112] and in the latter half of the Tang dynasty, it began to decline. Part of the decline of Xuanzang's Yogācāra was due to the unpopularity of its view that there are three final vehicles and therefore not all sentient beings can attain awakening.

Nevertheless, Yogācāra philosophy heavily influenced the indigenous schools that developed as the Chinese made Buddhism their own. The Chan and Huayan schools incorporated elements of Madhyamaka and Yogācāra. The Chan tradition in North China preferred the gradual cultivation to awakening, while Chan masters in South China preferred the sudden awakening approach. They often quote the Perfection of Wisdom sūtras, the *Śūraṃgama Sūtra*, Nāgārjuna's *Treatise on Wisdom*, as well as the *Descent to Laṅka Sūtra* and the *Sūtra Unraveling the Thought*. Later, the Southern Chan school became predominant, and most Chan masters in Taiwan, Japan, Korea, and Western countries are its descendants. This lineage traces its roots to the Sixth Patriarch Huineng, the founder of the southern tradition of Chan.

Yogācāra also influenced Pureland Buddhism, in that the pureland is said to be a creation of the mind. When the mind is pure, the environment is pure. As discussed in the previous chapter, the visualization of Amitābha or another buddha and his pureland in front of us is a reflection of the mind; it is only the mind.

During the Buddhist revival that took place in China at the end of the nineteenth century and well into the twentieth century, prominent figures such as the lay followers Ouyang Jingwu (1871–1943) and Han Qingjing and the monk Taixu (1890–1947) once again made Yogācāra popular, and new Buddhist institutes were established that favored the study of Yogācāra. Nowadays, Yogācāra influence is clearly present in Chinese Buddhism.

Several factors contributed to this renewed interest in Yogācāra. One was that in the nineteenth century, Yang Rengshan brought back many lost Yogācāra, Huayan, Tiantan, and Sanlun Chinese texts from Japan. The Chinese then compiled the entire Buddhist Tripiṭaka into one set, which took decades to do, and gifted them to Japan, Korea, and possibly Vietnam—countries that used Chinese characters until modern times. In addition, Chinese monks who studied in Tibet brought back Yogācāra texts that were not in the Chinese canon.

In response to Western science and philosophy, which were associated with imperialism, Chinese Buddhists became more interested in their own rich intellectual traditions, such as Yogācāra. In the Sino-Tibetan Buddhist Institute, founded in 1932 near Chongqing, China, studies included the Yogācāra texts by Asaṅga, Dharmapāla (531–61),[113] and Vasubandhu. Fazun, a scholarly monk-translator who visited Tibet and taught at the Sino-Tibetan Buddhist Studies Institute, noticed some differences between Yogācāra as presented in China and in Tibet. The following is a brief synthesis of Yinshun's perspective.

Yogācāra in China asserts eight consciousnesses and states that all dependently produced phenomena rely on the foundation consciousness to arise. Seeds on this storehouse consciousness produce the seven consciousnesses with their mental activities, the sense faculties and their objects, and the "external" world. These, or our contact with them, in turn, perfume the foundation consciousness with more seeds, and in this way cause and effect operate. For example, the seed of a visual consciousness produces a visual consciousness, the seed of green produces green, the seed of the faulty produces the faulty. These manifest phenomena then perfume the foundation consciousness with more seeds of the visual consciousness, more seeds to perceive green, and so on. Results arise due to these seeds as well as other conditioning factors that must be present for the seeds to ripen. In this way, truly existent causes produce truly existent effects.

Because seeds produce manifest objects and consciousnesses and these, in turn, place more seeds on the foundation consciousness, Yogācārins assert that apart from the mind, things do not exist. Although there are no objects independent of mind, objects that are the nature of mind exist. The perceiving mind and its object arise from the same seed on the foundation consciousness. Although both "external" objects and the perceiving mind seem to be independent of each other, this is erroneous and grasping things to exist this way is the wrong view that gives rise to attachment, anger, and other afflictions.

Based on this they explain the three natures—the imaginary, dependent, and thoroughly established natures. "External" objects being unrelated to the mind is the imaginary nature that phenomena lack. However, conventional things are based on the real, so the mind must truly exist. If it did not, nothing could exist. This is phenomena's dependent nature.

Not understanding that objects are only mind, sentient beings are confused. Afflictions arise and create karma, which keeps them bound in saṃsāra. However, when sentient beings understand through meditation that external objects do not exist and that objects arise due to the mind, then they can know that, based on phenomena's dependent nature, they are empty of the imaginary nature. This emptiness is their thoroughly established nature. Through this, the afflictive seventh consciousness is eliminated, and liberation is attained. In this way, both saṃsāra and nirvāṇa are established based on the mind.

Yinshun believes that the Yogācāra system is an ingenious aid that ultimately leads disciples with a certain disposition to the final Madhyamaka view. He quotes the *Sūtra Unraveling the Thought*, which explains that people who have accomplished five deeds have a mature capacity and are able to understand that all phenomena lack inherent nature. The five deeds are planting superior virtuous roots, clearing various afflictions, continuing to mature, frequently practicing the Mahāyāna teachings, and accumulating the superior collections of merit and wisdom. Those who have accomplished these five deeds have correct wisdom, understand the lack of inherent existence, and do not require the teaching in the *Sūtra Unraveling the Thought*.

However, people who have not done all five deeds regard the teaching on the emptiness of inherent existence as extremely difficult. Mistakenly thinking that emptiness means phenomena are totally nonexistent, they fall to the extreme of nihilism. Others object to this teaching, think that things inherently exist, and fall to the extreme of absolutism. Both groups believe that the view of emptiness of inherent existence is not the Buddha's teaching but was spoken by Māra.

For all these people who have modest faculties and have not accomplished all five deeds, the Buddha taught the *Sūtra Unraveling the Thought*. Although his actual thought was that all three natures lack true existence, he explained that some things truly exist while others do not. This teaching is suitable for people of both extremes who do not understand the view of no true existence. To teach these people, the Buddha said that some things—the dependent and thoroughly established natures—are ultimately real and others—the imaginaries—are not.

This teaching is suitable for people who believe that something real must exist before conventional descriptions and names can be given to them. If things were merely designated without any real foundation, even conventionalities could not exist. (Here the conventional includes the dependent and existent imaginaries.) Imaginaries such as unconditioned space exist due to conception, and dependent things exist due to causes and conditions.

Although Yogācāra is very popular in Chinese Buddhism, some people see Madhyamaka and the Perfection of Wisdom teachings as definitive because in some Yogācāra sūtras such as the *Laṅkavatāra* and *Śūraṃgama*,[114] the Buddha warned against mistakenly considering the foundation consciousness to be a self. Although Yogācāra texts state that the foundation consciousness is momentary and impermanent, reifying it nevertheless remains a danger due to sentient beings' innate misconceptions and grasping. Since

Yogācāra states that the foundation consciousness carries the karmic seeds to future lives, many people think of it as a permanent essence.

Madhyamaka explains the transference of karmic imprints to the next life without positing a real self. In his *Treatise on Wisdom* Nāgārjuna explains this by means of an analogy. The mind of the previous moment is like a stamp with a design embossed on it. When that stamp is pressed on soft wax, the design on the stamp is transferred to the wax, which can now transfer the design in the future. Similarly, the mind of the previous moment generates the mind of the next moment. The mind of the previous moment is gone, but the karmic seed has been transferred to the next moment of mind without there being a permanent self. In this way, all seeds are transferred from one moment to the next and from one life to the next. This process continues as long as the mind is under the influence of ignorance.

Yinshun says that later Yogācārins did not know that Maitreya and Asaṅga's teachings were for disciples with a certain disposition—those who have not accomplished the five deeds—but instead thought that people must rely on the explanation of the *Sūtra Unraveling the Thought* regardless of their disposition. Regarding these teachings as literal and definitive for everyone, they claim that these teachings clarify what was said in the Perfection of Wisdom sūtras so that people do not misunderstand and think that nothing exists. But these people also say that Nāgārjuna agrees with the explanation in the *Sūtra Unraveling the Thought*, and they disagree with the Madhyamaka presentation that all phenomena are empty of inherent existence and are merely conventionally designated.

Most Yogācāra treatises tend to be very philosophical and technical, and its methods of cultivation are not clear. This school was reinvigorated during the renewal movement in the early twentieth century thanks to the efforts of two erudite scholars, Ouyang Jian (1871–1943) and Han Qingjing (1884–1949), but it currently has no obvious living master or lineage. Nevertheless, Yogācāra is popular in Chinese Buddhism today.

REFLECTION

The *Sūtra Unraveling the Thought* speaks of five deeds accomplished by people who have mature capacity and can understand that all phenomena lack inherent nature. Think of the benefit of each of the five and then think how you could increase your practice of each one.

1. Planting superior virtuous roots by engaging in virtuous activities.

2. Clearing various afflictions by avoiding circumstances that trigger them and gaining familiarity with their antidotes.

3. Continuing to mature in the Dharma by hearing, thinking, and meditating on the teachings.

4. Frequently practicing the Mahāyāna teachings with the aspiration to attain full awakening.

5. Accumulating the superior collections of merit and wisdom by doing all actions with a bodhicitta motivation and dedicating the merit with awareness that the agent, object, and action are mutually dependent and lack inherent existence.

Tathāgatagarbha

Of the three philosophical systems that were widespread in China and East Asia in general, Madhyamaka was the first to develop in India, followed by Yogācāra, and then the Tathāgatagarbha system. They entered China in roughly the same order. The Tathāgatagarbha doctrine was not as influential in Indian Buddhism as it was in Tibet and China. Indian pandits wrote very few commentaries on it, whereas many great Indian scholar-adepts wrote commentaries and treatises about Madhyamaka and Yogācāra philosophy.

The Tathāgatagarbha system relies on the *Lion's Roar of Queen Śrīmālā Sūtra*, the *Descent into Lanka Sūtra*, the *Nirvāṇa Sūtra*, the *Tathāgatagarbha Sūtra*, the *Aṅgulimāla Sūtra*, the *Śūraṃgama Sūtra*, the *Sūtra of Perfect Awakening* (*Mahāvaipulyapurnabuddha Sūtra*), the *Treatise on the Awakening of Faith in the Mahāyāna* (*Mahāyānaśraddhotpāda Śāstra*) attributed to Aśvaghoṣa,[115] the *Treatise on the Discrimination of the Jewel Nature* (*Ratnagotravibhāga*) by Sāramati, and the *Treatise on the Sublime Continuum* by Maitreya, which was translated into Chinese in the sixth century.[116]

The idea of buddha essence was presented to the Chinese with the translation of the *Nirvāṇa Sūtra* by Dharmakṣema in 421. This sūtra states that its purpose is to reveal the supreme teaching—that sentient beings possess the buddha essence. Just as all streams flow to the sea, all sūtras and samādhis lead to the *Nirvāṇa Sūtra*. Seen as the parting teachings the Buddha gave prior to his parinirvāṇa, it immediately became popular and was accepted as authoritative by Chinese Buddhists. The first translation consisted of only the first part of the sūtra, which says that not all sentient beings can be awakened. But the later translation was of a longer sūtra and clarified that all sentient beings have the buddha essence and can attain full awakening.

The Chinese immediately felt affinity for the Tathāgatagarbha doctrine because its contents corresponded with some Confucian and Taoist ideas that were already prominent in society. Both Confucianism and Taoism contain the idea that every phenomenon has its own fundamental basis or nature. The Tathāgatagarbha doctrine speaks of a final reality, a supreme affirmative reality that is beyond all form and all designations. Suchness (thusness, *tathatā*) is a formless presence in the world, one that is already present but unknown to ignorant beings. This is similar to the idea of the Tao and was more acceptable to Chinese culture than the Madhyamaka view of emptiness, which is a lack of essence.

In addition, the Chinese gravitated toward the idea of human nature being good. In the fourth century BCE the Confucian scholar Mencius expressed the belief that since everyone has a positive human nature, each person can achieve a perfected human state. Lao Tzu also spoke of cultivating the original mind. These ideas found a voice in Buddhism with the explanation in the *Awakening of Faith* that all polluted things of saṃsāra arise due to the mistaken notions and activity of the mind, and awakening is a return to the original inherent purity of the mind that all sentient beings have. In this way, the Tathāgatagarbha philosophy brought Taoism and Buddhism together and fit in well with Chinese Confucian mentality.

Chinese culture accentuates the fundamental nature or character of phenomena more than their superficial change, whereas in India the impermanent, changing nature of phenomena was emphasized. The Chinese gravitated toward the Tathāgatagarbha notion of an ever-present—but not necessarily permanent—essential nature in sentient beings that is good and that enables them to attain awakening. As a result, some Chinese masters do not emphasize emptiness but instead teach the tathāgatagarbha or tathatā as an inherently existent, fundamentally pure and permanent essence of the mind that can act as the cause of awakening. For these masters, suchness is not synonymous with emptiness, as it is for Madhyamaka, but is an ultimate affirmative existence. This more positive approach helps many practitioners be optimistic that their minds can transform from their current defiled state into the mind of a buddha. This view appeals to some people more than Madhyamaka, which speaks of refutation and negation, emptiness and impermanence. However, although these people may believe the buddha essence to be a permanent entity, not all Chinese masters teach that tathāgatagarbha suchness differs from emptiness. Masters such as Huineng and Zhiyi see them as different expressions that are harmonious in meaning, and Jizang interprets tathāgatagarbha in terms of Madhyamaka.

Buddhism does not exist in a vacuum. In the process of being established in a new land, the Buddhadharma is influenced by the culture, religions, and value systems of that place. As it becomes established in a new place, Buddhadharma, in turn, influences that culture and the views there. As in India, Tibet, Sri Lanka, and other places, this was the case in China and is now the case in the West. The Dharma Jewel—true cessations and true paths—is the same everywhere and at all times, but the outward appearance of the Dharma—including its rituals and art and the expression of Buddhist philosophy—is influenced by the history, social institutions, present beliefs, economic situation, and so on of the land to which it migrates.

Tathāgatagarbha as the Eternal, Inherent Essence

The meaning of tathāgatagarbha or buddha essence varies according to the context and the people using the term. According to the *Awakening of Faith*, a supreme reality with affirmative attributes exists. Called suchness, it is a transcendental real existence that is known as the ultimate reality (*paramārthadhātu*), buddha reality (*buddhadhātu*), and the sphere of reality (*dharmadhātu*). Suchness as a supreme being is the body of supreme or ultimate truth (*paramārthakāya*); as the Dharma, suchness is the dharmakāya; and as the reality of the world, suchness is the form body (*rūpakāya*).

According to Tathāgatagarbha doctrine, this essence or self that transmigrates is the Buddha's essence, the nature of nirvāṇa. Tathāgatagarbha is an inherent nature possessed by all sentient beings that is not separate from wisdom (*jñāna*). From it everything arises—good and evil, saṃsāra and awakening. But it itself is pure and without defilements. Tathāgatagarbha is the pure nature of a buddha that is obscured by the defilements of sentient beings. When freed from the obscuring defilements, it is called the dharmakāya. The *Anūnatvāpūrṇatvanirdeśa Sūtra* says (WB 318): "The realm of sentient beings is the dharmakāya, and the dharmakāya is the realm of sentient beings." There is no difference between sentient beings and buddhas.

The dharmakāya of the Buddha in its unawakened state is the tathāgatagarbha. Replete with a buddha's qualities, it is permanent (because it is not born), steadfast (because it does not die), calm (because it does not suffer), and eternal (because it does not age). The *Śrīmālādevi Sūtra* and the *Nirvāṇa Sūtra* also say the tathāgatagarbha is endowed with transcendental qualities—permanence, bliss, selfhood, and purity. Conceptions of these four qualities are the four distortions the Buddha refuted when he taught the truth of duḥkha. The Tathāgatagarbha doctrine asserts that these four qualities cannot be applied to the mundane world of saṃsāra, but they can be perfected and used to describe the absolute, the tathāgatagarbha. The perfection of purity is due to having unrelenting and pure faith in the Mahāyāna, the perfection of self is a result of wisdom that refutes non-Buddhist ideas of self, the perfection of bliss is the culmination of concentration, and the perfection of permanence is due to the utmost great compassion. The *Awakening of Faith* says (TSB 221):

> [Since suchness] is neither born at the beginning of time nor perishes at the end of time, it is utterly permanent and steadfast. In its nature it is itself fully endowed with all excellent qualities. That is, its essence itself possesses the radiant light of great wisdom, [the capacity of] universally illuminating the dharmadhātu, true cognition, the inherently pure mind, permanence, bliss, selfhood, and purity; and calmness, eternality, and freedom.

This presentation is reminiscent of the Indian view of Brahmā, the source and creator of all (who is analogous to the dharmakāya) and the ātman (which is analogous to sentient beings). Its proponents cite the *Śrīmālādevi Sūtra* (WB 318):

> Tathāgatagarbha, separate from the conditioned form, is the eternal and immutable. So tathāgatagarbha is that which is depended upon, it is that which supports, and it is that which establishes.

Because it is eternal and immutable, tathāgatagarbha is the support or basis for everything—birth, death, nirvāṇa. This explanation eases the fear of those who are frightened by impermanence and selflessness. Yinshun explains (WB 319): "The existence of good and evil is based on tathāgatagarbha, but their existence does not have tathāgatagarbha as their substance, nor are they produced from the tathāgatagarbha." Just as the bright sun and storm clouds exist in the sky but do not have the sky as their substance and are not produced by the sky, so too both saṃsāra and nirvāṇa depend on the tathāgatagarbha. The aggregates, sense sources, afflictions, and so on depend on the tathāgatagarbha to exist, but they are not in accord with the tathāgatagarbha and are different from it. Because of them, saṃsāra exists. In this way tathāgatagarbha is the basis of defilements. All virtuous qualities that have existed from beginningless time also depend on the tathāgatagarbha and are not different from it.

Tathāgatagarbha is called "foundation of all" (*ālaya*). The foundation consciousness is based on the tathāgatagarbha, and everything arises from the foundation consciousness. The pure nature—tathāgatagarbha—exists in the foundation consciousness, and thus the nature of the mind is originally pure. This unpolluted core and essence of the mind—which is called the "true-mind"—differs from the mind in general. Yinshun describes the relationship of the buddha essence and foundation consciousness (WB 319):

> Although the inherent nature of tathāgatagarbha is pure, from beginningless time it has been permeated by the false and defiled residual habits of meaningless elaboration, which are then called foundation consciousness—just as the vast sky, when covered by floating clouds, becomes neither bright nor clear. The content of the foundation consciousness has a true aspect (tathāgatagarbha) and a karmic aspect (permeated by meaningless elaborations); the union of these two is *ālaya* (foundation of all).

This differs from the Yogācāra explanation. According to the Tathāgatagarbha doctrine the foundation consciousness exists dependent on the tathāgatagarbha. However, the tathāgatagarbha and the karmic aspect are not separate in the foundation consciousness. Our various births in saṃsāra arise from the defiled seeds on the foundation consciousness. Since the tathāgatagarbha is eternal, immutable, and inseparable from saṃsāra, it is said to transmigrate in the various realms as sentient beings are reborn. Nevertheless, it remains unpolluted. It is like space being square in a square container and being round in a round container. The tathāgatagarbha, which is the true form of the foundation consciousness, is part of the dharmakāya. When it is freed from the bonds of the defilements, the tathāgatagarbha is no longer called the foundation consciousness but is then called the dharmakāya.

What is the role of realizing emptiness in a system that is based on the ultimate truth being an affirmative phenomenon and sentient beings being originally awakened owing to their possessing the tathāgatagarbha? The realization of emptiness eliminates afflictive attachment so that the true nature can be perceived. Instead of being distracted by clinging to the appearances of phenomena, practitioners will be able to go deeper and see their true nature as it really is—pure and unsullied.

Zongmi (781–841), the fifth Huayan patriarch who also practiced Chan, regards the negative language of "unborn," "the empty state of being without the appearance of phenomena," "neither tainted nor pure," "without cause or effect," "neither ordinary nor ārya," and so forth as another way of getting at the true nature, the tathāgatagarbha. What is it that lacks these things? It is awareness, the knowing. He describes the phrase "empty tranquil awareness" (TSB 216):

> "Empty" means empty of all appearance of phenomena and is still a negative term. "Tranquil" just indicates the principle of the immutability of the true nature and is not the same as nothingness. "Awareness" indicates the revelation of the very essence and is not the same as discrimination. It alone constitutes the inherent essence of the true-mind.

According to the *Śrīmālā Sūtra*, "tathāgatagarbha" expresses the actual meaning of emptiness:[117]

> Bhagavat! The tathāgatagarbha wisdom is the tathagata's wisdom of emptiness. Bhagavat! All arhats, pratyekabuddhas, great powerful bodhisattvas have not (yet) seen and grasped the tathāgatagarbha. Bhagavat! There are two types of tathāgatagarbha wisdom of emptiness: (1) the empty tathāgatagarbha is separate from, free from, and different from the stores of defilements; (2) the tathāgatagarbha that is not empty is not separate from, not free from, and not different from the inconceivable buddhadharmas more numerous than the sands of the Ganges River . . . Only a buddha [fully] realizes the tathāgatagarbha, the extinction of all duḥkha, by destroying the stores of all defilements and cultivat[ing] the path that ends all duḥkha.

As in all Buddhist traditions, different practitioners often read sūtra passages differently, such that the meaning they derive from the passage varies. The above passage is from chapter 9 of the *Śrīmālā Sūtra*, whose title may be translated as "Emptiness Veils True Reality" or "True Reality Implicit in Emptiness." People who read the title in the first way may conclude that the teaching on emptiness is provisional and the Perfection of Wisdom sūtras are incomplete because they do not speak of the wondrous qualities of the tathāgatagarbha. A complete understanding of emptiness involves recognizing both the empty and nonempty aspects of the tathāgatagarbha wisdom of emptiness. *Awakening of Faith* concurs, saying that suchness is empty "because it is ultimately able to reveal what is real," and it is not empty "because it has its own essence and is fully endowed with undefiled and excellent qualities" (TSB 219).

People who read the title in the second way may conclude that a defining quality of the Tathāgatagarbha system is to make explicit the nonempty part of the wisdom of emptiness. The Perfection of Wisdom sūtras focus on emptiness and also speak extensively on the importance and practice of the six perfections and skillful means to guide sentient beings to buddhahood. Similarly, emptiness is expounded in the *Treatise on the Middle Way*, whereas the full range of the perfections, including detailed explanations of dharmas taught by the Buddha elsewhere, is fully expounded in Nāgārjuna's *Treatise on Wisdom*, which is a Madhyamaka text. Thus the full path to buddhahood is explained, together with the Buddha's excellent qualities in Madhyamaka texts.

Those who follow the Tathāgatagarbha doctrine accept the realization of emptiness as a necessary precondition to the realization of the buddha essence, but say that the realization of emptiness alone—that is, the śrāvakas' realization of emptiness—is incomplete. It is an important first step because it eliminates the idea that any of the aggregates are the person. The aggregates are impermanent and in the nature of duḥkha, so they are not suitable to be a self. Grasping a worldly self that is in the aggregates keeps us bound in saṃsāra, but eliminating that grasping is not the end of the path. In his final teaching, the *Nirvāṇa Sūtra*, the Buddha says that in each sentient being there is a true-self (*satya-ātman*), the buddha element (*buddhadhātu*), and an embryonic buddha (tathāgatagarbha, buddha essence) that is permanent and latent. Whereas the worldly self is impermanent, suffering, and unreal, the true-self is suchness (reality, *tattva*), full of virtuous qualities (*guṇa*, C. *gong de*), permanent (*nitya*, C. *bu huai*), immovable, ultimate, blissful, everlasting (*śāśvata*, C. *bu huai*), stable (*dhruva*), and peace. The *Awakening of Faith* asserts (CE 119):

> Reality is the permanent, immutable, true-mind, complete with pure qualities.

The true-self is like a treasure covered by the mud of defilements that just needs to be seen and uncovered. This self is inconceivable (*acintya*) and inexpressible; it cannot be known by reasoning and concept alone. By clearing away the defilements, this radiant and shining self can be known. Only by knowing this true-self can full awakening be attained.

The *Ratnagotravibhāga* says that the positive expression of the tathāgatagarbha was taught as an antidote for those who misunderstand emptiness as explained in the Perfection of Wisdom sūtras. These people mistakenly think that emptiness means the destruction of all impermanent things and that nirvāṇa can be attained only when phenomena have been made nonexistent. Furthermore, when some people hear that all phenomena are empty, they become discouraged and cannot generate the aspiration for full awakening.

Other people who want to attain full awakening think they are superior to those who have not and regard others' faults as inherent in those people. They do not see that those faults are adventitious and that others' true nature is empty of these defilements and endowed with all the qualities of the Tathāgata. Because they have this limited view, they cannot generate the compassion that sees self and others as equal. The Tathāgatagarbha doctrine was taught to remedy those defects of the teachings on emptiness. Therefore the *Sublime Continuum* explains the true meaning of emptiness (RGV 132–33):

> Nothing whatsoever is to be removed,
> not the slightest thing is to be added,
> perfectly view the perfect [truth;]
> seeing the perfect [truth] will liberate completely.[118]
>
> The element [buddha essence] is empty of the adventitious [stains],
> which differ from it;
> but it is not empty of the matchless properties
> that are, essentially, indivisible from it.

The *Flower Ornament Sūtra* contains a passage that many Chan practitioners say are the first words the Buddha said after his awakening (TSB 166):

> Oh spiritual children of the Buddha, there is no place where the wisdom of the Tathāgata does not reach. Why? Because there is not a single sentient being that is not fully endowed with the wisdom of the Tathāgata. It is only on account of their afflictive thinking, erroneous views, and attachments that they do not succeed in realizing it. When they become free from afflictive thinking, the all-comprehending wisdom, the spontaneous wisdom, and the unobstructed wisdom will then be manifest before them.

At that time the Tathāgata with his unobstructed pure eye of wisdom universally beheld all sentient beings throughout the dharmadhātu and said,

"How amazing! How can it be that these sentient beings are fully endowed with the wisdom of the Tathāgata and yet, being ignorant and confused, do not know it and do not see it? I must teach them the ārya path, enabling them to be forever free from afflictive thinking and to achieve for themselves the ocean of the broad and vast wisdom of the Tathāgata within themselves and so be no different from the buddhas."

Awakening of Faith explains the relationship between sentient beings' unawakened state and the ultimate awakened mind with the three types of *jue* (awareness/awakening): (1) original (pure) awareness/awakening that is equal in all sentient beings (C. *ben jue*), (2) initial awareness/awakening when they gain the first glimpse of the original awareness/awakening (C. *shi jue*), and (3) ultimate awareness/awakening (C. *jiu jing jue*). Practitioners start with original awareness/awakening, have the initial awareness/awakening, and by completing the entire path with all the perfections, attain ultimate awakening or buddhahood, at which time awakening is complete. Ultimate awakening is the same as the original awareness or fundamental knowing, but the process of mental development that occurs with Dharma practice must be completed. This is another way to explain the path to buddhahood.

Tathāgatagarbha as the Nature of the Buddha

In other contexts, tathāgatagarbha appears to mean the nature of the Buddha, a nature that is solely a buddha's but that sentient beings may attain when they become awakened. In some places in the *Nirvāṇa Sūtra*, the buddha essence is the supreme perfect awakening, the Tathāgata, the supreme emptiness, and the Middle Way. All of these qualities are associated with the Buddha, not with sentient beings, lending credence to buddha nature referring to the nature of a buddha.

When the sūtra says that sentient beings possess buddha nature, what does that mean? If they already possess the nature of a buddha, why do the sūtras teach what to practice and abandon to attain buddhahood? (MTC 162):

> At that time, the bodhisattva Siṃhanāda, the mahāsattva, addressed the Buddha, "World-honored One! If the Buddha

> and buddha essence are not different, what need is there for any sentient being to cultivate the path?
>
> The Buddha says, "Good spiritual child! It is not the case as your question [suggests]. Although the Buddha and buddha essence are not different, sentient beings are not yet completely endowed with [the virtues of a buddha].
>
> "Good spiritual child! It is just as a person who harbors the evil thought of harming his mother. Having harmed [her], he regrets it. Although his three actions [of body, speech, and mind] are good, we still call this person 'hell being.' For what reason? It is because this person will definitely fall into hell. Although this person does not have the aggregates, sense sources, and constituents of a hell [being], we can still call him 'hell being.'
>
> "Good spiritual child! That is why I say in various sūtras that when we see a person practicing virtues, we see a heavenly being, that when we see a person practicing negativities, we see a hell being. [It is because we are certain that] they will definitely obtain those results.
>
> "Good spiritual child! Since all sentient beings will definitely attain the supreme, perfect awakening, I say that all sentient beings alike possess buddha essence. [In fact], all sentient beings actually are not yet in possession of the thirty-two signs and the eighty marks [of a buddha]."

In our everyday speech, we often give the name of the result to the cause. We say "I planted some flowers today" when we plant the seeds that will grow and become flowers. Similarly, when we see the buddha essence in a human being, a frog, or a deva, we can say "I see a buddha" because we're giving the name of the resultant buddha to the cause, a sentient being.

When we have strong conviction in the workings of the law of karma and its effects, we may see someone engaging in harmful actions in this life, and knowing that he will experience the result of his actions in the future, we call him a "hell being." Even though he is still a human being, he is given a name that pertains to his future rebirth. In the same way, when we have strong conviction in sentient beings having buddha nature, we look at the present confused and suffering sentient beings and refer to them as buddhas.

Even though they are not buddhas at present, they are given a name indicating what they will become in the future.

The *Nirvāṇa Sūtra* goes on to explain that possession in general may be in the past, present, and future. When it is said that all sentient beings possess buddha nature, it is a case of future possession (MTC 163):

> All sentient beings will possess in the future the supreme, perfect awakening that is called buddha essence. All sentient beings possess alike at the present various bonds of defilements and so do not possess at present the [Buddha's] thirty-two signs and eighty marks. All sentient beings possessed in the past the cutting off of [some] defilements and so can see their buddha nature at present.

The *Nirvāṇa Sūtra* presents the causes of buddha nature to illustrate its claim that all sentient beings possess the nature of a buddha. Just as milk is the direct cause of yogurt and warmth is a cooperative condition, buddha nature is the direct cause of a buddha and practicing the six perfections is the cooperative condition. Just as we say milk has the nature of yogurt even before it has become yogurt, it is said that sentient beings have the nature of a buddha even though they are not yet buddhas. After they practice the six perfections, they will indeed become buddhas.

The *Nirvāṇa Sūtra* gives some examples illustrating how sentient beings are the cause of buddha nature: it is like a bag of gold hidden beneath the house of a poor woman and a diamond buried in the ground. These examples indicate that unbeknownst to them, sentient beings have a beautiful buddha nature that they cannot see or make use of at present.

On the one hand, it appears that these examples harken back to the Chinese view that all people have a positive nature and to the view of the early Chinese Yogācārins that there is an original pure mind in every sentient being. On the other hand, these examples can be seen not as making ontological statements about sentient beings' ultimate nature but as uplifting passages that encourage practitioners by giving them confidence in their ability to actualize the path.

Later in the *Nirvāṇa Sūtra*, some passages argue against seeing buddha nature as an inherent essence characterized by being permanent, blissful, pure, and self. In fact, people who think in this way are said to slander the Three Jewels. In chapter 3 of the sūtra, there are statements such as:[119]

> Being subject to the veils of afflictions and ignorance, there arises in sentient beings the afflictive mind. The self, they reckon, is selfless. The permanent (eternal), they reckon, is impermanent. The pure, they reckon, is impure. Bliss, they reckon, is duḥkha. Because they are subject to this veil of afflictions, although they may give rise to these ideas, they do not penetrate their meaning, just as a drunken person who in a place that is not spinning gives rise to the perception of it being spun. The self, then, is the buddha in meaning. The permanent is the dharmakāya in meaning. Bliss is nirvāṇa in meaning. The pure is the Dharma in meaning...
>
> The selfless is [subject to] birth and death. The self is the Tathāgata. The impermanent is the śrāvakas and solitary realizers. The permanent is the dharmakāya. Duḥkha is the outside [non-Buddhist] paths. Bliss is nirvāṇa. The impure is the existence of conditioned things. The pure is the Buddha and bodhisattvas' true Dharma. These are called uninverted [views]. Because of these non-inversions, one perceives both the words and their meanings.

The *Nirvāṇa Sūtra* differs from some other Tathāgatagarbha sūtras, such as the *Descent into Lanka Sūtra*, that establish a connection between the tathāgatagarbha, which is the original pure mind, and the Yogācāra notion of the foundation consciousness. This connection led some people to have a substantialist view of the buddha essence that is not found in the *Nirvāṇa Sūtra*, as seen in passages such as the following (MTC 98):

> [The truth of cessation of duḥkha] means the eradication of all defilements; and the eradication of defilements is called *permanence*. Since defilements are annihilated in the state of cessation of duḥkha, [the practitioner] experiences *bliss*. Since [the state of cessation] is the [true] condition that the buddhas and bodhisattvas aspire to, it is called *pure*. Since [a practitioner who

> has reached the state of cessation] will never again assume the twenty-five [forms of saṃsāric] existence,[120] it is called *transcendental.* Since it is transcendental, it is called *self.*

Here the four qualities of permanence, bliss, purity, and self are epithets of nirvāṇa, the true cessation of dukkha and its origins, and do not imply that nirvāṇa is an inherently existent reality.

Tathāgatagarbha in Tibetan Buddhism

Tathāgatagarbha, the buddha essence or buddha nature, has various meanings in China and Tibet, and over the centuries there have been many debates about its meaning. The Perfection of Wisdom sūtras emphasize the negation of inherent existence, whereas the *Tathāgatagarbha Sūtra* uses a very different language, one that affirms rather than negates. The latter describes the buddha essence as permanent; it is real selfhood and endowed with the transcendent excellences of a buddha. It is an affirmative, uncaused absolute that is the ultimate truth—not the nonaffirming negation that the Perfection of Wisdom sūtras assert is the ultimate nature of all phenomena.

In *Saṃsāra, Nirvāṇa, and Buddha Nature,* we discussed the Buddha's intended meaning and his purpose for making such statements and the logical inconsistencies that arise if they are taken literally and accepted as definitive.[121] Saying that the dharmakāya of the Buddha with its transcendent excellences exists complete within sentient beings at this moment is a skillful way of encouraging those who think that full awakening is beyond their capability. It also soothes their fears that realizing emptiness means that nothing exists and they would disappear. What the Buddha actually meant by such statements is that both the minds of sentient beings and the minds of buddhas are similar in being empty of inherent existence.

According to the Madhyamaka presentation, the tathāgatagarbha exists at the causal level in ordinary beings and in āryas, but the dharmakāya exists only at the resultant buddhahood. The nature dharmakāya of a buddha has the twofold purity—freedom from inherent existence and freedom from adventitious defilements—whereas the buddha essence does not, even though it is the emptiness of inherent existence. Although there is no difference in the experience of emptiness no matter what the base of that emptiness is—a person, a tree, something defiled, or one of the thirty-two signs of the Buddha's body—from the point of view of the base of that emptiness, the emptinesses of the defiled mind of sentient beings, the semi-defiled mind of āryas, and the pure mind of buddhas are considered different. The emptiness of a mind is one nature with that mind. Thus if that mind is defiled, as the minds of ordinary sentient beings are, the emptiness of that mind may also be considered defiled.[122]

Through realizing the suchness of our own minds, we ordinary beings will purify our minds so that they will become the minds of āryas. By continued meditation on the emptiness of the mind, the mind itself is purified and the dharmakāya of a buddha is attained. In this way, as the mind is freed from defilements, the emptiness of the mind of an ordinary being (the buddha essence of an ordinary being) will become the buddha essence of an ārya and then the nature dharmakāya of a buddha with the twofold purity. In addition, our transforming buddha nature will become the transforming buddha nature of an ārya and then the wisdom dharmakāya of a buddha.

Dolpopa Sherab Gyaltsen (1292–1361) and the Jonang tradition he supported insisted that the tathāgatagarbha is endowed with a twofold purity. This twofold purity is not freedom from inherent existence and freedom from adventitious defilements, which are both nonaffirming negations. Rather it is the naturally luminous, unconditioned ultimate reality that is endowed inseparably with the transcendent, limitless excellences of buddhahood.

Gyaltsab Darma Rinchen (1364–1432) responded to this claim, saying that although the mind's ultimate nature has never been polluted by afflictions and does not exist inherently, that does not mean that it is free from all adventitious defilements. He set out several unwanted consequences that would occur if the twofold purity was the nature of sentient beings:

- Sentient beings would already be buddhas but not know it, and buddhas would be ignorant, not knowing if they were buddhas or sentient beings.
- If the dharmakāya were one nature with a sentient being's mind, they would be related and one person could simultaneously be a sentient being and possess the dharmakāya of a buddha.

- Sentient beings would have a permanent self. They could never change, and without changing they would be unable to generate bodhicitta or wisdom or to progress through the paths and grounds to become buddhas.
- If sentient beings were buddhas from beginningless time, they would not need to again attain buddhahood. If they still needed to be awakened again, who would be practicing the path and attaining awakening—a sentient being or a buddha?
- If the dharmakāya obscured by adventitious defilements existed in the continuums of sentient beings, a purified dharmakāya and an obscured dharmakāya would exist at the same time in sentient beings. If an obscured dharmakāya does not exist in the continuums of sentient beings, then the purified dharmakāya and the continuum of a sentient being would be the same nature and sentient beings would already be free from all defilements.

These arguments are powerful; I recommend contemplating them repeatedly.

REFLECTION

1. Although the mind's ultimate nature has never been polluted by afflictions and lacks inherent existence, what are the inconsistencies of thinking that we are already buddhas?
2. Look at the state of your present mind with its attachment, anger, jealousy, pride, confusion, and so forth. Is this mind the mind of a fully awakened buddha?
3. Contemplate that you have the potential to become a buddha. However, having the potential to become something does not mean we are already that. The daisy seed has the potential to become a daisy, but it isn't a daisy right now.
4. If the idea that a buddha exists within you right now makes you optimistic about attaining buddhahood, understand that having the potential to become a buddha can too. The more you understand the emptiness of the mind, the more the afflictions will recede, bringing peace in your life. The

more you cultivate love and compassion, the more your heart will open and your self-confidence will increase.

Similar to some Chinese masters, Dolpopa presents the tathāgatagarbha as an affirmative phenomenon that is the ultimate truth. To many people, the tathāgatagarbha sounds very much like a soul or the permanent self (ātman) asserted by non-Buddhists. This issue arises in the *Descent into Laṅka Sūtra*, when Mahāmati asks the Buddha:[123]

> The Lord promulgates the tathāgatagarbha in the discourses, saying it is naturally luminous, primordially pure, endowed with the thirty-two signs [of a buddha] and existing within the bodies of all sentient beings. You say it is like a precious gem, wrapped in a filthy rag, being permanent, stable, and eternal, but wrapped by the defilements of the aggregates, elements, and sense sources. How is this tathāgatagarbha theory different from the ātman of the non-Buddhists? The non-Buddhists also espouse a self that is permanent, inactive, qualityless, all-pervading, and indestructible.

The Buddha replies (CE 63):

> Mahāmati, my teaching of the tathāgatagarbha is not the same as the non-Buddhist ātman. Mahāmati, the tathāgatas, arhats, perfect buddhas teach the essence of the meaning of words such as "emptiness," "perfect side" (as opposed to the imperfect side of saṃsāra), "nirvāṇa," "nonproduction," "signlessness," and "wishlessness," to prevent the naïve from fearing selflessness. Their discourse with reference to the tathāgatagarbha teaches the state of nonconceptuality, the non-apparent object.
>
> Mahāmati, present and future bodhisattvas should not become attached to it as a self. Mahāmati, for example, potters manufacture a variety of vessels out of one mass of clay particles with their hands, manual skill, a rod, water, thread, and efforts. Mahāmati, similarly the tathāgatas also teach the selflessness of

> phenomena, which is a dearth of all conceptual constructions. Endowed with the wisdom of that [selflessness] and with skillful means, they, like a potter, teach it with various expressions in words and letters either as the tathāgatagarbha or as selflessness.
>
> Thus Mahāmati, the teaching of the tathāgatagarbha is not the same as the non-Buddhist ātman. Mahāmati, to educate the non-Buddhists who are attached to the ātman, the tathāgatas teach emptiness through the teaching of the tathāgatagarbha.

Here, the Buddha clearly states that the teaching on tathāgatagarbha being an awakened buddha with all the transcendent excellences and existing in each sentient being is an interpretable teaching. In fact, tathāgatagarbha refers to emptiness, the ultimate truth.

The learned adept Sakya Pandita (1182–1251) agrees that the tathāgatagarbha is a provisional teaching taught to help those who fear selflessness and cling to inherent existence to approach the idea that all persons and phenomena lack inherent existence. It is not difficult to understand that some people—possibly even ourselves!—find attractive the notion of human beings having a pure, permanent, inborn essence that is naturally good. That is very comforting, especially if we were taught such beliefs as children. It makes death less frightening, because an intrinsically good person will definitely have a good rebirth, and because a permanent, eternal person will not totally cease at the time of death.

In addition, some people find the idea that nothing has an inherent essence frightening. They think that realizing selflessness would cause the self to vanish right then and there. To them, selflessness and emptiness are nihilistic and life-negating. Some people have misunderstood the philosophy of emptiness; others have never encountered it. Still others adhered to the notion of inherent existence in previous lives, planting seeds for this belief to continue in this life. Being a skillful teacher, the Buddha understands that many conditions need to come together for these people to understand and then feel comfortable adopting the teaching on selflessness.

It is for this reason that my responses vary when people ask me if Buddhists believe in God. When speaking to people who have a strong faith in God, I say that human beings are created in God's image, so it is only right that we respect and care for God's creation. This encourages them to live ethically, cultivate love and compassion, avoid violence as a way to resolve disputes, and forgive when they are harmed.

However, when I am questioned by Buddhists or scientists, I discuss dependent arising as a way to understand not only the functioning of everything in our world but also its emptiness of inherent existence. These people can accept the compatibility of dependent arising and emptiness without too much difficulty. Of course, realizing dependent arising and emptiness is a different matter, and that takes time in addition to much contemplation and meditation.

Nāgārjuna and the Indian Mādhyamikas all agree that the ultimate truth is a nonaffirming negation. When meditators realize emptiness directly, they perceive simply the absence of inherent existence. Apart from this, there is no other object apprehended—no pure mind, no inherently existent buddha, no permanent self. Nor is there the thought "This is emptiness."

Although the wisdom mind realizing emptiness nonconceptually does not affirm anything, it perceives an object—emptiness—which is an existent phenomenon. The mind directly realizing emptiness perceives only the absence of inherent existence, the mere lack of the object of negation. This understanding energizes, empowers, and strengthens the mind. But when a meditator develops a mind that meditates on nothingness, his mind has no energy or strength. A mind vividly realizing emptiness—the lack of inherent existence—contradicts the mind grasping inherent existence. A mind focused on nothingness cannot harm that grasping.

The *Nirvāṇa Sūtra* explains that the dharmakāya, which is present in the buddha essence of each and every sentient being, has four qualities: it is pure, self, bliss, and permanent. Taking the *Nirvāṇa Sūtra* as definitive, some people read this literally. They reason: True duḥkha has the attributes of being impure, not-self, duḥkha, and impermanent. Since those four attributes have been purified in the dharmakāya, what remains must be pure, self, bliss, and permanent. Therefore the tathāgatagarbha is a true self possessing these four attributes, and this is ultimate reality.

Still others, such as Tsongkhapa and his followers, take the Tathāgatagarbha doctrine to be a definitive teaching. They assert that its principal subject matter is the emptiness of inherent existence—the ultimate truth—and that Asaṅga's commentary on the *Sublime Continuum* is written from the Prāsaṅgika viewpoint. Stating that the tathāgatagarbha refers to the emptiness of the mind, they explain the statement that the dharmakāya and tathāgatagarbha are a pure, blissful, permanent true self in a novel way that supports the understanding of emptiness as the ultimate truth. The realization of emptiness is used by ordinary beings to eliminate afflictive obscurations and for ārya bodhisattvas to overcome cognitive obscurations. In the *Sublime Continuum*, Maitreya relates these four attributes to the dharmakāya (RGV 1.32):

> The [dharmakāya] is purity, since its nature is pure
> and [even] the remaining latencies are fully removed.
> It is true self, since all conceptual elaborations
> in terms of self and not-self are totally stilled.
> It is true bliss, since the aggregates
> of mental nature and their causes are reversed.
> It is permanence, since saṃsāra
> and the state beyond sorrow are realized as one.

Based on Asaṅga's commentary, Gyaltsab Darma Rinchen unpacks the meaning of this verse, explaining four types of people, each of whom has a prominent hindrance that necessitates a particular antidote. Each type of person and each antidote are correlated to one of the four attributes—purity, self, bliss, and permanence. As practitioners advance on the path, these attributes become perfections that are qualities of the dharmakāya.

But all of us start out as worldly beings migrating in saṃsāra. In the Buddha's teaching on the four truths, which form the structure of his doctrine, the four qualities of purity, self, bliss, and permanence are listed as qualities of true duḥkha. Worldly beings believe they have purity, self, bliss, and permanence, and they see these attributes in what doesn't in fact have them. They regard the body, which is foul, as pure; the self that is imputed as inherently existent; saṃsāric activities that never bring satisfaction as blissful; and their selves as permanent and eternal. Overwhelmed by ignorance, they continue to wander in saṃsāra.

Āryas who have gone beyond the world give the names of the four attributes to qualities of the buddhas, where they have different meanings and are referred to as perfections. There is much to ponder here, and doing so brings understanding and inspires us to practice.

The Four Attributes for Non-arhats

Let's begin with four types of people—those filled with desire, non-Buddhist philosophers, śrāvaka learners, and solitary realizer learners—their specific hindrances, and the antidotes to those.

People filled with desire who long for the pleasures of saṃsāra are not interested in awakening. They may have wrong views or simply lack interest in spiritual matters. They reject the Dharma, and the Mahāyāna Dharma in particular. Known as *icchantika* in Sanskrit, they are temporarily unable to attain liberation or awakening due to having such strong obscurations. To remedy their lack of interest in spiritual matters and lack of desire to free all sentient beings from saṃsāra, they need to cultivate confidence in and devotion to the Mahāyāna teachings. The antidote is to cultivate convictional faith in the Mahāyāna, which will lead them to take interest in and have the aspiration to enter the Mahāyāna.

Non-Buddhist philosophers are attached to incorrect doctrines. Grasping the inherent existence of persons and phenomena, they accept an independent, permanent creator, a primal substance out of which everything originates, a universal mind, or other false theories. To remove their obscurations, the wisdom realizing emptiness is needed.

Śrāvaka learners know the horrors of saṃsāra and seek to be free from it. Śrāvaka learners are practitioners on the śrāvaka path who are not yet arhats. Terrified of their own suffering in saṃsāra, they strive for personal liberation and shrink away from buddhahood. To mollify their fear, they must develop various blissful concentrations, such as the treasury of space, which are the union of serenity and insight accomplished by Mahāyāna practitioners.

Solitary-realizer learners still cherish their own welfare and liberation more than those of others. Solitary-realizer learners are those on the solitary-realizers' path who are not yet arhats. Lacking any sense of responsibility for the well-being of all sentient beings, they do not think, "I will free them from saṃsāra." To remedy their lack of interest in working for the benefit of all sentient beings, they must cultivate great compassion.

Although the above divisions are made according to the type of person, everyone who wishes to follow the Mahāyāna path to full awakening must abandon these four hindrances that interfere with realizing the emptiness of the mind and generating bodhicitta. They must also complete the method aspect of the path, and when cultivating the four perfections of the dharmakāya, they must avoid grasping them as inherently existent.

TYPES OF PERSONS, HINDRANCES, ANTIDOTES, AND THE PERFECTIONS

PERSONS	HINDRANCES	ANTIDOTE TO THE HINDRANCES, WHICH IS THE CAUSE OF THE PERFECTION	RESULTANT PERFECTION
Worldly people who desire saṃsāra and have no intention to get out of it	Hostility toward the Mahāyāna Dharma and great desire for sense pleasures and the peace of meditative stabilizations	Convictional faith and confidence in the Mahāyāna	Perfection of purity
Non-Buddhist philosophers	View of inherent existence of persons and phenomena, other wrong views	Meditation on the perfection of wisdom	Perfection of supreme self
Śrāvaka learners	Fear of one's own saṃsāric suffering, focus only on their own welfare and forsake other sentient beings	Meditative concentrations such as the treasury of space, which give rise to the bliss of concentration and are exclusive Mahāyāna samādhis with the union of serenity and insight	Perfection of bliss
Solitary-realizer learners	No regard for or sense of responsibility for other sentient beings' welfare	Great compassion	Perfection of permanence

The four perfections are qualities of a tathāgata that are not possessed by śrāvaka and solitary-realizer arhats or by bodhisattvas of the pure grounds—the three types of persons who have eradicated afflictive obscurations. Four additional obscurations prevent these highly realized adepts from attaining the four perfections of a tathāgata's dharmakāya. Whereas the hindrances of the worldly people, non-Buddhist philosophers, śrāvaka learners, and solitary-realizer learners pertain to polluted dependent origination, the obstacles of the three types of persons pertain to unpolluted dependent origination. Polluted dependent origination refers to how ordinary beings take rebirth in saṃsāra and attain liberation; unpolluted dependent origination concerns liberated beings and how they attain full awakening.

REFLECTION

1. Reflect on the four types of persons who are not yet free from saṃsāra. Consider their particular hindrances and the antidotes.
2. Do you share any of the hindrances and traits of these four types of persons? How can understanding them help you focus your Dharma practice to overcome the hindrances and cultivate and strengthen the antidotes?

The Four Perfections for Ārya Bodhisattvas

The four perfections refer to qualities of the dharmakāya. In some contexts, the dharmakāya refers to one of the three bodies of a buddha—the truth body of a buddha. Here, together with the tathāgatagarbha and the dharmadhātu, it refers to the ultimate truth.

The dharmakāya is the perfection of purity because its nature is pure and free from all latencies of afflictions and seeds of polluted karma. It possesses the twofold purity—natural freedom from inherent existence and freedom from adventitious defilements. This was actualized by recognizing that within the natural purity, the latencies of adventitious defilements are to be abandoned and have been abandoned. This point corresponds to those with great desire who dislike the Mahāyāna reversing their attraction to the impure objects of saṃsāra. It also applies to ārya bodhisattvas who, with firm devotion for the Mahāyāna teachings, meditate with unpolluted pristine wisdom and eliminate the two obscurations so that the emptiness of their minds becomes the ultimate sphere of reality (*dharmadhātu*) that is endowed with the two purities.

The dharmakāya is the perfection of (the true or supreme) self because all conceptual elaborations of inherent existence have been abandoned. This has been accomplished by recognizing that the ultimate nature of all persons and phenomena is their emptiness of inherent existence. All elaborations of their inherent existence have been negated. This corresponds to non-Buddhist philosophers, who cling to erroneous views of a self of persons and phenomena. They now realize the perfection of wisdom, directly perceive emptiness, and overcome their grasping inherent existence. This ceases their misconceptions that a creator, primal substance, universal mind, and so forth is the ultimate nature or a real self. The perfection of self is attained by meditating on the perfection of wisdom that realizes persons and phenomena to be naturally free from all elaborations of inherent existence. This wisdom knows that the self of persons and the self of phenomena imputed by erroneous philosophies are completely nonexistent. The dharmakāya is the perfection of self because it is pervaded by a pacification (emptiness) in which no dualistic appearances whatsoever arise.

The dharmakāya is free from grasping the self of persons asserted by non-Buddhist philosophers that causes them to fall to the extreme of saṃsāra; the pure-ground bodhisattvas are now free from the elaborations of self. The dharmakāya perceives the selflessness known by the śrāvakas and solitary realizers but does not fall to the extreme of personal nirvāṇa, making it free from the elaborations of not-self. Usually the two extremes are explained as the wrong views of absolutism and nihilism. Here they are explained from the viewpoint of the resultant dharmakāya in which buddhas do not dwell in saṃsāra or in nirvāṇa's peace.

From the perspective of what is perceived, freedom from the two extremes is two factors: the dharmakāya being free from the elaborations of self because the two selves of persons and phenomena have been negated, and the dharmakāya being free from the elaborations of not-self because the two selflessnesses are not perceived as inherently existent. The abandonment of all dualistic appearances by relying on selflessness is freedom from the elaborations of the mode of perception.

The dharmakāya is the perfection of bliss because the mental body and its causes—unpolluted karma and the latencies of ignorance—have been abandoned. Because they have eliminated all afflictive obscurations, arhats and pure-ground bodhisattvas are not reborn in saṃsāra in ordinary bodies made of flesh and bones. Instead they take a "mental body"—a body that is the nature of mind. The causes of a mental body are unpolluted karma and the latencies of ignorance. Nothing can obstruct the movement of this mental body, and it cannot be directly seen or known by those with lower realizations. With a mental body, arhats abide in meditative equipoise until the buddhas wake them from their personal peace and spur them to generate bodhicitta and follow the bodhisattva path to full awakening. Employing the supernormal power of creating emanations as the unique empowering condition, ārya bodhisattvas use their mental bodies to emanate thousands of bodies in the realms of saṃsāra to benefit sentient beings.

Although they are highly realized, pure-ground bodhisattvas still need to exert energy to generate the motivation to accomplish the welfare of sentient beings. In addition, because the causes of the mental body are not completely pure, it must be abandoned for them to become buddhas. Pure-ground bodhisattvas abandon the mental body and its causes by recognizing that the twelve links of unpolluted dependent origination, which are supported by the cognitive obscurations (not by ignorance, like the afflictive twelve links), are to be abandoned. They counteract these obscurations with the antidote, the perfection of wisdom, and become buddhas, whose dharmakāya is unending.

The perfection of highest bliss is unpolluted in that a tathāgata has abandoned the mental body and its causes. Because buddhas possess this highest bliss, by means of samādhis such as the treasury of space, they pervade all world systems, simultaneously teaching all sentient beings who are receptive disciples and benefiting others in whatever way possible.

The dharmakāya is the perfection of permanence since tathāgatas realize that saṃsāra and nirvāṇa are equal in being empty by nature. Pure-ground bodhisattvas actualize the ultimate severance from the extremes of saṃsāra and nirvāṇa by realizing that saṃsāra and nirvāṇa are indifferentiable in terms of being empty of inherent existence. By meditation on great compassion, ārya bodhisattvas become tathāgatas whose uninterrupted stream of great compassion for all sentient beings endures for all time. Being free of the subtle hindrances of the cognitive obscurations, tathāgatas have abolished the twelve links of afflictive dependent origination and the twelve links of unpolluted dependent origination. Having attained the four perfections, they abide in meditative equipoise as long as saṃsāra endures, and for that reason, the dharmakāya is called the perfection of permanence.

Perfections and Becoming a Tathāgata

PERFECTIONS OF THE DHARMAKĀYA	Perfection of purity	Perfection of supreme self	Perfection of bliss	Perfection of permanence
WHAT HAS BEEN ELIMINATED SO THE PERFECTION APPLIES TO THE DHARMAKĀYA	The dharmakāya is purity because its nature is pure and free from all latencies of afflictions and seeds of polluted karma.	The dharmakāya is the supreme or true self because all conceptual elaborations of persons and phenomena have been abandoned.	The dharmakāya is true bliss because the mental body and its causes, unpolluted karma and latencies of ignorance, have been abandoned.	The dharmakāya is permanent since saṃsāra and nirvāṇa are realized as being forever the same in terms of being empty of inherent existence.
WHAT BODHISATTVAS HAVE UNDERSTOOD	Within the natural purity, the latencies of physical, verbal, and mental defilements have been abandoned.	The ultimate nature of all persons and phenomena is their emptiness of inherent existence.	The twelve links of unpolluted dependent origination based on cognitive obscurations have been abandoned by meditation on the perfections of wisdom.	By knowing the equality of saṃsāra and nirvāṇa in being empty of inherent existence, pure-ground bodhisattvas actualize ultimate severance from the extremes of saṃsāra and nirvāṇa.
THE LINK TO HINDRANCES OF WORLDLY BEINGS, PHILOSOPHERS, AND FUNDAMENTAL VEHICLE LEARNERS	It reverses the love of impure saṃsāric things in people who have great desire and dislike the Mahāyāna.	It ceases clinging to erroneous views that grasp the self of persons and the self of phenomena by meditating on the perfection of wisdom that directly realizes emptiness.	Perfection of highest bliss is unpolluted bliss that has abandoned even the mental body of arhats and pure-ground bodhisattvas.	By meditation on great compassion, they become tathāgatas whose uninterrupted stream of great compassion for all sentient beings endures for all time.

WHAT PURE-GROUND BODHISATTVAS PRACTICE AND THE QUALITY OF A TATHĀGATA THEY ATTAIN	By devotion to the Mahāyāna Dharma, ārya bodhisattvas meditate with unpolluted pristine wisdom and eliminate the two obscurations so the emptiness of their minds becomes the ultimate sphere of reality endowed with the two purities.	By meditation on the perfection of wisdom, pure-ground bodhisattvas eliminate the elaborations of self because the selves of persons and phenomena have been abandoned. They eliminate the elaborations of not-self because the two selflessnesses are seen as empty. The tathāgatas do not dwell in saṃsāra or in nirvāṇa's peace.	By means of samādhis such as treasury of space, buddhas simultaneously teach all receptive disciples and benefit sentient beings in all world systems throughout limitless space.	All cognitive obscurations and the twelve links of unpolluted dependent origination have ceased. Tathāgatas abide in meditative equipoise as long as saṃsāra endures and simultaneously manifest in multiple bodies to benefit sentient beings.

In the presentation of afflictive dependent origination, clinging to purity, self, bliss, and permanence are hindrances. In the context of unpolluted dependent origination, these terms take on a different meaning that indicates the qualities of a buddha's dharmakāya.

The perfection of self requires special attention to understand it properly. The Tibetan Jonang tradition and some Chinese Buddhists say that the true self—the ultimate truth—is an affirmative phenomenon endowed with the qualities of a tathāgata. It is unchanging, not subject to death, peaceful by nature, and endures forever. It can never be harmed and is the nature of nirvāṇa. They explain their interpretation by quoting such sūtras as the *Nirvāṇa Sūtra*, which says:

> It is not true to say that all phenomena are devoid of a Self. The Self is reality (suchness, *tattva*), the Self is permanent (*nitya*), the

> Self is virtuous qualities (*guṇa*), the Self is everlasting (*śāśvata*), the Self is stable (*dhruva*), the Self is peace.

The Jonang followers accept the above passage literally and say it is a definitive teaching. They do not understand that the words "permanent" and so forth have different meanings in the context of the dharmakāya. However, those following Nāgārjuna and the Prāsaṅgika Madhyamaka school see the passage as interpretable because reasoning demonstrates that the ultimate truth is not an affirmative phenomenon or an inherently existent entity. Gyaltsab states that such a view is beyond the pale of Buddha's teachings, and clinging to this view indicates a person has a strong affinity with non-Buddhist philosophies.

As a Madhyamaka scripture, the *Sublime Continuum* asserts that the principal object of negation is an independent, absolute reality. When speaking of the perfection of self as a quality of the dharmakāya, the selflessness of persons and the selflessness of phenomena are called "self." The correct meaning of "supreme self" or "true self" refers to the emptiness of persons and phenomena perceived by a Buddha's pristine wisdom.

REFLECTION

1. Contemplate each perfection and see how the names of attributes of true duḥkha have been given different meanings so they become attributes of a buddha's dharmakāya.
2. Imagine what it would be like to reverse your desire for saṃsāric pleasures, to relinquish grasping inherent existence, to abandon a mental body (after you gain one as an ārya), and to overcome all self-centeredness. Imagining having the four perfections fortifies our aspiration to cultivate them with joyous effort.

Conclusion

The sūtras that speak of the tathāgatagarbha give the impression that a buddha with complete wisdom and merit and the signs and marks of an awakened being already exists within each sentient being. Yinshun states that this resembles the idea of an ātman—a permanent self or soul—and in both Tibet and China, Madhyamaka masters say that the idea of a permanent, pure mind in sentient beings is incompatible with the Buddha's fundamental idea of selflessness.

The earliest Chinese commentaries on *Awakening of Faith* by Jinyin Huiyuan (523–87) and Fazang explain true-mind and original awakening as pristine wisdom in nature. The Huayan and Chan master Zongmi embraced Tathāgatagarbha doctrine, considering it the Buddha's final teaching about ultimate reality. Zongmi wrote extensively about the true self and original awakening and described the philosophical implications of the Tathāgatagarbha doctrine. The Mādhyamika master Jizang saw the Tathāgatagarbha doctrine as important, but interpreted it in accordance with Madhyamaka philosophy. Some Chan practitioners say the tathāgatagarbha is a sort of huatou or koan, in this case an ontological koan. Others say buddha nature is a dependent arising and is compatible with Madhyamaka.

Many contemporary Chinese Buddhist masters accept the teachings on emptiness as the foundation of the Dharma that cannot be negotiated. Yinshun explains that non-Buddhists find it extremely difficult to understand the idea that the person and all other phenomena are empty of inherent existence yet exist nominally. They cannot accept that rebirth occurs without a real self that goes from one life to another and on to awakening. They fear that if the self is empty, it will cease completely at the time of death. Thus as a skillful means to soothe their fear, the Buddha taught the Tathāgatagarbha doctrine.

Similarly, for the purpose of teaching and encouraging ordinary people who are weak-minded, contemporary Chinese masters often teach buddha nature, saying that everyone is endowed with an inborn potential to become a buddha. Having studied Candrakīrti's texts, Yinshun considers Madhyamaka to be the highest teaching and says his personal view accords with that of Candrakīrti. However, he accepts the Tathāgatagarbha doctrine as a skillful means when teaching ordinary people. Speaking about an eternal pure mind shows that the ignorant mind is not sentient beings' essence and spurs sentient beings to eliminate their ignorance. But there is danger that people become attached to the view of the pure mind, thinking that it is permanent and independent. Thus, after they are encouraged by contemplating buddha nature, Yinshun teaches them Madhyamaka to show that the pure mind is neither permanent nor truly existent.

Although the tathāgatagarbha is said to be eternal, immutable, and existing in all realms of saṃsāra as well as in nirvāṇa, the Buddha's actual intention in saying this is not that an affirmative, ultimate, independent, absolute reality exists. Buddha essence does not refer to an inherently existent ātman or soul. Rather, tathāgatagarbha and the "foundation of all" refer to the emptiness of inherent existence. Emptiness is the fundamental nature within which everything exists; it is a nonaffirming negation, not an affirmative ultimate reality. Yinshun says (WB 323):

> The Buddha took this undifferentiated nature of things [emptiness] to be his nature and body, so it is called the buddha nature and the dharmakāya.

In conclusion, the Buddha uses diverse means to lead sentient beings to the correct view. Ordinary people and non-Buddhist theists do not accept impermanence and selflessness. To the contrary, they fear selflessness and emptiness. To these people, the Buddha teaches the Tathāgatagarbha doctrine—that the buddha essence abides in all beings. This eases their fear and inspires them with hope. As they practice and gradually accumulate merit, they come to see that their fear was unfounded. They release grasping an inherent ultimate reality and come to understand that tathāgatagarbha refers to emptiness. In this way, they will embrace the Madhyamaka view.

To those who have not yet completed the five deeds—and especially for those who have practiced the Fundamental Vehicle and are ready to progress—the Buddha teaches Yogācāra. By practicing with this view, they diminish the force of afflictions, accumulate merit, and complete the five deeds. Then they are prepared to adopt the Madhyamaka view.

This way of guiding people is analogous to three shops that sell medicine. One shop is without frills and sells the medicine directly, without adding sugar or putting the medicine in an attractive container. The people who get the medicine here follows the instructions, take the full dose, and recover quickly. However, only people who know the value of the medicine get it at this shop; others shy away because the medicine does not look appetizing and it tastes terrible. This medicine is the Madhyamaka view.

Another shop makes the same medicine into sugar-coated tablets that can be easily swallowed and sells the tablets in beautiful bottles. More people buy it at this shop and more lives are saved. This form of the medicine is the Yogācāra view.

Nevertheless, young children cannot swallow the tablets, so a third shop mixes the medicine with a lot of sugar and forms it into bunnies, footballs, and dolls and sells it in colorful and intriguing packages with puzzles on the back. The children love this medicine, take it without complaining, and recover. This form of the medicine is the Tathāgatagarbha doctrine.

Skillful means are needed to help sentient beings. However, we must look out for possible dangers. People may buy the medicine in the nice bottles and intriguing boxes and, rather than take the medicine, flaunt the packaging, saying their bottle or box is more attractive than anyone else's. This is like people who outwardly adopt a view but do not practice it and instead make it into an identity and object of pride. They compete with others, arguing who has the best view, but do not use that view to transform their minds.

Another danger is mixing the medicine with so much sugar that there is hardly any healing power in the cleverly crafted bunnies, footballs, and dolls. This is like diluting the Dharma so much in order to attract many followers that the teachings people hear cannot completely cure the afflictions.

Of course each Chinese school views its own tenets as the most accurate. Zhiyi considers Tiantai based on the *Lotus* and *Nirvāṇa* sūtras as the definitive teaching, and Chan masters view Yogācāra, Tathāgatagarbha, and Madhyamaka as expedient means. In later generations Chan masters seem to prefer Tathāgatagarbha, although they individually hold different views on its meaning. Nevertheless, all schools accept the differences among them and respect one another.

If we understand the Buddha's skillful means and his intended meaning for teaching each view, we will not go astray. We will respect all Buddhist traditions, their teachers, and their practitioners as disciples of the Buddha.

15 | Madhyamaka in China

IN THE PREVIOUS chapters we spoke about Yogācāra and the Tathāgatagarbha doctrine as two of the three prominent philosophical systems in Chinese Buddhism. Now we turn to Madhyamaka to see how this philosophical view took root and developed in China.

Madhyamaka: Empty Nature, Mere Name

Madhyamaka (C. *Zhongguan*)[124] is the riveting philosophy fleshed out by Nāgārjuna and elaborated by Indian scholar-adepts over many centuries to investigate the ultimate mode of existence. Madhyamaka has three branches according to place and time: (1) *Indian Madhyamaka* began with Nāgārjuna in the first or second century, was passed to his disciple Āryadeva, and was commented on by Buddhapālita, Bhāvaviveka, Candrakīrti, Śāntarakṣita, Śāntideva, and others. (2) *Chinese Madhyamaka* began in the fifth century with the Central Asian translator Kumārajīva. It became prominent with Jizang and remained as a separate school until the Tang dynasty. Now its tenets have been incorporated in indigenous Chinese traditions. (3) *Tibetan Madhyamaka* is exemplified by the works of Baltsab Nyima Drak, Longchen Rabjam, Drom Tonpa, Ju Mipham, Rendawa, Gorampa, Gampopa, Tsongkhapa, and other Tibetan commentators, who lived many centuries after the flourishing of Madhyamaka in India and China.

Chinese and Tibetan Madhyamaka have a common ancestor in Indian Madhyamaka. However, their later developments differ due to the Chinese and Tibetan masters who wrote treatises and commentaries on it. Piṅgala's commentary on the *Treatise on the Middle Way* belongs to the early

Madhyamaka and is followed in China.[125] At the time he wrote it, the debate between Buddhapālita and Bhāvaviveka had not yet occurred, and Yogācāra had not yet become prominent. Thus Piṅgala's commentary is very different from later developments of Madhyamaka in India with Candrakīrti, Śāntideva, and Śāntarakṣita. At their time, Yogācāra was active and non-Buddhists posed various challenges, so Madhyamaka had to critique their assertions and in the process unpack Nāgārjuna's meaning. Madhyamaka philosophy continued to develop in Tibet, with many texts written on its various facets. These texts brought out the deeper meanings of Madhyamaka philosophy, elaborating on the refutations of the lower philosophical tenets systems and delving into the Svātantrika-Prāsaṅgika distinction.

In addition, the approach to philosophy differed in Chinese and Tibetan cultures. The tenet systems began to develop in India, and Tibetans then expanded, systematized, and ranked them based on the sophistication of their views. However, in China, the Buddhist masters ranked sūtras and treatises in a schema that showed their progressive understanding of the path. Philosophical debates performed in public were the norm in India and later in Tibet, whereas Chinese culture emphasized harmonizing elements over argumentation and the discrimination of details. For example, Nāgārjuna's *Refutation of Objections*, which criticizes non-Buddhists and Buddhist essentialists such as the Sarvāstivādins, was translated into Chinese early on. However, the Chinese did not pay close attention to this treatise, as its philosophical, epistemological, and logical analysis did not appeal to the Chinese intelligentsia who had been educated in Confucian classics. Because it was not becoming for gentlemen to argue and debate, most Chinese practitioners did not see the value of debating philosophical tenets. They trusted what Nāgārjuna taught and accepted it as true. The Chinese were very practical, and their major concern was how to realize the truth disclosed by Nāgārjuna. To do this, they developed their own typologies and ways of explaining Madhyamaka doctrine.

Madhyamaka arrived in Tibet several centuries after it came to China. As a result, some of the Madhyamaka texts used in each country are shared in common, while others differ. Although the Tibetans and the Chinese share the *Treatise on the Middle Way* and portions of Āryadeva's writings, the Chinese rely on Nāgārjuna's *Twelve Gate Treatise* and *Treatise on Wisdom*, neither of which is found in Tibetan Buddhism.

Madhyamaka in China faced difficulties due to the political environment. During the persecution of Buddhism in the Tang dynasty,[126] most Madhyamaka books were destroyed. After this, Madhyamaka did not continue as a distinct school and there was not significant development in Madhyamaka thought. However, many of its tenets had already been incorporated into the indigenous Chinese Tiantai, Huayan, Chan, and Pureland schools.[127] In modern times, due to the translations of Fazun and the writings and teachings of Yinshun, there is renewed interest in Madhyamaka. In particular, Yinshun advocated that Chinese Buddhism return to the Indian tradition and especially to Madhyamaka philosophy.

Sanlun School

When Buddhist texts first went to China, some translators used Taoist terms to express Buddhist concepts in classical Chinese, much as some translators use Christian vocabulary to express Buddhist ideas in English. As a result, some Taoist concepts were mixed with Buddhadharma; this was especially problematic with the Perfection of Wisdom sūtras, leading to initial misunderstanding of the doctrine of emptiness. However, this was corrected by the great translator Kumārajīva, whose orthodox presentation and translations[128] of *Treatise on the Middle Way*, Piṅgala's commentary, and numerous other works by Nāgārjuna were done circa 410 CE.

The Sanlun or Three Treatise school relies on three principal texts to explain the Madhyamaka view:

1. The *Treatise on the Middle Way* (*Mūlamādhyamakakārikā*, C. *Zhong lun*) by Nāgārjuna was translated by the great Madhyamaka scholar Kumārajīva. The root text of the *Treatise* is published together with a commentary by the Indian Mādhyamika Piṅgala. This commentary is one of the oldest commentaries on this text, and of the various commentaries on the *Treatise on the Middle Way* that were translated into Chinese, this is the only one widely studied in Chinese Buddhism at present. The *Treatise on the Middle Way* was translated into Tibetan, but Piṅgala's commentary was not. However, a commentary called the *Akutobhayā* (T. *Ga las 'jigs med*), ostensibly by Nāgārjuna (although that is debated), was translated into Tibetan in the early ninth century.

Modern scholars believe that one Indian text served as the source for both Piṅgala's commentary and the *Akutobhayā* because they are very similar.

2. The *Twelve Gate Treatise* (*Dvādaśamukha Śāstra*, C. *Shiermen lun*) is attributed to Nāgārjuna and was translated by Kumārajīva. Written in prose, it covers many of the same themes as the *Treatise on the Middle Way*. Neither the Sanskrit original nor a Tibetan translation is available.
3. *The Hundred* (*Śataka Śāstra*, C. *Bai lun*)[129] by Āryadeva was translated by Kumārajīva. The original *Śata Śāstra* was twenty chapters, each with five verses. Kumārajīva is said to have condensed it to ten chapters, each with five stanzas. He also paraphrased some passages of Vasu's commentary, changed the wording to make the meaning clearer, and deleted passages he considered unhelpful for the Chinese. *The Hundred* found in the Chinese canon appears to be a combination of Āryadeva's verses with the commentary of Vasu.[130] The Tibetan canon does not contain *The Hundred* but it does have Āryadeva's *The Four Hundred* (*Catuḥśatakaśāstrakārikā*).

The fourth prominent Madhyamaka text in China, the *Treatise on Wisdom*, is also by Nāgārjuna. This lengthy text speaks extensively of both the method and wisdom aspects of the path and is widely relied upon by practitioners of all schools of Chinese Buddhism. The chapter on the perfection of generosity is a good example of the breadth and depth of Nāgārjuna's thought. Madhyamaka reasoning forms the bones and marrow and appeals to readers who want to study and meditate on emptiness. There are also extensive discussions on causality, compassion, and bodhicitta interwoven with wonderful stories that appeal to readers who want to cultivate the distinguishing features of the Mahāyāna. The chapters on the rest of the perfections are similarly structured.

Many other Madhyamaka works are also found in the Chinese canon, and translations were made of other detailed Indian commentaries devoted to the refutation of wrong views of both Buddhists and non-Buddhists. Of these, the best was perhaps by Jizang, who despite his Chinese name was, like Kumārajīva, a scholar-monk native to Central Asia. Regarded as the founder of the East Asian Madhyamaka school, Jizang wrote strictly within the doctrinal scope of Indian Madhyamaka.

Kumārajīva considered the Madhyamaka doctrine to be the highest and most accurate and taught it to his disciples. Daosheng (360–434) continued transmitting Madhyamaka in China, and Kumārajīva's chief disciple Sengzhao (378–413) spread this teaching widely among the literati of the time. Sengrui, Senglang, Sengquan, Falang, and Jizang were also prominent Mādhyamikas. The Madhyamaka doctrine continued to spread in the fifth-to-seventh centuries and had a strong impact on other Buddhist schools. After Jizang's time, Sanlun declined as a separate school, chiefly because its important ideas had been absorbed into other schools. It particularly influenced Zhiyi, the great Tiantai master, and has had a far-reaching effect on Chinese Buddhism to this day.

Nāgārjuna's Influence in China

Nāgārjuna's texts are not limited to those on emptiness but include teachings on a wide variety of topics on the method side of the path as well. As a result, they have had a major impact on many of the subsequent schools that arose in China. Nāgārjuna is a lineage master in the Chan (Zen), Pureland, and Tiantai schools. Some of his works are in both the Tibetan and Chinese canons. The Chinese canon contains some works by Nāgārjuna that are not found in the Tibetan canon.

In many of his texts, Nāgārjuna stresses the importance of bodhicitta, saying that if practitioners follow the path to arhatship, they may never become buddhas. Whether this is his final belief or not, it certainly acts to dissuade those contemplating an arhat's nirvāṇa from following that route and directs them to the Mahāyāna path. At the end of the *Treatise on Wisdom*, Nāgārjuna states that all sentient beings will attain buddhahood. Nāgārjuna emphasizes that bodhisattvas must not only generate bodhicitta and engage in the six perfections, but also practice the thirty-seven harmonies with awakening. In his *Treatise on the Detailed Explanation of the Ten Grounds*, he espouses the Pureland practice.[131]

Nāgārjuna's *Treatise on Wisdom* was translated and abridged by Kumārajīva. An exegesis on the *Twenty-Five-Thousand Stanza Perfection of Wisdom Sūtra*, the *Treatise on Wisdom* frequently quotes the *Treatise on the Middle*

Way and refutes wrong conceptions of the view as well as expounds the entire bodhisattva path. Although it is a commentary on the Perfection of Wisdom sūtras, it employs a variety of approaches. When it lays out the classifications of phenomena and teachings about topics such as karma, it relies on the Sarvāstivāda approach. When it discusses topics that all Buddhist traditions accept, it uses the explanation in the āgamas. When discussing monastic discipline, it speaks from the Vinaya perspective, and when exploring the bodhisattva path, it refers to the presentation in the *Jātaka*, *Avadāna*, and Mahāyāna sūtras such as the *Dense Array Sūtra* (*Ghanavyūha Sūtra*). While the *Treatise on Wisdom* will sometimes refer to the Abhidharma when analyzing phenomena, this is never its ultimate approach. The ultimate view espoused in the *Treatise on Wisdom* is pure Nāgārjunian Madhyamaka. Because it extensively describes both the bodhisattva deeds and the ultimate nature, the *Treatise on Wisdom* is the chief text that many Chinese practitioners from all schools rely on to learn both method and wisdom.

The *Treatise on Wisdom* is a huge work and differs from Nāgārjuna's other, more terse works in that it gives a more elaborate explanation of all the concepts, persons, history, and practices involved with that sūtra.[132] Elucidating most of the themes from the *Treatise on the Middle Way*, it uses a variety of means, such as dialectical arguments, stories, examples, metaphors, analogies, similes, anecdotes, and sūtra quotations, making it a rich and engaging text. The entire Sanskrit original cannot be found, although a few fragments were discovered in Central Asia. It was not translated into Tibetan. The *Treatise on Wisdom* has continuously been popular with Chinese Buddhists and has had a strong impact on all Chinese schools.

The Madhyamaka View

When Chinese Madhyamaka masters are asked, "What is emptiness?" their brief response is "dependent arising." They cite Nāgārjuna's homage at the beginning of the *Treatise on the Middle Way* in which he bows to the Buddha because he taught dependent arising, which is free from ceasing, arising, discontinuation, permanence, coming, going, difference, and identity. Because all things arise dependent on causes and conditions, they lack *svabhāva*—inherent nature. This level of dependent arising refers to causality as expressed in the twelve links as well as to causality in general.

Chinese Mādhyamikas also speak of dependent arising in terms of mutual or relational dependence. Produced and unproduced phenomena depend on each other. They are identified and established in relation to each other. In China, the notion of inherent existence was refuted principally by pointing out the contradictions between inherent existence and dependent arising. Although early Chinese Mādhyamikas did not specifically set out dependence on mere term and concept, they definitely accepted it.

Emptiness is spoken of in multiple ways: One is dependent arising as the meaning of emptiness as Nāgārjuna stated in the *Treatise on the Middle Way*. Another is the eighteen types of emptiness as expressed in the Perfection of Wisdom sūtras, in which the types of emptiness are designated and differentiated dependent on the objects that are the bases of emptiness. In this way, the *Treatise on Wisdom* shows that being empty and arising dependently are not contradictory and are mutually complementary.

Another way of revealing emptiness is through the meaning of *svabhāva*—inherent existence or self-nature—the object of negation. According to Yinshun, there are, in general, three defining points:[133]

1. Being alone, independent (*ekatā*). This word also means standing by itself, established by itself, independent and unrelated to others. Existence in this manner is refuted by causal dependence; things that arise due to causes and conditions do not stand by themselves, they depend on others and therefore do not exist under their own power.
2. Permanent and unchanging (*nityatā*). An eternal, permanent, unchanging soul or self cannot exist. This is refuted by realizing I is a changing phenomenon that depends on causes and conditions and cannot be static and unchanging. Being dependent, it is not established by itself and cannot maintain itself.
3. Having control; self-sufficient, substantially existent (*svāmin*). This could be read as two terms. The first two characters—*zhu zai* (*vaśitva* or *īśvara*)[134]—mean controller, ruler, autonomous, under its own power. *Zhen shi* (*dravyasat*, *bhūta-sat*, *svatantra*, or *satya*) means substantial existence or real, true existence. This term indicates something that is in control of its own actions and fate. However, whatever arises due to causes and conditions cannot exist under its own power; it cannot control or rule over itself or anything else.

In the *Treatise on Wisdom*, Nāgārjuna sometimes mentions all three characteristics when speaking of the object of negation. At other times, he mentions one or two. This does not necessarily indicate a difference in the object of negation, although it may, depending on the wrong view he is refuting. Some of the text is in the form of question and answer, with the challenging questions representing the views of non-Buddhists, the Buddhist Sarvāstivādins, or Buddhist essentialists. In these cases, Nāgārjuna refutes the assertion according to the term the opponents use, and in cases where there is more than one meaning of a term, he will use the meaning of the opponent he is refuting.[135]

The *Perfection of Wisdom Sūtra in 100,000 Lines* speaks of three kinds of designation:[136]

1. *Designation by name* (*nāma-prajñapti*, C. *ming jia*) refers to nominal existence. Names are designated by means of conventions. These names correspond to the meaning or to the object and are given merely due to convention. Although sentient beings designate names to objects, ignorance confuses the name with the object and the name with the meaning, thinking that the name and the object/meaning are the same, although they are not. The names are just pointers. For example, if someone calls us a derogatory name, we get offended because we equate that name with ourselves when in fact the name is simply a word.

   The Chinese word *jia*, which here is translated as "designated," also means illusory. Phenomena are false like illusions because they are merely designated.
2. *Dependent designation* (*upādāya-prajñapti*, C. *shou jia*) means "designated or imputed in relation to": phenomena are designated in relation to other phenomena and specifically in relation to their bases of designation. This is the word Nāgārjuna uses in the verse from the *Treatise on the Middle Way* (MMK 24.18):

   > That which is dependent arising
   > is explained to be emptiness.
   > That, being a dependent designation,
   > is itself the Middle Way.

A person is designated in dependence on the collection of its parts—the body and mind. The person is not designated on its own, but in relation to the collection of the aggregates. Ignorance is deceptive because it grasps the collection of the aggregates as being a real person. In other situations, ignorance grasps a collection of parts as being a real whole.

3. *Designated phenomena* (*dharma-prajñapti*, C. *fa jia*) refers to dependent arising in the sense of dependence on causes and conditions. When we analyze things seeking the smallest parts that compose them, we may come to believe that these smallest particles exist independent of everything else and have an inherent nature that is never lost. That is incorrect because they exist by depending on their causes and conditions. Thus these tiny particles that are the fundamental building blocks of all larger objects are also empty of true existence. Their appearance of being independent is false because they exist in relation to other things. This counters the Sarvāstivāda view that the fundamental particles of the four elements exist inherently.

Because things are designated in these three ways, they are empty of inherent existence. The Perfection of Wisdom sūtras assert that both conditioned and unconditioned phenomena lack inherent existence. Causal dependence cannot prove the emptiness of unconditioned phenomena because they do not depend on causes and conditions for their existence. However, they are relationally dependent on conditioned things. Unconditioned phenomena cannot exist by themselves; they are identified, defined, and exist in relation to conditioned things. Being dependent in this way, unconditioned phenomena are empty of inherent existence. For this reason, when the Perfection of Wisdom sūtras speak of eighteen types of emptiness, they include the emptiness of the unproduced and the emptiness of the unconditioned.

The unconditioned and the conditioned are mutually dependent on each other. One cannot exist without the other. They are not one and the same; neither are they separate and unrelated. The unconditioned, emptiness, is the true nature of the conditioned. The Perfection of Wisdom sūtras say that emptiness is the nature (*svabhāva*) of phenomena. They also say that phenomena are empty of essential nature. As explained in chapter 4, the term "nature" has diverse meanings according to the context. When saying that the nature of phenomena is emptiness, "nature" refers to the ultimate nature—that all phenomena lack inherent existence. When saying that phenomena are empty of nature, "nature" refers to inherent existence, a mode of existence that they have never had. When the Perfection of Wisdom sūtras state that the nature of phenomena is that they have no nature, the first usage of "nature" refers to their ultimate mode of existence and the second usage indicates that they lack inherent existence. Yinshun explains (WB 305–6):

> From the karmic results of birth and death to the attainment of the accomplishments of the three vehicles, and even nirvāṇa . . . all things exist only in name, only conventionally.
>
> All things in ordinary worldly existence are established by perception through names and speech, but based on extraordinary investigation, they have no inherent nature and cannot be established . . . This does not mean that emptiness, the nonexistence of an inherent nature, annihilates everything and denies the establishment of all things, however. On the contrary, if things were not empty and without an inherent nature, but instead had an inherent nature, then they would be things with a fixed existence. A thing that really existed and had an inherent nature would not need to arise from conditions. In such a case, that which had not arisen could not arise, that which had not ceased could not cease, and ordinary people would remain ordinary people and could not become buddhas!

As Nāgārjuna said in *Treatise on the Middle Way*, if emptiness did not exist, nothing could be established; but because emptiness exists, everything can be established. From the conventional viewpoint, things are like illusions, and from the ultimate perspective, they are empty of inherent existence. These two perspectives do not contradict each other. The two truths are mutually supportive.

Jizang and the Madhyamaka School

As we have seen, Madhyamaka philosophy came into China very early—several centuries before it came to Tibet. During the intervening centuries,

Madhyamaka philosophy in India developed considerably, as did the terminology used to express it. After Madhyamaka went to Tibet, its terminology and refutations were further developed. It was only in the twentieth century, with Fazun's translations, that the Chinese came to know of the developments in Tibetan Buddhism. Meanwhile Madhyamaka philosophy developed in China under the guidance of Chinese Madhyamaka masters. This development is reflected in the teachings of the great Madhyamaka master Jizang, to whose activities in the late sixth and early seventh centuries we will now turn.

Jizang's family was from Parthia in Central Asia. He was ordained as a child, and people quickly recognized his genius in using reasoning and explaining the Dharma. In the chaotic times at the end of the Northern and Southern dynasties, he collected, preserved, and studied Buddhist scriptures, living with other monks in old monasteries in the mountains to avoid the tumult in the cities. Later, at the invitation of the crown prince, he relocated, eventually living in Xian (Chang-an), the capital. He composed more than forty treatises and commentaries, and he frequently lectured on Sanlun and the *Lotus Sūtra*. He also taught the Perfection of Wisdom sūtras, the *Treatise on Wisdom*, the *Flower Ornament Sūtra*, and the *Vimalakīrti Sūtra*. His writings centered on the above texts as well as on the *Nirvāṇa Sūtra*, *Diamond Sūtra*, and *Śrīmālā Sūtra*, and he wrote detailed commentaries on each of the three principal Sanlun treatises. The first two patriarchs of Japanese Madhyamaka, Huiguan and Zhizang, studied with him. Although Jizang's interest went beyond Sanlun, his confidence and devotion to it wasn't swayed. Instead, he used Sanlun to interpret the *Lotus Sūtra*, the *Nirvāṇa Sūtra*, and other sūtras that were well-known at his time.

After the first spurt of enthusiasm for the Madhyamaka teachings that were translated and propagated by Kumārajīva and his followers in the early fifth century, Chinese interest shifted to the *Satyasiddhi Śāstra* and the *Nirvāṇa Sūtra*. Then in the mid-sixth century, interest in Madhyamaka was again revived by Senglang, who lived a reclusive life on Mount She. His disciples, especially Falang (507–81), taught Madhyamaka more widely. Falang's chief disciple, Jizang, then took the lead, reviving Madhyamaka in China. Jizang's work represents the evolution of Madhyamaka thought in China up to that time.

In the time between the introduction of Madhyamaka to China and the revival of Madhyamaka with Jizang, the Buddhist landscape had changed considerably. In Kumārajīva's time, Buddhist thinkers were also familiar with Taoist thought, so Kumārajīva and his followers made great effort to explain Buddhist principles correctly, to differentiate them from Taoist principles, and to clarify previous misunderstandings in which the two had been mixed. By Jizang's time, specialists in many of the main sūtras and treatises had arrived from India, and the Chinese were writing their own commentaries on these. There was now a distinct Buddhist vocabulary and distinct Buddhist concepts, so that mixture with Taoist ideas was no longer a big problem. The task for Jizang was to be consistent and faithful to Madhyamaka principles, to bring out their implications, and to apply them when examining the sūtras and treatises of other Buddhist schools.

Jizang holds that the principal theme of Sanlun is refutation of the false to reveal the correct. "The correct" can be spoken of in terms of its essence and its function. The essence is the true character of all things, which is intangible and beyond word and thought. It is neither conventional nor ultimate. The function of the correct is using skillful means to help sentient beings realize this true character of all phenomena that transcends words and concepts. "The false" refers to wrong views, which fall into four categories: (1) non-Buddhist theories of the substantiality of persons and phenomena, (2) Abhidharma notions of an objective self but a subjective not-self, (3) Satyasiddhi's assertion that emptiness is an absolute truth, and (4) the grasping mind of a Mahāyāna practitioner.

Non-Buddhist Ideas

Jizang refuted many non-Buddhist theories in his commentary on *The Hundred*. The first nine chapters of Āryadeva's *The Hundred* refute wrong views, and the last chapter refutes the reification of emptiness itself. The first refutation counteracts grasping the self of persons, followed by refuting grasping a self of phenomena and grasping emptiness. Grasping and attachment to self are singled out among all the afflictions for several reasons. First, non-Buddhists consider the self as the principal truth or reality; they also believe that liberation is attained through abandoning selfish attachment to the self. They maintain that the afflictions must be eliminated, but the self must remain to attain liberation, so eliminating the self is not necessary. Furthermore, the self is the subject that meditates on emptiness and attains liberation. Falang, Jizang's teacher, said that rather than fear the afflictions we should fear this self. This non-Buddhist view of self is tenacious and difficult to uproot, so we should be afraid of it and put effort into eliminating it. Eliminating misconceptions of the self is therefore a priority.

In the āgamas the Buddha explains sixty-two wrong views of the self that are to be overcome. Hearing all the false reasons the non-Buddhists give for clinging to the self, we can see that giving up wrong views requires wisdom and effort.

On Abhidharma and Satyasiddhi Tenets

Abhidharmikas and the Satyasiddhi thinkers analyze things by dissecting them into components to determine that no self is there. Jizang, on the other hand, mainly uses consequences in his reasoning process to show the errors in the logic of those who assert inherent existence. He noticed that meditating according to the views of the Abhidharma and Satyasiddhi schools could lead to the extremes of absolutism or nihilism. Those meditating according to the Abhidharma negate the self but not phenomena, leaving the root of saṃsāra intact. They also identify something as the carrier of karma from one life to another. These beliefs lead to the extreme of absolutism.

Jizang's strongest refutations were directed toward the views of the Satyasiddhi school. Although the *Satyasiddhi Treatise* (*Sattyasiddhi Śāstra*), an Indian Abhidharma text by Harivarman (250–350), was initially propagated by Kumārajīva and his followers as an introduction to Madhyamaka and Mahāyāna thought, it became so popular that some people saw its teaching on emptiness to be the same as Madhyamaka. But practitioners of this treatise failed to differentiate between emptiness and nonexistence and failed to apply the understanding of emptiness to the bodhisattva path. Having strong conviction in Nāgārjuna's thought and wanting to maintain its purity, Jizang was afraid that naïve people would not be able to discern the difference between the limited or distorted views held by Satyasiddhi and the correct view espoused by Sanlun. Seeing it as his personal responsibility to clarify this, he criticized the Satyasiddhi view and directed people to follow Madhyamaka.

On Yogācāra Ideas

At Jizang's time, the *Compendium on the Mahāyāna* by Asaṅga and the *Commentary on the Ten Grounds* and the *Explanation of the Compendium of Mahāyāna*, both by Vasubandhu, were popular. They were some of the first translations of Indian treatises introducing Yogācāra concepts to the Chinese. The Yogācāra idea of the foundation consciousness was influenced by the popular Tathāgatagarbha doctrine, which posits a buddha essence that abides eternally, without arising or ceasing. Followers of the *Commentary on the Ten Grounds* considered the foundation consciousness to be this originally pure consciousness present in each sentient being and said that other consciousnesses carried the karmic seeds that led to rebirth in saṃsāra. The followers of the *Compendium on the Mahāyāna*, on the other hand, believed the foundation consciousness was a defiled consciousness that stored the karmic seeds and a ninth consciousness, the *amala* (the pure consciousness), was the originally pure mind in sentient beings. Both of these groups maintained that while sentient beings' nature was pure, ignorance was responsible for saṃsāra and the eradication of ignorance was liberation.

According to Jizang, Asaṅga and Vasubandhu sought to overcome sentient beings' confidence in the existence of external objects and phenomena. The idea of mind-only (*vijñaptmātra*) was useful in that it explained phenomena as mental constructs arising from the mind. Jizang, however, did not consider the idea of foundation consciousness as part of the original Yogācāra teachings, but saw it as an addition by later masters in China. He criticized the ideas of a foundation consciousness and an original pure mind as contradictory to the basic principles of selflessness and emptiness that are at the core of the Buddha's teachings. However, he did not criticize Asaṅga and Vasubandhu, whom he held in high regard, but attributed these wrong views to misunderstandings formed by their Chinese followers who relied on the *Compendium on the Mahāyāna* and the *Commentary on the Ten Grounds*. By saying that the mind is truly existent, and this truly existent mind is the basis for attaining liberation, these Chinese followers were asserting a position tantamount to the non-Buddhist ātman. Furthermore, these people mistakenly believed that the three naturelesses were the ultimate, inherent identity of things. In *A Treatise on the Profound (Teachings of the) "Vimalakīrti Sūtra,"* Jizang refutes these ideas (PTE 85):

> Regarding the meaning of the mind-only [proposed] by Vasubandhu, he means to bring an end to the object through the subject. When the object ceases, the subject also ceases. Being untrammeled, [one] naturally realizes the truth. [Vasubandhu] does not mean that the object is falsely constructed and the mind is truly existent. The later scholars do not understand his idea. Therefore they should be rebuked.

On the Tathāgatagarbha Doctrine

The topic of buddha nature arose infrequently in early Indian and Chinese Madhyamaka literature and seldom appears in the Perfection of Wisdom sūtras, the *Vimalakīrti* or *Lotus* sūtras, or in the three principal Sanlun treatises. The *Nirvāṇa Sūtra* was especially well received in China, and many of the teachers of the Satyasiddhi, Yogācāra, and Madhyamaka schools wrote and taught on its principal themes. Tao-lang, a Sanlun master who was active in revitalizing Madhyamaka, wrote on the *Nirvāṇa Sūtra*, *Lotus Sūtra*, and Madhyamaka, and Jizang saw himself as the heir to the tradition of combining these three. While Jizang's initial training was in Madhyamaka and he was well grounded in it, the *Lotus* and *Nirvāṇa* sūtras were very popular at his time, so he could hardly ignore them, especially since the *Nirvāṇa Sūtra* was thought to contain the Buddha's final—and thus most important—teachings. Jizang saw buddha essence as a fundamental Mahāyāna idea and devoted a chapter to it in his *Treatise on the Profound Mahāyāna* (C. *Dasheng xuanlun*). He speaks of buddha nature not in a substantialist way, which would contradict basic Madhyamaka tenets, but in a way that accords with emptiness as taught by Nāgārjuna.

Jizang understands buddha nature to be the nature of the Buddha, and gives other words associated with the highest truth and ultimate reality as synonyms of buddha nature: the reality of phenomena (*dharmatā*), suchness (*tathatā*), dharma element (*dharmadhātu*), one vehicle, and ultimate limit of reality (*bhūtakoṭi*). Buddha nature is the Middle Way that is beyond dualistic views. An example is his reading of the following passage in the *Nirvāṇa Sūtra* (MTC 161):

> The buddha essence is called the supreme emptiness; the supreme emptiness is called wisdom. Concerning emptiness, [the śrāvakas

> and solitary realizers] do not see [both] emptiness and non-emptiness. The wise see [both] emptiness and non-emptiness, [both] permanence and impermanence, [both] duḥkha and bliss, [both] self and not-self. Emptiness is [the nature of] all saṃsāra; non-emptiness is [the nature of] mahānirvāṇa, and so forth. Not-self is [the nature of] saṃsāra, and self is [the nature of] the mahānirvāṇa.
>
> Seeing the emptiness of all [saṃsāra] without seeing the non-emptiness of [nirvāṇa] is not called the Middle Way, and so forth. Seeing the not-self of all [saṃsāra] without seeing the self [of nirvāṇa] is not called the Middle Way. The Middle Way is called buddha essence.

Some people take this passage to mean that the wisdom knowing the supreme emptiness knows empty, impermanent, duḥkha, and not-self as attributes of saṃsāra and their opposites—nonempty, permanent, bliss, and self as attributes of nirvāṇa. They state that this is the Middle Way. This interpretation of the Middle Way differs from the traditional meaning of the Middle Way as being the abandonment of dualistic extremes.

However, Jizang reads "the wise" as the subject of the third sentence, saying the passage should be read: "Concerning emptiness, [the wise] do not see emptiness and non-emptiness" and so on up to "the wise do not see either self or not-self." None of these dualistic views is the Middle Way or the nature of the Buddha. He says (MTC 173):

> Thus in abandoning [the thought of] non-emptiness, [the wise] steer clear of the extreme of absolutism, and in abandoning [the thought of] emptiness, [the wise] steer clear of the extreme of nihilism. The same is the case with respect to "not seeing wisdom and non-wisdom." Hence, we take the Middle Way to be the buddha nature.

That which has avoided extremes and goes beyond dualism is the Middle Way, which is the buddha nature. Understanding this, Jizang was critical of the eleven theories that were discussed in Chinese Buddhist circles as being the direct cause of the buddha nature. The *Nirvāṇa Sūtra* says that the direct cause of the buddha nature is sentient beings, and there was much speculation about just what factor(s) in sentient beings this refers to. Among the theories put forth as the cause of the buddha essence were the five aggregates and mind, the original pure mind resplendent with numerous virtues, the foundation consciousness, the *amala* (ninth) consciousness, the supreme truth, and the supreme emptiness. According to Jizang, these all rang of substantialist thinking and were unacceptable.

In the earlier part of the *Nirvāṇa Sūtra*, buddha essence is portrayed as an inherent possession of sentient beings—something akin to the original pure mind—while in later parts it is seen as something newly acquired upon attaining buddhahood. To Jizang this means that neither one of these represents the Buddha's ultimate intention. Instead, Jizang believes the Buddha employs skillful means, and because sentient beings hold the view of impermanence—here probably meaning instability or self-deception—he counteracts that by teaching that all sentient beings originally possess the buddha essence and thus have the ability to attain buddhahood. But sentient beings do not understand this as skillful means and think the buddha nature is an inherent essence with specific attributes. To remedy that wrong conception, the Buddha then speaks of the buddha nature as acquired upon attaining buddhahood. However, in fact the buddha nature is neither inherent nor acquired; it is beyond such dualities.

The Buddha has several reasons for teaching that sentient beings possess buddha nature: They will know their own potential and practice well, so they will become buddhas. They will recognize that all other sentient beings have buddha nature and will respect them, treat them with kindness and compassion, and not harm them by killing, stealing, and so on. Knowing that they can attain a buddha's supreme wisdom, sentient beings will not be satisfied with the paths of the śrāvakas and solitary realizers. Sentient beings will not fall into nihilism by thinking there is no continuity of mind after death, and they will have the confidence that they will definitely become buddhas. Advocating the Middle Way of nonduality as the buddha nature, Jizang says (MTC 182):

> By "tathāgatagarbha" is meant the womb [*garbha*] of the Tathāgata. Since [sentient beings] miss [the truth of] nonduality, they entertain dualistic views. As these dualistic views envelop

> [the truth of] nonduality, the way of nonduality cannot manifest itself. Hence, these dualistic views are the womb of [the truth of] nonduality. Further, the way of nonduality, being concealed by dualistic views, [like an embryo concealed in a womb,] is called "tathāgatagarbha."

Sentient beings, in their ignorance, do not understand nonduality, and the truth of nonduality is hidden by their womb-like dualistic views. They believe that what is nondual is dual and thus abide in saṃsāra. In this state, the truth of nonduality is known as the tathāgatagarbha. But when all erroneous and dualistic views are eliminated by means of wisdom, the truth of nonduality shines forth. In this state, it is known as the dharmakāya. Understood in this way, tathāgatagarbha and dharmakāya refer to the same state of nonduality at different times and do not imply any type of pure inherent essence. Jizang says in *A Treatise on the Profound Mahāyāna* (PTE 84):

> If the dharmakāya originally existed, how could it be acquired by causes? If it is acquired by causes, it would not exist originally. If it were not acquired by causes, this would be the same as a non-Buddhist position. If it existed originally, how could it be named the Middle Way? If this pure thing that is free from the four phrases and hundred errors existed originally, it should expel the false by itself; how could it be covered by afflictions? If one who later attains the tenth ground can expel afflictions, why can't the eternally abiding dharmakāya expel [afflictions]?

In short, the Tathāgatagarbha notion of a permanent, pure mind and the Yogācāra idea of foundation consciousness are absolutist ways of thinking that are in line with the non-Buddhist view of ātman. Because the mind is empty, it may be transformed from its ordinary state to an awakened state. Both the afflicted mind and the awakened mind lack inherent existence. There is nothing to grasp and no one who grasps. The experience of emptiness is designated correct insight, wisdom, buddha nature, and dharmakāya. But none of these exist inherently.

Noncraving and Freedom from Elaborations

Jizang emphasizes that practitioners must remain loyal to noncraving and not inadvertently get derailed by false grasping. In *A Treatise on the Profound Vimalakīrti Sūtra* (*Jing-ming xuan-lun*), he says (MTC 101):

> Practitioners of the Way want to forsake the false ways and seek the true way, and thus are bound by [their longing for] the Way. Practitioners of meditation [try to] stop disturbances and seek calmness, and thus are bound by [their fondness for] meditation. Pursuers of scholarship claim that there is wisdom [to be cultivated], and thus are bound by [their love of] wisdom. They further say, "We should practice contemplating non-arising so as to eliminate the mind of craving." As a result, they are bound by [the idea of] non-arising. Living in the midst of bondages, they want to abandon bondages, not really knowing that [the attempts to abandon bondages] are all [additional] bondages.

If we get caught up in conceptions about the path or in certain meditation experiences to the detriment of realizing the true nature, we are deceiving ourselves. Conversely, we must be careful not to become attached to noncraving. Other Buddhist schools refute wrong views, and when doing so, they establish some special view. For example, the Sarvāstivādins assert partless particles, the Satyasiddhi followers stop at nirvāṇa and lack great compassion, and Yogācārins put forth the foundation consciousness. As Mādhyamikas we refute wrong views and abandon grasping to any and all ideas and practices, including the idea and practice of noncraving.

Jizang's criteria for establishing any statement as true is its usefulness in refuting wrong views and cultivating noncraving. In other words, there is no absolute truth to cling to, no absolute teaching that is the best teaching to give to everyone at all times. Scriptures are for the purpose of refuting wrong ideas, not for establishing fixed Buddhist dogmas. When wrong ideas have been abandoned, speech stops. This pragmatic approach influences how he evaluates the diversity of teachings (MTC 106):

> There are altogether three ways of [looking at these diverse explanations]: First, if their disciples all achieve awakening [on listening to them], none of these explanations is wrong. Second, if on hearing them, their disciples all become deluded, none of these theories is right. Third, there may be occasions [when an explanation leads to] awakening at one place and produces confusion at another place. Then it is called "true" at one place and is named "false" at another place.

Along the same line, Mādhyamikas do not set up wisdom in opposition to defilements. Seeing that all phenomena are empty, they know there is no arising of truly existent defilements and thus practitioners do not need to eradicate these defilements. By understanding this, they will be able to abandon defilements. Liberation is a state in which all duality has been abandoned.

Bodhisattvas can be effective in their work to benefit sentient beings due to their understanding of nonduality. Using the example of Vimalakīrti, Jizang says (MTC 108):

> Vimalakīrti remained in the impure [realm] without becoming impure, and he was not bound by [impure] things. He stayed in the pure [realm] without becoming [attached to] the pure, and he was not bound by pure [things]. Roaming over both the impure and pure [realms], he was not bound by [the wish] to negate impure and pure [things]. Never acting [despite his appearance of being in action], he was not bound by [the longing for] impure or for pure [things]. Hence, he was known as having achieved liberation.

Saṃsāra is not inherently bad and to be abandoned, and nirvāṇa is not inherently good and to be attained. Saṃsāra and nirvāṇa are established in mutual dependence, and the discrimination between saṃsāra and nirvāṇa is only skillful means based on convention. Mādhyamikas hold the view of the equality of saṃsāra and nirvāṇa in that both are empty (MTC 109):

> It is so because phenomena are neither of saṃsāra nor of nirvāṇa. It is only because sentient beings are deluded that saṃsāra comes

> into being. To stop saṃsāra, [the Buddha] for the moment talks of nirvāṇa. When saṃsāra is eliminated, nirvāṇa will also cease.

Subduing elaborations is the purpose of Nāgārjuna and Āryadeva's teachings, and liberation is attained by correct insight that is free from elaborations. Elaboration connotes conceptual proliferation and reification, and when we view emptiness with a mind of elaboration, there is a subjective factor that causes our perception of emptiness to deviate from emptiness itself. When we conceptually cognize emptiness, the true nature is concealed by language and concepts, and nondual reality is seen in a dual way. Subject and object are seen as distinct, and we conjecture many differences among objects. In this way, conceptualization reifies everything—even emptiness—and we come to regard what is imagination as fact. This is the basis for mundane conventional knowledge, which is erroneous from the viewpoint of āryas and refuted by Indian Mādhyamikas and Chinese Sanlun followers.

Those who don't understand noncraving believe that there must be something real that serves as a support for what is imputed. If that real support is negated, they say nothing is left. In that case, there would be no basis for the Buddha's teachings, and without a basis, it would be impossible to lead disciples on the correct path. Jizang responds that if we cling to anything, we miss the point. Our meditation will not be correct and we will be unable to cease the two extremes and attain awakening. He quotes Nāgārjuna's renowned passage (MMK 24.14):[137]

> For him to whom emptiness makes sense,
> everything makes sense.
> For him to whom emptiness does not make sense,
> nothing becomes sense.

It is only because all phenomena are empty that conventional things exist and conditioned phenomena function properly. On the ultimate level, emptiness is the final reality of all phenomena. On the conventional level, the illusion-like appearances of conventionalities exist within emptiness and because of emptiness.

To reach the other shore, we must establish the right view of nonabiding, then meditate correctly, and finally end all elaborations. As long as we think in rigid categories—Buddhist and non-Buddhist, existence and nonexistence, and so on—we cannot realize emptiness. When we realize that each teaching was given dependent on conditions, we will stop attachment to a particular teaching and will treat things equally with an open mind. Realization of dependent arising leads to the correct view, which brings correct contemplation in which preferences, aversions, confrontations, as well as subject and object duality subside. This is the cessation of elaborations.

As we do away with our biases and craving, we'll see that there are many approaches to emptiness. The Pāli tradition, especially the Abhidharma, employs dissecting phenomena into their components as the method to realize emptiness. The Perfection of Wisdom sūtras use negations to indicate that emptiness is beyond language and concepts. Madhyamaka uses reasoning to refute conjectures, and this leads to direct perception of emptiness.

Emptiness is not nonexistence; it can be perceived directly with the mind. But when we use the realization of emptiness to refute true existence, we should not grasp emptiness as truly existent. In addition, a conceptual understanding of emptiness should not be confused with the direct experience of emptiness.[138]

Jizang advocates a gradual approach to uproot elaborations, as taught by his teacher Falang. The practice leading to the state beyond false discriminations has five steps.

1. Initially, practitioners must cultivate ethical conduct. While cultivating virtue, they learn that nonvirtue is associated with elaborations and true virtue with non-elaboration.
2. They see that virtue arising from a craving mind is due to elaborations, and this differs from the non-elaboration of a mind that does not crave.
3. They recognize that discernment between craving and noncraving or any kind of dual opposition is due to elaborations, whereas nonduality is non-elaboration.
4. They cultivate the understanding that duality and nonduality are two extremes and discriminating them is conjoined with elaborations. Only when language and all conceptualization vanish will the state of non-elaborations be present.

5. Practitioners realize that holding on to non-elaborations in contrast to elaborations is still a kind of elaboration.

In this progression, the correctness of the preceding step is negated to present the correctness of the subsequent step. In this way the coarser afflictions held in the earlier step are pacified and practitioners work on subtler afflictions in the next step. In this process nothing positive is affirmed; instead, there is continuous dismantling of the mind's conceptually constructed view until there is nothing left to remove and reality is directly perceived.

The *Lotus Sūtra* says, "Such a dharma is inexpressible [because in that state] the expression of language ceases and quiets." This is emptiness; emptiness is suchness, correct Dharma, and the pure, fundamental nature. It cannot be spoken of as existent or nonexistent. It is only truly known by āryas, whose wisdom realizing suchness is nondual with suchness. The experience of this direct perception of emptiness is illustrated by a Chinese proverb, "Only the person drinking the water will know whether it is warm or cold." Emptiness is knowable, but it isn't truly existent; its identity is dependent. Someone who is thirsty should know when he sees a mirage that no water is there. Otherwise, he may lose his way when seeking freedom from thirst. Likewise, we should know that teachings on emptiness do not refer to an absolute truth. Water, suchness, the desire for water or suchness, the one who desires—all these are unreal.

In the direct experience of emptiness, there is no subject or object, no conception, no words. Sengzhao says (PTE 263):

> The true state is unspeakable. All that is being said is unreal, [like a] play. The wondrous state transcending words is utterly empty.

Nevertheless, the Buddha must use words and signs to help sentient beings realize what is without name and identity. The Buddha's teachings lead to this pure state, but he must employ words, expressions, and reasoning in accord with the audience's disposition to lead them to what is beyond words, expressions, and reasoning. His intent is to liberate all sentient beings, not to establish a philosophical system that would increase attachment to mistaken conceptualization.

A term does not correspond with an objective referent; phenomena exist merely nominally and are empty of their own inherent nature. Still, language can and must be used to point practitioners to the true nature, suchness.

All phenomena have the same ultimate nature; they are all empty of inherent existence. All phenomena—including the arguments used to refute inherent existence and emptiness itself—are empty. The emptiness of one thing is the emptiness of all, in that when directly perceived, the emptiness of one thing and the emptiness of another cannot be distinguished. Jizang makes a special point of saying that emptiness itself lacks inherent existence and that reifying emptiness or grasping onto ideas about emptiness interferes with liberation. He also emphasizes that the reasoning, consequences, and other words and concepts used to refute wrong views should not be clung to, for they too lack inherent existence. Nevertheless, these function to refute all misconceptions. All discourses are skillful means to benefit disciples.

Mādhyamikas do not assert any theses. Their teachings are not an expression of a fixed position, and they do not proclaim any absolute truth or reality. After teachings have served the purpose of benefiting someone, they are released and not clung to. Jizang calls this way of teaching "question and answer based on emptiness."

Mādhyamikas present their opponents with absurd consequences that would arise from the opponents' contradictory assertions and ask them to respond. This shows them the absurdity of their way of thinking. This is a path of refutation without assertion, in which what is incorrect is eliminated and nothing new is fabricated to replace it. Non-Madhyamaka opponents cling to the notion that their refutations must substantially exist in order to refute anything. Nāgārjuna disagrees; in the *Twelve Gate Treatise* he says, "By virtue of the principle of emptiness, all things are established."

Thus the refutation of all (truly existent) phenomena does not destroy the foundation of Sanlun's teachings. Rather, it uproots elaborations so that we will realize emptiness; in that way the incorrect is abandoned and the correct is revealed. Mādhyamikas say that non-truly existent arguments refuting non-truly existent assertions is like one illusory character in a magical show stopping another illusory character: it appears but is not real. Words and statements come into existence due to causes and conditions; they don't exist independently. Nevertheless, they can still express the teachings on dependent arising so that people will realize that emptiness is the true nature of phenomena.

Although in general the Chinese intelligentsia saw debate as unfitting for gentlemen and viewed setting forth illogical consequences as sophistry, Jizang did not shy away from these. He saw consequences as an efficient way to uncover and release misconceptions. Rather than assert positive theses by using syllogisms, he challenged others in accordance with their views for the purpose of exposing the incongruity of their ideas.

Mādhyamikas do not seek to give people new information to replace their incorrect knowledge. When the Buddha refutes that a (truly existent) phenomenon exists, he does not propound another view that a phenomenon is nonexistent, because holding that a phenomenon does not exist is another extreme to be negated, and the Buddha's aim is to eliminate all misconceptions with correct insight. The Buddha may sometimes use the word "nonexistent," but his purpose is to counteract the disease of clinging to existence. Jizang calls this practice "removing the old [illness] without developing a new [illness]." Reifying emptiness or being attached to reasoning would be a new illness.

Manner of Teaching

Everything exists only nominally. Words lack objective referents. Reasoning, consequences, and arguments exist nominally and are empty of inherent existence, as are the theses they establish; there is no objective, independent truth. Because things are empty yet exist nominally, language can be used to lead others to the realization of the ultimate nature. Words have a purpose, for they can be employed to eliminate misconceptions and reification. However, the words should not be clung to and concepts must not be solidified into objective truths; doing so would be the opposite of the purpose of wise words.

Language is conventional and we should not let ourselves be trapped by it. When we understand that every teaching is given dependent on conditions, we stop grasping on to a particular teaching and treat all teachings equally with an open mind because they are skillful means to lead beings of various dispositions. Thus Jizang is practical and freely employs whatever is suitable to lead others to correct realizations. He is not confined in the methods he uses to help sentient beings drowning in saṃsāra due to their ignorance. In a suitable situation he may present his opponents' assertions, even though they are erroneous, if that is helpful to his audience. Sometimes Jizang uses empirical evidence to refute wrong views, at other times he uses consequences. He employs whatever is useful without asserting any thesis of his own, unlike other thinkers who posit theses and then argue with others to defend them. Once someone's wrong views are eliminated, the teachings used to accomplish that are released and not clung to as an absolute truth. Jizang calls this way of teaching "question and answer based on emptiness," explaining that it originated with the Buddha and was used by Nāgārjuna and Āryadeva to aid their disciples.

Once all wrong views are abandoned, correct insight arises automatically. At the end of the process of negation, if one reaches a conclusion and expounds a "correct thesis" or an absolute truth, he has become "Mara's subject" because he is again caught in clinging. Madhyamaka is not for the sake of winning arguments but solely for the purpose of liberating sentient beings.

This path is gradual, as expressed in the five steps for abandoning elaboration mentioned above. At the conclusion of these five, practitioners arrive at the nondual realization of emptiness, which is inexpressible and transcends all conventions. The ultimate nature, suchness, cannot be said to be existent or nonexistent, nor can it be adequately described by words and concepts. It can only be experienced through direct perception. Yet in the direct perception there is neither subject nor object, only pure emptiness.

The Two Truths

The two truths were a prominent topic in Chinese Buddhism by the early sixth century, and each of the schools had its own way of explaining them. The two truths are also a central subject that is essential to understand in Sanlun. In the *Profound Meaning of the Three Treatises* (C. *Sanlun xuanyi*), Jizang says (PTE 244):

> The two truths are the root of Buddhism. By virtue of the two truths, buddhas train themselves and transform others.

And in the *Meaning of the Two Truths* (C. *Erdi yi*), he says (PTE 244):

> Whoever understands the two truths understands the four [main Sanlun] treatises entirely. Whoever does not understand the two truths does not understand the four treatises . . . Whoever understands the two truths is free from nihilism and absolutism, walks the Middle Way, realizes the buddha nature, and attains the dharmakāya. Hence, you should know it is a great benefit to know the two truths.

What are the two truths? In the *Treatise on the Middle Way*, Nāgārjuna's verse delineating the two truths (MMK 24.8–9) is followed by Piṅgala's commentary (MTC 136):

> The Buddha's teaching of the Dharma
> is based on two truths:
> a truth of worldly convention
> and an ultimate truth.
>
> Those who do not understand
> the distinction between these two truths
> do not understand
> the Buddha's profound teaching.
>
> With respect to the conventional truth, all phenomena are in nature empty. Yet [the standpoint of] the world is false, and hence there arise false phenomena which are [regarded as] real from the standpoint of the world. The sages and āryas know the false nature of the worldly standpoint and hence they know that all phenomena are empty and nonarising. [This] is the ultimate truth [seen] from the standpoint of the āryas and is called "true." The buddhas have recourse to these two truths to teach the Dharma to sentient beings.

Jizang speaks of the two truths as "standpoint" as well as "instruction." As a standpoint, ordinary people regard the things they encounter as truly existent, whereas āryas directly perceive their emptiness. Conventionalities are expressible and belong to the realm of words and concepts, but the experience of emptiness is inexpressible. Seen in this way, the two truths have definite meanings and are comprised of specific objects.

In terms of the two truths as instruction, they are taught to eliminate wrong views. Dependent arising is taught to counteract grasping inherent existence, and emptiness is taught to overcome the notion that dependently arising things exist objectively. But both "conventional existence" and "ultimate emptiness" are expressions that are empty and exist only nominally. The teachings of dependently arising existence as conventional truth and of the emptiness of inherent existence as the ultimate truth are nominal expressions. They are applied provisionally to benefit sentient beings, but are empty. From this perspective, the two truths do not have definitive meaning, nor do they correspond to objective referents.

The things ordinary people agree to be true—such as that object being a car and the other object being a person—are false. In fact, conventional existence is empty. Whereas conventional truths are called "reality," only ultimate truth has the meaning of reality, for it is what is known by āryas. Emptiness is reality, but teachings on it are given in terms of conventional truths. These teachings point practitioners toward emptiness by showing them the way to realize it. However, holding the slightest idea of emptiness in one's mind obscures emptiness, and all elaborations about reality as well as the conceptual notion of emptiness must be eliminated.

Just as a raft is used to cross a river but is not clung to once we have reached the other shore, the Dharma teachings support us in gaining realizations but should not be clung to once we have reached nirvāṇa. Āryas employ conventionalities to teach emptiness since ordinary people use these. Conventional truths talk about the specific features of phenomena, such as their being dependent arising and actions bringing results. Conventional truth is the truth of conditionality that sentient beings need to understand. Understanding it is the gateway to understanding ultimate truth.

Both conventional truths and emptiness are necessary—without understanding both, we cannot end duḥkha; they are two sides of the same coin. Ordinary people who lack wisdom cannot perceive ultimate truth, but their not perceiving ultimate truth doesn't make it false.

Conventional and ultimate truths mutually depend on each other; they are called "existence" and "emptiness," respectively. This demarcation is dualistic, even though the two truths, as well as existence and emptiness, are designated in relation to each other. Existence implies nonexistence, and emptiness implies nonemptiness. Emptiness is the emptiness of existence and existence is the existence of emptiness; they are mutually dependent. In this way, Madhyamaka meditators are called to go beyond the two extremes of nihilism and absolutism and beyond the duality of inherent existence in which both existence and emptiness are reified. In this way, the Middle Way is neither (inherently) existent nor empty, because neither existence nor emptiness exist independent of each other.

Jizang does not see the two truths as separate realms or principles, for this would be a form of dualistic thinking, whereas Madhyamaka goes beyond dualistic thinking and the attachment it breeds. To adapt to the understanding of sentient beings, the Buddha says there are two truths. Jizang says (MTC 141):

> By [the two truths as] instruction, [it is meant that] the [true] principle is originally nondual, and that it is for the sake of the objects [of instruction] that it is spoken of as dual. Hence [the two truths] are called "instruction."

The true principle is noncraving, which is the abandonment of all thoughts of duality. To help sentient beings overcome their dualistic ways of thinking, the buddhas say their beliefs are conventional and worldly and praise the ultimate and supreme. But sentient beings then reify the ultimate, see it as solid and desirable, and view the two truths as totally separate.

The Middle Way is the way of noncraving. It is freedom from fixed ontological opinions. It is suchness, totally empty and free from elaborations. In addition to relinquishing the four pairs of contraries that are negated in the homage to the *Treatise on the Middle Way*,[139] suchness is the abandonment of dualities such as suffering and bliss, defilement and non-defilement, ignorance and the abolition of ignorance, wisdom and non-wisdom, and so forth. The Middle Way should not become an object of our craving either. The true Middle Way goes beyond the duality of middle and non-middle, just as genuine noncraving goes beyond attachment and noncraving.

In this way Jizang stresses the importance of not grasping emptiness as truly existent and not grasping truly existent conceptions of emptiness. After using the reasonings to establish emptiness to refute true existence, we should not grasp emptiness as truly existent. In the same way, we must take care not to construct emptiness with a conceptual mind and think our conceptual construct is emptiness. The ultimate is beyond all duality, including the duality of duality and nonduality.[140] Without adhering to or reifying any of these, we should see everything as illusion-like so that our minds are not attached to anything. Then lacking all support, birth and death will cease and the state of supreme bliss will emerge.

The mind is empty of inherent existence, and thus it is possible to transform it from its afflictive state to an awakened state. Both the afflictive mind and the awakened mind are empty. There is nothing to refute and nothing to establish. There is no person who craves and nothing to crave. When ignorance and afflictions are abandoned, the empty universe remains. This state is beyond all words and concepts, although it may be called correct insight, buddha nature, and dharmakāya for the sake of sentient beings.

Wisdom

Wisdom knows and does not know. Jizang explains (PTE 233):

> Wisdom (*prajñā*) knows suchness. Therefore it knows. Since it realizes suchness, within and without unite perfectly and the observed object and the observing subject cease. Therefore it does not know [truly existent subject and object]. Although the observed object and the observing subject cease, objects and cognizers appear as they are. Hence it knows there is nothing to be known; the no-knowing is precisely the knowing.

Wisdom directly realizes emptiness, the ultimate nature. Therefore wisdom knows. However, it knows suchness in a totally nondual manner. In that experience, there is no subject (wisdom) within and no object (suchness) without. Thus wisdom does not know anything and there is nothing to be known.

Wisdom knows suchness, and suchness is neither existence nor nonexistence; it is ungraspable. Because there is no reified object to be known, wisdom does not know. However, its manner of not knowing is not like that of an inanimate object or an ignorant person. It does not know because there is no objective, inherently existent object for it to know. Insight into this unknowability is true knowledge. In this way, wisdom knows the entire variety of things as well as their true nature, emptiness. Sengzhao explains this in *Wisdom Has No Knowing* (PTE 234):

> Thus an ārya with knowingless wisdom intuits the signless ultimate reality. In the ultimate reality, there is no absence of [things such as] the hare and the horse. As for wisdom, there is nothing to the utmost it does not reflect. For this reason, it meets [things] precisely [as they are]; it associates with things without affirming anything. Calm and in repose, it has no knowing, yet there is nothing that it does not know.

Wisdom knows the ultimate nature of all phenomena nondually. It also knows conventional truths whose emptinesses it apprehends. Being totally unencumbered by conception and elaboration of reified existence, this wisdom reflects all objects just as they are, just like a mirror that reflects everything without fabrication, reification, selection or rejection, affirmation or denigration. This wisdom knows in a way totally unlike worldly cognizers with their subjects and objects, discrimination, reasoning, assumptions, and theories. From the perspective of an ārya in meditative equipoise on emptiness, this worldly knowledge is mistaken and afflictive. Piṅgala says (PTE 235):

> All things are empty in nature. Since the worldly beings are upside down, they fabricate things and perceive them as real. The āryas with true insight know it is erroneous. Thus they know all things are empty and nonarising.

Being "upside down" worldly beings who perceive phenomena in a mistaken way, let's do our best to create the causes and conditions to gain an ārya's direct unmistaken realization of emptiness.

REFLECTION

1. Review the Madhyamaka topics as explained in the Chinese Sanlun school.
2. Which topics are explained in a way similar to the explanation according to Madhyamaka in Tibet?
3. Are there differences in how Madhyamaka is explained in China and Tibet? How does thinking about the differences help clarify your understanding of the Madhyamaka view?

Renewed Interest in Madhyamaka

The first half of the twentieth century saw renewed Chinese interest in Madhyamaka thought, prompted by several Chinese monks who studied with excellent teachers in Tibetan monasteries. One of these monks, Fazun Shih (1902–80), a brilliant scholar and translator, rendered some later Madhyamaka works from Tibetan to Chinese. His Dharma colleague Yinshun (1906–2005) read these translations. Candrakīrti's *Supplement* and Tsongkhapa's chapter on insight in the *Great Treatise on the Stages of the Path* had a strong impact on him. A prolific writer, Yinshun wrote a commentary on the *Treatise on the Middle Way* and explained the Madhyamaka view in many of his other works, sparking other Chinese Buddhists' interest in this philosophy.

For many centuries the Tathāgatagarbha doctrine as found in the Huayan tradition had been considered the highest teaching. However, Yinshun questioned the origins of some of the sūtras and commentaries explaining tathāgatagarbha. Stressing the importance of going back to Indian Buddhist sources, he emphasized the Madhyamaka view and saw the Tathāgatagarbha doctrine as one of the Buddha's skillful means—an expedient teaching that leads sentient beings to the ultimate teaching of Madhyamaka and the Perfection of Wisdom. In this way, Fazun and Yinshun revived the Madhyamaka school so that more practitioners are now learning and meditating on it, and more scholars are studying its principal texts. Nowadays there are monastics and lay practitioners who follow Madhyamaka philosophy and teach it in some of the Buddhist institutes in Taiwan.

16 | Buddhist Renewal

IN THE EARLY twentieth century an age of Buddhist reform and renewal began in China. This reflected the change occurring in many other areas of Chinese society at that time. Aside from the social, political, and economic chaos of the declining Qing dynasty, the 1911 Xinhai Revolution, and the Republican era that ensued, imperialistic European countries as well as Japan were challenging China. This awakened the Chinese to the problems in their own institutions, the difficulties of maintaining their own cultural and religious traditions, and the need for reform.

Buddhism was challenged in many ways. Encountering modernity and Western science, Buddhists wondered what role Buddhism played in these. The fall of the Qing dynasty stopped the imperial patronage and support of the Saṅgha. Many people—both monastic and lay—saw stagnation in the Saṅgha: monasteries had accumulated great tracts of land and wealth, monastic discipline had declined, as had the level of monastic education, and many monastics spent their time chanting at funerals for pay. The government, military, industry, and educational institutions wanted to confiscate the monasteries' land and buildings and use them for secular purposes—army barracks, schools, governmental offices, and so on, things that were desperately needed for China to find its place in a modernizing world.

This social change provoked a variety of reactions among Chinese citizens. Some people wanted to recover and strengthen native Chinese traditions. In this regard, reformers such as Taixu, who was perhaps the most well-known Chinese monk in the early twentieth century, wanted to return to the Buddhist scholasticism of the Tang dynasty as well as take up what was good about modernity, such as modern educational methods. A charismatic leader, Taixu sought to raise the prestige of Buddhism in society and to spread the Dharma. His method was to shift the focus of Buddhism from rituals to philosophical study, to incorporate the best from secular knowledge, and to be more socially engaged by using the Buddha's teachings to benefit people here and now. He began new educational institutes for the Saṅgha and renewed the study of Madhyamaka texts translated by Kumārajīva in the fourth and fifth centuries and Yogācāra texts translated by Xuanzang in the seventh century.

Beginning around the time of the conference of the World Parliament of Religions held in Chicago in September 1893, Buddhists slowly started to expand their identity so that it was no longer strictly bound to their particular Buddhist tradition, their own monastery, or their own teacher. Taixu advocated this approach to spread the Dharma and unify the Saṅgha nationally and internationally. To that end he traveled to Europe and throughout Asia, making contacts with Buddhists of other traditions and establishing branches of the World Buddhist Studies Institute. He encouraged Chinese students to go to Tibet, Japan, and Sri Lanka to study and set up seminaries in China where Tibetan, Japanese, and Pāli scriptures were taught.

Observing monastics performing many rituals for the deceased and for spirits and beings in other realms, Taixu sought to shift the focus of the Saṅgha to benefiting human beings in the present. He saw Buddhists chanting in order to be born in a pureland in future lives and wanted to bring the emphasis of Buddhist practice back to benefiting sentient beings here and now. Rather than having his disciples do rituals to appease the gods and spirits, he directed them to learn the Dharma. Thus he formulated "Humanistic Buddhism" (*renjian fojiao*), which stresses the importance of cultivation in this life, improving human society, and creating a pureland on earth.

Taixu expressed his philosophy for revitalizing Chinese Buddhism: "When I herein speak of the renewal of the status of Chinese Buddhism, [I mean we should] take Chinese Buddhism, which has evolved and changed over two thousand years, as the base, and then when encountering China's present and future needs, absorb and choose the special characteristics of Buddhism from each time and each place."[141] He respected and wanted to maintain Chinese Buddhist doctrines, and at the same time supplement them with knowledge gained from other Buddhist traditions. Furthermore, he wanted Chinese Buddhist forms to be suitable for a modernizing society in order to attract the respect and participation of the younger generation. To bring this about, he reformed monastic education and promoted Buddhist social-welfare projects.

Taixu's wish to revitalize, popularize, and spread Buddhism met with many challenges. In the first quarter of the twentieth century, Confucian thinkers asserted Confucianism to be the unique Chinese approach that was best suited to interact with a changing world. Confucians such as Liang Shuming (1893–1988) dismissed Buddhism as irrelevant to helping China confront modernity and Westernization. Although Liang saw Buddhist teachings as being the most profound, he said that because they emphasized introspection and preparing for future lives, spreading them would inhibit China's modernization.[142]

Taixu saw things differently; his task was to convince China's intellectuals and leaders of the value of his view. Later, during the turbulent years when Republicans and Communists were battling for control physically and philosophically, he faced the challenge of helping Buddhism negotiate the changing political climate in China. Challenges also arose from Christian missionaries, both in China before 1949 and in Taiwan after that, as well as from secular culture, consumerism, and the media.

Several well-known monks who worked with Taixu or shared his ideals made significant contributions in this area as well. For example, at one government meeting to discuss religious reform during the Republican Period, Master Xuyun (Empty Cloud) single-handedly stopped a government decision to allow monks to get married, as many non-Buddhists had suggested. Buddhists opposed this but were afraid to speak out. Because Xuyun was well respected by Buddhists and government officials alike, he successfully spoke out against this policy, which would have been catastrophic for Buddhism in China. Xuyun (1840–1959) and Laiguo (1881–1953) helped to preserve the Chan lineage in those turbulent times. Their awakening stories are recorded.

Nowadays Chinese Buddhism has adopted the Humanistic Buddhism of Taixu and Yinshun based on the idea of creating a pureland on Earth. This multilayered approach seeks to purify the world we live in by enacting the bodhisattvas' deeds as well as to purify our minds through meditation and concentration.

Fazun and the Sino-Tibetan Buddhist Studies Institute

Among the seminaries Taixu began was the World Buddhist Institute's Sino-Tibetan Buddhist Studies Institute in Chongqing, which for many years was directed by his disciple Fazun. This institute was open from 1932 to 1950, but unfortunately succumbed to the turmoil of the communist takeover of China. Fazun was a brilliant Chinese monk who had studied in Tibet—and was admitted to Drepung Monastery—from 1925 to 1934.[143] Inspired by the dedication and sacrifices of the ancient Chinese translators who brought the Dharma to China centuries ago, he delved into the study of the great treatises of the Nālandā tradition, and Tsongkhapa's works in particular, and translated many texts from Tibetan into Chinese—both Indian treatises that had not been previously translated and Tibetan commentaries. Among his excellent translations were Candrakīrti's *Madhyamakāvatāra* and Tsongkhapa's *Lamrim Chenmo.*

In addition to his translation work, Fazun established a curriculum at the Sino-Tibetan Buddhist Studies Institute that included intense study of both Tibetan language and the great treatises studied at Gelug monasteries in a liberal and progressive academic atmosphere. Taixu's emphasis on the international aspect of Buddhism made Chinese monastics receptive and eager to learn these treatises. Fazun's work was well received also because the Madhyamaka and Yogācāra texts that he translated supported the rejuvenation of the study of China's centuries-old Yogācāra and Madhyamaka texts. This was one expression of Taixu's idea of "mutual benefit," with Chinese Buddhism being enriched by texts in the Tibetan canon and Tibetan Buddhism benefiting from texts in the Chinese canon.

Fazun introduced new educational methods and new material into Chinese seminaries. He also promoted what he considered to be the correct form of Buddhist philosophy. Referring to the wrong views of Hva Shang Mahāyāna—the Chinese monk who taught "mindless chanting" and "thoughtless meditation" and who was defeated in the debates at Samye, Tibet, at the end of the eighth century—Fazun said, "This is also a major cause of the teaching's decline, because those who have this misconception do not recognize the classic scriptures and their commentaries to be instructions and therefore belittle their value."

Fazun became a great translator of important texts written by Indian and

Tibetan scholar-adepts from Tibetan into Chinese,[144] especially after he moved to Beijing in 1950. Unfortunately, many of them were not published and were subsequently destroyed during the Cultural Revolution.

In addition to supporting Fazun in translating numerous Tibetan texts, the Sino-Tibetan Buddhist Studies Institute also published Tibetan grammar books, as well as Fazun's *The Political and Religious History of the Tibetan People* (*Xizang minzu zhengjiao shi*). Printed around 1940, this book explained Tibetan history from the Tibetan point of view.[145] In this book, Fazun introduced aspects of Tibetan history and Tibetan interpretations of events that were not well known in China. He explained that Tibetans saw Buddhism coming into Tibet primarily from India and felt a strong connection to the Indian sources. This was contrary to some Chinese assumptions that Tibetan Buddhism was due solely to the marriage of the Chinese princess Wencheng and the Tibetan king Songtsen Gampo in 641 and the Chan monks who went to Tibet in later centuries. This book may not have sat well with the Sinocentric version of history held by many Chinese; those who had a high regard for the Marxist approach to history did not like it either.

The Interface between Tibetan and Chinese Buddhism

During the Republican period in China (1911–49), Buddhist institutes sprung up. They expanded monastic education and involved more lay people in the study, practice, and propagation of the Dharma. These changes reinvigorated Chinese Buddhism. Three of these institutes were the Chinese School of Buddhist Doctrine (Zhina neixue yuan), begun in 1921 and led by Ouyang Jian (1871–1943); the Society of the Third Time (Sanshi xuehui), founded in 1927 and directed by Han Qingjing (1884–1949); and Wuchang Buddhist College, started in 1922 by Taixu (1889–1947). These Buddhist institutes nurtured the next generation of scholars, among whom were Lu Cheng (1896–1989), Han Jingqing (1912–2003), and Fazun. Interested in Tibetan Buddhism and fluent in Tibetan language, these three scholars contributed greatly to the translation of Tibetan Buddhist works into Chinese and to the spread of those teachings in China.

What stimulated this new interest in Tibetan Buddhism? In part it surely had to do with the general trend in China at that time of assessing China's social institutions and role in the modern world. In addition, some of these Chinese Buddhist scholars were questioning the Sinification of Buddhism that had gone on for the previous thousand years. They wanted to reassess traditional Chinese Buddhist doctrines by examining their Indian roots, and since Tibet had preserved the Nālandā tradition from India, interest arose in the Indian texts found in the Tibetan canon.

The scholar Lu Cheng compiled a list of works in the Tibetan canon that he thought must be translated into Chinese to expand Buddhist material available to Chinese practitioners and scholars. Similarly, he listed texts in the Chinese canon that he recommended be translated into Tibetan so that Tibetans would better understand Chinese Buddhism. In this way, both communities would be enhanced by having texts from India that heretofore had not been translated into their language. Lu Cheng also translated Indian texts from Tibetan into Chinese and edited a concise version of the Chinese Tripiṭaka with references to the Sanskrit, Pāli, and Tibetan texts.[146]

Han Jingqing founded the Maitreya Center in Beijing and taught Buddhist philosophy there.[147] Many of his translations—which include the major works of Dignāga, Dharmakīrti, and Sthiramati—are still unpublished. Other translators were also busy, including Yang Huaqun, who translated Dharmakīrti's *Drop of Reasoning*, and Liu Xiaolan, who translated Vasubandhu's *Exposition on the Three Natures.*

Nenghai (1886–1967) was another of the Chinese monastics who learned the Tibetan language and studied in Tibet during the Republican period. He studied with Kangsar Rinpoche at Drepung Gomang Monastery in Tibet, and after returning to China he established several monasteries where Tibetan Buddhism formed the mainstay of the curriculum and practice.

There was increased interest among Chinese lay followers in Tibetan Buddhism too, especially in tantra. As a result, several Tibetan lamas toured and taught in China. They and their Chinese disciples also translated and published tantric materials. The Republican period saw the establishment of several institutes in different areas of China for the study and practice of Tibetan Buddhism; some were oriented toward monastics, others toward lay followers.

As part of the ongoing Buddhist renewal, in the twentieth century there arose the Critical Buddhism movement when some scholars began to reexamine traditional doctrines of Chinese Buddhism—such as original awakening and buddha essence—and question if they were in accord with the Buddha's teachings on emptiness and selflessness. There was also discussion about the Yogācāra doctrine of the Faxiang school of Xuanzang and Kuiji, which many people regard as the foundation of authentic Buddhism. In some cases, their doubts centered around the authenticity of the texts that these doctrines are based on, such as *Awakening of Faith*; in other instances, they questioned the traditional Chinese interpretation of authentic sūtras, Indian treatises, and commentaries. Some scholars advocated returning to Buddhism's Indian roots to understand the correct view. In contrast, others such as Taixu accepted the tathāgatagarbha scriptures, including *Awakening of Faith*, as authentic Buddhist scriptures, and proposed a new interpretation of the tathāgatagarbha doctrine and original-awakening theory in which there was no notion of sentient beings as already awakened with all the Buddha's qualities present in their minds.

Chinese Buddhism in the Twentieth Century

Taixu's thought has had a major impact on prominent Chinese masters in the twentieth and twenty-first centuries who reestablished Buddhism in Taiwan and did their best to preserve it in China. Taixu's disciple Yinshun was very impressed with Tsongkhapa's works and organized his own text, *The Way to Buddhahood*, by speaking of three levels of motivation as Tsongkhapa did in his *Great Treatise*. In his works on emptiness, Yinshun principally cites Nāgārjuna's *Commentary on the Great Perfections of Wisdom*, but also quotes the *Great Treatise* as well as Fazun's new translation of Candrakīrti's *Supplement*. His emphasis on Madhyamaka and the perfection of wisdom generated renewed interest in this view among Chinese Buddhists. Yinshun also taught many of the teachers of Humanistic Buddhism in the modern Buddhist revival in Taiwan.

These two masters, Taixu and Yinshun, differed in their reaction to the academic study of Buddhism in colleges and universities. Taixu was enthusiastic about the rational approach in academia and its potential to stimulate Chinese Buddhism, yet he was also hesitant to completely embrace academia because academics' critical approach challenged the authority of Chinese Buddhism and the Chinese rendering of Buddhist history. Taixu sought to use academia and science to connect the internationally diverse Buddhist traditions, and at the same time to show the distinct and special features of Chinese Buddhist thought.

Yinshun, on the other hand, returned to the Indian source material and adopted the critical approach of academia. Yinshun believed in the truth and constancy of the Buddha's message of the Dharma, but he also realized that the Buddha and those who followed him needed to use skillful means to make the teachings interesting and accessible to the audience at different times and places. He saw these adaptations in general as being true to the Dharma and useful, but he was concerned that, if carried to excess, they would lead to the degeneration of Buddhism. To discriminate between appropriate and deviant adaptations he advocated that we first discern the fundamental points of the Buddhadharma and the Buddha's unique insights into the four truths. Then by tracing Buddhism's historical development, we will know the adaptations that occurred in different places, cultures, and historical periods.[148] Following this, critical analysis should be applied to discern adaptations that embodied Buddhist principles but manifested them in ways that suited the time, place, and people, from adaptations that deviated from Buddhist principles and teachings. Then we must go about eliminating the deviant practices and theories and encouraging the ones that are true to the Buddha's teachings.

Among the many good monastic teachers in Taiwan today, four are known for their contribution to Buddhist teachings and to the reestablishment of Buddhadharma in Taiwan. Hsing Yun (b. 1927) founded the Fo Guang Shan Buddhist organization, which is now the largest Buddhist temple in Taiwan with hundreds of branches in Taiwan and internationally. His monastic and lay disciples focus on Humanistic Buddhism and engage in projects to serve society: they have established several colleges and schools, as well as orphanages, homes for the elderly, and drug detox centers. Hsing Yun has published many books that help people apply Buddhist principles in their daily lives.

Sheng Yen (Shengyan, 1931–2009) was a Chan master and a Buddhist scholar who published many academic articles and books. He founded the Institute of Chung-Hwa Buddhist Culture in New York, the Institute of Chung-Hwa Buddhist Studies, and the Dharma Drum Mountain. The latter consists of a monastery, a Buddhist institute for monastics, and a college for graduate and post-graduate studies in Buddhism and Buddhist informatics.

Wei Chueh (Weijue, 1928–2016) founded the Lin Quan Temple and Chung Tai Chan Monastery where he organized many Chan retreats and became known for his lucid teaching style, emphasizing both scriptural understanding and Chan meditation.

Cheng Yen (Zhengyan, b. 1937) is a Buddhist nun, teacher, and philanthropist. Early in her monastic life she did retreat in the mountains, making one bow for each word of the *Lotus Sūtra*. She too emphasizes Humanistic Buddhism and founded the Buddhist Compassion Relief Tzu Chi Foundation, a worldwide Buddhist charity that includes hospitals, medical colleges, and relief work for natural disasters. Environmentally aware, Tzu Chi makes blankets from discarded plastic and teaches recycling and reuse to eliminate waste. It also has a satellite television station that airs programs twenty-four hours a day and features motivational talks to Cheng Yen's disciples every morning and evening.

Jinghui (1933–2013) was a student of the revered Chan master Xuyun (Hsu Yun, popularly called Empty Cloud, 1840–1959). He remained in mainland China and became the abbot of two temples in Hubei Province and served as the vice president of the Buddhist Association of China. He conducted Chan meditation retreats and taught the Chan theory and practice.

These and other masters have dedicated their lives to the Buddhadharma in different ways and are shining examples of unwavering devotion and diligence. There are other, smaller Buddhist monasteries that are also very active, notably the Luminary Buddhist Monastery and Institute founded by Bhikṣuṇī Wuyin, who is respected for her training and education of bhikṣuṇīs. She and her bhikṣuṇī disciples have been instrumental in teaching Vinaya to Western nuns.

Buddhism in Contemporary China and Taiwan

Buddhism in present-day Chinese cultural areas is diverse. Many temples and monasteries in China proper were destroyed during the Cultural Revolution, their monastics being forced to return to lay life or go into hiding.[149] Now temples are being rebuilt and some Buddhist institutes opened in China, but as in Tibet, the government maintains a level of control over monastics, who are sometimes relegated to being tour guides for visiting tourists. The government appoints or changes abbots, and monastics cannot freely give Dharma talks outside of monasteries without government approval. One reason some monasteries are deficient in Dharma is that after the Cultural Revolution there has been a severe shortage of well-trained elders to teach the current generation of saṅgha members. In recent years the government has ordered the destruction of buildings in some large Buddhist institutes, such as Larung Gar, and forced some monastics to disrobe. Some Buddhist masters who live in Taiwan now go on teaching tours in Mainland China.

Buddhism is flourishing in Taiwan. There are temples, monasteries, and now Dharma centers. Chan and Pureland are the most popular practices. Some Chinese temples have introduced meditation as taught in the Theravāda tradition, which they do in addition to traditional Chinese rituals and chanting. A few have incorporated teachings from the Tibetan tradition, although those who are interested in Tibetan Buddhism usually attend a Tibetan Dharma center in Taiwan or study in Dharamsala, India.

Many large temples in Taiwan emphasize social-welfare projects that benefit the impoverished and the ill. Some temples operate television and radio stations that broadcast Dharma talks and other Buddhist programs. Some Buddhist organizations have started Buddhist universities as well as elementary and high schools that are open to children no matter their religion. Many have begun publishing companies, which they use to produce and distribute Buddhist books, videos, and audio recordings of Dharma teachings, often for free distribution.

Taixu's and Yinshun's differing views on academia have influenced the present development of Buddhism in Taiwan, where a university education in Buddhism is highly regarded. Many monastics have gone and still go to Japan for their Buddhist education. In recent years more Chinese monastics have attended Western universities to study Buddhism as well as Sanskrit, Pāli, and Tibetan languages. In previous years, going to a university abroad was seen as superior to studying in a monastery. However, in recent years more and more Chinese Buddhist monasteries are establishing their own institutes of higher education, many of which have received university accreditation.

Notes

1. The Mahāyāna consists of four bodhisattva paths—the paths of accumulation, preparation, seeing, and meditation—as well as the buddha path—the path of no-more-learning.
2. Chapters 4 and 5 of *Searching for the Self* describe the main tenets of each of the Buddhist tenet systems, including their assertions on veiled and ultimate truths.
3. For translations of Tsongkhapa's *Middle Stages of the Path* and *Great Treatise on the Stages of the Path*, see TT and LC, respectively.
4. See chapter 8 of *The Foundation of Buddhist Practice* for more on the eight worldly concerns, the disadvantages of our attachment and aversion toward them, and how to overcome these exaggerated emotional reactions that consume so much of our life.
5. For more on first-link ignorance, see chapter 7 of *Saṃsāra, Nirvāṇa, and Buddha Nature.*
6. Superficial causes of error are, for example, hallucinations caused by drugs, seeing the scenery move because you're in a moving vehicle, or a dysfunctional ear faculty or eye faculty so that you don't hear properly or see correctly. Deeper causes of error are, for example, grasping inherent existence.
7. All consciousnesses exist conventionally and from this perspective are called "conventional consciousnesses" even if their object is emptiness, an ultimate truth. As explained in chapter 3, consciousnesses perceiving emptiness may be called "ultimate consciousnesses," but they are not actual ultimates. Only emptiness is an actual ultimate.
8. See chapter 4 of *In Praise of Great Compassion.*
9. For more about what can and cannot bear analysis and what is found and not found by ultimate analysis, see chapter 8 of *Realizing the Profound View.*
10. It is unclear if Rāhula refers to the arhat with that name or to the Buddha's son who was a monk.
11. For more about emptiness dawning as the meaning of dependent arising and dependent arising dawning as the meaning of emptiness, see chapters 9 and 10 in *Realizing the Profound View.*
12. This verse is chanted often in Tibetan monasteries. The English phonetics for it are: *Ma sam jo may sherab parol chin/ Makye migag namkhai ngowo nyi/ So sor rang rig yeshe choyulwa/ Du sum gyalway yum la chag tsal lo.*

13. A probing awareness may be conceptual or nonconceptual. An example of the latter is an ārya's nonconceptual meditative equipoise that directly and nonconceptually realizes emptiness. Although this mind is not actively probing or analyzing, it is based on having done so and is a union of serenity and insight.
14. This list is from MP 386–87.
15. Panchen Sonam Dragpa, who wrote the textbooks for Drepung Loseling and Gaden Shartse Monasteries, differs. He claims that true cessation and nirvāṇa have different objects of negation: a true cessation is the absence of an affliction, whereas an emptiness is the absence of inherent existence. Thus a true cessation is an ultimate truth but not an emptiness. In this way, he asserts two types of ultimate truths: true cessations and emptinesses.
16. For more on how defilements are removed on the śrāvaka and solitary-realizer paths, see chapter 7 of *Courageous Compassion*, and for how they are removed on the bodhisattva path, see chapters 8–10 of *Courageous Compassion*. For more about nirvāṇa, see chapter 11 of *Saṃsāra, Nirvāṇa, and Buddha Nature.*
17. For more on the natural purity of the mind, see chapters 13 and 14 of *Saṃsāra, Nirvāṇa, and Buddha Nature.*
18. For more on objects negated by the path and objects negated by reasoning, see chapter 8 of *Searching for the Self.*
19. Please review chapter 2 of *The Foundation of Buddhist Practice* and chapter 6 of *Searching for the Self.*
20. "Self" can refer to the conventionally existent I or to inherent existence, depending on the context. Here it refers to an inherently existent I or to inherent existence in general, not to a conventional I.
21. The literal translation of *lha'i ngar rgyal* is "divine pride." Here "pride" means self-confidence.
22. See chapter 2 of *The Foundation of Buddhist Practice* for more about reliable cognizers and other types of awarenesses.
23. Nothing is findable when searched for on the ultimate level because nothing exists inherently. In this case, the existence of water in the mirage does not require ultimate analysis to be refuted. Another person's correct conventional cognizer knows there is no water there.
24. For more on the Sāṃkhya tenets, see Sopa and Hopkins, *Cutting through Appearances*, 158–67.
25. See part 2 of FEW for more about Dolpopa's view and the Gelug Prāsaṅgikas' refutation of it.
26. Only emptiness appears to a nondualistic wisdom realizing emptiness. This mind correctly apprehends its apprehended object, emptiness.
27. See chapter 14 in *Realizing the Profound View* for more on the *Kaccānagotta Sutta* (*Advice to Kātyāyana Sūtra*) in Sanskrit.
28. For more about this example, see Cabezón, *A Dose of Emptiness*, 334–45.
29. From the viewpoint that the same object, the fluid, is viewed in three different ways, we could say that there is one basis of designation that has three different

designations. But from the viewpoint that there are three designated objects, we could say there are three bases of designation.

30. In this example, the fluid is seen differently by the three beings. However, in other cases, the beings of one realm may not see something in a place where beings of another realm see an obstructive object. For example, humans may see a flowing river while hungry ghosts see just a dry riverbed. The human beings cannot cross that area due to the deep water, but the hungry ghosts can easily walk across the dry riverbed.
31. Other ancient monastic universities in India and Bangladesh include Vikramaśīla (Bihar), Valabhi (Gujarat), Odantapurī (Bihar), Taxila (Punjab), Somapura (Bengal), Pushpagiri (Orissa), and Jagaddala (Bangladesh).
32. See chapter 5 of *Searching for the Self* for more on the criteria various tenet systems employ to discern definitive and interpretable scriptures.
33. These are: (1) rely principally not on the person but on the teaching, (2) with respect to the teaching, rely not on mere words but on their meaning, (3) with respect to the meaning, rely not on the interpretable meaning but on the definitive meaning, and (4) with respect to the definitive meaning, rely neither on sense consciousnesses nor on conceptual consciousnesses but on the nondual wisdom that realizes emptiness directly and nonconceptually. See chapter 8 of *Approaching the Buddhist Path*.
34. Tsongkhapa said that beginning with Bhāvaviveka, Svātantrika Mādhyamikas accepted the *Sūtra Unraveling the Thought* as definitive although their interpretations of it differed from that of the Yogācāra. Bhāvaviveka believed the Buddha did not teach the nonexistence of external objects.
35. The *Pratyutpanna Buddha Saṃmukhāvasthita Samādhi Sūtra*, translated from the Tibetan by Paul Harrison, PhD diss., Australian National University, 1979, p. 37. This sūtra is an early Mahāyāna sūtra, which probably came to be known around the first century BCE. It is found in both the Tibetan and Chinese canons. It was first translated from Sanskrit to Chinese by the Kushan Buddhist monk Lokakṣema in 179 CE.
36. It is said that Asaṅga's own beliefs accord with Madhyamaka, as shown in his commentary on the *Sublime Continuum* (*Uttaratantra*, aka *Ratnagotravibhāga*). It's not unusual to say that a revered teacher wrote a text from the viewpoint of a particular tenet system to benefit certain disciples although his personal beliefs accord with another tenet system. Such is also the case with Asaṅga's brother Vasubandhu, who wrote the *Treasury of Knowledge* from the Vaibhāṣika perspective and the commentary on that text from the Sautrāntika perspective, whereas he was actually a Yogācārin and authored texts from that perspective as well. Tibetans say the *Sublime Continuum* was composed by Maitreya and transmitted by Asaṅga; the Chinese say it was composed by Sāramati.
37. For more on latencies and their being neutral, see chapter 5 of *Saṃsāra, Nirvāṇa, and Buddha Nature*.
38. See p. 60 of *The Foundation of Buddhist Practice* for more on the five similarities.

39. See chapter 2 of *Saṃsāra, Nirvāṇa, and Buddha Nature* for more on the god realms.
40. It is not clear whether the Reasoning Proponents say that the potency that is the observed object condition and the potency that is the empowering condition for a sense consciousness are on the mental consciousness or a preceding sense consciousness of a similar type.
41. The notion of latencies and seeds differs in the various tenet systems. In terms of how karma is carried, Vaibhāṣikas do not speak of karmic seeds or latencies. Some Vaibhāṣikas assert an abstract composite called "acquisition" (*prāpti*, T. *'thob pa*) that is bound to the mental continuum, and other Vaibhāṣikas assert an abstract composite named "non-wastage" (*avipraṇāśa*, T. *chud mi za ba*), which is like a guarantor for a debt. Sarvāstivādins say that physical and verbal actions are imperceptible forms that continue to exist and are capable of producing effects. Sautrāntikas introduce the notion of karmic seeds, which Yogācārins and Mādhyamikas also accept. Yogācārins expand on the notion of seeds and latencies, saying that karmic seeds influence sentient beings' rebirth, experiences, habits, and which environment they are reborn into, whereas other latencies are the substantial cause for a cognition and the object cognized. Although all other systems accept seeds and latencies as inherently existent, Prāsaṅgikas assert that they are empty of inherent existence.
42. Tsongkhapa states in his *Ocean of Eloquence* (OOE 74):

    [Question:] Are such residual latencies as these substantially the same as, or separate from, the consciousness that is their basis?

    [Answer:] Those residual latencies are neither substantially the same as nor different from the basis.

    [Question:] Why are they not the same?

    [Answer:] They are not the same because (a) seeds would then have an objective support (*ālambana*) and aspect (*ākāra*) [as does a consciousness], (b) the seeds of the five states of rebirth would get muddled up, and (c) the realms would get muddled up as well.
43. Annotated translation of this text is in Cabezón, *A Dose of Emptiness*, 62.
44. Hopkins, *Reflections on Reality*, 220–21.
45. The latencies of the view of self are usually said to cause the afflictive mentality to view the foundation consciousness and think "I." Here it seems the meaning of the term is extended to include apprehending that objects exist by their own character as the referent of conceptual consciousnesses.
46. We may think that our visual consciousness perceives a turtle's moustache and external objects, so such consciousnesses must exist. However, a turtle's moustache and external objects do not exist, so they cannot be perceived. Therefore consciousnesses that "perceive" them also do not exist. We are merely perceiving the appearance of such nonexistent objects. That false appearance and the consciousness perceiving the false appearance exist.
47. Appearances of being established by their own character as the basis of entity (as

in "this is a table") and attribute (as in "this is the color of the table") are existent imaginaries.

48. For Yogācārins *ultimately existent* means existing by its own character without being posited through the force of conventions. *Existence by its own character* means having some mode of existing by its own character. While other-powered natures exist this way, they don't exist by their own character *as referents or bases of terms and concepts. Existing from its own side* means existing without being merely imputed by conception.
49. See Hopkins, *Absorption in No External World* and *Reflections on Reality.*
50. Although Yogācārins speak of common objects, it is difficult to pinpoint what a common object could be.
51. William Magee, "A Tree in the West: Competing Tathāgatagarbha Theories in Tibet." *Chung-Hwa Buddhist Journal* 19 (2006): 445–511.
52. For more on affirming negations and nonaffirming negations, see *Realizing the Profound View,* 33–35. In brief, affirming negations negate one thing while affirming another. A having-ceased negates something existing now but affirms that it did exist in the past and ceased.
53. This chart explains the relationship between when the object is present and when the consciousness apprehending it is present, according to the presentation of the other tenet systems:

	FIRST MOMENT	SECOND MOMENT	THIRD MOMENT	FOURTH MOMENT
Visual object (pot)	Pot is not yet in the sphere of vison	Pot is the observed object condition of the first moment of visual consciousness apprehending pot	Pot is the observed object condition of the second moment of visual consciousness apprehending pot	Pot is the observed object condition of the third moment of visual consciousness apprehending pot
Visual consciousness	—	—	First moment of visual consciousness apprehending pot	Second moment of visual consciousness apprehending pot

54. *Mirror Clearly Reflecting the Meaning of the Middle Way: A Commentary Elucidating the Meaning of the Introduction to the Middle Way,* by the First Dalai Lama Gyalwa Gedun-drub, trans. Fedor Stracke (https://happymonkspublication.org

/wp-content/uploads/2018/07/HMP_Mirror-Clearly-Reflecting-the-Meaning-of-the-Middle-Way-ed7.pdf), 74.

55. For an extensive explanation of this, see Vose, *Resurrecting Candrakīrti.*
56. See Jeffrey Hopkins, "A Tibetan Delineation of Different Views of Emptiness in the Indian Middle Way School: Tsong-kha-pa's Two Interpretations of the *Locus Classicus* in Candrakīrti's *Clear Words* Showing Bhāvaviveka's Assertion of Commonly Appearing Subjects and Inherent Existence," *Tibet Journal* 14, no. 1 (1989): 10–43.
57. See *Saṃsāra, Nirvāṇa, and Buddha Nature* for more on the twelve links.
58. Buddhist essentialists have another way of describing substantial existence that is not an object of negation: substantially existent objects can be identified without depending on identifying another object. We can identify the color red without identifying anything else. However, to identify a person, we must cognize their body, speech, or mind first.
59. The term *svalakṣaṇa*, translated as self-character, own character, or specifically characterized, has different meanings depending on the context. To Vaibhāṣikas and Sautrāntikas it means the object is established by its own character as the referent of a conceptual consciousness. In another context, Sautrāntikas say it means appearing uniquely to an awareness and is synonymous with functioning thing. To Yogācārins it means existing from its own side without being merely imputed by terms and conception, and applies only to dependent and consummate phenomena. This means the object exists but is not merely posited by terms and concepts. Svātantrikas say that there is no existence by its own character as defined by Yogācārins because Yogācārins equate that with true existence, which Svātantrikas refute. Svātantrikas have their own description of existence by its own character: phenomena exist by their own mode of subsistence within their appearing to and being imputed by a nondefective awareness. They assert phenomena exist by their own character conventionally, but not ultimately.
60. See chapter 2 for an explanation of superficial causes of error.
61. *Tsong-kha-pa Lo-sang-drak-pa's Extensive Explanation of (Candrakīrti's) Supplement to (Nāgārjuna's) "Treatise on the Middle": Illumination of the Thought*, trans. Jeffrey Hopkins, unpublished manuscript, 115.
62. Some Prāsaṅgika scholars, however, say that because there is not a commonly appearing subject, an inference proving emptiness can be created only by a consequence.
63. If you wish to delve into some of these issues and learn more about the structure of syllogisms and consequences, see Lopez, *A Study of Svātantrika*, chap. 5.
64. For more on the eight approachers and abiders, see chapter 7 of *Courageous Compassion*.
65. Since the appearance of inherent existence cognized by sentient beings is an existent phenomenon and the Buddha knows all existents, it is said that he knows these mistaken appearances. However, he does not know them because his mind is mistaken but because he perceives what sentient beings perceive.
66. Apperception is rejected by the Vaibhāṣikas, Sautrāntika-Svātantrikas, and

Prāsaṅgikas because if it existed, the subject and object of a cognition would be confused. Some scholars say the Sautrāntika-Scripture Proponents also reject apperception.

67. For more on the diamond slivers refutation, see chapter 6 of *Realizing the Profound View.*
68. Some examples of a framework: When we say, "This happened before I was born," it locates an event in time in relation to the time of my birth. When I say, "When I was ten years old," it indicates a connection between me in the present and me in the past.
69. This topic is also discussed in the diamond slivers reasoning explained in chapter 6 of *Searching for the Self.*
70. Yogācāra-Svātantrikas assert that an object's emptiness of being an entity other than the reliable cognizer apprehending it is the coarse selflessness of phenomena. The emptiness of true existence of all phenomena is the subtle selflessness of phenomena.
71. For more on the way in which the tenet systems see the ignorance that is the root of saṃsāra, see chapters 3 and 7 in *Saṃsāra, Nirvāṇa, and Buddha Nature.*
72. Same entity here means they are the same in being virtuous, nonvirtuous, or neutral. Same time means they arise and cease at the same time.
73. Although Vasubandhu adopted the Vaibhāṣika perspective when writing the *Treasury of Knowledge* and the Sautrāntika perspective when writing his commentary on it, it is said that he was actually a Yogācārin. It was from the Yogācāra perspective that he refuted partless particles.
74. There is debate on this point. Jamyang Shepa asserts that Sautrāntika-Reasoning Proponents accept that minute particles have parts.
75. Here "end" refers to the last part of the continuum of an object; the end exists while the object exists. Once the last part or end part has ceased, the object has ended. For example, death is the end or last part of a life; death occurs during the life. Once death has been completed, the life has ceased and has thus ended.
76. See chapter 10 in *Realizing the Profound View* for the Buddha's intent and the culmination of analysis on the correct view.
77. See chapter 8 in *Realizing the Profound View* for an explanation of the three criteria to establish conventional existence.
78. See *Realizing the Profound View* to learn the various ways to refute inherent existence and to arrive at the correct view free from the extremes of absolutism and nonexistence.
79. The higher training of concentration is discussed in detail in chapters 6–10 in *Following in the Buddha's Footsteps.*
80. Please see chapter 6 in *Following in the Buddha's Footsteps* for the description of these three meditation objects.
81. Please see chapter 9 in *Approaching the Buddhist Path* for more about the four principles.
82. See chapter 2 in *The Foundation of Buddhist Practice* for more on the various types of reliable cognizers.

83. These are also called the four types of attention: the four types of attention or mental engagement explained in the context of cultivating serenity—tight focus, intermittent focus, uninterrupted focus, and spontaneous focus. See chapter 7 in *The Foundation of Buddhist Practice* for more on the four.
84. The *Kāśyapaparivarta Sūtra* is in the *Ratnakūṭa Sūtra*.
85. When using the breath to cultivate serenity, the sign or *nimitta* that appears as concentration deepens is the conceptual appearance of the breath that is appearing to that conceptual consciousness. This is the actual meditation object of serenity, not the breath itself.
86. The Tibetan word *mi rtog pa* can also be translated as "nonconceptual," but that is not the meaning here.
87. The definitions of serenity and insight are from Jetsun Chokyi Gyaltsen.
88. Bhikkhu Soma, *The Way of Mindfulness: The Satipaṭṭhāna Sutta and Its Commentary* (Colombo, Sri Lanka: Ajirārāma Press, 1949), 19.
89. For a more in-depth explanation of illusion-like appearances, see chapter 11 of *Realizing the Profound View*.
90. See chapter 6 of *In Praise of Great Compassion* for an in-depth explanation of the three types of compassion that Candrakīrti spoke about.
91. This is similar to a meditation in Tibetan Buddhism where we are instructed to observe: Where did that thought come from? Where does it abide? Where does it go when it ceases?
92. See chapters 11 and 12 in *Searching for the Self* for more about serenity and insight as practiced in the Pāli tradition.
93. These are the ten imperfections as listed in Vism 20.105. The ten can be listed in different ways. See *Courageous Compassion*, 224, for a different list and more explanation of these ten imperfections.
94. Although we often think "path" refers to something outside of ourselves that we practice, as in "practicing the path" or "being on the path," in the Pāli tradition the sūtras consider the "path" as a course of action, whereas in the Pāli Abhidharma and commentaries, as well as in the Sanskrit tradition, a path is a consciousness with some level of realization.
95. This presentation of going from an ordinary being to a nonreturner is unusual, although it is also found in the Sarvāstivāda Abhidharma. Perhaps the object of meditation is what enables all five lower fetters to be eradicated at once. The meditator was in the first dhyāna, having attained that through suppressing the five hindrances, which include sensual desire and malice. This temporary weakening of those two hindrances in dhyāna could make it possible for them to be eradicated when first penetrating dhyāna with wisdom. Thus in addition to the three fetters that are usually removed with the first penetration of nirvāṇa, these other two are also cut off.

    There were many disciples who reached the stages of nonreturner and arhatship in a single life during the Buddha's lifetime, and presumably this occurred in later centuries as well. It isn't necessary to proceed through each stage in order over a period of lives. There are a number of ways to go from the state of an ordinary being to the state of an arhat. For example, some may actualize the path and fruit of each stage sequentially over a period of lives, culminating in arhatship. Someone with sharp faculties can quickly go to the fruit of nonreturner or even to arhatship. She first penetrates nirvāṇa and becomes a stream-enterer, the first stage of awakening. Quickly arising from that meditation, she immediately enters meditation again and attains the second stage, that of a once-returner. Again emerging from the meditation quickly and immediately entering meditation once more, she eradicates all five lower fetters and attains the third stage of awakening, that of a nonreturner. Whether this person has to pass through each path and fruit is an open question. The sūtra gives the impression that one goes directly to the higher path and fruit—either nonreturner or arhatship—but the commentary explains that one rapidly passes through each lower path and fruit sequentially.

96. The ten fetters are the five lower fetters plus desire for existence in the form realm, desire for existence in the formless realm, arrogance, restlessness, and ignorance. The pollutants are the pollutant of sensuality, the pollutant of existence, and the pollutant of ignorance. See chapter 3 in *Saṃsāra, Nirvāṇa, and Buddha Nature* for more on the fetters and pollutants.
97. There is one Chinese written language. Mandarin is the official dialect, one of the many spoken dialects of Chinese.
98. The rigorous Buddhologist Jan Nattier writes: "Where Kumārajīva's work can be compared with an extant Indic manuscript—that is, in those rare cases where part or all of a text he translated has survived in a Sanskrit or Prakrit version—a somewhat surprising result emerges. While his translations are indeed shorter in many instances than their extant (and much later) Sanskrit counterparts, when earlier Indic-language manuscript fragments are available they often provide exact parallels of Kumārajīva's supposed 'abbreviations.' What seems likely to have happened, in sum, is that Kumārajīva was working from earlier Indian versions in which these expansions had not yet taken place." See Nattier, *A Few Good Men: The Bodhisattva Path according to the Inquiry of Ugra (Ugraparipṛcchā)* (Honolulu: University of Hawai'i Press, 2003).
99. *Siddhānta* may also be translated as "tenets."
100. These teachings may talk about the six pāramitās but not completely expound wisdom or emptiness; they may promote the ten virtuous deeds and five precepts or scold the śrāvakas for being small-minded to encourage them to generate bodhicitta.
101. In Chinese, the term *fo-hsing* (buddha nature or buddha essence) is the translation of several terms—*buddhadhātu* (buddha element), *buddhagotra* (buddha nature or buddha lineage), *buddhagarbha* (buddha essence), and *tathāgatagarbha* (tathāgata essence). The meaning of these terms varies according to the context. Here, we are investigating the potential for all sentient beings to attain full awakening.
102. All references to the ten stages are from the *Awakening of Faith in the Mahāyāna* (*Dasheng oixin lun*). The reconstructed Sanskrit title is *Mahāyāna Śraddhotpādaśāstra*. It is usually attributed to Aśvaghoṣa, although not all scholars agree.

Although some scholars question the authenticity of this text, others praise it for embodying all aspects of Mahāyāna practice, including the six pāramitās, serenity and insight, a detailed analysis of subtle and coarse afflictions, levels of consciousness, and so forth. It is a masterpiece of organization, pulling all these themes together coherently. This text combines qualities of Tathāgatagarbha and Yogācāra. It became popular in China, Japan, and Korea, and practitioners from those countries wrote commentaries on it. It harmonizes the Tathāgatagarbha and Yogācāra doctrines.

103. The *Awakening of Faith* speaks of two kinds of suchness (C. *zhen ru*): that which transcends words and that which is predicated in words. Suchness that transcends words indicates that all things are just the one-mind and that phenomena are differentiated only due to deluded thinking. Suchness predicated on words has two aspects. The first is called the "truly empty because it is ultimately able to reveal what is real," and the second is called "the truly nonempty because it is in its very essence fully endowed with undefiled excellent qualities."

104. The word *jue* in the Chinese term *ben jue* can mean either awareness or awakening. So *ben jue* is sometimes translated as "original awakening." In this case, "primordially pure awareness" expresses the meaning better.

105. According to the subtlest passages of the *Śūraṃgama Sūtra*, the ultimate true-mind is inseparable from all phenomena and transcends the duality of self and others, permanence and change.

106. *The Śūraṅgama Sūtra, with Excerpts from the Commentary by the Venerable Master Hsüan Hua: A New Translation* (Ukiah, CA: Buddhist Text Translation Society, 2009), 52.

107. Original text from the Huayan Sūtra, CBETA 2022. Q1, T09, no. 278, 449c13–15. Translated by Bhikṣu Jian Hu, private correspondence, August 15, 2022.

108. "Hva Shang" is a title referring to an abbot or other esteemed person; "Hva Shang Mahāyāna" means a Mahāyāna abbot. H. H. the Dalai Lama says that during the time of Śāntarakṣita there were Chinese monks at Samye, and these monks were translating texts from Chinese into Tibetan. If they had had such distorted views of meditation, Śāntarakṣita would have refuted them himself and would not have asked Kamalaśīla to come in later years to debate with Hva Shang Mahāyāna. His Holiness's conclusion is that Hva Shang Mahāyāna's corrupted view of Chan was not shared by all Chinese practitioners.

Until the manuscript *On the Determination of the Right Tenets of Mahāyāna Sudden Awakening* was found in the Dunhuang caves, the Chinese had no record of this debate. This text records the actual Dharma exchanges between Hva Shang and Kamalaśīla and concludes that Hva Shang won the debate. Contemporary scholars have researched the debate, some concluding that there was not an actual debate but rather an extended correspondence between the two participants with many questions and answers about meditation.

109. In India it does not seem that a difference was made between Yogācāra, Vijñaptimātra, Vijñānavāda, and Cittamātra, although there are diverse ideas about the referents of these terms in China.

110. Chinese Buddhist historians call Yogācāra studies before Xuanzang "old Weishi," and those after Xuanzang that were based on his translations "new Weishi." "Weishi" means Consciousness-Only. "Faxiang" also refers to Yogācāra.
111. Woncheuk's commentary on the *Āryagambhīrasaṃdhinirmocana Sūtra* called *'Phags pa dgongs pa zab mo nges par 'grel pa'i mdo rgya cher 'grel pa* is found in the Tibetan Tengyur. The practice of outlining Dharma texts was already done in China; Woncheuk's commentary brought that practice to Tibet.
112. The Huichang persecution of Buddhism (841–46) harmed all Buddhist schools, especially those study-intensive ones whose important, foundational treatises were destroyed en masse, some not to be recovered from Japan until the nineteenth and twentieth centuries. Chan and Pureland survived better than others.
113. Dharmapāla (531–61) was an Indian monk and abbot of Nālandā. He was a great debater and, despite his short life, wrote several books that are now found in the Chinese canon. Xuanzang followed Dharmapāla's Yogācāra tradition, which was called the Faxiang school in China. This tradition was later transmitted to Japan by Dosho (629–710).
114. The *Śūraṃgama Sūtra* is considered primarily a Tathāgatagarbha sūtra with elements of Yogācāra and Madhyamaka. It mentions the foundation consciousness and afflictive consciousness, but only in a few places and without elaboration.
115. Aśvaghoṣa lived in first- or second-century India. There is no known extant Sanskrit version of the text, and it was not translated into Tibetan. The earliest versions of this text are in Chinese. Paramārtha is said to have translated it in 553. Śikṣānanda edited or translated another version of the text around 695–700.
116. In China, *Ratnagotravibhāga* and its commentary are said to be authored by the Indian scholar Sāramati (350–450). Sāramati seems to be unknown to the Tibetans. In the Tibetan tradition, this text is known as the *Sublime Continuum* (*Mahāyānottaratantra Śastra*). The root verses are said to be by Maitreya, and Asaṅga wrote a prose commentary on them. Some of the Tibetan commentaries on this text have been written by Dolpopa, Go Lotsawa, and Ju Mipham.
117. CBETA 2022. Q1, T12, no. 353, 221c13–23. Translated by Bhikṣu Jian Hu, private correspondence, August 15, 2022.
118. See chapter 14 in *Saṃsāra, Nirvāṇa, and Buddha Nature* for the Prāsaṅgika explanation of this verse.
119. *The Great Parinirvāṇa Sūtra*, trans. Charles Patton, redacted from the Chinese of *Dharmakshema* by Huiyan, Huiguan, and Xie Lingyun, T375.12.605a–611a (http://www.buddhism.org/Sutras/2/GreatParinirvana.htm).
120. These forms include hell beings, hungry ghosts, animals, human beings, asuras, and the many levels of devas.
121. See chapters 13 and 14 in *Saṃsāra, Nirvāṇa, and Buddha Nature*.
122. In fact, emptiness is not defiled; its nature is free from adventitious stains. In the case of sentient beings, the emptiness of their minds is said to be "defiled" because the mind, which is the base of that emptiness, is defiled and its emptiness is one nature with that mind.
123. Robert A. F. Thurman, *The Central Philosophy of Tibet: A Study and Translation*

of Jey Tsong Khapa's "Essence of True Eloquence" (Princeton, NJ: Princeton University Press, 1991), 347.

124. Yinshun's name for this system may also be translated as Empty-Name-Only (*xingkong weiming lun*). He also gives a more descriptive name, "the doctrinal system that establishes liberation and saṃsāra on the basis that the nature of all phenomena is empty and that all phenomena exist as mere provisional designations."
125. Piṅgala (aka Qingmu), also known as "Blue Eyes," is the author noted in the text. However, there has been much discussion among scholars about who Piṅgala actually was. See C. W. Huntington, "The 'Akutobhayā' and Early Indian Madhyamaka," 184–88; and Brian Bocking, *Nāgārjuna in China*, 395–405. Unfortunately the Sanskrit original of Piṅgala's commentary is no longer available.
126. Although in general the Tang dynasty saw a flourishing of Buddhism, under the Emperor Wuzong (814–46), a series of edicts were issued in 842–845 that decimated the Saṅgha. The Huang Chao Rebellion (874–884), while not specifically aimed against Buddhism, led to the destruction of many monasteries.
127. Thankfully, many Madhyamaka texts had been taken to Japan before the persecution, so almost a thousand years later, in the late Qing dynasty, they were brought back to China.
128. Kumārajīva greatly improved translation methods. Some academic scholars say that he omitted some material when he translated, and if his translations are compared to later Nepalese Sanskrit texts, this seems to be the case. However, if they are compared to early Sanskrit texts, it is clear that he did not omit anything in his translations.
129. For an English translation see Giuseppe Tucci, *Pre-Diṅnāga Buddhist Texts on Logic from Chinese Sources* (Nepal: Pilgrims Books House, 1998). Originally published as no. 49 in Gaekwad's Oriental series in Baroda by the Oriental Institute in 1929.
130. The identity of the Bodhisattva Vasu is unclear. Some say it is Vasubandhu, but many others doubt that is the case.
131. This text has been translated into English. See Dharmamitra, *Nāgārjuna's Treatise on the Ten Bodhisattva Grounds*.
132. Portions of Nāgārjuna's *Treatise on Wisdom* have been translated into English. See Dharmamitra, *Nāgārjuna on the Six Perfections*; and Smitheram, *Great Perfection of Wisdom Treatise*.
133. From an interview with Bhikṣu Houkuan Shih, May 17, 2009. The Sanskrit terms for the first and third qualities are educated guesses; none of the scholars I asked was sure what the Sanskrit and Tibetan terms are for these. The same is true for the Sanskrit equivalent for *zhen shi*.
134. *Vaśitva* also means self-mastery, self-command, freedom of will, power or dominion over all material elements. *Īśvara* also means owner, ruler, chief, to create and destroy at will.
135. Chinese translations, in general, are not as precise as Tibetan translations, in the sense that in a Tibetan translation one Sanskrit term has one Tibetan equiva-

lent term, so it is easy to translate back from Tibetan to Sanskrit. This is not the case in Chinese, however, due to differences in the fundamental structure of the language.

136. Nāgārjuna mentions these three types of designation in the *Treatise on Wisdom*, fascicle 41.
137. The Chinese translation of this verse reads: It is because of emptiness/ that all phenomena are possible./ Without emptiness/ no phenomenon is possible. Translation by Bhikṣu Jian Hu.
138. This is similar to the approach of the Sakya scholar Goram Sonam Senge (1429–89), who says that after refuting inherent existence, our innate grasping mind grasps emptiness as inherently existent. All contrived ideas thinking "This emptiness is the Madhyamaka view" is not the Madhyamaka view. All thought, even thinking "The person is empty of true existence," involves grasping true existence. While Tsongkhapa says that all thought is mistaken in that it is mediated by conceptual appearance, it does not necessarily grasp true existence. However, he agrees with Gorampa's point that inferential realization of emptiness, while being a positive and necessary step on the path, can in no way compare to the experience of direct nonconceptual realization of emptiness. At buddhahood all conceptual processes have ceased and the Buddha's wisdom remains.
139. These are ceasing and arising, discontinuation and permanence, coming and going, and difference and identity.
140. Compare this with Gorampa in his *Distinguishing the Views: Moonlight for the Main Points of the Mahāyāna* (unpublished translation by Guy Newland):

    But when refuting that [inherent existence], one may grasp at the emptiness of truth . . . So grasping emptiness must be refuted. Therefore since grasping both and grasping neither also must be refuted, it is impossible to find an object that can be grasped as any of the four extremes. The lack of any such grasping [at any of the four extremes of existence, nonexistence, both, and neither] is what is designated by the phrase "realizing the Madhyamaka view." But if one grasps at any extreme, saying, "This is the Madhyamaka view," then whether one grasps at emptiness, nonemptiness, or something else, one has not avoided grasping extremes, so it is not the Madhyamaka view.

141. Brenton Sullivan, "Venerable Fazun and His Influence on Life and Education at the Sino-Tibetan Buddhist Institute," MA thesis, University of Kansas, 2007, 76.
142. Interestingly, the year before Liang died, he publicly announced that he was a Buddhist but never told anyone for fear of being ridiculed. He accepted past, present, and future lives and said that in his previous life he was a Chan monk!
143. Several young Chinese monks went to Tibet around the same time as Fazun. One of them, Nenghai (1886–1967), upon his return to China established a monastery that followed Tsongkhapa's teachings. Another, Bisong (aka Xing Suzhi 1916–), traveled to Tibet in 1937. Studying at Drepung Monastery, in 1945 he

passed an examination before the regent of Tibet and became the first Chinese geshe lharampa. Today he lives in Los Angeles where he is active in the Buddhist community.

144. Among his excellent translations were Atiśa's *Lamp of the Path* (*Bodhipathapradīpa*), Tsongkhapa's *Great Treatise on the Stages of the Path, Great Treatise on the Stages of the Tantric Path* (C. *Mizongdao cidi guanglun*), and *Illuminating the Intent*, and Maitreya's *Distinguishing Dharma and Dharmatā* (*Dharmadharmatāvibhāga*). Of the five great treatises studied in Gelug monasteries, Vasubandhu's *Treasury of Knowledge* and Nāgārjuna's *Treatise of the Middle Way* had already been translated into Chinese long before Buddhism went to Tibet. Fazun translated the *Ornament of Clear Realization* (which in China was not considered one of Maitreya's works) and wrote a commentary on it, Dharmakīrti's *Commentary on Reliable Cognition* (C. *Facheng*) with a commentary by the First Dalai Lama, Dignāga's *Pramāṇasamuccaya*, Candrakīrti's *Supplement to the "Treatise on the Middle Way"* (C. *Yuecheng*), and Tsongkhapa's *Explanation of the Bhikshu Precepts* (C. *Bichu xuechu*).

145. Fazun relied on Tibetan sources such as Butön's religious and political *History of Buddhism in Tibet* (fourteenth century) and Tukwan Lobsang Chokyi Nyima's (1732–1802) *History of the Origin and Development of the Religions*.

146. Among Lu Cheng's translations from Tibetan into Chinese are Dignāga's *Pramāṇasamuccaya* and *Hetucakraḍamaru*; he also retranslated Asaṅga's *Compendium of the Mahāyāna* and Dignāga's *Alambanaparīkṣā* into Chinese.

147. Among Jingqing's translations from Tibetan into Chinese are Asaṅga's *Compendium of the Mahāyāna*; Vasubandhu's *Exposition on the Three Natures* (*Trisvabhāvanirdeśa*), which he wrote a commentary on; Vasubandhu's commentary on *Distinguishing Dharma and Dharmatā*; Dharmakīrti's *Drop of Reasoning* (*Nyāyabindu*); Sāgaramegha's commentary on the *Bodhisattva Grounds*; and others. He wrote a commentary on *Treatise on the Establishment of the Doctrine of Mind Only* (*Vijñaptimātratāsiddhi Śāstra*) and translated works from later Indian writers, including Kamalaśīla, Vimuktisena, and others.

148. Here Yinshun described the development of Buddhism in India in five stages: (1) the śrāvaka-based period when practitioners sought liberation, (2) the bodhisattva-inclined period that branched off from the śrāvaka tradition, (3) the bodhisattva-based period when both the śrāvaka and bodhisattva traditions were taught, (4) the tathāgatagarbha-inclined period that branched off from the bodhisattva tradition, and (5) the tathāgatagarbha-based period when Buddhism adopted theistic beliefs and worship.

149. For example, when I (Chodron) visited mainland China in 1994, I met some Chinese nuns who, during the Cultural Revolution, were forced to walk through their town wearing dunce caps and placards that disparaged Buddhism. Their temple was confiscated by the government and turned into a warehouse. During this time they lived with their families and did not wear robes, but kept their precepts.

When the political climate changed years later, they put on their robes and began living together as a saṅgha community again.

150. Sometimes the second type of dependent arising is said to be dependence on parts.

Glossary

absolutism (eternalism or view of permanence, *śāśvatānta*, *bhavadiṭṭhi*, T. *rtag lha*). The belief that phenomena inherently exist.

abstract composites (*viprayukta-saṃskāra*, T. *ldan min 'du byed*). Impermanent phenomena that are neither forms nor consciousnesses.

acquired afflictions (*parikalpita*, T. *kun btags*). Afflictions learned in this life through contact with false philosophies and psychologies.

acquisition (*prāpti*, T. *'thob pa*). Asserted by Vaibhāṣikas, it is an abstract factor that is like a rope ensuring that karma attaches to the person's mindstream and will go to the next life.

adventitious (*āgantuka*, T. *glo bur*). In Buddhism: not in the nature of the mind.

affirmative negation (*paryudāsapratiṣedha*, T. *ma yin dgag*). A negation that is realized upon explicitly eliminating an object of negation and projects an affirmative or positive phenomenon in the wake of that negation.

afflictions (*kleśa*, T. *nyon mongs*). Mental factors that disturb the tranquility of the mind. These include disturbing emotions and wrong views.

afflictive consciousness (I-consciousness, *kliśtamanas*, T. *nyon yid*). Asserted by Yogācāra-Scripture Proponents: observing the foundation consciousness, it generates the sense of a self-sufficient substantially existent person and grasps the person to exist in this way.

afflictive ignorance (*kliṣṭāvidya*, T. *ngon mongs can gyi ma rig pa*). Lower schools: grasping a self-sufficient substantially existent person and all other coarser forms of ignorance that prevent liberation. Prāsaṅgikas do not differentiate afflictive and unafflictive ignorance because they assert all ignorance is an obscuration preventing liberation.

afflictive obscurations (*kleśāvaraṇa*, T. *nyon sgrib*). Obscurations that mainly prevent liberation; afflictions and their seeds.

aging (*sthityanyathātva*, *jarā*, T. *ṭhitassa aññathatta*). Alteration of that which exists.

aggregates (*skandha*, T. *phung po*). The four or five components that make up a living being: form (except for beings born in the formless realm), feelings, discriminations, miscellaneous factors, and consciousnesses.

analysis (*vicāra*, T. *dpyod pa*). A mental factor that examines an object in detail.

analytical meditation (*vicārabhāvanā*, T. *dpyad sgom*). Meditation done to understand an object.

appearing object (*pratibhāsa-viṣaya,* T. *snang yul*). The object that actually appears to a consciousness. The appearing object of a conceptual consciousness is a conceptual appearance of something.

apperception (*svasaṃvedana*, T. *rang rig*). A "secondary" consciousness that knows the main consciousness itself directly and nondualistically. Asserted by some tenet systems, it is negated by Prāsaṅgikas and others.

apprehended object (*muṣṭibandhaviṣaya*, T. *'dzin stangs kyi yul*). The main object with which the mind is concerned—that is, the object that the mind is getting at or perceives. Synonymous with engaged object.

approachers and abiders (T. *zhugs gnas*). Practitioners of the Fundamental Vehicle. Approachers are working to attain the fruit of stream-enterer, once-returner, nonreturner, or arhat, which are certain to be attained in that very life. Abiders are those who have eliminated or reduced the corresponding fetters of that stage and become a stream-enterer, once-returner, nonreturner, or arhat.

arhat (foe destroyer, T. *dgra bcom pa*). Someone who has eliminated all afflictive obscurations and attained liberation.

arising/production (*utpada*, *jāti*, *uppāda*, T. *skye ba*). The coming into being of an impermanent phenomenon that wasn't present before.

ārya (*ariya*). Someone who has directly and nonconceptually realized the emptiness of inherent existence.

attain its entity. Come into existence.

autonomous syllogism (*svatantra-prayoga*, T. *rang rgyud kyi sbyor ba*). A syllogism where the parties involved agree that all parts of the syllogism inherently exist; Svātantrikas' preferred form of reasoning.

basis of designation (basis of imputation, T. *btags gzhi*). The collection of parts or factors in dependence on which an object is designated or imputed.

beings who will never attain awakening (*icchantika*, T. *'dod chen pa*). Beings who lack the buddha element, as held by the Yogācāra-Scripture Proponents.

bodhicitta (altruistic intention, T. *byang chub sems*). A main mental consciousness induced by an aspiration to bring about the welfare of others and accompanied by an aspiration to attain full awakening oneself.

bodhisattva (T. *byang chub sems dpa*). Someone who has uncontrived bodhicitta.

bodhisattva ground (*bhumi*, T. *sa*). A consciousness in the continuum of an ārya bodhisattva characterized by wisdom and compassion. It is the basis for the development of good qualities and the basis for the eradication of ignorance and mistaken appearances.

brahma-like conduct (*brahmaçarya*, T. *tshangs spyod*). Pure conduct, especially sexual abstinence.

buddha nature (*buddhagotra*, T. *sang rgyas kyi rigs*, C. *fo xin*). Chinese Buddhism: suchness; the emptiness of the mind endowed with all excellent qualities. Syn. *pure mind*.

character natureless (*laksaṇa-niḥsvabhāvatā*, T. *mtshan nyid ngo bo nyid med pa*). A quality of imaginaries—that they do not exist by their own character.

character (*lakṣaṇa*, T. *mtshan nyid*). Nature.

characteristics (*lakṣaṇa*, T. *mtshan nyid*). Attributes or features of an object.

coarse afflictions (T. *nyon mongs rags pa*). Afflictions prompted by and underlain by grasping a self-sufficient substantially existent person.

cognitive faculty/sensory faculty (*indriya*, T. *dbang po*). The subtle material in the gross sense organ that enables perception of sense objects; for the mental consciousness, it is previous moments of any of the six consciousnesses.

cognitive obscurations (*jñeyāvaraṇa*, T. *shes sgrib*). Obscurations that mainly prevent full awakening; the latencies of ignorance and the subtle dualistic appearance that they give rise to.

collection of merit (*puṇyasaṃbhāra*, T. *bsod nams kyi tshogs*). A virtuous action motivated by bodhicitta that is a main cause of attaining the form body of a buddha.

collection of wisdom (*jñānasaṃbhāra*, T. *ye shes kyi tshogs*). A virtuous mental action motivated by bodhicitta that is a main cause of attaining the truth body of a buddha.

conceived object (*adhyavasāya-viṣaya*, T. *zhen yul*). The object conceived by a conceptual consciousness. Syn. *apprehended or engaged object of a conceptual consciousness.*

concentration (*samādhi*, T. *ting nge 'dzin*). A mental factor that dwells single-pointedly for a sustained period of time on one object; a state of deep meditative absorption; single-pointed concentration that is free from discursive thought.

conceptual appearance (*artha-sāmānya*, T. *don spyi*). A mental image of an object that appears to a conceptual consciousness.

conceptual consciousness (*kalpanā*, T. *rtog pa'i shes pa*). A consciousness that knows its object by means of a conceptual appearance.

conceptuality (*kalpanā*, T. *rtog pa*). Thought; a mind that knows its object via a conceptual appearance.

conceptualizations (*vikalpa viparyāsa*, T. *rnam rtog*). Distorted thoughts that range from exaggerating the desirability or beauty of an object to grasping impermanent things as permanent, and so forth.

concomitant (*saṃprayukta*, T. *mtshungs ldan*). Accompanying or occurring together in the same mental state.

conditionality (causal dependence, *hetupratyayāpekṣa*, T. *rgyu rkyen la ltos pa*). (1) Dependence on causes and conditions; (2) all three forms of dependence.

confusion (*moha*, T. *gti mug*). Ignorance.

consciousness (*jñāna*, T. *shes pa*). That which is clear and cognizant.

consequence (*prāsaṅga*, T. *thal 'gyur*). A form of reasoning that shows the other party the inconsistencies in their assertions; the form of reasoning widely used by the Prāsaṅgikas.

consummate or thoroughly established nature (*pariniṣpanna svabhāva*, *pariniṣpannalakṣaṇa*, T. *yongs grub kyi mtshan nyid*). Asserted by Yogācārins: the suchness of phenomena and the emptiness of external objects—that is, the emptiness of subject and object arising from different substantial entities and the emptiness of an object existing by its own character as the referent of its name.

conventional analysis (T. *tha snyad dpyod byed kyi rigs pa*). Investigating the conventional nature and function of objects; any analysis that is not aimed at realizing the emptiness of inherent existence.

conventional consciousnesses (*vyavahāra-vijñāna*, T. *tha snyad pa'i shes pa*). (1) Ordinary conventional consciousnesses that are not influenced by a realization of emptiness; (2) special conventional consciousnesses that are influenced by reasoning analyzing the ultimate.

conventional existence (*saṃvṛtisat*, T. *kun rdzob tu yod pa*). Existence.

conventional truths (*saṃvṛtisatya*, T. *kun rdzob bden pa*). That which is true from the perspective of true-grasping; objects found by a conventional reliable cognizer perceiving a false knowable object. Syn. *veiled truths*.

cooperative conditions (*sahakari-pratyaya*, T. *lhan cig byed pa'i rkyen*). Causes that aid the main or substantial cause in producing its result.

counterpervasion (*vyatirekavyāpti*, T. *ldog khyab*). The contrapositive of the major premise; the relationship between the opposite of the predicate and the opposite of the reason: if something is not the predicate, it is necessarily not the reason.

creator god (T. *dbang phyug*, T. *'jig rten bkod pa po*). An independent being who created the world, such as Īśvara.

death (*maraṇa*, T. *'chi ba*). The last moment of a lifetime when the subtlest clear light mind manifests.

deceptive (*moṣa*, *visaṃvādaka*, T. *slu ba*). (1) Erroneous; (2) not existing in the way it appears.

defilement (stain, *mala*, T. *dri ma*). Either an afflictive obscuration or a cognitive obscuration. Syn. *stain*.

definite karma (T. *nges pa'i las*). Actions that are consciously done and accumulated (there was an intention to act).

definitive (*nītārtha*, *nītattha*, T. *nges don*). Prāsaṅgikas: A sūtra or statement that mainly and explicitly teaches ultimate truths.

dependent arising (*pratītyasamutpāda*, T. *rten cing 'brel ba 'byung ba*, *rten 'byung*, *rten 'brel*). This is of three types: (1) causal dependence—things arising due to causes and conditions; (2) mutual dependence—phenomena existing in relation to other phenomena;[150] and (3) dependent designation—phenomena existing by being merely designated by terms and concepts.

dependent designation (*upādāya prajñapti*, T. *brten nas gdags pa*). Being designated by term and concept.

dependent or other-powered natures (*paratantra svabhāva*, *paratantralakṣaṇa*, T. *gzhan dbang gi mtshan nyid*). Functioning things; phenomena that are produced by causes and conditions.

designated object (*prajñapti*, *paññatti*, T. *btags don*). The object designated by term and concept in dependence on its basis of designation.

desire realm (*kāmadhātu*, T. *'dod khams*). One of the three realms of cyclic existence; the realm where sentient beings are overwhelmed by attraction to and desire for sense objects.

dhyāna (*jhāna*, T. *bsam gtan*). A meditative stabilization of the form realm.

different (*nānātva*, T. *tha dad*). Phenomena that are diverse.

different nature (T. *ngo bo tha dad*). Two things that can exist at different times and different places.

direct cause (*sājñātkāraṇa*, T. *dngos rgyu*). A cause that immediately precedes its result. Parents are the direct cause of a child.

direct perceiver (*pratyakṣa*, T. *mgon sum*). Sautrāntikas: A nonmistaken knower that is free from conceptuality. Prāsaṅgikas: A manifest phenomenon.

direct reliable cognizer (*pratyakṣa-pramāṇa*, T. *mgon sum tshad ma*). Lower schools: A nondeceptive awareness that newly knows its object directly. Prāsaṅgikas: a nondeceptive awareness that knows its object directly or conceptually without depending on a reason.

discerning discrimination (*pratyavekṣaṇā*, T. *so sor rtog pa*). Correct examination or investigation; awareness of individual characteristics of cause and effect or emptiness; conceptual understanding of the meaning.

distorted conception (inappropriate attention, *ayoniśo-manaskāra*, T. *tshul bzhin ma yin pa'i yid la byed pa*, *tshul min yid byed kyi rnam rtog*). Distorted thoughts that project exaggerations and erroneous qualities on objects that lead to the arising of afflictions.

dualistic appearance (*dvayābhatā*, T. *gnyis snang*). (1) The sense that subject and object are distinct and cut off; (2) the appearance of inherent existence.

duḥkha (*dukkha*, T. *sdug bsngal*). The unsatisfactory experiences of cyclic existence.

eight worldly concerns (*aṣṭalokadharma*, T. *'jig rten chos brgyad*). Attachment to material gain, fame, praise, and pleasure and aversion to loss, disrepute, blame, and pain.

elaborations (proliferations, *prapañca papañca*, T. *spros pa*). Ignorance and other mental fabrications that obscure the ultimate nature of phenomena, their emptiness.

empowering condition (*adhipati-pratyaya*, T. *bdag pa'i rkyen*). The sense faculty that connects the object with a consciousness so that cognition of the object occurs.

emptiness (*śūnyatā*, T. *stong pa nyid*). Madhyamaka: The lack of true existence.

engaged object (*pravṛtti-viṣaya*, T. *'jug yul*). The main object with which the mind is concerned. Syn. *apprehended object*.

erroneous (*viparyaya*, T. *log pa*, *phyin ci log pa*). Wrong, incorrect, perverted.

erroneous awareness (wrong awareness, *viparyayajñāna*, T. *log shes*). A mind that is wrong with respect to its apprehended object.

essentialists (proponents of true existence, *vastusat-padārthavādin*, T. *dngos por smra ba*). Buddhist and non-Buddhist philosophers following a non-Madhyamaka tenet system who assert that the person and aggregates truly exist.

exalted knower (*jñāna*, T. *mkhyen pa*). A realization of someone who has entered a path. It exists from the path of accumulation through the buddha ground. Exalted knower, path, ground, pristine wisdom, and clear realization are mutually inclusive.

example (*sadṛṣṭānta*, T. *mthun dpe*). A part of a syllogism that is easier to understand and helps us to understand the thesis.

existence by its own character (*svalakṣaṇasat*, T. *rang gi mtshan nyid kyis yod pa*). Prāsaṅgika: Existence such that when the object designated is sought, it is findable. Existence that does not depend on being merely imputed by term and concept. Svātantrika: When the object is sought with ultimate analysis, it is findable.

existence as its own suchness (*tattvasiddhi*, T. *de kho na nyid du grub pa*). Synonymous with true existence.

existence from its own side (*svarūpasiddhi*, T. *rang ngos nas grub pa*). Existence such that the object designated is findable in its basis of designation.

existence through its own power (*svairīsiddhi*, T. *rang dbang du grub pa*). Existence through the object's own mode of being. Autonomous existence without depending on other factors.

existent (*bhāva*, *sat*, T. *yod pa*). That which is perceivable by mind. Syn. *phenomenon*.

external objects (*bāhyārtha*, T. *phyi don*). (1) Sense objects. (2) In Yogācāra: objects that appear distant and cut off from the consciousness perceiving them; objects that do not arise from the same latency as the consciousness cognizing it.

extreme of absolutism (*śāśvatānta*, *bhāvānta*, T. *yod pa'i mtha'*). The extreme of eternalism; believing that phenomena inherently exist.

extreme of nihilism (*ucchedānta*, *abhāvānta*, T. *med pa'i mtha'*). The extreme of nonexistence; believing that our actions have no ethical dimension; believing that nothing exists.

falsity (*mṛṣā*, *mithya*, T. *brtsun pa*). A phenomenon that appears truly existent, whereas it is empty of true existence.

fetters (*saṃyojana*, T. *kun tu sbyor ba*). Factors that keep us bound to cyclic existence and impede the attainment of liberation. The five lower fetters—view of a personal identity, deluded doubt, view of rules and practices, sensual desire, and malice—bind us to rebirth in the desire realm. The five higher fetters—desire for existence in the form realm, desire for existence in the formless realm, arrogance, restlessness, and ignorance—prevent a nonreturner from becoming an arhat.

focal object (*iṣaya*, T. *dmig pa*). The main object the mind refers to or focuses on.

form realm (*rūpadhātu*, T. *gzugs kyi khams*). The saṃsāric realm in which beings have bodies made of subtle material; they are born there due to having attained various states of concentration.

formless realm (*ārūpyadhātu*, T. *gzugled kyi khams*). The saṃsāric realm in which sentient beings do not have a material body; they are born there due to having attained various states of meditative absorption.

foundation consciousness (mind-basis-of-all, *ālayavijñāna*, T. *kun gzhi rnam shes*). A storehouse consciousness on which all latencies and karmic seeds are placed; it carries these from one life to the next and is the self according to the Yogācāra-Scripture Proponents.

four mental engagements (*catur manaskāra*, T. *yid la byed pa bzhi*). Four ways in which the mind engages with the meditation object when cultivating serenity—forceful, interrupted, uninterrupted, and spontaneous.

four truths of the āryas (*catvāry āryasatyāni*, T. *'phags pa'i bden pa bzhi*). The truth of duḥkha, its origin, its cessation, and the path to that cessation.

free from conceptuality (*kalpanā-apodha*, T. *rtog bral*). Without the appearance of a conceptual appearance.

fruition (*vipaka*, T. *smin pa*). A result; a neutral phenomenon included in the continuum of a sentient being that arises from a cause that is not neutral—that is, it arises from a cause that is either virtuous or nonvirtuous.

full awakening (*samyaksaṃbodhi*, T. *yang dag par rdzog' pa'i sangs rgyas*). Buddhahood; the state in which all obscurations have been abandoned and all good qualities developed limitlessly.

Fundamental Vehicle (T. *theg dman*). The path leading to the liberation of śrāvakas and solitary realizers.

future sprout (T. *myu gu ma 'ongs pa*). A [factor of] nonarising of the sprout due to the noncompletion of its conditions, even though the causes for its arising exist. It exists before the sprout has arisen.

future in relation to the sprout (T. *myu gu'i ma 'ongs pa*). The result of the sprout, which comes after the time of the sprout.

general characteristics (*sāmānya-lakṣaṇa*, *sāmañña-lakkhaṇa*, T. *spyi mtshan*). Characteristics, such as impermanence, unsatisfactoriness, and not-self, that are common to all functioning things.

grasping inherent existence (*svabhāvagraha*, T. *rang bzhin gyi grub pa 'dzin pa*). Grasping persons and phenomena to exist truly or inherently. Syn. *grasping true existence* (Prāsaṅgikas).

grasping true existence (true-grasping, *satyagraha*, T. *bden 'dzin*). Grasping persons and phenomena to exist with an intrinsic essence.

having-ceased (*naṣṭa*, T. *zhig pa*). An affirmative negation that is the "having happened" or "having ceased" of an event or an object.

higher knowledge (*vidyā*, *vijjā*, T. *rig pa*). Pāli tradition: the sublime knowledge that arises at the end of the path. Sanskrit tradition: pure awareness or knowledge.

ignorance (*avidyā*, T. *ma rig pa*). A mental factor that is obscured and grasps the opposite of what exists. There are two types: ignorance regarding ultimate truth and ignorance regarding karma and its effects.

imaginaries (*parikalpita*, T. *kun btags*). As asserted by Yogācārins, imaginaries are merely imputed by thought. Some are existent phenomena, others are nonexistents.

immediately preceding condition (*samanantara-pratyaya*, T. *de ma thag rkyen*). A moment of mind that acts as a cause for a perceiving consciousness to arise in the next moment.

impermanence (*anitya*, *anicca*, T. *mi rtag pa*). Momentariness; not remaining in the next moment. Coarse impermanence is the ending of a specific thing; subtle impermanence is something not remaining the same in the very next moment.

imputed or imaginary natures (*parikalpita svabhāva*, *parikalpitalakṣaṇa*, T. *kun btags kyi mtshan nyid*). One of the three natures asserted by the Yogācāra school. Imputed by conception. Some imaginaries are existent, others are not.

imputedly existent (*prajñaptisat*, T. *btags yod*). (1) Something that exists by being merely designated by term and concept; (2) things imputed by thought that are abstract, conceptual entities; (3) something that can be identified only by cognizing one of its parts or attributes.

inappropriate attention. *See* distorted conception.

independent (*sva-tantra*, T. *rang dbang*). Prāsaṅgikas: inherent, self-powered, not dependent on anything else. Other tenet systems: not dependent on causes and conditions.

individual self-knowledge (self-realized wisdom, *pratyātmagati*, T. *so sor rang rig*). Direct knowledge or experience free from dualistic thought. A pristine wisdom realizing emptiness that is a personal direct experience of Reality.

inference (*anumāna*, T. *rjes su dpag pa*). A conclusion reached through a syllogism on the basis of evidence and reasoning.

inferential reliable cognizer (*anumāna-pramāṇa*, T. *rjes dpag tshad ma*). An awareness that knows its object—a slightly obscure phenomena—nondeceptively, purely in dependence on a reason.

inherent existence (*svabhāvasiddhi*, *sabhāvasiddha*, *T. rang bzhin gyis grub pa*). Existence with its own self-powered nature able to set itself up.

innate (*sahaja*, T. *lhan skyes*). Existing with the mind from beginningless time; something not acquired anew in this life.

insight (*vipaśyanā*, *vipassanā*, T. *lhag mthong*). A wisdom of thorough discrimination of phenomena conjoined with special pliancy induced by the power of analysis (and with serenity).

insight knowledge (P. *vipassanā-ñāṇa*). Mundane (*lokiya*) knowledge of the three characteristics gained through insight. It leads to supramundane (*lokuttara*) path knowledge that realizes the four truths and nirvāṇa.

insight wisdom (P. *vipassanā-paññā*). Knowledge of the three characteristics gained through insight and leading to stream-entry.

interpretable (*neyārtha*, *neyyattha*, T. *drang don*). A scripture or statement that speaks about the variety of phenomena and/or cannot be taken literally.

investigation (*vitarka*, T. *rtog pa*). A mental factor that seeks a rough idea about an object.

karma. Intentional action of body, speech, or mind.

karmic seeds (T. *las kyi sa bon*). The potencies from previously created actions that will bring their results.

knowable object (*jñeya*, T. *shes bya*). That which is suitable to serve as an object of an awareness.

latencies (*vāsanā*, T. *bag chags*). Predispositions, imprints, or tendencies.

latencies of the branches of cyclic existence (*bhavāṅgavāsanā*, T. *srid pa'i yan lag gi bag chags*). Latencies that cause the appearance of the object as an external form, separate from the consciousness apprehending it.

latencies for expressions or verbalization (*abhilāpavāsanā*, T. *mngon brjod kyi bag chags*). Latencies to use language, to accept conventions, and to conceptualize. This aspect comes from our having repeatedly used language in the past.

latencies of a similar type (*samakulavāsanā*, T. *rigs mthun gyi bag chags*). Yogācāra: latencies to produce a similar type of apprehended object and apprehending consciousness in the future.

latencies of the view of self (*ātmadṛṣtivāsanā*, T. *bdag lta'i bag chags*). Latencies that cause an awareness in which the afflicted mentality views the foundation consciousness and thinks "I."

liberated path (*vimuktimārga*, T. *rnam grol lam*). Induced by the uninterrupted path preceding it, a wisdom directly realizing emptiness that has completely eradicated a portion of defilements; a path that has temporarily suppressed a portion of the manifest afflictions.

liberation (*mokṣa*, T. *thar pa*). A true cessation that is the abandonment of afflictive obscurations; nirvāṇa, the state of freedom from cyclic existence.

liberation (*vimukti*, *vimutti*, T. *rnam grol*). Sanskrit tradition: complete freedom from saṃsāra; Pāli tradition: a conditioned event that brings nirvāṇa.

Madhyamaka (T. *dbu ma*). A Mahāyāna tenet system that refutes true existence.

mahāsiddha (T. *grub chen*). A great adept who has profound realizations and meditative attainments.

manifest afflictions (T. *nyon mongs mngon gyur*). Afflictions active in the mind at the present moment (contrasted with seeds of afflictions).

manifest (*pratyakṣa*, T. *mngon gyur*). An existent is a manifest object in relation to an awareness that clearly realizes it; a phenomenon that can be known for the first time without relying on a correct reason is a manifest object.

meditative equipoise on emptiness (T. *stong nyid rtogs pa'i mnyam bzhag ye shes*). An ārya's mind focused single-pointedly on the emptiness of inherent existence.

mental consciousness (*mano-vijñāna*). A consciousness that knows mental objects, in contradistinction to sense consciousnesses that know sense objects.

mental continuum (*cittasaṃtāna*, T. *sems kyi rgyun*). The continuum of a mind from one moment to the next, even spanning lifetimes.

mental factor (*caitta*, T. *sems byung*). An aspect of mind that accompanies a primary consciousness and fills out the cognition, apprehending particular attributes of the object or performing a specific function.

mere veilings (*saṃvṛtimātra*, T. *kun rdzob tsam*). Objects perceived by arhats and pure-ground bodhisattvas as false, like illusions. "Mere" negates their being truly existent.

merely designated by name (T. *ming du btags pa tsam*). The mode of existence asserted by Prāsaṅgikas.

mind (*citta*, T. *sems*). That which is clear and cognizant. The part of living beings that cognizes, experiences, thinks, feels, and so on. In some contexts it is equivalent to primary consciousness.

Mind Only (*cittamātra*, T. *sems tsam pa*). A philosophical school, also called Yogācāra, that asserts phenomena are the nature of mind.

mindfulness (*smṛti*, *sati*, T. *dran pa*). A mental factor that brings to mind a phenomenon of previous acquaintance without forgetting it and prevents distraction to other objects.

mindstream (*cittasaṃtāna*, T. *sems kyi rgyun*). The continuity of mind.

mistaken consciousnesses (*bhrānta*, T. *'khrul ba*). (1) Conceptual consciousnesses whose objects appear by means of conceptual appearances; (2) consciousnesses that cannot recognize the appearance of inherent existence as false.

mistaken awareness (*bhrānti-jñāna*, T. *'khrul shes*). An awareness that is mistaken in terms of its appearing object.

momentary (*kṣaṇika*, T. *skad cig ma*). Not enduring to the next moment without changing.

monastic (*pravrajita*, T. *rab tu byung ba*). Someone who has received monastic ordination; a monk or nun.

mutual dependence (T. *phan tshun ltos grub*). Dependence that involves phenomena being posited and attaining their conventional identity in relation to each other, such as an object and its parts, or cause and effect.

nature truth body (*svabhāvika dharmakāya*, *svabhāva-kāya*, T. *ngo bo nyid sku*). The buddha body that is the emptiness of a buddha's mind and the true cessations in that buddha's continuum.

natureless (*niḥsvabhāva*, T. *ngo bo nyid med pa*). Lacking a certain nature; emptiness.

negation (*pratiṣedha*, T. *dgag pa*). An object comprehended by an awareness upon the explicit elimination of an object of negation. Equivalent to exclusion (*apoha*, T. *sel ba*), other exclusion (*anyāpoha*, T. *gzhan sel*), and isolate (*vyatireka*, *ldog pa*).

nihilism (*ucchedānta*, *vibhavadiṭṭhi*, T. *med mtha'*). The belief that our actions have no ethical dimension; the belief that nothing exists.

nimitta (T. *mtshan ma*). In the context of cultivating serenity: the sign that appears to the mind as concentration deepens.

nirvāṇa (T. *mya ngan las 'das pa*). The state of liberation of an arhat; the emptiness of a mind that has been totally cleansed of afflictive obscurations.

nominal truths (*vyavahārasatya*, T. *tha snyad bden pa*). *See* conventional truths.

nominally different (T. *tha snyad du tha dad*). Two phenomena are nominally different when they are not the same thing and can be distinguished by conception.

nonabiding nirvāṇa (*apratiṣṭita-nirvāṇa*, T. *mi gnas pa'i myang 'das*). A buddha's nirvāṇa that does not abide in either the extreme of cyclic existence or the extreme of personal liberation.

nonaffirming negation (*prasajyapratiṣedha*, T. *med dgag*). A negative phenomenon in which, upon the explicit elimination of the object of negation by an awareness, an affirmative phenomenon or an affirmative negation is not suggested or established in place of the object of negation.

nonconceptual consciousness (*nirvikalpaka*, T. *rtog med shes pa*). A consciousness that apprehends its object directly, not by means of a conceptual appearance.

nondeceptive (*avisaṃvādi*, *amoṣa*, T. *mind slu ba*). (1) Incontrovertible, correct; (2) existing the way it appears to a reliable cognizer directly realizing it.

nonduality (T. *gnyis snang nub pa*). The nonappearance of subject and object, inherent existence, conventional truths, and conceptual appearances in an ārya's meditative equipoise on emptiness.

nonerroneous (*aviparīta*, T. *phyin ci ma log pa*). Correct, right.

nonexistent (*asat*, *abhāva*, T. *med pa*). That which is not perceivable by mind.

nonmistaken (*abhrānta*, T. *ma 'khrul ba*). (1) Sautrāntikas: not mistaken with respect to a consciousness's appearing object; (2) Prāsaṅgikas: without the appearance of inherent existence.

non-thing (*abhāva*, T. *dngos med*). (1) A permanent phenomenon; (2) a phenomenon that cannot perform a function; (3) that which doesn't exist.

non-wastage (*avipraṇāśa*, T. *chud mi za ba*). Asserted by some Vaibhāṣikas, it is likened to an IOU, voucher, or seal that ensures karma will go from one life to the next.

object (*viṣaya*, T. *yul*). That which is known by an awareness.

object of negation (*pratiṣedhya*, T. *dgag bya*). What is negated or refuted.

objective existence (*visayasiddhi*, T. *yul ngos nas grub pa*, *yul steng nas grub pa*). Existence by its own nature without being posited through the power of conventional designation.

observed object (*ālambana*, T. *dmigs yul*). The basic object that the mind refers to or focuses on while apprehending certain aspects of that object.

observed-object condition (*ālambana-pratyaya*, T. *dmigs pa'i rkyen*). The object perceived by a sense direct perceiver, which is also one of the conditions producing that mind.

one (*ekatva*, T. *gcig*). A singular phenomenon; a phenomenon that is not diverse; identical.

one-mind (C. *ixin*). Chan: Implies the union of serenity and insight. Tathāgatagarbha: the mind that is the basis of saṃsāra and nirvāṇa.

one nature (*eka-prakṛtika*, T. *rang bzhin gcig pa*). Two phenomena are one nature when they arise, abide, and cease simultaneously and do not appear separate to direct perception. Syn. *one entity* (*ekarūpatā*, T. *ngo bo gcig pa*).

ordinary being (*pṛthagjana*, T. *so so skye bo*). Someone who is not an ārya.

own-characteristics (specific characteristics, *svalakṣaṇa*, *salakkhana*, T. *rang mtshan*). The specific characteristics unique to each phenomenon. Things have their own characteristics, but they do not exist by their own character. Sautrāntikas: own-characterized is synonymous with impermanent. Yogācāra: all other-powered and consummate natures are own-characterized. Prāsaṅgikas: inherent existence.

past sprout (T. *myu gu 'das pa*). The factor of having ceased of the sprout that has already arisen.

past in relation to the sprout (T. *myu gu'i 'das pa*). What happened before the sprout came into existence.

path (*mārga*, T. *lam*). An exalted knower that is conjoined with uncontrived renunciation.

path knowledge (P. *magga-ñāṇa*). A supramundane path that knows the four truths and nirvāṇa.

path of accumulation (*sambhāramārga*, T. *tshogs lam*). First of the five paths. In the Śrāvaka or Solitary Realizer Vehicle, it begins when one aspires for liberation day and night; in the Mahayana, it begins when one has uncontrived bodhicitta.

path of meditation (*bhāvanāmārga*, T. *sgom lam*). The fourth of the five paths. This begins when a meditator begins to eradicate innate afflictions from the root.

path of no-more-learning (*aśaikṣamārga*, T. *mind slob lam*). The last of the five paths; arhatship or buddhahood.

path of preparation (*prayogamārga*, T. *sbyor lam*). The second of the five paths. It begins when a meditator attains the union of serenity and insight on emptiness.

path of seeing (*darśanamārga*, T. *mthong lam*). The third of the five paths. It begins when a meditator first has direct, nonconceptual realization of the emptiness of inherent existence.

permanent (*nitya*, *nicca*, T. *rtag pa*). Unchanging, static, not momentarily changing. It does not mean eternal.

permanent, unitary, independent self (T. *rtag gcig rang dbang can gyi bdag*). A soul or self (ātman) asserted by non-Buddhists.

person (*pudgala*, T. *gang zag*). A living being designated in dependence on the four or five aggregates.

pervasion (*anvayavyāpti*, T. *rjes khyab*). The major premise of a correct syllogism; the relationship between the reason and the predicate: whatever is the reason is necessarily the predicate.

pollutant (*āsrava*, *āsava*, T. *zag pa*). A set of three or four deeply rooted defilements: sensual desire, existence (craving to exist in a saṃsāric form), and ignorance; some lists add view.

polluted (*āsava*). Under the influence of ignorance or its latencies.

posit (*vyavasthāna*, T. *bzhag pa*). To establish, determine, or postulate an object; to designate.

positive (affirmative, *vidhi*, T. *sgrub pa*). A phenomenon that is not realized by the conceptual consciousness apprehending it by explicitly eliminating an object of negation.

potency (*sakti*, T. *nus pa*). The energy or ability to bring a result.

Prāsaṅgika Madhyamaka (T. *dbu ma thal gyur ba*). A Mahāyāna tenet system that asserts that all phenomena lack inherent existence both conventionally and ultimately.

predicate (*sādhya dharma*, T. *bsgrub bya'i chos*). What is to be proven in a syllogism.

present sprout (T. *myu gu da ltar*). The sprout that has arisen but has not ceased.

present in relation to the sprout (T. *myu gu'i da ltar*). The time the sprout exists.

primal substance (*prakṛti, pakati*, T. *spyi gtso bo*). Asserted by the non-Buddhist Sāṃkhya school: fundamental nature; a truly existent substance out of which everything is created.

primary consciousness (*vijñāna*, T. *rnam par shes pa*). A consciousness that apprehends the presence or basic entity of an object; they are of six types: visual, auditory, olfactory, gustatory, tactile, and mental.

primary mental consciousness (*mano-vijñāna*, T. *yid kyi rnam shes*). A primary mental consciousness that knows mental and physical phenomena, as opposed to sense consciousnesses that know only physical objects.

pristine wisdom (*jñāna*, T. *ye shes*). A type of wisdom that opposes grasping inherent existence and knows emptiness inferentially or directly.

probing awareness (*yuktijñāna*, T. *rigs shes*). A consciousness using reasoning to analyze the ultimate or conventional nature of an object. It can be either conceptual or nonconceptual.

production natureless (*utpatti-niḥsvabhāvatā*, T. *skye ba ngo bo nyid med pa*). A quality of dependent natures: they arise from causes that are a different nature than themselves and do not arise from causes that are the same nature as themselves.

pure mind (C. *qinjing xin*). Syn. *buddha nature.*

pureland (*kṣetraśuddhi*, T. *dag zhing*). Places created by the unshakable resolve and merit of buddhas where all external conditions are conducive for Dharma practice.

reality (*dharmatā*, T. *chos nyid*). Emptiness.

realization (*adhigama*, T. *rtogs pa*). An awareness that eliminates superimpositions on an object and is able to induce ascertainment of a phenomenon. It may be either inferential or direct.

reason (sign, *liṅga*, T. *rtags*). The part of a syllogism that proves the thesis.

reason applies to the subject (*pakṣadharma*, T. *phyogs chos*). One of the three criteria of a correct syllogism; the minor premise; the relationship between the subject and the reason, specifically that the reason is a property of the subject.

reliable cognizer (*pramāṇa*, T. *tshad ma*). Prāsaṅgika: a nondeceptive awareness that is incontrovertible with respect to its principal object and that enables us to accomplish our purpose.

samādhi. *See* concentration.

Sāṃkhya (Enumerator, T. *grangs can pa*). A school of Hindu philosophy that asserts a primal substance and says that effects exist in a nonmanifest state in their causes.

saṃsāra (cyclic existence, T. *'khor ba*). The cycle of rebirth that occurs under the control of afflictions and karma; the mental and physical aggregates that are under the control of afflictions and karma.

Sautrāntika (T. *mdo sde pa*). A Fundamental Vehicle tenet system that asserts that functional things are ultimate truths and phenomena that exist by being imputed by thought are conventional truths.

seed (*bija*, T. *sa bon*). The potency to bring a result.

self (*ātman*, *attā*, T. *bdag*). (1) A person; (2) inherent existence; (3) a permanent, monolithic, independent soul.

self-grasping (*ātmagrāha*, T. *bdag 'dzin*). Grasping a wrong mode of existence of persons or other phenomena; Prāsaṅgikas: grasping inherent existence.

self-realized wisdom. *See* individual self-knowledge.

selflessness of persons (*pudgalanairātmya*, T. *gang zag gi bdag med*). Prāsaṅgika: the nonexistence of a self-sufficient substantially existent person is the coarse selflessness of persons; the nonexistence of an inherently existent person is the subtle selflessness of persons.

selflessness of phenomena (*dharmanairātmya*, T. *chos kyi bdag med pa*). Prāsaṅgikas: the nonexistence of an inherently existent object other than a person.

self-sufficient, substantially existent person (T. *gang zag rang rkya thub pa'i rdzas yod*). A person that can be identified without identifying its aggregates; a self that is the controller of the body and mind. Such a self does not exist.

sense direct reliable cognizers (T. *dbang po'i mngon sum tshad ma*).

Prāsaṅgika: incontrovertible awarenesses that know their objects—sights, sounds, smells, tastes, and tangible objects—directly by depending on a physical cognitive faculty.

sentient being (*sattva*, T. *sems can*). Any being with a mind, except for a buddha.

serenity (*śamatha*, T. *zhi gnas*). Sanskrit tradition: concentration arisen from meditation that is accompanied by the bliss of mental and physical pliancy in which the mind abides effortlessly without fluctuation for as long as we wish on whatever virtuous object the mind has been placed. Pāli tradition: one-pointedness of mind; the eight attainments (meditative absorptions) that are the basis for insight.

signlessness (*ānimitta*, T. *mtshan ma med pa*). The emptiness that is the absence of inherent existence of the cause of any phenomenon.

six perfections (*ṣaḍpāramitā*, T. *phar phyin drug*). The practices of generosity, ethical conduct, fortitude, joyous effort, meditative stability, and wisdom that are motivated by bodhicitta.

slightly obscure phenomena (*kimcidparokṣa*, T. *cung zad lkog gyur*). Phenomena that ordinary beings can initially know only through factual inference.

solitary realizer (*pratyekabuddha*, T. *rang rgyal*). A person following the Fundamental Vehicle who seeks liberation, emphasizes understanding the twelve links of dependent arising, and does not rely on a spiritual guide during their last rebirth before attaining liberation.

śrāvaka (hearer, P. *sāvaka*, T. *nyan thos*). Someone practicing the Fundamental Vehicle path leading to arhatship who emphasizes meditation on the four truths.

stabilizing meditation (*sthāpyabhāvanā*, T. *'jog sgom*). Meditation to focus and concentrate the mind on an object.

subject of a syllogism (*dharmin*, T. *chos can*). The object being discussed in a syllogism.

substantial cause (*upādāna-kāraṇa*, T. *nyer len gyi rgyu*). The cause that becomes the result, as opposed to cooperative conditions that aid the substantial cause in becoming the result.

substantially established (*dravyasidda*, T. *rdzas grub*). Lower schools: an object that can be known directly without first identifying another object. Prāsaṅgikas: syn. *true existence*.

substantially existent (*dravyasat*, *dabbasat*, T. *rdzas yod*). (1) Vaibhāṣikas: an object that can be identified even when broken into smaller pieces or moments of time. (2) Sautrāntikas through Svātantrikas: an object that can be known directly without another object being identified. (3) Prāsaṅgikas: inherently existent.

subtle afflictions (T. *nyon mongs phra mo*). Afflictions stemming from grasping inherent existence (contrasted with coarse afflictions).

suchness (*tattva*, T. *de kho na nyid*, C. *zhen ru*). Emptiness, the way things really are.

superimposition (*samāropa*, T. *sgro btags*, *sgro 'dogs*). The imputing or projecting of something that does not exist—for example, a self of persons.

supramundane (transcendental, *lokottara*, *lokuttara*, T. *'jig rten las 'das pa*). Pertaining to the elimination of fetters and afflictions; pertaining to āryas.

Svātantrika Madhyamaka (T. *dbu ma rang rgyud pa*). A Mahāyāna tenet system asserting that phenomena do not exist inherently on the ultimate level but do exist inherently on the conventional level.

syllogism (*prayoga*, T. *sbyor ba*). A statement consisting of a subject, predicate, and reason, and in many cases an example.

tathāgata (T. *de bzhin gshegs pa*). A buddha.

tenet (*siddhānta*, T. *grub mtha'*). A philosophical assertion or belief.

tenet system/school (T. *grub mtha'i lugs*). A set of philosophical assertions regarding the basis, path, and result that is shared by a group of people.

thesis (*pratijñā*, T. *dam bca'*). What is to be proven—the combination of the subject and the predicate—in a syllogism.

thing (*bhava*, *vastu*, T. *dngos bo*). (1) something that can perform a function, syn. *product*; (2) phenomena.

thought (*kalpanā*, *rtog pa*). Conceptual consciousness.

three characteristics. Three qualities of conditioned phenomena: impermanence, duḥkha, and selfless (not-self).

three criteria for existent phenomena. It is known to a conventional consciousness; its existence is not invalidated by another conventional reliable cognizer; it is not invalidated by a mind analyzing emptiness.

three criteria of a correct inference or syllogism (T. *tshul gsum*). Presence of the reason in the subject, pervasion or entailment, and counterpervasion.

three natures (*trisvabhāva*, T. *mtshan nyid gsum*). A classification of all phenomena in the Yogācāra presentation into imaginary, dependent (other-powered), and consummate natures.

three pure grounds (T. *dag pa sag sum*). The last three stages of a bodhisattva—the eighth, ninth, and tenth grounds. Prāsaṅgikas: bodhisattvas on these grounds have eradicated afflictive obscurations and are eradicating cognitive obscurations.

three realms (*tridhātuka*, *tedhātuka*, T. *khams gsum*). Desire, form, and formless realms.

three types of beings (T. skyes bu gsum). Śrāvaka arhats, solitary-realizer arhats, and pure-ground bodhisattvas, all of whom have eradicated afflictive obscurations.

true cessation (*nirodhasatya*, T. *'gog bden*). The cessation of a portion of afflictions or all afflictions; the cessation of a portion of cognitive obscurations or all cognitive obscurations.

true existence (*satyasat*, T. *bden par yod pa*). Prāsaṅgika: existence in its own right without being merely imputed by name and concept. Svātantrika: establishment as its own mode of abiding without being posited through the force of appearing to a nondefective awareness.

true-grasping. *See* grasping true existence.

true-mind (C. *zhen xin*). Chan: the mind that is originally pure and complete with pure qualities.

true-self (*satya-ātman*, C. *zhen wo*). Chan: suchness (reality, *tattva*); the true, pure, fundamental nature of the mind that is full of virtuous qualities (*guṇa*) and is permanent (*nitya*), immovable, ultimate, blissful, everlasting, stable (*dhruvá*), and peace.

true-suchness (*tathatā*, C. *zhen ru*). The way phenomena exist.

truth body (*dharmakāya*, T. *chos sku*). The buddha body that includes the nature truth body and the wisdom truth body.

twelve links of dependent origination (*dvādaśāṅga-pratītyasamutpāda*, T. *rten 'brel yan lag bcu gnyis*). A system of twelve factors that explains how we take rebirth in saṃsāra and how we can be liberated from it.

two truths (*satyadvaya*, *saccadvaya*, T. *bden pa gnyis*). Ultimate truths and veiled (conventional) truths.

ultimate analysis (T. *don dam pa'i dpyod pa*). Analysis that examines what an object really is and its deeper mode of existence.

ultimate existence (*paramārthasiddhi*, T. *don dam par grub pa*). Prāsaṅgika: existence such that when the object is sought with ultimate analysis, it is found. Svātantrika: existence by an object's own uncommon mode of subsistence without being posited by the force of appearing to a nondefective awareness.

ultimate natureless (*paramārtha-niḥsvabhāvatā*, T. *don dam pa ngo bo med pa*). A quality of consummate natures; the ultimate nature of phenomena that is perceived by the ultimate purifying consciousnesses.

ultimate truth (*paramārthasatya*, *paramattha-sacca*, T. *don dam bden pa*). The ultimate mode of existence of all persons and phenomena; emptiness; objects that are true and appear true to their main cognizer, a wisdom nonconceptually and directly realizing emptiness.

unafflictive ignorance (*akliṣṭāvidyā*, T. *nyon mongs can ma yin pa'i ma rig pa*). Lower schools: not knowing things that are far away in distance or time, the subtle qualities of the Buddha, and subtle facets of the law of karma and its effects. Prāsaṅgikas do not differentiate afflictive and unafflictive ignorance because they assert all ignorance is an obscuration preventing liberation.

unfortunate states (*apāya*, T. *ngan song*). Unfortunate states of rebirth as a hell being, hungry ghost, or animal.

unimpaired (T. *gnod pa med pa*). Not hindered by any of the superficial causes of error.

uninterrupted path (*ānantarya-mārga, T. bar chad med lam*). A wisdom directly realizing emptiness that is in the process of eliminating some portion of defilements; a path that is in the process of temporarily suppressing some portion of manifest afflictions.

union of serenity and insight (*śamatha-vipaśyanā-yuganaddha*, T. *zhi lhag zung 'brel*). Absorption in which the bliss of mental and physical pliancy has been induced by analysis. This marks the first moment of the path of preparation.

unpolluted (*anāsrava*, T. *zag med*). Not under the influence of ignorance.

Vaibhāṣika (T. *bye brag smra ba*). A Fundamental Vehicle tenet system that accepts directionally partless particles and temporally partless moments of consciousness as ultimate truths and asserts truly established external objects.

veiled truths (*saṃvṛtisatya*, *sammuti-sacca*, T. *kun rdzob bden pa*). Objects that are true only from the perspective of ignorance; objects that appear to exist inherently to their main cognizer. This includes all phenomena except ultimate truths. Syn. *conventional truths.*

veilings (*saṃvṛti*, T. *kun rdzob*). Objects of perceivers of falsities. All phenomena that are not ultimate truths are veilings. Syn. *conventionalities.*

veiler (*saṃvṛti*, T. *kun rdzob*). Ignorance; a mind that veils, conceals, and obscures the ultimate nature of phenomenon—their emptiness—and superimposes true existence on them.

view of a personal identity (view of the transitory collection, *satkāyadṛṣṭi*). An afflictive view that grasps an inherently existent I or mine (according to the Prāsaṅgika).

Vinaya (T. *'dul ba*). Monastic discipline.

wind (*prāṇa*, T. *rlung*). One of the four elements; energy in the body that influences bodily functions; subtle energy on which levels of consciousness ride.

wisdom truth body (*jñāna dharmakāya*, T. *ye shes chos ku*). The buddha body that is a buddha's omniscient mind.

wishlessness (*apraṇihita*, T. *smon pa med pa*). The ultimate nature of the effects of things.

worldly consciousnesses (T. *'jig rten pa'i shes pa*). Sense and mental consciousnesses in the mindstreams of ordinary beings and āryas that perceive veiled truths.

Yogācāra (Cittamātra, T. *rnal 'byor spyod pa, sems tsam pa*). A Mahāyāna tenet system that asserts the true existence of other-powered natures but does not assert external objects.

Yogācāra-Svātantrika Madhyamaka (T. *rnal 'byor spyod pa'i dbu ma rang rgyud pa*). A Mahāyāna tenet system that does not assert external objects, asserts six consciousnesses, and refutes inherent existence ultimately but not conventionally.

yogi (T. *rnal 'byor pa*). A meditator on suchness.

yogic direct reliable cognizers (T. *rnal 'byor mngon sum tshad ma*). Nondeceptive mental consciousnesses that know their objects by depending on a union of serenity and insight.

Recommended Reading

Abhidharmakośabhāṣyam of Vasubandhu. Sanskrit edition. 4 vols. French translation from the Sanskrit by Louis de La Vallée Poussin. English translation from the French by Leo M. Pruden. Fremont, CA: Asian Humanities Press, 1991.

Blumenthal, James. *The Ornament of the Middle Way: A Study of the Mādhyamaka Thought of Śāntarakṣita*. Ithaca, NY: Snow Lion Publications, 2004.

Bocking, Brian. *Nāgārjuna in China: A Translation of the Middle Treatise*. Lewiston, NY: Edwin Mellen Press, 1995.

Cabezón, José Ignacio. *A Dose of Emptiness: An Annotated Translation of the sTong thun chen mo of mKhas grub dGe legs dpal bzang*. Albany: State University of New York Press, 1992.

Cozort, Daniel. *Unique Tenets of the Middle Way Consequence School*. Ithaca, NY: Snow Lion Publications, 1998.

Dharmamitra, Bhikshu, trans. *Nāgārjuna on the Six Perfections: An Ārya Bodhisattva Explains the Heart of the Bodhisattva Path: Exegesis on the Great Perfection of Wisdom Sūtra: Chapters 17–30, by Ārya Nāgārjuna*. Seattle: Kalavinka Press, 2008.

———, trans. *Nāgārjuna's Treatise on the Ten Bodhisattva Grounds: The Daśabhūmika Vibhāṣā, by Ārya Nāgārjuna*. Seattle: Kalavinka Press, 2019.

———, trans. *Marvelous Stories from the Perfection of Wisdom: 130 Didactic Stories from Ārya Nāgārjuna's "Exegesis on the Great Perfection of Wisdom Sūtra."* Seattle: Kalavinka Press, 2009.

Diamond Cutter Sūtra. http://emahofoundation.org/images/documents/DiamondSutraText.pdf.

Gregory, Peter N. *Tsung-mi and the Sinification of Buddhism*. Honolulu: University of Hawai'i Press, 2002.

Hopkins, Jeffrey. *Meditation on Emptiness*. Boston: Wisdom Publications, 1996.

———. *Absorption in No External World*. Boulder, CO: Snow Lion Publications, 2017.

———. *Reflections on Reality*. Berkeley: University of California Press, 2007.

———. *Tsong-kha-pa's Final Exposition of Wisdom*. Ithaca, NY: Snow Lion Publications, 2008.

Huntington, C. W. "The 'Akutobhayā' and Early Indian Mādhyamaka." PhD diss., University of Michigan, Ann Arbor, 1986.

Jane, Wen-ling. "Practice and Theory of Emptiness: A Study of Jizang's Commentary on the 'Refutation of Emptiness' of the Bailun." PhD diss., Columbia University, 2009.

Jinpa, Thupten, trans. *Illuminating the Intent: An Exposition of Candrakīrti's Entering the Middle Way, by Tsongkhapa*. Somerville, MA: Wisdom Publications, 2021.

———. *Self, Reality, and Reason in Tibetan Philosophy*. New York: RoutledgeCurzon, 2002.

Kapstein, Matthew, ed. *Buddhism between Tibet and China*. Boston: Wisdom Publications, 2009.

Klein, Anne Caroline. *Path to the Middle: Oral Mādhyamika Philosophy in Tibet*. Albany: State University of New York Press, 1994.

Lang, Karen. *Āryadeva's Catuḥśataka: On the Bodhisattva's Cultivation of Merit and Knowledge*. Copenhagen: Akademisk Forlag, 1986.

Lindtner, Christian. *Master of Wisdom: Writings of the Buddhist Master Nāgārjuna*. Berkeley, CA: Dharma Publishing, 1997.

Liu, Ming-Wood. *Mādhyamaka Thought in China*. New York: E. J. Brill, 1994.

Lopez, Donald S. *A Study of Svātantrika.* Ithaca, NY: Snow Lion Publications, 1987.

Magee, William. *The Nature of Things: Emptiness and Essence in the Geluk World.* Ithaca, NY: Snow Lion Publications, 1999.

Newland, Guy. *Appearance and Reality.* Ithaca, NY: Snow Lion Publications, 1999.

———. *Introduction to Emptiness: As Taught in Tsong-Kha-Pa's Great Treatise on the Stages of the Path.* Ithaca, NY: Snow Lion Publications, 2009.

Ngawang Samten, Geshe, and Jay L. Garfield, trans. *Ocean of Reasoning: A Great Commentary on Nāgārjuna's "Mūlamādhyamakakārikā," by rJe Tsong Khapa.* New York: Oxford University Press, 2006.

Perdue, Daniel E. *Debate in Tibetan Buddhism.* Ithaca, NY: Snow Lion Publications, 1992.

Smitheram, Robert. *The Great Perfections of Wisdom Treatise.* Hacienda Heights, CA: Fo Guang Shan International Translation Center, 2017.

Sopa, Geshe Lhundup, and Jeffrey Hopkins. *Cutting through Appearances: Practice and Theory of Tibetan Buddhism.* Ithaca, NY: Snow Lion Publications, 1989.

Tegchok, Khensur Jampa. *Insight into Emptiness.* Edited by Thubten Chodron. Boston: Wisdom Publications, 2012.

———. *Practical Ethics and Profound Emptiness: A Commentary on Nagarjuna's Precious Garland.* Translated by Bhikshu Steve Carlier. Edited by Thubten Chodron. Somerville, MA: Wisdom Publications, 2017.

Thabkhe, Geshe Yeshe. *The Rice Seedling Sūtra.* Somerville, MA: Wisdom Publications, 2020.

Tsong-ka-pa. *Compassion in Tibetan Buddhism.* Translated and edited by Jeffrey Hopkins. Ithaca, NY: Snow Lion Publications, 1980.

Vose, Kevin. *Resurrecting Candrakīrti: Disputes in the Tibetan Creation of Prāsaṅgika.* Boston: Wisdom Publications, 2009.

Wu, Jiang. *Enlightenment in Dispute: The Reinvention of Chan Buddhism in Seventeenth-Century China.* New York: Oxford University Press, 2008.

Zhang Jianfei, and Yang Nianqun. *In Search of Truth in the Snow Mountains: An Oral History of a Han Lama Dictated by Xing Suzhi*. China: SDX Joint Publishing Company, 1991.

Yinshun, Venerable. *A Sixty-Year Spiritual Voyage on the Ocean of Dharma*. Translated by Yu-lung L. Avis, Po-Hui Chang, and Maxwell E. Siegel. Noble Path Buddhist Education Fellowship, 2009.

Yin-shun, Venerable. *The Way to Buddhahood: Instructions from a Modern Chinese Master*. Boston: Wisdom Publications, 2012.

Zhixu. *Mind-Seal of the Buddhas: Patriarch Ou-i's Commentary on the Amitābha Sūtra*. Translated by J. C. Cleary. San Francisco: Sūtra Translation Committee of the United States and Canada, 1997.

Zhiyi. *The Essentials of Buddhist Meditation*. Seattle: Kalavinka Press, 2008.

Index

F

R

S

About the Authors

The Dalai Lama is the spiritual leader of the Tibetan people, a Nobel Peace Prize recipient, and an advocate for compassion and peace throughout the world. He promotes harmony among the world's religions and engages in dialogue with leading scientists. Ordained as a Buddhist monk when he was a child, he completed the traditional monastic studies and earned his geshe degree (equivalent to a PhD). Renowned for his erudite and open-minded scholarship, his meditative attainments, and his humility, Bhikṣu Tenzin Gyatso says, "I am a simple Buddhist monk."

Peter Aronson

Bhikṣuṇī Thubten Chodron has been a Buddhist nun since 1977. Growing up in Los Angeles, she graduated with honors in history from the University of California at Los Angeles and did graduate work in education at the University of Southern California. After years studying and teaching Buddhism in Asia, Europe, and the United States, she became the founder and abbess of Sravasti Abbey in Washington State. A popular speaker for her practical explanations of how to apply Buddhist teachings in daily life, she is the author of several books on Buddhism, including *Buddhism for Beginners*. She is the editor of Khensur Jampa Tegchok's *Insight into Emptiness*. For more information, visit sravastiabbey.org and thubtenchodron.org.

Also Available from the Dalai Lama and Wisdom Publications

Buddhism
One Teacher, Many Traditions

The Compassionate Life

Ecology, Ethics, and Interdependence
The Dalai Lama in Conversation with Leading Thinkers on Climate Change

Essence of the Heart Sūtra
The Dalai Lama's Heart of Wisdom Teachings

The Essence of Tsongkhapa's Teachings
The Dalai Lama on the Three Principal Aspects of the Path

The Fourteenth Dalai Lama's Stages of the Path, vol. 1
Guidance for the Modern Practitioner

The Fourteenth Dalai Lama's Stages of the Path, vol. 2
An Annotated Commentary on "Oral Transmission of Mañjuśrī"

The Good Heart
A Buddhist Perspective on the Teachings of Jesus

Imagine All the People
A Conversation with the Dalai Lama on Money, Politics, and Life as It Could Be

Kalachakra Tantra
Rite of Initiation

The Life of My Teacher
A Biography of Kyabjé Ling Rinpoché

Meditation on the Nature of Mind

The Middle Way
Faith Grounded in Reason

Mind in Comfort and Ease
The Vision of Enlightenment in the Great Perfection

MindScience
An East-West Dialogue

Opening the Eye of New Awareness

Practicing Wisdom
The Perfection of Shantideva's Bodhisattva Way

Science and Philosophy in the Indian Buddhist Classics, vol. 1
The Physical World

Science and Philosophy in the Indian Buddhist Classics, vol. 2
The Mind

Science and Philosophy in the Indian Buddhist Classics, vol. 3
Philosophical Schools

Science and Philosophy in the Indian Buddhist Classics, vol. 4
Philosophical Topics

Sleeping, Dreaming, and Dying
An Exploration of Consciousness

The Wheel of Life
Buddhist Perspectives on Cause and Effect

The World of Tibetan Buddhism
An Overview of Its Philosophy and Practice

Also Available from Thubten Chodron

Insight into Emptiness
Khensur Jampa Tegchok
Edited and introduced by Thubten Chodron

"One of the best introductions to the philosophy of emptiness I have ever read."—José Ignacio Cabezón

Practical Ethics and Profound Emptiness
A Commentary on Nagarjuna's Precious Garland
Khensur Jampa Tegchok
Edited by Thubten Chodron

"A beautifully clear translation and systematic explanation of Nagarjuna's most accessible and wide-ranging work. Dharma students everywhere will benefit from careful attention to its pages."—Guy Newland, author of *Introduction to Emptiness*

Awakening Every Day
365 Buddhist Reflections to Invite Mindfulness and Joy

Buddhism for Beginners

The Compassionate Kitchen

Cultivating a Compassionate Heart
The Yoga Method of Chenrezig

Don't Believe Everything You Think
Living with Wisdom and Compassion

Guided Meditations on the Stages of the Path

How to Free Your Mind
Tara the Liberator

Living with an Open Heart
How to Cultivate Compassion in Daily Life

Open Heart, Clear Mind

Taming the Mind

Working with Anger

About Wisdom Publications

Wisdom Publications is the leading publisher of classic and contemporary Buddhist books and practical works on mindfulness. To learn more about us or to explore our other books, please visit our website at wisdomexperience.org or contact us at the address below.

Wisdom Publications
132 Perry Street
New York, NY 10014 USA

We are a 501(c)(3) organization, and donations in support of our mission are tax deductible.

Wisdom Publications is affiliated with the Foundation for the Preservation of the Mahayana Tradition (FPMT).